Select chapters from

Public Speaking
for College & Career

Ninth Edition

Hamilton Gregory
Asheville-Buncombe Technical Community College

Edited by Andrea Patterson & Elwanda Ingram

With Chapter 2 and the appendix from

Communication Works

Tenth Edition

Teri Kwal Gamble
College of New Rochelle

Michael Gamble
New York Institute of Technology

Winston-Salem State University

 Learning Solutions

Boston   Burr Ridge, IL   Dubuque, IA   New York   San Francisco   St. Louis
Bangkok   Bogotá   Caracas   Lisbon   London   Madrid
Mexico City   Milan   New Delhi   Seoul   Singapore   Sydney   Taipei   Toronto

Select Chapters from
Public Speaking for College & Career, Ninth Edition
with additional material
Winston -Salem State University

This book is a McGraw-Hill Learning Solutions textbook and contains select material from the following sources:
Public Speaking for College and Career, Ninth Edition by Hamilton Gregory. Copyright © 2010 by The McGraw-Hill Companies, Inc.
Communication Works, Tenth Edition by Teri Kwal Gamble and Michael Gamble. Copyright © 2010 by The McGraw-Hill Companies, Inc.
Both reprinted with permission of the publisher. Many custom published texts are modified versions or adaptations of our best-selling textbooks. Some adaptations are printed in black and white to keep prices at a minimum, while others are in color.

1 2 3 4 5 6 7 8 9 0 WDD WDD 12 11 10

ISBN-13: 978-0-07-744922-3
ISBN-10: 0-07-744922-3

Learning Solutions Manager: Judson Harper
Production Editor: Lynn Nagel
Printer/Binder: Worldcolor
Winston-Salem State University student and faculty photos courtesy of Garrett Garms, University Photographer

CONTENTS

Part 2
Developing a Focus

Part 3
Preparing Content

Part **4**
Organizing the Speech

Chapter 7   **The Body of the
Speech   130**

Part 5
Presenting the Speech

Part 6
Types of Public Speaking

Preface

Soncerey L. Montgomery, Ph.D.
Assistant Professor of Speech
Winston-Salem State University

Althea B. Bradford, M.A.
Instructor of Speech
Winston-Salem State University

Our daily interactions and experiences with students at Winston-Salem State University (WSSU), an Historically Black College and University (HBCU) founded in 1892, remind us that nurturing young minds is a social responsibility. As facilitators of the learning process in this educational milieu, we realize the university's greatest resource is its students. We share the same sensitivity to and acute awareness of providing a supportive environment for our students. As such, we embrace every opportunity to contribute decisively to the rich educational legacy upon which our institution was founded. Equally important, we realize that we, as faculty, must identify and build upon the strengths of our students. What we do inside the classroom can make the difference between students' ability to succeed or fail. So it is with noble intentions that we equip students with the tools needed to be successful in the classroom and beyond.

Our hope is that this textbook will serve as a vehicle that jumpstarts conversations and addresses issues related to the sustainability of our students. Our colleagues who helped to customize this textbook represent several generations of teaching; thus, our approaches and styles vary. Some lean more toward theory and application while others focus primarily on developing public speaking skills in our students. However, no expense is spared in terms of the importance of teaching our students the value of public speaking. In a society where self-expression and collective expression are both measures of communicative competence, we are committed to serving our students so that they are able to think critically and solve problems rationally – regardless of race, gender or class. As such, we will continue to work diligently to ensure that students at this university receive the best education possible while preparing for graduate studies or a career. Serving as examples for our students, we model what our HBCUs are designed to produce even as our students explore new avenues of achievement. We are on a healthy trajectory to enhance the educational experiences of our students. In fact, every day we are making efforts to tap into their full potential. We are confident that our students have the drive to become critical thinkers and problem solvers. Undeniably, these competencies make them assets to this institution as well as our global society. They, too, may one day teach at one of our nation's highly regarded universities, develop their own businesses, or become heads of corporations and countries.

We begin with a brief discussion of the motivating factors that led speech faculty at WSSU to customize the textbook. For example, we want this textbook to be more than an echo of Western thinking; instead it is intended to help students embrace multiple ways of viewing the world. We also want to amplify the voices of our students and encourage them to stay connected to their culture, for they are indeed agents of change. Because of Winston-Salem State University's long-standing commitment to effectively preparing students for careers and graduate or professional school, we are confident that this textbook will yield even greater results for those enrolled in the required speech course at this university.

The purpose of Fundamentals of Speech, an introductory speaking course, is to help students understand the importance of personal and public communication skills in their day-to-day lives. This course is designed to stimulate and encourage an appreciation for the personal benefits that will accrue as students develop improved public speaking and communication skills. Undeniably, communication is central to all that we do – whether it is sending a text message, making a presentation, studying abroad, standing in line at the grocery store, or relaxing on the couch. Moreover, effective communication skills are essential to successful living and productivity. For example, students encounter people one-on-one regularly, such as talking to advisors and instructors, health care professionals, and peers. Communication is multi-faceted and so are those who engage in it. Therefore, we must adapt to the changing needs of our students, our educational environment and our society at large. For example, the political climate of society has changed with the election of the country's first African American President, Barack Obama. Many students at this university have embraced this shifting paradigm. Casual conversations and formal classroom speeches have reflected President Obama's consciousness of the importance of education, interdependence between cultural groups and the ability to speak effectively in a variety of settings.

We have a responsibility to help our students understand the complex world of communication by giving them practical ways to apply what is taught. Therefore, we focus on the study and application of basic elements, techniques, and processes essential to effective public speaking. The ultimate goal of this course is to give students the tools needed to speak in public in a variety of situations and to help them master speaking techniques. This textbook has been decidedly customized to ensure that this goal is met.

The textbook explores the vast and dynamic nature of communication. It also highlights the importance of cultural competence in communication encounters. Admittedly, however, the textbook is not intended to be an exhaustive study of human communication. Rather it focuses primarily on fundamentals of speech preparation and presentation, giving adequate coverage of various principles and aspects of the development process in each chapter. Preparation in effective public speaking is a requisite. Therefore, some of the key chapters in this textbook focus on building skills and helping students reach competency and efficiency in nonverbal communication, interpersonal communication, interviewing skills and cultural studies, to name a few. The chapters are fundamentally linked to other aspects of critical inquiry such as information literacy, written communication, and critical reading.

Communication is ever-changing and so are our students. Yet, the basic need to hone effective communication skills does not change from semester to semester. Our students still need opportunities inside and outside of the classroom to apply basic public speaking skills and demonstrate competency in oral expression. Edward R. Murrow, one of the most notable American broadcast journalists, writes, "The newest computer can merely compound, at speed, the oldest problem in the relations between human beings, and in the end the communicator will be confronted with the old problem, of what to say and how to say it." The need to polish communication skills transcends time, generations and even technology. Therefore, as speech faculty, we remain committed to educating students to be personally and professionally successful in the 21st century.

During a talk to schoolchildren on "Animal Attack and Defense" at the American Museum of Natural History in New York, Hassan Mohamed, a student at Colgate University, explains how mountain goats defend themselves against predators. By volunteering to be a museum educator, this student demonstrates that public speaking is an excellent way to contribute to one's community.

Introduction to Public Speaking

chapter 1

OUTLINE

Benefits of a Public Speaking Course

The Speech Communication Process
Elements of the Process
Overview of the Process

The Speaker's Responsibilities
Maintain High Ethical Standards
Enrich Listeners' Lives
Take Every Speech Seriously

Speech Introducing Yourself or a Classmate
Sample Self-Introduction Speech
Sample Speech Introducing a Classmate

Quick Guide to Public Speaking
Preparation
Delivery

OBJECTIVES

After studying this chapter, you should be able to:

1. Explain at least three benefits of a public speaking course.

2. Identify and explain the seven elements of the speech communication process.

3. Describe the main responsibilities that speakers have toward their listeners.

4. Prepare a speech introducing yourself or a classmate.

When Meggan Carter enrolled in a public speaking class as a freshman

at the University of Mary in Bismarck, North Dakota, she—like many other students—assumed that she would never need public speaking skills in "the real world."

But events proved her wrong. During her senior year, as part of a statewide antismoking campaign, she stepped forward to testify at a hearing of the North Dakota Senate. There were over 200 people in the hearing room. Television cameras recorded her remarks, which were telecast on the evening news to thousands of state residents. Her comments were also reported in newspapers and TV news programs across the nation.[1]

Carter's goal was to persuade the legislators to ban smoking in all public buildings in North Dakota. As part of her argument, she said that to earn money for school expenses, she had worked as a server at a restaurant that permitted smoking. "I would wake up the next day after work," she said, "and I would be coughing up a lot of junk." She also reported what she had learned from interviews with a lung disease specialist and other physicians about the long-term harm caused by tobacco.[2]

Meggan Carter waits to address a hearing of the North Dakota Senate.

Unfortunately for her, a few days after she spoke, the North Dakota Senate rejected the proposed ban. It was a bitter disappointment for Carter, but she believes that she "possibly changed the lives of some people for the better." If she got at least one person to quit smoking or persuaded one person to abstain from trying tobacco, she says, her efforts were successful.

Carter credits her public speaking class with enabling her to prepare and deliver her presentation. For example, right before she began speaking, she was nervous, but she controlled her jitters by applying what she had learned in class: "Be thoroughly prepared and know all the in's and out's of the topic." A videotape of her presentation shows her speaking with confidence and conviction, displaying strong gestures and good eye contact.[3]

As Meggan Carter discovered, a public speaking class can bolster your self-confidence, as you develop your abilities to prepare and present a spoken message in college, career, and community. A bonus is the chance to make a contribution to others. You can touch lives—whether you are training new employees, demonstrating a useful product, or advocating a worthwhile cause.

Benefits of a Public Speaking Course

Many college graduates look back on all the courses they took in college and say that public speaking was one of the most valuable.[4] Here are some of the reasons why this course is considered so important.

1. **You learn how to speak to a public audience.** Knowing how to stand up and give a talk to a group of people is a rewarding skill you can use throughout your life. Imagine yourself in these public speaking scenarios:

- In one of your college classes, you must give a 30-minute presentation on a research project.
- To 50 colleagues at work, you give a brief speech appealing for contributions to the United Way charity drive.
- In court you explain to a jury why a traffic accident was not your fault.
- To a gathering of neighbors, you explain your ideas for curbing crime in the neighborhood.

You will encounter many such occasions that require public speaking ability.

2. **You learn skills that apply to one-on-one communication.** Although the emphasis of this course is on speaking to groups, the principles that you learn also apply to communication with individuals.[5] Throughout your lifetime you will be obliged to talk in situations such as these:

- In a job interview, a human resources manager says, "We've got 50 well-qualified applicants for this job. Why should we hire you?" If you know how to give a reply that is brief, interesting, and convincing, you obviously improve your chances of getting the job. In a public speaking course, you learn how to organize and present persuasive messages.

- You sit down with a bank executive to ask for a loan so that you can buy a new car. The skills of nonverbal communication (such as eye contact and facial expression) that you learn in a public speaking course should help you convey to the banker that you are a trustworthy and reliable person who will repay the loan.

After taking a public speaking course, many students report that their new skills help them as much in talking to one person as in addressing a large audience.

3. You develop the oral communication skills that are prized in the job market. When you go to a job interview, which of the following is most likely to influence the employer when he or she decides whether to hire you?

- The reputation of your school
- Your grade-point average
- Letters of reference
- Technical knowledge in your field
- Oral communication skills—speaking and listening
- Written communication skills—reading and writing

Research shows that "oral communication skills" is the correct answer—a finding that surprises many students.[6] Surely "technical knowledge in your field" is the most important factor for jobs in science and technology, isn't it? Not according to employers. You can be brilliant in your field, says one executive, but if you can't communicate successfully with co-workers and the public, your brilliance is of little value.[7]

Once you have a job, being a good communicator can help you win promotions. "If a dozen equally skilled technicians are competing for the job of manager, the winner is most likely to be the one with the best communication skills," says Cristina Silva, human resources manager of a plant in Los Angeles.[8]

connectpublic speaking.com
See "Career Opportunities" on *Connect Public Speaking.*

4. You work in an ideal environment for gaining experience and building confidence. The classroom is a perfect place to practice and develop your skills because it is an unthreatening setting. (No one will deny you a job or a raise on the basis of your classroom speeches.) Your audience is friendly and sympathetic—all your classmates are going through the same experience.

The critiques given by your instructor (and, in some cases, by fellow students) are valuable parts of the course. If, for example, you say "um" or "uh" so often that it distracts your listeners, you are probably unaware of this unconscious habit. Being told of the problem is the first step toward correcting it.

If you are like most students, your public speaking class will cause you to gain self-confidence. You will enjoy the pride that comes from meeting a challenge and handling it successfully.

5. You can make a contribution to the lives of other people. While attending a funeral service for a beloved aunt, Karen Walker heard the minister give a brief eulogy and then say, "Would anyone like to say a few words at our 'open mike'?" A few people went to the microphone and shared some reminiscences, but most audience members were silent. "I wanted to pay tribute to my aunt, but I was too scared," said Walker. "I felt really bad because there were a lot of important things about my aunt and her life that were never said." A few years later, Walker took a public speaking class, and a year or so afterward, she attended another funeral–for her grandfather. "This time I vowed that I would not pass up the opportunity to honor a wonderful person. I asked to be part of the service, and I spoke about my childhood memories of my grandfather."

The eulogy, said Walker, was appreciated by her family members, who told her that she had expressed beautifully what they would have said if they had possessed the courage and the skills to stand up and speak. "It gave me a good feeling to know that I could represent the family in this way," she said.

Being able to speak in public–offering a toast, sharing information, providing encouragement, attempting persuasion–can bring pleasure and joy to yourself and to others. Walker said that her success was possible because of what she had learned in her public speaking class.[9]

Your Thoughts

Who is the most engaging public communicator (politician, teacher, minister, etc.) you have ever encountered? What are the reasons for his or her success?

The Speech Communication Process

When a speaker gives a speech, does communication take place?

Sometimes yes, sometimes no. The reason for the lack of universal success is that *speaking and communicating are not the same thing.* You can speak to a listener, but if the listener does not understand your message in the way you meant it to be understood, you have failed to communicate it.[10] Here's an example:

> A job recruiter coached one young woman on how to present herself at a job interview. She was told to "dress your best." On the day of the interview, she showed up wearing a prom dress.
> The recruiter had meant "wear your best business attire," but the young woman had interpreted the advice as "wear the fanciest clothes you own."[11]

This incident illustrates that speaking and communicating are not synonymous. A speaker can give information, but true, effective communication fails to take place if listeners misinterpret the message. According to Hitachi, Ltd., of Japan: "Communication is not simply sending a message. It is creating true understanding–swiftly, clearly, and precisely."[12]

To help you give a speech that truly communicates, it is helpful to understand the process of speech communication, as shown in Figure 1.1. Studying this process can yield valuable insights–not only into speechmaking, but also into your daily interactions with other people.

Elements of the Process

The speech communication process has seven distinct components.

Speaker

When you are a **speaker,** you are the source, or originator, of a message that is transmitted to a listener. Whether you are speaking to a dozen people or 500, you bear a great responsibility for the success of the communication. The key question that you must constantly ask yourself is not "Am I giving out good information?" or "Am I performing well?" but, rather, "Am I getting through to my listeners?"

speaker
the originator of a message sent to a listener

Listener

The **listener** is the recipient of the message sent by the speaker. The true test of communication is not whether a message is delivered by the speaker but whether

listener
the receiver of the speaker's message

Figure 1.1
The Speech Communication Process

In this model of the speech communication process, a **speaker** creates a **message** and sends it via a **channel** to the **listener,** who interprets it and sends **feedback** via a channel to the speaker. **Interference** is whatever impedes accurate communication. The **situation** refers to the time and place in which communication takes place.

The speech communication process is often dynamic, with communicators sending and receiving messages in rapid sequence, sometimes even simultaneously. In this informal business presentation, the speaker sends messages while receiving feedback (both verbal and nonverbal) from listeners. At various times, a speaker and a listener may exchange roles.

it is accurately received by the listener. "A speech," says management consultant David W. Richardson of Westport, Connecticut, "takes place in the minds of the audience."[13]

If communication fails, who is to blame—the speaker or the listener? Depending on the situation, the blame could be placed on either, or both. Although speakers share part of the responsibility for communication, listeners also must bear some of the burden. They must try hard to pay attention to the speaker, fighting off the temptation to daydream or think about personal concerns. They must listen with an open mind, avoiding the tendency to prejudge the speaker or discount a speaker's views without a fair hearing.

Message

The **message** is whatever the speaker communicates to the listeners. The message is sent in the form of *symbols*–either *verbal* or *nonverbal*.

Verbal symbols are words. It's important for you to recognize that words are not things; they are *symbols* of things. If you give me an apple, you transfer a solid object from your hand to mine. But if you're making a speech and you mention the word "apple," you are no longer transferring a concrete thing. You are transferring a symbol.

Nonverbal symbols are what you convey with your tone of voice, eyes, facial expression, gestures, posture, and appearance.

So far, the process sounds simple and obvious, but now we enter a danger zone. As a speaker transmits verbal and nonverbal symbols, the listeners must interpret them. Unfortunately, listeners may end up with a variety of interpretations, some of them quite different from what the speaker intended. Consider a simple word like *apple*. One listener may think of a small green fruit, while another conjures an image of a big red fruit. One listener may think of crisp tartness, while another thinks of juicy sweetness. If a simple word can evoke a variety of images, imagine the confusion and misunderstanding that can arise when abstract words such as *imperialism, patriotism,* and *censorship* are used. The term *censorship* may mean "stamping out filth" to some listeners, but it may mean "total government control of the news media" to others.

As a speaker, strive to use symbols that will cause the listener to arrive at a meaning that is as close as possible to the one in your mind. Don't say, "Smoking may cause you a lot of trouble." The vague verbal symbols at the end of the sentence–"a lot of trouble"–might be interpreted by some listeners to mean "coughing," by others to mean "stained teeth," or by still others to mean "cancer." Be specific: "Smoking may cause lung cancer."

Sometimes a speaker's verbal symbols contradict his or her nonverbal symbols. If you say to an audience, "I'm delighted to be here tonight," but your face has a mournful expression and your tone of voice is regretful, the listeners are getting a mixed message. Which will they believe: your words or your nonverbal behavior? Listeners usually accept the nonverbal behavior as the true message. In this case, they will believe that you are *not* delighted to be there.

The solution to this problem is to make sure the nonverbal part of your message reinforces, rather than contradicts, the verbal part. In other words, smile and use a friendly tone of voice when you say, "I appreciate the opportunity to speak to you tonight."

message
whatever is communicated verbally and nonverbally to the listener

Your Thoughts

When nonverbal and verbal messages are contradictory, why do you think listeners tend to accept the nonverbal as the true message?

Channel

The **channel** is the medium used to communicate the message. A speech can reach an audience by means of a variety of channels: radio, television, the Internet, a public-address system, or direct voice communication.

channel
the pathway used to transmit a message

For public speaking in the classroom, your primary channel is auditory (your voice), accompanied by a visual channel (gestures, facial expressions, visual aids).

For some speeches in the workplace, you may have a public-address system. This channel can be very effective (if the system works well and the acoustics in the room are good), because it enables you to speak in an easy, conversational style without having to raise your voice.

Feedback

feedback
verbal and nonverbal responses made by a listener to a speaker

Feedback is the response that the listeners give the speaker. Sometimes it is *verbal,* as when a listener asks questions or makes comments during a lecture. In most public speeches and certainly in the ones you will give in the classroom, listeners refrain from giving verbal feedback until the question-and-answer period at the end of the speech.

Listeners also give *nonverbal* feedback. If they are smiling and nodding their heads, they are obviously in agreement with your remarks. If they are frowning and sitting with their arms folded, they more than likely disagree with what you are saying. If they are yawning and looking at you with a glazed expression, they are probably bored or weary. ("A yawn," wrote English author G. K. Chesterton, "is a silent shout.")

If you receive negative feedback, try to help your listeners. If, for example, you are explaining a concept, but some of your listeners are shaking their heads and giving you looks that seem to say, "I don't understand," try again, using different words, to make your ideas clear.

Interference

interference
anything that obstructs accurate communication of a message

Interference is anything that blocks or hinders the accurate communication of a message. There are three types:

- *External* interference arises outside the listener: someone coughing, a baby crying, people talking loudly in the hall, or an air-conditioning breakdown that leaves the listeners hot and sticky and preoccupied with their discomfort.
- *Internal* interference comes from within the listener. Some listeners might be daydreaming or worrying about a personal problem. Some might be too tired to expend mental energy on listening. As a speaker, you can help listeners overcome internal distractions by making your speech so lively and interesting that the audience feels compelled to listen to you.
- *Speaker-generated* interference occurs when the speaker uses words that are unfamiliar to the audience, or that are interpreted in a way that the speaker did not intend. If the speaker wears bizarre clothing, some listeners might scrutinize the attire instead of concentrating on the speech.

Sometimes listeners will strive to overcome interference—for example, straining to hear the speaker's words over the noise of a truck roaring down the street outside. At other times, though, some listeners will fail to make the extra effort, and no communication takes place.

When you are a speaker, watch for any signs of interference and, if possible, take steps to overcome the problem. If a plane roars overhead, causing your listeners to lean forward to hear your words, you can either speak louder or pause until the plane's noise has subsided.

Interference can be caused by a daydreaming listener.

Tips for Your Career

Tip 1.1 Seek Feedback*

Probably unaware of what he was doing, one college professor during his lectures would roll his tie all the way up to his collar, release it, and then roll it up again. Students in the class were distracted by this habit. One day they made bets on how many times he would roll the tie up during class.

Such distracting mannerisms and foibles can mar your speechmaking, and you may not even be aware of what you're doing. You may, for example, develop the unconscious habit of smoothing your hair or straightening your clothes as you talk. The best way to discover and discard these quirks is to get feedback (in the form of an evaluation) from your listeners.

Although feedback is valuable for pinpointing delivery problems, it is even more important as a way to assess the *content* of your speech: Are your remarks enlightening or confusing to the listeners?

You don't need an evaluation of every speech in your career, but you should seek feedback occasionally. Strive to get both positive and negative input, so that you can keep the good while eliminating the bad. Here are four good methods:

1. **Ask several friends or colleagues for a critique of your speech.** Don't make an imprecise request like "Tell me how I do on this" because your evaluators will probably say at the end of your speech, "You did fine—good speech," regardless of what they thought of it, to avoid hurting your feelings. Instead give them a specific assignment: "Please make a note of at least three things that you like about the speech and my delivery, and at least three things that you feel need improvement." Now your listeners know they can be frank and not worry about hurting your feelings; as a result, you are likely to get helpful feedback.

2. **Pass out evaluation forms to all your listeners.** Ask them to make comments anonymously and then drop the forms in a box near the exit. The form can contain the requests mentioned above, or you can create your own items.

3. **Invite a small group of listeners to sit down with you after a meeting to share their reactions.** This is especially useful in finding out whether the listeners understood and accepted your message. Try to listen and learn without becoming argumentative or defensive.

4. **Have a presentation videotaped.** Invite colleagues to watch the tape with you and help you evaluate it. Because many people are *never* pleased with either themselves or their speeches on videotape, colleagues often can provide objectivity. For example, an introduction that now seems dull to you might strike your colleagues as interesting and captivating.

*The sources for Tips are cited in the Notes section at the end of the book.

Situation

The **situation** is the context—the time and the place—in which communication occurs. Different situations call for different behaviors by both speaker and listener. A speaker who delivers a eulogy in the stately hush of a cathedral would not crack jokes, but in an entertaining after-dinner speech at a convention, jokes would be appropriate. In some settings, listeners can cheer and clap, but at other times, they must remain silent.

Time of day plays a part in how receptive an audience is. Many listeners, for example, tend to be sluggish and sleepy between 3 and 5 P.M. If you give a presentation during that period, make it lively. Perhaps you could use colorful visual aids and involve listeners in a hands-on project to keep them engaged. If your speech is a long one, you might invite listeners to stand up and stretch at the halfway point to shake off their sleepiness.

When you prepare a speech, find out as much as possible about the situation: Where will the speech be given, indoors or outdoors? What is the nature of the

situation
the setting in which communication takes place

connectpublic
speaking.com
For an interactive
exercise on the
speech commu-
nication process,
visit Chapter 1
on *Connect Public
Speaking.*

occasion? How many people are likely to be present? By assessing these variables in advance, you can adapt your speech to make it appropriate to the situation.

Overview of the Process

Look once again at Figure 1.1. The diagram at the top of the page is deliberately simplified to help clarify the different components. Don't interpret the diagram as meaning that speakers and listeners ordinarily take turns at communicating. As suggested by the photo below the figure, communicators often send and receive messages at the same time. Thus, communication is not a ball tossed back and forth between speaker and listener, but two (or more) balls tossed simultaneously. For example, you go into your boss's office to ask for a raise. As you start your (verbal) message, she is giving you a friendly, accepting smile, a (nonverbal) message that seems to say that she is glad to see you. But as your message is spelled out, her smile fades and is replaced by a grim expression of regret—negative feedback. "I wish I could give you a big raise," she says, "but I can't even give you a little one." As she is saying these last words, she interprets your facial expression as displaying disbelief, so she hastily adds, "Our departmental budget just won't permit it. My hands are tied." And so on . . . a lively give-and-take of verbal and nonverbal communication.

The Speaker's Responsibilities

A speaker who stands before an audience has certain responsibilities that a conscientious person should accept. Here are some guidelines.

Maintain High Ethical Standards

The standards of conduct and moral judgment that are generally accepted by honest people in our society are called *ethics.* In public speaking, ethics focuses on how speakers handle their material and how they treat their listeners.[14] Speakers should be honest and straightforward with listeners, avoiding all methods and goals that are deceitful, unscrupulous, or unfair.

Because ethics is such an important concern, the icon in the margin of this page will appear throughout this book at points where ethical issues are discussed. Let's examine three important ethical responsibilities of the speaker.

Never Distort Information

As an ethical speaker, you should always be honest about facts and figures. Distorting information is not only dishonest—it's foolish. Let's say that in your career, you persuade some colleagues to take a certain course of action but it is later discovered that you got your way by distorting facts and statistics. Henceforth your colleagues will distrust everything you propose—even if you have sound logic and impeccable evidence on your side. "A liar will not be believed," said the Greek fabulist Aesop, "even when he [or she] speaks the truth."[15]

Respect Your Audience

Some speakers show disrespect for their listeners, talking down to them as if they were ignorant or foolish. Speaking in a scolding, condescending tone, one speaker told an audience of young parents, "I know you people

Ethical Issue

Your Thoughts **?**

If you are crusading for a good cause, is it okay to falsify a few minor statistics to advance your argument? Defend your answer.

don't believe me, but you are wasting your time and your money if you buy instructional videos on how to be a good mother or father."

Speakers who are disdainful and arrogant might adopt a more respectful attitude if they heed the wisdom contained in two observations by the American humorist Will Rogers: "Everybody is ignorant, only on different subjects" and "There is nothing as stupid as an educated man if you get him off the thing he was educated in."[16] When you are the expert on a subject, remember that your "ignorant" listeners, on other topics, can reverse roles with you.

Reject Stereotyping and Scapegoating

Do you agree with the following statement?

> Psychiatrists are therapists who can cure mental illness in about one week. Their primary method is to hypnotize their patients and delve into repressed memories from childhood.

This image is badly distorted and exaggerated, but it is accepted as true by millions of Americans because it is the way psychiatrists are portrayed in many Hollywood films.[17]

Psychiatrists are victims of the common practice of stereotyping. A **stereotype** is a simplistic or exaggerated image that humans carry in their minds about groups of people. For example, "Lawyers are shrewd and dishonest" is a popular stereotype.

stereotype
an oversimplified or exaggerated image

Stereotyping can occur in public speaking classes. When trying to choose a speech topic, some males think that women are uninterested in how to repair cars, while some females think that men are uninterested in creative hobbies such as knitting and needlepoint.

You should reject stereotypes because they are "mental cookie cutters," forcing all people in a group into the same simple pattern. They fail to account for individual differences and the wide range of characteristics among members of any group. Some lawyers are dishonest, yes, but many are not. Some women are uninterested in repairing cars, yes, but some are avid mechanics.

While avoiding stereotyping, you also should reject its close cousin, scapegoating, which is the creation of a **scapegoat**–a person or a group unfairly blamed for some real or imagined wrong. For example, some people blame recent immigrants to the United States and Canada for every imaginable problem in society. Because many immigrants are Hispanic, the most frequently targeted scapegoats today are Hispanics (whether or not they are immigrants). As a result, the FBI reports that hate crimes against Hispanics have increased in recent years, surpassing 900 per year.[18]

scapegoat
an individual or a group that innocently bears the blame of others

Note: The preceding advice does not mean that you should disregard differences among your listeners. As we will see in Chapter 4, you should be sensitive and responsive to the needs and interests of listeners of different ages, cultures, and backgrounds. What is being condemned here is the use of unfair, exaggerated, or simplistic notions about individuals or groups.

Enrich Listeners' Lives

Before a speech, some speakers make remarks such as these to their friends:

- "I hope not many people show up."
- "When I ask for questions, I hope no one speaks up."
- "I want to hurry and get this over with."

Often these comments are made because the speaker is nervous. As you will discover in Chapter 2, I am sympathetic to speakers who experience stage fright. Nevertheless, I dislike hearing such remarks, because it's obvious that the speaker is focused on his or her own emotions rather than upon the audience.

Instead of viewing a speech as an ordeal, consider it an opportunity to make a contribution to the lives of your listeners. One of my students, Mary Crosby, gave a classroom speech on poisonous spiders—what they look like, how to avoid them, what to do if bitten, and so on. She had spent 6 hours researching the topic. If the 17 of us in the audience had duplicated her research, spending 6 hours apiece, we would have labored for 102 hours. Thus, Crosby saved us a great deal of time and effort and, more importantly, enriched our lives. (Most of us, of course, probably never would have taken the time to do this research, so her speech was all the more valuable.)

Take Every Speech Seriously

Consider two situations that some speakers erroneously assume are not worth taking seriously: classroom speeches and small audiences.

Classroom speeches.   Contrary to what some students think, your classroom speeches are as important as any speeches that you may give in your career or community, and they deserve to be taken seriously. They deal with real human issues and they are given by real human beings. As a teacher, I look forward to classroom speeches because I learn a lot from them. In recent years, I have learned how to save the life of a person choking on food, how to garden without using pesticides, and how to set up a tax-free savings account for my children.

Small audiences.   Some speakers mistakenly think that if an audience is small, or a great deal smaller than they expected, they need not put forth their best effort. You should try as hard to communicate with an audience of 5 as you would with an audience of 500. James "Doc" Blakely of Wharton, Texas, tells of a colleague who traveled to a small town in the Canadian province of Saskatchewan to give a speech and found that only one person had shown up to hear him. He gave the lone listener his best efforts, and later that listener started a national movement based on the speaker's ideas.[19]

connectpublic
speaking.com
View Christine
Fowler's self-
introduction speech
"Scars and Bruises"
on *Connect Public
Speaking.*

Speech Introducing Yourself or a Classmate

A speech introducing yourself or a classmate to the audience is often assigned early in a public speaking class. The speech gives you an opportunity to use an easy topic to gain experience. It also gives you and other members of the class a chance to learn key information about one another—so that future classroom speeches can be tailored to the needs and interests of the audience.

Strive to show your audience what makes you or your classmate interesting and unique. Unless your instructor advises otherwise, you can use the following checklist. Depending upon your time limits, you may not be able to include all items.

Background Information
- Name
- Marital status
- Hometown

- Family information
- Work experience
- Academic plans
- Post-graduation goals

Unique Features

- Special interests (hobbies, sports, clubs, etc.)
- One interesting or unusual thing about yourself or your classmate
- One interesting or unusual experience

The last three items are especially important because they give the audience a glimpse into the qualities, interests, and experiences that make you or your classmate unique.

Sample Self-Introduction Speech

Robert Schnitzhofer introduces himself to a public speaking class.

With a Name Like This . . .

INTRODUCTION

I'm Robert Schnitzhofer, and yes, I know, Schnitzhofer is a strange name. When I was a kid, I wished I had a name like Brad Pitt—short and tough-sounding. But now I see my name as an advantage, which I will explain in a few minutes.

BODY

I am enrolled in the culinary program, and after I graduate, I hope to open a bakery that specializes in wedding and birthday cakes. Not ordinary cakes—I want to offer sophisticated and elegant desserts.

I like a lot of different types of music. Some of my favorites are Gnarls Barkley, the White Stripes, Erykah Badu, and Drive-By Truckers. My favorite Web site is YouTube.com. My favorite movie of all time is *Jerry Maguire*.

Going back to my name: I was teased as a child, but now I enjoy having an odd name that people have never heard before. It's a good conversation starter. I tell people about my great-great grandfather Albert Schnitzhofer, who emigrated from Switzerland. I found out that he owned a bakery in Zurich. It's kind of intriguing to think that my interest in baking might be genetic. From a business point of view, I think having an unusual name will be an advantage. It will catch people's attention—stand out in the crowd.

CONCLUSION

Smucker's is a company that makes jams and jellies, and they have a slogan that you have probably heard on TV: "With a name like Smucker's, it has to be good." Someday when I open my business, I will call it Schnitzhofer Bakery, and I already have a slogan: "With a name like Schnitzhofer, we have to be good."

Sample Speech Introducing a Classmate

In this speech, Sara Newton introduces classmate Elizabeth Hernandez.

A Life-Changing Gift

INTRODUCTION

When Elizabeth Hernandez graduated from high school, she received a present that changed her life. It was a digital camera system, with several different lenses—including a zoom telephoto lens.

BODY

Elizabeth began going to soccer games, tennis matches, and other sports events, taking pictures with the telephoto lens. Some of her pictures were so good, she submitted them to the local newspaper. To her surprise, the paper printed all of them. The photo editor at the paper told Elizabeth that she ought to consider a career in photojournalism.

That's exactly what Elizabeth has decided to do. She is a photojournalism major, and she makes money on the side with freelance photography. Last summer she landed an assignment taking publicity pictures for a basketball camp.

Elizabeth loves to hike in wilderness areas, and of course she always takes her camera with her. Her other special interests are chatting with friends on Facebook and searching the Internet for—you guessed it—interesting photos.

CONCLUSION

Thanks to a wonderful high school graduation gift, Elizabeth Hernandez has found her passion and her career.

connectpublic
speaking.com
Connect Public Speaking has four speeches that need improvement, followed by improved versions. View them to learn how to avoid common mistakes.

Quick Guide to Public Speaking

To help you with any major speeches that you must give before you have had time to study this entire book, we will take a look at the key principles of preparation and delivery.

The guide below assumes that you will use the most popular method of speaking–extemporaneous–which means that you carefully prepare your speech but you don't read or memorize a script. Instead you look directly at your listeners and talk in a natural, conversational way, occasionally glancing at notes to stay on track.

The extemporaneous style and three other methods of speaking–manuscript (reading a document), memorization (speaking from memory), and impromptu (speaking with little or no time to prepare)–will be fully discussed in Chapter 10.

Preparation

Audience. The goal of public speaking is to gain a response from your listeners–to get them to think, feel, or act in a certain way. To reach the listeners, find out as much as you can about them. What are their ages, gender, racial and ethnic backgrounds, religion, and educational level? What are their attitudes toward you and the subject? How much do they already know about the subject? When you have completed a thorough analysis of your listeners, adapt your speech to meet their needs and interests.

Topic. Choose a topic that is interesting to you and about which you know a lot (either now or after doing research). Your topic also should be interesting to the listeners–one they will consider timely and worthwhile. Narrow the topic so that you can comfortably and adequately cover it within the time allotted.

If you love them, hot air balloons would make a good topic.

Purposes and central idea. Select a general purpose (to inform, to persuade, etc.), a specific purpose (a statement of exactly what you want to achieve with your audience), and a central idea (the message of your speech boiled down to one sentence). For example, suppose you want to inform your audience about fraud and abuse in the U.S. government's student-aid program. You could create objectives such as these:

General Purpose: To inform

Specific Purpose: To tell my listeners what happens when some unscrupulous schools abuse the federal student-aid program

Next, ask yourself, "What is my essential message? What big idea do I want to leave in the minds of my listeners?" Your answer is your central idea. Here is one possibility:

Central Idea: By manipulating the student-aid program, some schools cheat both taxpayers and students.

This central idea is what you want your listeners to remember if they forget everything else.

Finding materials. Gather information by reading books and periodicals (such as magazines and journals), searching for information on the Internet, interviewing knowledgeable people, or drawing from your own personal experiences. Look for interesting items such as examples, statistics, stories, and quotations. Consider using visual aids to help the audience understand and remember key points.

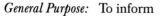

connectpublic speaking.com
For handy guidelines, see "Checklist for Preparing and Delivering a Speech."

Organization. Organize the body of your speech by devising two or three main points that explain or prove the central idea. To continue the example from above, ask yourself this question: "How can I get my audience to understand and accept my central idea?" Here are two main points that could be made:

I. Some schools resort to fraud and abuse of the student-aid program to scoop millions of dollars from the federal treasury.
II. Despite an investment of time and money, many students receive little or no useful training and end up saddled with debt.

The next step is to develop each main point with support material such as examples, statistics, and quotations from experts. Underneath the first main point, these two items could be used to illustrate the misuse of tax dollars:

• To expand student enrollment, some schools have rounded up homeless people and enrolled them for classes that they never attend, says James Thomas, the U.S. Department of Education inspector general.

Tips for Your Career

In a survey by the author, 64 business and professional speakers were asked to cite the most common mistakes made by public speakers in the United States today. Here are the mistakes that were listed most often.

1. **Failing to tailor one's speech to the needs and interests of the audience.** A *poor* speaker bores listeners with information that is stale or useless. A *good* speaker sizes up the listeners in advance and gives them material that is interesting and useful.

2. **Being poorly prepared.** A good speech does not just happen. The speaker must spend hours researching the topic, organizing material, and rehearsing the speech before he or she rises to speak. Therese Myers, head of Quarterdeck Office Systems, says, "I've learned that slapping together a presentation during an hour on the plane the day before doesn't cut it. Now I take at least two weeks to prepare a talk."

3. **Trying to cover too much in one speech.** Some speakers are so enthusiastic and knowledgeable about their topic that they try to cram a huge amount of material into a single speech. As Arnold "Nick" Carter, a corporate executive in Chicago, puts it: "They try to put ten pounds of information in a one-pound bag."

   Covering too much material causes the listeners to suffer from "information overload." They simply cannot absorb huge quantities of information in one sitting.

4. **Failing to maintain good eye contact.** Listeners tend to distrust speakers who don't look them in the eye. Yet some speakers spend most of their time looking at their notes or at the floor or at the back wall.

   Myers offers this advice: "Instead of addressing the room, talk for a few seconds to one person, then another, then another, then another." This not only helps with eye contact, but also makes you feel more at ease "because it's like having a one-on-one conversation."

5. **Being dull.** A speech can be made boring by poor content or by poor delivery. To avoid being dull, you should (a) choose a subject about which you are enthusiastic, (b) prepare interesting material, (c) have a strong desire to communicate your message to the audience, and (d) let your enthusiasm shine forth during your delivery of the speech.

- Three Texas schools received $7.4 million in student-aid payments for training security guards, but security experts testified that the training time had been inflated and that $260,000 would have been a reasonable cost, according to an investigation by *U.S. News & World Report*.

Transitions. To carry your listeners smoothly from one part of the speech to another, use transitional words or phrases, such as "Let's begin by looking at the problem," "Now for my second reason," and "Let me summarize what we've covered."

Introduction. In the first part of your introduction, grab the attention of the listeners and make them want to listen to the rest of the speech. Attention-getters include fascinating stories, intriguing questions, and interesting facts or statistics. Next, prepare listeners for the body of the speech (by stating the central idea and/ or by previewing the main points). Give any background information or definitions that the audience would need in order to understand the speech. Establish credibility by stating your own expertise or by citing reliable sources.

Conclusion. Summarize your key points, and then close with a clincher (such as a quotation or a story) to drive home the central idea of the speech.

Outline. Put together all parts of the speech (introduction, body, conclusion, and transitions) in an outline. Make sure that everything in the outline serves to explain, illustrate, or prove the central idea.

Speaking notes.   Prepare brief speaking notes based on your outline. These notes should be the only cues you take with you to the lectern.

Practice.   Rehearse your speech several times. Don't memorize the speech, but strive to rehearse ideas (as cued by your brief speaking notes). Trim the speech if you are in danger of exceeding the time limit.

Delivery

Self-confidence.   Develop a positive attitude about yourself, your speech, and your audience. Don't let fear cripple you: nervousness is normal for most speakers. Rather than trying to banish your jitters, use nervousness as a source of energy—it actually can help you to come across as a vital, enthusiastic speaker.

Approach and beginning.   When you are called to speak, leave your seat without sighing or mumbling, walk confidently to the front of the room, spend a few moments standing in silence (this is a good time to arrange your notes and get your first sentences firmly in mind), and then look directly at the audience as you begin your speech.

Eye contact.   Look at all parts of the audience throughout the speech, glancing down at your notes only occasionally. Avoid staring at a wall or the floor; avoid looking out a windo...

Speaking rate. ...e that makes it easy for the audience to absorb your ideas—neith...   ...st.

Expr... ...und as animated as it does when you carry on...

Clarity a... ...words distinctly and speak loud enough so that all lis... ...you. Avoid verbal fillers such as *uh, ah, um, er, okay, ya know*...

Gestures and mov... If it's appropriate, use gestures to accompany your words. Make them naturally and gracefully, so that they add to, rather than distract from, your message. You may move about during your speech, as long as your movements are purposeful and confident—not random and nervous. Refrain from jingling keys or coins, riffling note cards, or doing anything that distracts the audience.

Posture and poise.   Stand up straight. Try to be comfortable, yet poised and alert. Avoid leaning on the lectern or slouching on a desk.

Use of notes.   Glance at your notes occasionally to pick up the next point. Don't read them or absentmindedly stare at them.

connectpublic speaking.com
Connect Public Speaking has practice tests for each chapter in the book.

Stand up straight, look at your listeners, and use gestures.

Enthusiasm. Don't simply go through the motions of "giving a speech." Your whole manner–eyes, facial expression, posture, voice–should show enthusiasm for your subject, and you should seem genuinely interested in communicating your ideas.

Ending and departure.   Say your conclusion, pause a few moments, and then ask– in a tone that shows that you sincerely mean it–"Are there any questions?" Don't give the appearance of being anxious to get back to your seat (by pocketing your notes or by taking a step toward your seat).

Resources for Review and Skill Building

connectpublic
speaking.com

Connect Public Speaking provides resources for study and review, including sample speech videos, an Outline Tutor, and practice tests.

Summary

A public speaking course helps you develop the key oral communication skills (speaking well and listening intelligently) that are highly prized in business, technical, and professional careers. You gain both confidence and experience as you practice those skills in an ideal environment–the classroom–where your audience is friendly and supportive.

The speech communication process consists of seven elements: speaker, listener, message, channel, feedback, interference, and situation. Communication does not necessarily take place just because a speaker transmits a message; the message must be accurately received by the listener. When the speaker sends a message, he or she must make sure that the two components of a message–verbal and nonverbal–don't contradict each other.

Communicators often send and receive messages at the same time, creating a lively give-and-take of verbal and nonverbal communication.

Speakers should maintain high ethical standards, never distorting information, even for a good cause. They should respect their audiences and avoid taking a condescending or contemptuous attitude. They recognize the diversity to be found in today's audiences and reject stereotypes.

Good communicators don't view a speech as an ordeal to be endured, but as an opportunity to enrich the lives of their listeners. For this reason, they take every speech seriously, even if the audience is small.

Key Terms

channel, *9*	listener, *7*	situation, *11*
feedback, *10*	message, *9*	speaker, *7*
interference, *10*	scapegoat, *13*	stereotype, *13*

Review Questions

1. Why are communication skills important to your career?

2. Name five personal benefits of a public speaking course.

3. What are the seven elements of the speech communication process?

4. Why is speaking not necessarily the same thing as communicating?

5. If there is a contradiction between the verbal and nonverbal components of a speaker's message, which component is a listener likely to accept as the true message?

6. If communication fails, who is to blame—the speaker or the listener?

7. What two channels are most frequently used for classroom speeches?

8. What are the three types of interference?

9. What are stereotypes? Give some examples.

10. According to a survey, what is the number one mistake made by public speakers?

Building Critical-Thinking Skills

1. Describe an instance of miscommunication between you and another person (friend, relative, salesperson, etc.). Discuss what caused the problem, and how the interchange could have been handled better.

2. One of the elements of the speech communication process—feedback—is important for success in business. Imagine that you work in a travel agency and you have to give presentations on crime prevention to clients who have purchased overseas tours. How would you seek and use feedback?

Building Teamwork Skills

1. Working in a group, analyze a particular room (your classroom or some other site that everyone is familiar with) as a setting for speeches (consider size of the room, seating, equipment, and potential distractions). Prepare a list of tips that speakers can follow to minimize interference and maximize communication.

2. Taking turns, each member of a group states his or her chosen (or probable) career, and then group members work together to imagine scenarios (in that career) in which oral communication skills play an important part.

Despite a speech impediment that causes him to stutter, Jarvis McInnis is a popular speaker in the Gulf Coast region of the United States. A student at Tougaloo College, McInnis is shown addressing the Mississippi State Senate (after being honored as one of the state's top students). His secret for controlling nervousness and minimizing stuttering is to spend a great deal of time in preparation and practice. "If I don't prepare well, I stutter and stumble," he says. "But if I prepare thoroughly, my stuttering is barely noticeable, and the butterflies in my stomach are under control."

Controlling Nervousness

OBJECTIVES

After studying this chapter, you should be able to:

1. Describe the four kinds of fear that engender nervousness in speechmaking.

2. Explain why controlled nervousness is beneficial for a public speaker.

3. Apply techniques that can be used before and during a speech to control nervousness.

After pop singer Kelly Clarkson won the first season of

American Idol and became a top star, she received invitations to give speeches, but she declined them all. "I have never been nervous while singing," she said, "but when it comes to public speaking, I stumble on my words, sweat, and pull at my clothes."[1]

Only a few months after saying those words, however, she became an official spokesperson for NASCAR, giving presentations throughout the country. Not only was she speaking in public, but she was speaking with confidence and poise.

What happened?

"A good friend of mine helped me understand that when you give a speech, nothing bad is going to happen to you," she said. "If I open my mouth and make a mistake, people won't look down on me. Actually, they will probably like me because they will see that I'm the same as everyone else."[2]

If you experience nervousness as a public speaker, you are not alone. Most people—even performers such as Clarkson—suffer from stage fright when called upon to speak in public.[3] In fact, when researchers ask Americans to name their greatest fears, the fear of speaking to a group of strangers is listed more often than fear of snakes, insects, lightning, deep water, heights, or flying in airplanes.[4]

With the tips offered in this chapter, you will be able to control your nervousness and—like Kelly Clarkson—become a confident speaker.

Thanks to the insight of a friend, singer Kelly Clarkson is able to speak in public with confidence and poise.

Reasons for Nervousness

Is it foolish to be afraid to give a speech? Is this fear as groundless as a child's fear of the boogeyman? I used to think so, back when I first began making speeches. I was a nervous wreck, and I would often chide myself by saying, "Come on, relax, it's just a little speech. There's no good reason to be scared." But I was wrong. There *is* good reason to be scared; in fact, there are *four* good reasons.

1.   **Fear of being stared at.**   In the animal world, a stare is a hostile act. Dogs, baboons, and other animals sometimes defend their territory by staring. Their hostile gaze alone is enough to turn away an intruder. We human beings have similar reactions; it is part of our biological makeup to be upset by stares. Imagine that you are riding in a crowded elevator with a group of strangers. Suddenly you realize that the other people are staring directly at you. Not just glancing. *Staring.* You probably would be unnerved and frightened because a stare can be as threatening as a clenched fist—especially if it comes from people you don't know. That is why public speaking can be so frightening. You have a pack of total strangers "attacking" you with unrelenting stares while you are obliged to stand alone, exposed and vulnerable—a goldfish in a bowl, subject to constant scrutiny.

2.   **Fear of failure.**   In stressful social situations, most people are afraid of looking stupid. We say to ourselves, "What if I make a fool of myself?" or "What if I say something really dumb?"

3.   **Fear of rejection.**   What if we do our best, what if we deliver a polished speech, but the audience still does not like us? It would be quite a blow to our egos because we want to be liked and, yes, even loved. We want people to admire us, to consider us wise and intelligent, and to accept our ideas and opinions. We don't want people to dislike us or reject us.

4.   **Fear of the unknown.**   Throughout our lives we are apprehensive about doing new things, such as going to school for the first time, riding a bus without our parents, or going out on our first date. We cannot put a finger on exactly what we are afraid of, because our fear is vague and diffused. What we really fear is the unknown; we worry that some unpredictable disaster will occur. When we stand up to give a speech, we are sometimes assailed by this same fear of the unknown because we cannot predict the outcome of our speech. Fortunately, this fear usually disappears as we become experienced in giving speeches. We develop enough confidence to know that nothing terrible will befall us, just as our childhood fear of riding in a bus by ourselves vanished after two or three trips.

Many musicians say that fear keeps them from being flat and unenergetic.

All four of these fears are as understandable as the fear of lightning. There is no reason to be ashamed of having them.

The Value of Fear

In the first hour of my public speaking class, many students tell me that one of their goals is to eliminate all traces of nervousness. My response may surprise you as much as it surprises them: *You should not try to banish all your fear and nervousness. You need a certain amount of fear to give a good speech.*

You *need* fear? Yes. Fear energizes you; it makes you think more rapidly; it helps you speak with vitality and enthusiasm. Here is why: When you stand up to give a speech and fear hits you, your body goes on

adrenaline
a hormone, triggered by stress, that stimulates heart, lungs, and muscles and prepares the body for "fright, flight, or fight"

"red alert," the same biological mechanism that saved our cave-dwelling ancestors when they were faced with a hungry lion or a human foe and had to fight or flee to survive. Though not as crucial to us as it was to our ancestors, this system is still nice to have for emergencies: if you were walking down a deserted street one night and someone tried to attack you, your body would release a burst of **adrenaline** into your bloodstream, causing fresh blood and oxygen to rush to your muscles, and you would be able to fight ferociously or run faster than you have ever run in your life. The benefit of adrenaline can be seen in competitive sports: athletes *must* get their adrenaline flowing before a game begins. The great home-run slugger Reggie Jackson said during his heyday, "I have butterflies in my stomach almost every time I step up to the plate. When I don't have them, I get worried because it means I won't hit the ball very well."[5]

Many public speakers have the same attitude. John Farmer, a criminal trial attorney in Norton, Virginia, who has argued high-profile murder cases before the Virginia Supreme Court as well as in local courts, was asked if he still gets nervous in the courtroom. "Oh, yes," he replied, "the day I stop being nervous is the day that I'll stop doing a good job for my clients."[6]

In public speaking, adrenaline infuses you with energy; it causes extra blood and oxygen to rush not only to your muscles but also to your brain, thus enabling you to think with greater clarity and quickness. It makes you come across to your audience as someone who is alive and vibrant. Elayne Snyder, a speech teacher, uses the term **positive nervousness,** which she describes in this way: "It's a zesty, enthusiastic, lively feeling with a slight edge to it. Positive nervousness is the state you'll achieve by converting your anxiety into constructive energy. . . . It's still nervousness, but you're no longer victimized by it; instead you're vitalized by it."[7]

positive nervousness
useful energy

If you want proof that nervousness is beneficial, observe speakers who have absolutely no butterflies at all. Because they are 100 percent relaxed and cool, they give speeches that are dull and flat, with no energy, no zest. There is an old saying: "Speakers who say they are as cool as a cucumber usually give speeches about as interesting as a cucumber." Most good speakers report that if they don't have stage fright before a public appearance, their delivery is poor. One speaker, the novelist I. A. R. Wylie, said, "I rarely rise to my feet without a throat constricted with terror and a furiously thumping heart. When, for some reason, I *am* cool and self-assured, the speech is always a failure. I need fear to spur me on."[8]

Your Thoughts **?**

Many musicians make a distinction between "good nervousness" and "bad nervousness." What does this distinction mean? How does it apply to public speakers?

Another danger in being devoid of nervousness: you might get hit with a sudden bolt of panic. A hospital official told me that she gave an orientation speech to new employees every week for several years. "It became so routine that I lost all of my stage fright," she said. Then one day, while in the middle of her talk, she was suddenly and inexplicably struck with paralyzing fear. "I got all choked up and had to take a break to pull myself together."

Many other speakers have reported similar cases of sudden panic, which always hit on occasions when they were too relaxed. I once suffered such an attack, and the experience taught me that I must get myself "psyched up" for every speech. I remind myself that I need nervous energy to keep my listeners awake and interested. I encourage my butterflies to flutter around inside, so that I can be poised and alert.

Guidelines for Controlling Nervousness

We have just discussed how a complete lack of nervousness is undesirable. What about the other extreme? Is *too much* nervousness bad for you? Of course it is, especially if you are so frightened that you forget what you were planning to say, or if your breathing is so labored that you cannot get your words out. Your goal is to keep your nervousness under control so that you have just the right amount—enough to energize you, but not enough to cripple you. How can you do this? By paying heed to the following tips for the three phases of speechmaking: the planning stage, the period immediately before the speech, and during the speech.

In the Planning Stage

By giving time and energy to planning your speech, you can bypass many anxieties.

Choose a Topic about Which You Know a Great Deal

Nothing will get you more rattled than speaking on a subject about which you know little. If you are asked to talk on a topic with which you're not comfortable, decline the invitation (unless, of course, it is an assignment from an instructor or a boss who gives you no choice). Choose a topic about which you know a lot (or about which you can learn by doing extensive research). This will give you enormous self-confidence; if something terrible happens (for example, you lose your notes), you can improvise because your head will be filled with information about the subject. Also, familiarity with the topic will allow you to handle yourself well in the question-and-answer period after the speech.

Prepare Yourself Thoroughly

Here is a piece of advice given by many experienced speakers: *The very best precaution against excessive stage fright is thorough, careful preparation.* You have heard the expression "I came unglued." In public speaking, solid preparation is the "glue" that will hold you together.[9] Joel Weldon of Scottsdale, Arizona (who quips that he used to be so frightened of audiences that he was "unable to lead a church group in silent prayer"), gives his personal formula for controlling fear: "I prepare and then prepare, and then when I think I'm ready, I prepare some more."[10] Weldon recommends five to eight hours of preparation for each hour in front of an audience.[11]

Start your preparation far in advance of the speech date so that you have plenty of time to gather ideas, create an outline, and prepare speaking notes. Then practice, practice, practice. Don't just look over your notes—actually stand up and rehearse your talk in whatever way suits you: in front of a mirror, a camcorder, or a live audience of family or friends. Don't rehearse just once—run through your entire speech at least four times. If you "give" your speech four times at home, you will find that your fifth delivery—before a live audience—will be smoother and more self-assured than if you had not practiced at all.

Never Memorize a Speech

Giving a speech from memory courts disaster. Winston Churchill, the British prime minister during World War II who is considered one of the greatest orators of modern times, learned this lesson as a young man. In the beginning of his career, he would write out and memorize his speeches. One day, while giving a memorized talk to Parliament, he suddenly stopped. His mind went blank. He began his last sentence all over. Again his mind went blank. He sat down in embarrassment and shame. Never again did Churchill try to memorize a speech. This same thing has happened to many others who have tried to commit a speech to memory. Everything goes smoothly until they get derailed, and then they are hopelessly off the track.

Even if you avoid derailment, there is another reason for not memorizing: you will probably sound mechanical, like a robot. In addition to considering you dull and boring, your audience will sense that you are speaking from your memory and not from your heart, and they will question your sincerity.

Imagine Yourself Giving an Effective Speech

Let yourself daydream a bit: picture yourself going up to the lectern, nervous but in control of yourself, then giving a forceful talk to an appreciative audience. This visualization technique may sound silly, but it has worked for many speakers and it might work for you. Whatever you do, don't let yourself imagine the opposite—a bad speech or poor delivery. Negative daydreams will add unnecessary fear to your life in the days before your speech, and rob you of creative energy—energy that you need for preparing and practicing. Actress Ali MacGraw says, "We have only so much energy, and the more we direct toward the project itself, the less is left to pour into wondering 'Will I fail?'"[12]

Notice that the daydream I am suggesting includes nervousness. You need to have a realistic image in your mind: picture yourself as nervous, but nevertheless in command of the situation and capable of delivering a strong, effective speech.

positive imagery
visualization of successful actions

This technique, often called **positive imagery,** has been used by athletes for years. Have you ever watched professional golf on TV? Before each stroke, golfers carefully study the distance from the ball to the hole, the rise and fall of the terrain, and so on. Many of them report that just before swinging, they imagine themselves hitting the ball with the right amount of force and watching it go straight into the cup. Then they try to execute the play just as they imagined it. The imagery, many pros say, improves their game.

Baseball pitchers use visualization to help them throw a well-placed pitch.

Positive imagery works best when you can couple it with *believing* that you will give a successful speech. Is it absurd to hold such a belief? If you fail to prepare, yes, it is absurd. But if you spend time in solid preparation and rehearsal, you are justified in believing in success.

Know That Shyness Is No Barrier

Some shy people think that their shyness blocks them from becoming good speakers, but this is erroneous. Many shy introverts have succeeded in show business: Brad Pitt, Gwyneth Paltrow, Mick Thompson, Halle Berry, Diane Sawyer, Mariah Carey, Elizabeth Hurley, and David Letterman, to name just a few.[13] Many less-famous people also have succeeded. "I used to stammer," says Joe W. Boyd of Bellingham, Washington, "and I used to be petrified at the thought of speaking before a group of any size." Despite his shyness, Boyd joined a Toastmasters club to develop his speaking skills. Two years later, he won the Toastmasters International Public Speaking Contest by giving a superb speech to an audience of over 2,000 listeners.[14]

Shift Focus from Self to Audience

Before a speech, some speakers increase their anxiety by worrying about whether listeners will like them. This is a big mistake, says Johnny Lee, a specialist in preventing workplace violence, who controls his nervousness by focusing on his audience rather than on himself. To worry about yourself and your image, he says, "is a kind of vanity—you are putting yourself above your audience and your message."[15]

Carlos Jimenez, a member of a Toastmasters club in Northern California, says that focusing on himself is an act of inexcusable selfishness. "Who am I to worry about whether I will be perceived as a brilliant, eloquent expert. Who am I to think that the way I look and talk is more important than the people who are sitting in the audience? I look at public speaking as a way to help people, and I can't really help people if my mind is filled with 'me, me, me' instead of 'you, you, you.'"[16]

One good way to shift the focus from self to audience is to change your "self-talk." Whenever you have a self-centered thought such as, "I will make a total fool out of myself," substitute an audience-centered thought such as, "I will give my listeners information that will be very useful in their lives." This approach not only will liberate you from the grip of anxiety but also will empower you to connect with your audience.

Plan Visual Aids

Research shows that using a visual aid helps reduce anxiety.[17] Visual aids can help you in two ways: (1) you shift the audience's stares from you to your illustrations and (2) you walk about and move your hands and arms, thereby siphoning off some of your excess nervous energy. Whatever illustrations you decide to use, make sure they are understandable, appropriate, and clearly visible to everyone in the room.

connectpublic speaking.com
For additional tips, see "Speech Phobia" in the Supplementary Readings on *Connect Public Speaking.*

Make Arrangements

Long before you give your speech, inspect the place where you will speak and anticipate any problems: Is there an extension cord for the slide projector? Do the windows have curtains so that the room can be darkened for your slide presentation? Is there a chalkboard? Some talks have been ruined and some speakers turned into nervous wrecks because, at the last moment, they discover that there isn't an extension cord in the entire building.

Devote Extra Practice to the Introduction

Because you are likely to suffer the greatest anxiety at the beginning of your speech, you should spend a lot of time practicing your introduction.

Most speakers, actors, and musicians report that after the first minute or two, their nervousness moves to the background and the rest of the event is relatively easy. Ernestine Schumann-Heink, the German opera singer, said, "I grow so nervous before a performance, I become sick. I want to go home. But after I have been on the stage for a few minutes, I am so happy that nobody can drag me off." Perhaps happiness is too strong a word for what you will feel, but if you are a typical speaker, the rest of your speech will be smooth sailing once you have weathered the turbulent waters of the first few minutes.

Immediately before the Speech

Here are a few tips for the hours preceding your speech:

Verify Equipment and Materials

On the day of your speech, arrive early and inspect every detail of the arrangements you have made. Is the needed equipment in place and in good working order? If there is a public-address system, test your voice on it before the audience arrives so that you can feel at ease with it. Learn how to adjust the microphone.

Greet listeners as they arrive.

Get Acclimated to Audience and Setting

It can be frightening to arrive at the meeting place at the last moment and confront a sea of strange faces waiting to hear you talk. If you arrive at least one hour early, you can get acclimated to the setting and chat with people as they come into the room. In this way, you will see them not as a hostile pack of strangers but as ordinary people who wish you well.

Henry Heimlich is the creator of the famed Heimlich Maneuver for rescuing people who are choking. Even though he frequently gives lectures throughout the world, Dr. Heimlich says, "I am always a little nervous wondering how a particular audience will accept me and my thoughts. It is good to meet some of the audience socially before lecturing to them, in order to relate to their cultural and intellectual backgrounds. You are then their 'friend.'"[18]

Danielle Kennedy of Sun Valley, Idaho, says that when she began her speaking career, she was so nervous she would hide out in a bathroom until it was time for her to speak. Now, she says, she mingles with the listeners as they arrive and engages them in conversation. "This reminds me that they are just nice people who want to be informed. I also give myself pleasant thoughts. Things like: 'Can you imagine, these people drove 100 miles just to hear me. I am so lucky. These people are wonderful.' I get real warm thoughts going by the time I get up there."[19]

Use Physical Actions to Release Tension

We have seen that adrenaline is beneficial, providing athletes and public speakers with wonderful bursts of energy, but it also has a bad side. When your body goes on red alert, you get pumped up and ready for action, but you also get trembling hands and jittery knees. If you are an athlete, this is no problem because you will soon be engaged in vigorous physical activity that will drain off excess nervous energy. As a public speaker, you lack such easy outlets. Nevertheless, there are several tension releasers you can use:

connectpublic
speaking.com
For additional techniques for relaxation, go to *Connect Public Speaking,* and click on WEBLINKS.

- Take a few deep breaths. Be sure to inhale slowly and exhale slowly.
- Do exercises that can be performed quietly without calling attention to yourself. Here are some examples: (1) Tighten and then relax your leg muscles. (2) Push your arm or hand muscles against a hard object (such as a desktop or a chair) for a few moments, then release the pressure. (3) Press the palms of your hands against each other in the same way: tension, release . . . tension, release . . .

During the Speech

Here are some important pointers to keep in mind as you deliver a speech.

Pause a Few Moments before Starting

All good speakers pause a few moments before they begin their talk. This silence is effective because (1) it is dramatic, building up the audience's interest and curiosity; (2) it makes you look poised and in control; (3) it calms you; and (4) it gives you a chance to look at your notes and get your first two or three sentences firmly in mind.

Many tense, inexperienced speakers rush up to the lectern and begin their speech at once, thus getting off to a frenzied, flustered start. In the back of their mind, they have the notion that silence is a terrible thing, a shameful void that must be filled up immediately. To the contrary, silence is a good breathing space between what went before and what comes next. It helps the audience tune in to the speaker and tune out extraneous thoughts.

Deal Rationally with Your Body's Turmoil

If you are a typical beginning speaker, you will suffer from some or all of the following symptoms as you begin your talk:

- Pounding heart
- Trembling hands
- Shaky knees
- Dry, constricted throat
- Difficulty in breathing
- Quivering voice
- Flushed face

You usually suffer the greatest discomfort during the first few minutes of a speech, but then things get better. If, however, your symptoms get worse as you go along, it might be because your mind has taken a wrong path. Examine the two paths diagrammed in Figure 2.1. If you take Route A, you are trapped in a vicious circle. Your mind tells your body that disaster is upon you, and your body responds by feeling worse. This, in turn, increases your brain's perception of disaster.

You can avoid this rocky road by choosing Route B, in which your mind helps your body stay in control. The mental trick is to remind yourself that nervousness is an ally that can help energize you. Tell yourself that your symptoms, rather than being a prelude to disaster, are evidence that you are keyed up enough to give a good speech.

Think of Communication, Not Performance

Regard your task as *communication* rather than *performance.* Dr. Michael T. Motley of the University of California, Davis, says that speakers who suffer from excessive anxiety make the mistake of thinking of themselves as *performing* for listeners, whom they see as hostile evaluators. Such people say, "The audience will ridicule me if I make a mistake. I'll be embarrassed to death." But in fact, says Dr. Motley,

Your Thoughts ■

"It is folly for a speaker to focus on his or her personal appearance." Do you agree? Defend your answer.

Figure 2.1

The alternative paths that a speaker feeling stressed might take.

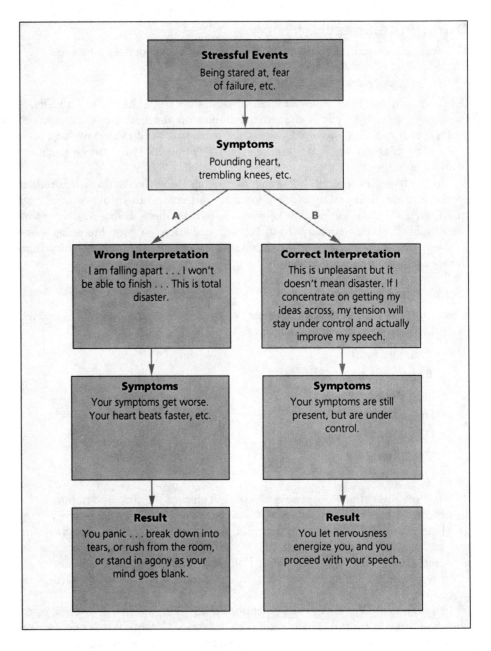

audiences are more interested in hearing what you have to say "than in analyzing or criticizing how [you] say it." Audiences "usually ignore errors and awkwardness as long as they get something out of a speech."[20]

When speakers stop worrying about "How well am I performing?" and start thinking about "How can I share my ideas with these people?" two things usually happen: (1) their anxiety comes down to a manageable level and (2) their delivery improves dramatically. By treating speechmaking as more like one-on-one communication than as a stage exhibition, they tend to talk *with* people, instead of orate *at* them; they tend to speak conversationally rather than in a stiff, unnatural way.

When one of my students, Maxine Jones, began her first classroom speech, her voice sounded artificial and cold; but after a few moments, she sounded animated and warm, as if she were carrying on a lively conversation. This caused her to become more interesting and easier to follow. Later she explained her transformation: "At first I was scared to death, but then I noticed that everyone in the room was looking at me with curiosity in their eyes, and I could tell that they really wanted to hear what I was saying. I told myself, 'They really *care* about this information—I can't let them down.' So I settled down and talked to them as if they were my friends. I got so involved with explaining things to them that I didn't worry too much about being scared."

What Jones discovered is confirmed by athletes. Most tennis players, for example, are gripped by nervous tension before a match, but if they concentrate on hitting the ball, their tension recedes into the background. Likewise, public speakers may be filled with anxiety before a speech, but if they concentrate on communicating with the audience, their anxiety moves to a back burner, where it provides energy for the task.

Know That Most Symptoms Are Not Seen

Some speakers get rattled because they think the audience is keenly aware of their thumping heart and quaking hands. You, of course, are painfully aware of those symptoms, but—believe it or not—your audience is usually oblivious to your body's distress. Remember that people are sitting out there wanting to hear your ideas. They are not saying to themselves, "Let's see, what signs of nervousness is this person displaying?" I have had students tell me after a speech that they were embarrassed about their jittery performance, yet I and the other listeners in the class saw no signs of nervousness. We were listening to the ideas and failed to notice the speaker's discomfort. Various studies have found the same thing to be true: audiences are unaware of the symptoms that the speakers think are embarrassingly obvious.[21] In other words, you are probably the only one who knows that your knees are shaking and your heart is pounding.

Dick Cavett, who spent many years as a TV talk-show host, notes that a TV performer's level of stage fright "varies from night to night. The best thing to do is tell yourself it doesn't show one-eighth as much as you feel. If you're a little nervous, you don't look nervous at all. If you're very nervous, you look slightly nervous. And if you're totally out of control, you look troubled. It scales down on the screen." People who appear on a talk show, says Cavett, should

Troy Collins, a native of Virginia who works for the Los Angeles Police Department, displays nervous tension as he waits to enter the ring for a sumo wrestling match in Washington, D.C. Before an event, many athletes are gripped by nervous tension, but when the action starts, they focus on performing their maneuvers, and the tension moves to a back burner, where it provides ongoing energy. Likewise, if public speakers concentrate on communicating with their audience, their anxiety recedes into the background, where it acts as a source of power.

always remind themselves that everything they are doing *looks* better than it *feels*. "Your nervous system may be giving you a thousand shocks, but the viewer can only see a few of them."[22] The same thing holds true for a speech: you look better than you feel.

Never Mention Nervousness or Apologize

Despite what I've just said, there may be times when an audience does notice your nervousness—when, for example, your breathing is audibly labored. In such a case, resist the temptation to comment or apologize. Everyone knows that most people get nervous when they talk in public, so why call attention to it or apologize for it?

Commenting about nervousness can create two big dangers. First of all, you might get yourself more rattled than you were to begin with. I remember listening to a teacher who was giving a talk to a PTA meeting one night. In the middle of her remarks, she suddenly blurted out, "Oh my god, I knew I would fall apart." Up to that time, I had not been aware of any discomfort or nervousness. She tried to continue her talk, but she was too flustered. She gave up the effort and sat down with a red face. I don't know what kind of internal distress she was suffering, of course, but I am certain that if she had said nothing about her nervousness, she could have dragged herself through the speech. When she sat down, I felt irritated and disappointed because I had been keenly interested in her remarks. How selfish of her, I thought, to deprive me of the second half of her speech simply because she was nervous. I know that my reaction sounds insensitive, but it underscores an important point: your listeners don't care about your emotional distress; they only want to hear your ideas.

The second risk in mentioning symptoms is that your audience might have been unaware of your nervousness before you brought it up, but now you have distracted them from your speech and they are watching the very thing you don't want them to scrutinize: your body's behavior. If you say, "I'm sorry that my hands are shaking," what do you think the audience will pay close attention to, at least for the next few minutes? Your hands, of course, instead of your speech. Keep your audience's attention focused on your ideas, and they will pay little or no attention to your emotional and physical distress.

Don't Let Your Audience Upset You

If you are like some speakers, you get rattled when you look out at the audience and observe that most listeners are poker-faced and unsmiling. Does this mean they are displeased with your speech? No. Their solemn faces have nothing to do with you and your speech. This is just one of those peculiarities of human nature: in a conversation, people will smile and nod and encourage you, but

Actress Penelope Cruz listens to a speaker at a film festival in Berlin. Is she displeased with the speaker's remarks? Is she angry? Is she bored? Don't jump to conclusions. Perhaps this is just her habitual expression when she's absorbed in listening to an interesting subject. Speakers should not let such expressions upset them. Some listeners who look displeased are actually quite pleased.

Tips for Your Career

A psychologist tells of the time when he was speaking at a convention as the presiding officer. At one point, he wanted to praise an associate, who was sitting next to him at the head table, for her hard work in planning the convention. "As I began my words of tribute," he said, "my mind suddenly went blank, and I couldn't remember her name! It was awful. This was a woman I had worked with for years. She was like a sister."

Fortunately, he said, everyone was wearing name tags, so he leaned over, saw her name, and used it in his remarks—without the audience suspecting his memory lapse.

Such lapses are common, but don't be alarmed. There is a simple solution: Prepare a card with all basic information—names, dates, phone numbers—and keep the card with your other notes for easy access.

This "card trick" is used by many ministers, politicians, and other public speakers. "When I perform weddings, even if I'm an old friend of the couple," says one minister, "I have their names printed in big letters on a card that I keep in front of me."

Use a card for any familiar passages, such as the Lord's Prayer or the Pledge of Allegiance, that you are supposed to recite or to lead the audience in reciting. You may never need to read the card, but it's nice to have a backup in case of emergency.

Please don't misinterpret this tip to mean that you should write out an entire speech. Brief notes—a few words or phrases—are still recommended. Use the "card trick" only for names, numbers, and wordings that must be recalled with complete accuracy.

Officiating at a wedding, a minister directs the bride to put the ring on the groom's finger. At public ceremonies, many ministers avoid embarrassment by having key information (such as the names of bride and groom) on a card in front of them.

when listening to a speech in an audience, the same people will wear (most of the time) a blank mask. The way to deal with those stony faces is to remind yourself that your listeners want you to succeed; they hope that you will give them a worthwhile message. If you are lucky, you will notice two or three listeners who are obviously loving your speech; they are nodding in agreement or giving you looks of appreciation. Let your eyes go to them frequently, for they will give you courage and confidence.

If you are an inexperienced speaker, you may get upset if you see members of an audience whispering to one another. You may wonder, "Are these people making negative comments about me?" If the listeners are smiling, it's even worse: You ask yourself, "Did I say something foolish? Is there something wrong with my clothes?" If this happens to you, keep in mind that your rude listeners are probably talking about something other than the quality of your speech or your personal appearance. Most likely, they are just sharing some personal gossip. If

connectpublic
speaking.com
For an interactive exercise on nervousness, visit Chapter 2 on *Connect Public Speaking.*

by chance they *are* whispering about something you've said, it's not necessarily negative. They may be whispering that they agree with you 100 percent.

What if you see faces that look angry or displeased? Don't assume the worst. Some people get a troubled look on their face whenever they concentrate on a speaker's message. Michelle Roberts, a defense attorney in Washington, D.C., studies the facial expressions of every juror when she addresses the jury during a trial, but she has learned that sour faces do not necessarily signify disapproval. "Sometimes jurors seem like they're scowling and actually they're with you."[23]

What if a listener stands up and walks out of the room? For some inexperienced speakers, this is a stunning personal setback, a cause for alarm. Before you jump to conclusions, bear in mind that the listener's behavior is not necessarily a response to your speech: he or she may have another meeting to attend or may need to use the rest room or may have become ill suddenly. But what if the listener is indeed storming out of the room in a huff, obviously rejecting your speech? In such a case, advises veteran speaker Earl Nightingale, "don't worry about it. On controversial subjects, you're bound to have listeners who are not in agreement with you—unless you're giving them pure, unadulterated pap. Trying to win over every member of the audience is an impossible and thankless task. Remember, there were those who disagreed with wise, kind Socrates."[24]

Act Poised

To develop confidence when you face an audience, act as if you already are confident. Why? Because playing the role of the self-assured speaker can often transform you into a speaker who is genuinely confident and poised. In various wars, soldiers have reported that they were terrified before going into combat, but nevertheless they acted brave in front of their buddies. During the battle, to their surprise, what started off as a pretense became a reality. Instead of pretending to be courageous, they actually became so. The same thing often happens to public speakers.

Look Directly at the Audience

If you are frightened of your audience, it is tempting to stare at your notes or the back wall or the window, but these evasions will only add to your nervousness rather than reduce it.

Force yourself to establish eye contact, especially at the beginning of your speech. Good eye contact means more than just a quick, furtive glance at various faces in front of you; it means "locking" your eyes with a listener's for a couple of seconds. Locking eyes may sound frightening, but it actually helps to calm you. In an article about a public speaking course that she took, writer Maggie Paley said, "When you make contact with one other set of eyes, it's a connection; you can relax and concentrate. The first time I did it, I calmed down 90 percent, and spoke . . . fluently."[25]

Don't Speak Too Fast

Because of nervous tension and a desire to "get it over with," many speakers race through their speeches. "Take it slow and easy," advises Dr. Michael T. Motley of the University of California, Davis. "People in an audience have a tremendous job of information-processing to do. They need your help. Slow down, pause, and guide the audience through your talk by delineating major and minor points carefully. Remember that your objective is to help the audience understand what you are saying, not to present your information in record time."[26]

To help yourself slow down, rehearse your speech in front of friends or relatives and ask them to raise their hands whenever you talk too rapidly. For the actual delivery of the speech, write yourself reminders in large letters on your notes (such as "SLOW DOWN"). While you are speaking, look at your listeners and talk directly to them in the same calm, patient, deliberate manner you would use if you were explaining an idea to a friend.

Get Audience Action Early in the Speech

I said earlier that it's a bit unnerving to see your listeners' expressionless faces. In some speeches, you can change those faces from blank to animated by asking a question. (Tips on how to ask questions will be discussed in Chapter 8.) When the listeners respond with answers or a show of hands, they show themselves to be friendly and cooperative, and this reduces your apprehension. When they loosen up, you loosen up.

Eliminate Excess Energy

For siphoning off excess energy during the speech, you can use visual aids (as mentioned earlier) and these two tension releasers:

- Let your hands make gestures. You will not have any trouble making gestures if you simply allow your hands to be free. Don't clutch note cards or thrust your hands into your pockets or grip the lectern. If you let your hands hang by your side or rest on the lectern, you will find that they will make gestures naturally. You will not have to think about it.
- Walk about. Though you obviously should not pace back and forth like a caged animal, you can walk a few steps at a time. For example, you can walk a few steps to the left of the lectern to make a point, move back to the lectern to look at your notes for your next point, and then walk to the right of the lectern as you speak.

In addition to reducing tension, gestures and movement make you a more exciting and interesting speaker than someone who stands frozen in one spot.

Accept Imperfection

If you think that you must give a perfect, polished speech, you put enormous—and unnecessary—pressure on yourself. Your listeners don't care whether your delivery is perfect; they simply hope that your words will enlighten or entertain them. Think of yourself as merely a package deliverer; the audience is more interested in the package than in how skillfully you hand it over.

Making a mistake is not the end of the world. Even experienced speakers commit a fair number of blunders and bloopers. If you completely flub a sentence or mangle an idea, you might say something like, "No, wait. That's not the way I wanted to explain this. Let me try again." If you momentarily forget what you were planning to say, don't despair. Pause a few moments to regain your composure and find your place in your notes. If you can't find your place, ask the audience for help: "I've lost my train of thought—where was I?" There is no need to apologize. In conversation, you pause and correct yourself all the time; to do so in a speech makes you sound spontaneous and natural.

If you make a mistake that causes your audience to snicker or laugh, try to join in. If you can laugh at yourself, your audience will love you—they will see that you are no "stuffed shirt." Some comedians deliberately plan "mistakes" as a technique for gaining rapport with their audiences.

Welcome Experience

If you are an inexperienced speaker, please know that you will learn to control your nervousness as you get more and more practice in public speaking, both in your speech class and in your career. You should welcome this experience as a way to further your personal and professional growth.

One student told her public speaking instructor at the beginning of the course that she just *knew* she would drop out of the class right before her first speech. She stayed, though, and developed into a fine speaker. She later got a promotion in her company partly because of her speaking ability. "I never thought I'd say this," she admitted, "but the experience of giving speeches—plus learning how to handle nervousness—helped me enormously. Before I took the course, I used to panic whenever I started off a talk. I had this enormous lump in my throat, and I thought I was doing terrible. I would hurry through my talk just to get it over with." But as a result of the course, she said, "I learned to control my nervousness and use it to my advantage. Now I'm as nervous as ever when I give a speech, but I make the nervousness work *for* me instead of *against* me."

In your career, rather than shying away from speaking opportunities, seek them out. An old saying is true: experience is the best teacher.

After reading this chapter, if you feel that you need additional tips on managing your anxiety, see the article entitled "Speech Phobia" in the Supplementary Readings on Connect Public Speaking (connectpublicspeaking.com).

Resources for Review and Skill Building

connectpublic
speaking.com

Connect Public Speaking provides resources for study and review, including sample speech videos, an Outline Tutor, and practice tests.

Summary

The nervousness engendered by stage fright is a normal, understandable emotion experienced by most public speakers. The major reasons for speakers' nervousness are (1) fear of being stared at, (2) fear of failure, (3) fear of rejection, and (4) fear of the unknown.

Instead of trying to eliminate nervousness, welcome it as a source of energy. Properly channeled, it can help you give a better speech than you would deliver if you were completely relaxed.

The best way to avoid excessive, crippling nervousness is to pour time and energy into preparing and practicing your speech. Then, when you stand up to speak, deal rationally with your nervous symptoms (such as trembling knees and dry throat); remind yourself that the symptoms are not a prelude to disaster but instead are evidence that you are keyed up enough to give a good speech. Never call attention to your nervousness and never apologize for it; the listeners don't care about your emotional state—they just want to hear your message. Concentrate on getting your ideas across to the audience; this will get your mind where it belongs—on your listeners and not on yourself—and it will help you move your nervousness to a back burner, where it can still simmer and energize you without hindering your effectiveness.

Key Terms

adrenaline, *26*   positive imagery, *28*   positive nervousness, *26*

Review Questions

1. What are the four main reasons for speakers' nervousness?

2. Why are fear and nervousness beneficial to the public speaker?

3. Why is delivering a speech from memory a bad method?

4. Is shyness a liability for a speaker? Explain your answer.

5. How can a speaker reduce excessive tension before a speech?

6. Does an audience detect most of a speaker's nervous symptoms? Explain your answer.

7. Why should you never call attention to your nervousness?

8. Explain the idea "Think of communication, not performance."

9. Why should speakers not be upset when they see the solemn faces of their listeners?

10. Why should a speaker act as if he or she is confident?

Building Critical-Thinking Skills

1. In an experiment, psychologist Rowland Miller asked college students to do something embarrassing, such as singing "The Star-Spangled Banner," while classmates watched. Those students who reported a great degree of embarrassment thought that their classmates would consider them fools and like them less, but Miller found just the opposite: The classmates expressed greater regard for the easily embarrassed students after the performance than before. What lessons can a public speaker draw from this research?

2. Imagine that while you are speaking to an audience, you notice that (a) everyone is very quiet, (b) a man in the front is rubbing his neck, and (c) a woman is looking in her purse. Using two columns on a piece of paper, give a negative interpretation of these events in the first column, and then give a positive interpretation in the adjacent column.

Building Teamwork Skills

1. In a group, make a list of the nervous symptoms that group members have experienced before and during oral communication in public. (This may include being asked for comments during a class discussion.) Then discuss ways to control nervousness.

2. Worrying about future events, say mental-health therapists, can be helpful at certain times and harmful at other times. In a group, discuss the pros and cons of worrying, giving examples from everyday life. Then decide which aspects of speech preparation and delivery deserve to be worried about and which do not.

An ethnic Uighur student in China listens to an instructor. When listeners are engaged and attentive, they not only learn a lot but also help to energize and encourage the speaker.

Listening

OBJECTIVES

After studying this chapter, you should be able to:

1. Explain the difference between hearing and listening.

2. Describe eight keys to effective listening.

3. Define three major responsibilities that listeners have toward speakers.

4. Know how to give and receive evaluations of speeches.

Causing 1.6 million deaths each year, tuberculosis is an

infectious disease that strikes most often in low-income areas of the world. Because it is rare in North America, news media sounded an alarm in 2007 when an American, Andrew Speaker, contracted the disease and was quarantined by the U.S. government. Some experts feared that he could set off a national epidemic of tuberculosis.

The patient was treated at Denver's National Jewish Medical and Research Center by Dr. Gwen Huitt, one of the nation's top infectious-disease specialists. Shortly after she began treatment, Dr. Huitt conducted a press conference to educate the public on what was happening. During the conference, which was televised by several cable TV networks, she discussed the nature of the disease and mentioned that "tuberculosis infects one-third of the world's population." She was trying to make the point that millions of people are exposed to the TB bacterium, but most of them do not die.[1]

Unfortunately, some TV viewers thought she said that one-third of the world's population would be killed by the disease. Scared individuals telephoned doctors' offices with queries—until authorities reassured the public that there was no cause for panic.[2] Further reassurance was given two months later when the patient was released in good condition.[3]

As Dr. Gwen Huitt tries to calm public fears, some TV viewers fail to listen correctly.

Dr. Huitt was totally innocent in the public misunderstanding—she had spoken clearly and concisely. Her experience, however, illustrates a common problem in all levels of society—ineffective listening. When new or difficult material is presented, almost all listeners are faced with a challenge because human speech lacks the stability and permanence of the printed word. Oral communication is fast-moving and impermanent—"written on the wind."

This chapter is designed to help you become a better listener. It also should help you become a better speaker. As you become more aware of the difficulties of the listening process, you will be able to make adjustments in your presentations to ensure that everyone in your audience receives your message clearly and accurately.

The Problem of Poor Listening Skills

A parent says to a child, "Are you listening to me?"

The child replies, "I hear you. I hear you."

Although in conversation we sometimes use the words "hear" and "listen" interchangeably, they are not synonymous. **Hearing** occurs when your ears pick up sound waves being transmitted by a speaker. **Listening** involves making sense out of what is being transmitted. As Keith Davis put it, "Hearing is with the ears, listening is with the mind."[4]

hearing
the process by which sound waves are received by the ear

listening
the act of interpreting and evaluating what is being said

Listening is a major part of daily life. People spend an estimated 50 to 70 percent of their communication time listening. In almost all jobs, employees spend far more time listening than they spend reading and writing.

And yet, despite all this time devoted to listening, research shows that most of us are not very effective as listeners. According to tests by Dr. Lyman K. Steil of the University of Minnesota in St. Paul, here is what happens after the average person listens to a 10-minute oral presentation:

- Ten minutes later: The listener has heard, understood, properly evaluated, and retained only about 50 percent of what was said.
- Two days later: The listener's comprehension and retention have dropped to only 25 percent of what was said.[5]

You might think that our chief problem is failing to retain information, but actually our biggest error is miscomprehending and distorting what we hear. The results can be disastrous. Throughout the world, instructions are misunderstood, equipment breaks down from improper use, productivity declines, profits sag, sales are lost, feelings are hurt, morale is lowered, rumors get started, and health is harmed.[6] Dr. Steil estimates that listening mistakes each week in American business might cost as much as a billion dollars.[7]

How to Listen Effectively

Many businesses have discovered that they can boost productivity and sales by teaching their employees to listen more effectively. Here are some of the techniques that are taught.

Prepare Yourself

Listening to difficult material is hard work, so prepare yourself as thoroughly as a runner prepares for a race.

Prepare yourself *physically*. Get plenty of sleep the night before. If necessary, exercise right before the speech or lecture. Let's suppose that you will be sitting in a warm room in mid-afternoon and are therefore likely to become drowsy and lethargic. You could take a brisk walk before entering the room to make yourself alert.

Prepare yourself *intellectually*. If the subject matter of the speech is new or complex, do research or background reading beforehand. In this way, the speech will be much easier to understand. The American philosopher Henry David Thoreau once said, "We hear and apprehend only what we already half know."

Be Willing to Expend Energy

When you listen to a comedian cracking jokes on TV, do you have to work hard to pay attention? Of course not. You simply sit back in a comfortable chair and enjoy the humor. It is easy, effortless, relaxing.

If you are like many listeners, you assume that when you go into a room for a lecture or a speech on a difficult subject, you should be able to sit back and absorb the content just as easily as you grasp a comedian's jokes. This is a major misconception, because the two situations are quite different. Listening to light material requires only a modest amount of mental effort, while listening effectively to difficult material requires work. You must be alert and energetic, giving total concentration to the speech, with your eyes on the speaker, your ears tuned in to the speaker's words, and your mind geared to receive the message.

According to Dr. Ralph G. Nichols, who did pioneering work on listening skills at the University of Minnesota, listening "is characterized by faster heart action, quicker circulation of the blood, and a small rise in body temperature."[8]

If you tend to drift away mentally whenever a speaker begins to talk about unfamiliar or difficult material, try to break yourself of the habit. Vow to put as much energy as necessary into paying attention.

Listening often requires intense concentration.

Listen Analytically

You should analyze a speech as it is being presented—not to nitpick or poke holes in it, but to help you understand and remember the speaker's message, and to determine which parts of the speech are valuable to you and which are worthless. There are two elements that you should examine analytically: the main ideas and the support materials.

Focus on main ideas. Some listeners make the mistake of treating all of a speaker's utterances as equal in importance. This causes them to "miss the forest for the trees": they look so hard at individual sentences that they fail to see the "big picture," the larger meaning.

Try to distinguish the speaker's primary ideas from the secondary material—such as facts, figures, and stories—that are used to explain, illustrate, or prove the primary ideas. If a speaker tells an interesting story, for example, ask yourself, "Why is the speaker telling me this? What main idea is the speaker trying to get across to me by telling this story?"

Main points are more important than support materials, as you can see in the sample notes in Figure 3.1.

Evaluate support materials. Effective speakers use support materials (such as stories, statistics, and quotations) to explain, illustrate, or prove their main points. As a listener, you should evaluate those supports, asking yourself these questions:

- Is each main point amplified with support materials?
- Do the support materials seem to be accurate and up-to-date? Are they derived from reliable sources or are they merely hearsay?
- Do they truly explain or prove a point?

Learning to listen analytically not only will help you become a better listener but also will help you improve the quality of your own speeches. You will find yourself avoiding the mistakes you see in the speeches of others.

Your Thoughts ❓

Sometimes listening can be treated as passive receiving, while at other times it should be regarded as active participation. Give examples of when each approach is appropriate.

Take Notes

You should take notes whenever you listen to a speech—for the following reasons:

1. *Note taking gives you a record of the speaker's most important points.* Unless you have superhuman powers of memory, there is no way you can remember all of a speaker's key ideas without taking notes.

2. *Note taking sharpens and strengthens your ability to listen analytically.* When you take notes, you force your mind to scan a speech like radar, looking for main points and evidence. You end up being a better listener than if you did not take any notes at all.[9]

3. *Note taking is a good way to keep your attention on the speaker and not let your mind wander.* For this reason, it's a good idea to take notes on *all* speeches—not just on important lectures at school. A colleague explains why he takes notes at every meeting he attends, even though he often throws his notes away soon afterward:

   I take notes at any talk I go to. I review the notes right after the meeting to solidify the key points in my mind. Afterwards, I may save the notes for my files or for some sort of follow-up, but I usually throw them away. This doesn't mean that I had wasted my time by taking notes. The act of writing them helped me to listen actively and analytically. It also—I must confess—kept me from daydreaming.

There are many ways of taking notes, and you may have already developed a method that suits you. Some listeners use a variety of methods because speakers have different organizational and delivery styles, and a method that works with one speaker might not work with another.

Whatever system you use, your notes should include major points, with pertinent data or support materials that back up those points. You also may want to leave space for comments to yourself or questions that need to be asked.

Two methods are shown in Figure 3.1 . In Option A, the first column is designated for main ideas and the second column for support materials. The third column is for your responses—questions and concerns that come to mind during the

connectpublic
speaking.com
See "Listening
Profile" and
"Notes" template
in Supplementary
Readings on *Connect
Public Speaking*.

Figure 3.1

Two methods of note taking are shown as Option A and Option B.

Speaker's Words

"Many people don't pledge to become organ donors because they think there is a surplus of organs available. This is tragic because there is actually a dire shortage in all parts of the country, according to the *Los Angeles Times*. Many patients will die while waiting for a desperately needed organ. The situation is especially grim for liver and heart patients. Last year, according to the United Network for Organ Sharing, 7,467 patients were on the national waiting list for a liver; 954 of them—13 percent—died while waiting. For people needing hearts: 3,698 were on the list; 746 died while waiting—that's 20 percent. According to the *Times*, the situation is even worse than these statistics indicate: thousands of people needing organs, such as those injured in car accidents, die before their names can reach the official waiting lists."

Option A
The speaker's message is analyzed and sorted. (See text for details.)

Main Ideas	Support material	Response
Shortage of organs	All parts of U.S.	
Many will die waiting	Liver—13% died last year	
	Heart—20% died	Why is heart stat higher?
Situation worse than it looks	1000s die before names can reach lists	

Option B
Because it is sometimes hard to distinguish between main ideas and subpoints while a speaker is talking, some listeners jot down one item per line.

Shortage of organs

All parts of U.S.

Many will die waiting

Liver—13% died last year

Heart—20% died—why higher?

Situation worse than it looks

1000s die before names can reach lists

Later, the listener can analyze the notes, using a highlighter to focus on key ideas and a red pen for follow-up items.

Shortage of organs

All parts of U.S.

Many will die waiting

Liver—13% died last year

Heart—20% died—why higher?

Situation worse than it looks

1000s die before names can reach lists

Tips for Your Career

Tip 3.1 Take Notes in Important Conversations and Small-Group Meetings

Whenever your superiors and colleagues talk to you (either one-on-one or in a group meeting) about work-related matters, take notes. Not only does this give you a written record of important discussions, but it also is a compliment, a nonverbal way of saying, "Your ideas are important to me—so important that I want to make sure I get them down correctly." Contrary to what some may think, taking notes does *not* signify to others that you have a poor memory.

One of the most common gripes of employees is that "the boss never listens to what we say." So, if you are ever in a supervisory position, take notes whenever one of your subordinates comes to you with a suggestion or a complaint. Doing so demonstrates that you value the employee's comments and are prepared to take action if necessary. Even if you can't take action, the employee's morale is boosted because you have shown you truly listen and truly care.

Can you ever rise so high in your career that you no longer need to take notes? Not if you're Robert Stempel, former chairman of General Motors. Though he headed one of the world's largest corporations and could have hired a platoon of secretaries to take notes for him, Stempel took his own notes at management meetings.

speech. When the question-and-answer period begins, you can scan the response column and ask questions. (If a question that you jotted down is answered later in the speech itself, your effort hasn't been wasted; having raised the question will cause you to listen to the explanation with special interest.) The response column also can be used to plan follow-up research. (For example, you might remind yourself: "Look up more info on this in library.") The response column does not require an entry for each of the speaker's points; use it only as needed.

Option B is a good choice when a speaker talks fast and does not present his or her material in an easily recognized pattern or does not clearly distinguish between main points and subpoints. Write one note per line. Later use a highlighter to mark the key ideas and a red pen to circle items that you need to follow up on.

Whatever method you use, don't try to write down every sentence that the speaker says. Summarize; put the speaker's ideas into your own words. This will help you make sure that you are understanding the speaker's message. If you try to copy all utterances, as if you were a court stenographer, you would wear your hand out, and you would fall into the habit of transcribing without evaluating.

Soon after a presentation, review your notes and, if necessary, clarify them while the speaker's words are still fresh in your mind. If any parts of your notes are vague or confusing, seek help from another listener (or the speaker, if available).

Resist Distractions

Concentrating on a speech is made difficult by four common types of distractions: (1) *auditory*–people coughing or whispering, a noisy air conditioner, loud music from an adjacent room; (2) *visual*–cryptic comments on the board from a previous meeting, a nearby listener who is intriguing to look at, an appealing magazine on the desk or table; (3) *physical*–a headache or stuffy nose, a seat that is too hard, a room that is too hot or too cold; (4) *mental*–daydreams, worries, and preoccupations.

Tips for Your Career

Tip 3.2 Learn How Listeners Show Respect in Different Cultures

While Gail Opp-Kemp, an American artist, was giving a speech on the art of Japanese brush painting to an audience that included visitors from Japan, she was disconcerted to see that many of her Japanese listeners had their eyes closed. Were they turned off because an American had the audacity to instruct Japanese in their own art form? Were they deliberately trying to signal their rejection of her?

Opp-Kemp later found out that her listeners were not being disrespectful. Japanese listeners sometimes close their eyes to enhance concentration. Her listeners were paying tribute to her by meditating upon her words.

Someday you may be either a speaker or a listener in a situation involving people from other countries or members of a minority group in North America. Learning how different cultures signal respect can help you avoid misunderstandings. Here are some examples:

- In the deaf culture of North America, many listeners signify applause not by clapping their hands but by waving them in the air.

- In some cultures (both overseas and in some minority groups in North America), listeners are considered disrespectful if they look directly at the speaker. Respect is shown by looking in the general direction but avoiding direct eye contact.

- In some countries, whistling by listeners is a sign of approval, while in other countries, it is a form of jeering.

For detailed information about different cultures, visit the author's Web site (connectpublicspeaking.com), select STUDENT EDITION, click on WEBLINKS, and explore links for this page.

Mental distractions are often caused by the fact that your mind runs faster than a speaker's words. As a listener, you can process speech at about 500 words per minute, while most speakers talk at 125 to 150 words a minute. Thus, your brain works three or four times faster than the speed needed for listening to a speech. This gap creates a lot of mental spare time, and we are tempted to spend the time daydreaming.

How can you resist distractions? By using rigorous self-discipline. Prepare yourself for active listening by arriving in the room a few minutes early and getting yourself situated. Find a seat that is free from such distractions as blinding sunlight or friends who might want to whisper to you. Make yourself comfortable, lay out paper and pen for taking notes, and clear your mind of personal matters. When the speech begins, concentrate all your mental energies on the speaker's message.

This is what fake listening looks like.

Avoid Fake Listening

Many members of an audience look directly at a speaker and seem to be listening, but in reality they are just pretending. Their minds are far away.

If you engage in fake listening, you might miss a lot of important information, but even worse, you risk embarrassment and ridicule. Imagine that you are engaged in fake listening during a meeting and your boss suddenly asks you to comment on a statement that has just been made. You don't have a clue. You are speechless, and you look very foolish.

If you have the habit of tuning speakers out while pretending to listen, one of the best ways to force yourself to pay attention is to take notes, as discussed earlier.

Give Every Speaker a Fair Chance

Don't reject speakers because you dislike their looks or their clothes or the organization they represent. Instead, focus on their message, which might be interesting and worthwhile.

If speakers have ragged delivery, or they seem shaky and lacking in confidence, don't be too quick to discount the content of their speech.

Wyatt Rangel, a stockbroker, relates an incident:

> At a dinner meeting of my investment club, one of the speakers was a woman from Thailand who had lived in the U.S. only a year or so, and she spoke English with a heavy accent. It took a lot of concentration to understand what she was saying, and frankly I didn't think a recent immigrant could give me any worthwhile information. I was tempted to tune her out, but I made the effort, and I'm glad I did. She had some good insights into Asian corporations, and I was able to parlay her tips into financial gain a few months later.

Give every speaker a fair chance. You may be pleasantly surprised by what you learn.

Control Emotions

Some listeners don't listen well because they have a powerful emotional reaction to a topic or to some comment the speaker makes. Their strong emotions cut off intelligent listening for the rest of the speech. Instead of paying attention to the speaker's words, they "argue" with the speaker inside their heads or think of ways to retaliate in the question-and-answer period. They often jump to conclusions, convincing themselves that the speaker is saying something that he or she really is not.

During many question-and-answer periods, I have seen listeners verbally attack a speaker for espousing a position that any careful listener would know was not the speaker's true position.

When you are listening to speakers who seem to be arguing against some of your ideas or beliefs, make sure you understand exactly what they are saying. Hear them out, and *then* prepare your counterarguments.

Your Thoughts

Why do you think that the Chinese character for "listen" consists of pictures of the ear, the eye, and the heart?

The Listener's Responsibilities

As we discussed in Chapter 1, the speaker who is honest and fair has ethical and moral obligations to his or her listeners. The converse is also true: the honest and fair listener has ethical and moral obligations to the speaker. Let's examine three of the listener's primary responsibilities.

Avoid Rudeness

Are you a polite listener? To make sure that you are not committing acts of rudeness, consider the advice in the following two sections.

Follow the Golden Rule of Listening

If you were engaged in conversation with a friend, how would you feel if your friend yawned and fell asleep? Or started reading a book? Or talked on a cell phone? You would be upset by your friend's rudeness, wouldn't you?

Many people would never dream of being so rude to a friend in conversation, yet when they sit in an audience, they are terribly rude to the speaker. They fall

connectpublic
speaking.com
For interactive
exercises, visit
Chapter 3
on *Connect Public
Speaking*.

asleep or study for a test or carry on a whispered conversation with their friends. Fortunately, a public speaking class cures some people of their rudeness. As one student put it:

> I had been sitting in classrooms for 12 years and until now, I never realized how much a speaker sees. I always thought a listener is hidden and anonymous out there in a sea of faces. Now that I've been a speaker, I realize that when you look out at an audience, you are well aware of the least little thing somebody does. I am ashamed now at how I used to carry on conversations in the back of class. I was very rude, and I didn't even know it.

Ethical Issue

Follow the Golden Rule of Listening: "Listen unto others as you would have others listen unto you." When you are a speaker, you want an audience that listens attentively and courteously. So when you are a listener, you should provide the same response.

Reject Electronic Intrusion

In recent years, a new kind of rudeness has become rampant throughout society, says reporter Julie Hill. "Hardly a meeting, presentation, movie, or even church service is not interrupted by the ringing of at least one cell phone and then (even more annoying) the sound of a one-way conversation from the idiot who actually takes the call."[10]

Your Thoughts **?**

What do you think is the best way to solve the problem of electronic rudeness? Defend your answer.

These outrages are committed by people who should know better. "A business student in Milwaukee," writes Hill, "stumbled through an in-class presentation that was worth 20 percent of his grade, painfully aware that his professor was chatting on a cell phone through most of it."[11]

Cell phones are just one of many distractions that mar presentations today. Some listeners use laptop computers and wireless devices to engage in text messaging, e-mailing, browsing the Internet, or playing electronic games. In 2003, citizens in Norway were outraged when TV cameras caught a member of parliament playing a game on his handheld computer during a crucial debate on whether Norway should send troops to the war in Iraq.[12]

Refrain from using a laptop computer during a presentation unless you need to take notes on the speaker's remarks. In this case, ask the speaker for permission beforehand. During the presentation, show the speaker that you are respectfully paying attention by looking at him or her frequently (rather than keeping your eyes focused nonstop on your computer).

To avoid rude and insulting behavior, follow these rules of courtesy:

- Don't speak on a cell phone or a wireless headset during a presentation. Even whispers are distracting.
- Before a meeting begins, turn off any electronic equipment that might beep, chirp, or ring.
- Remove earphones that are connected to devices such as iPods.
- If you are subject to an emergency call (for example, if you are a firefighter or a paramedic), set your cell phone or pager to vibrate mode. When you are alerted that a message has arrived, leave the room quietly and then answer the call. Don't be disruptive by standing outside the door and shouting into the phone.

Tips for Your Career

Tip 3.3 Confront Electronic Rudeness

If you are like most speakers, you will be irritated or even unnerved if you see listeners who are immersed in their private world of electronic devices. It is hard to communicate effectively with people who are tuning you out.

What can you do to capture their full attention?

If possible, forbid the use of electronic devices. During her tenure as CEO of eBay, Inc., Meg Whitman banned electronic devices from her Monday morning staff meetings. "Talking on a cell phone or working on a laptop during a meeting is rude and insulting," she says. A similar ban has been enforced by other executives and by many military officers, high school teachers, and college professors.

What if you lack the power to order a ban? If possible, ask the person in charge of a group to request—before you rise to speak—that all equipment be turned off. But what if those strategies aren't possible, and you see that some of your listeners are using electronic equipment? Try saying something like this: "I hate to inconvenience anyone, but I have a problem. I have trouble concentrating on what I want to say when I look out and see people working on their computers or talking on their cell phones. I would appreciate it if you would help me out and turn off your equipment while I'm speaking." By emphasizing *your* difficulties rather than attacking *their* rudeness, you enhance your chances of gaining compliance.

One final strategy that has been used successfully by some speakers: In the introduction of your speech, use an attention-getter that is so compelling that listeners become totally absorbed in listening to you. (Samples of attention-getters are presented in Chapter 8.)

A Dutch official holds placards to request that guests refrain from taking pictures and having cell phones on during the wedding of Prince Constantij and Princess Laurentien in the Netherlands. Making requests in advance is one of the best ways to prevent electronic distractions.

- Use the vibrate option sparingly, because if you get up and leave a room to respond to a friend's routine call, you are creating an unnecessary disruption.

- If you receive permission from a speaker to use a laptop or some other device, confine yourself to taking notes. Save games, text messages, and e-mail for later.

Refrain from Multitasking

Some students object to the preceding guidelines, claiming that they are multitaskers, capable of using electronic devices and listening to the speaker at the same time. But they are overlooking two important issues:

1. When listeners avert their eyes and perform nonlistening activities, the speaker usually interprets the behavior as disrespect and rejection.

2. Although multitaskers think they are performing all activities effectively, studies show that their comprehension suffers. For example, researchers at Cornell University arranged for two groups of students to listen to the same lecture and then take a test immediately afterward. One group was allowed to use their laptops to browse the Internet during the lecture, while the other group was asked to keep their laptops closed. When tested, the students with open laptops remembered significantly less information from the lecture than did the students with closed laptops.[13]

Many other research studies show that in most situations, multitaskers—young and old alike—are likely to misunderstand information and make mistakes.[14] As Publilius Syrus, a Roman slave who lived 2,000 years ago, said, "To do two things at once is to do neither."[15]

Provide Encouragement

Encourage the speaker as much as possible—by giving your full attention, taking notes, leaning slightly forward instead of slouching back in your seat, looking directly at the speaker instead of at the floor, and letting your face show interest and animation. If the speaker says something you particularly like, nod in agreement or smile approvingly. (If the speaker says something that offends you or puzzles you, obviously you should not give positive feedback; I am not recommending hypocrisy.)

The more encouragement a speaker receives, the better his or her delivery is likely to be. Most entertainers and professional speakers say that if an audience is lively and enthusiastic, they do a much better job than if the audience is sullen or apathetic. From my own experience, I feel that I always do better in giving a speech if I get encouragement. Maybe just a few people are displaying lively interest, but their nods and smiles and eager eyes inspire me and energize me.

When we help a speaker to give a good speech, we are doing more than an act of kindness; we are creating a payoff for ourselves: the better the speaker, the easier it is to listen. And the easier it is to listen, the better we will understand, remember, and gain knowledge.

Find Value in Every Speech

Sometimes you will be obliged to hear a speech that you feel is boring and worthless. Instead of tuning the speaker out and retreating into your private world of daydreams, try to exploit the speech for something worthwhile. Make a game of it: see how many diamonds you can pluck from the mud. Is there any new information that might be useful to you in the future? Is the speaker using techniques of delivery that are worth noting and emulating?

If a speech is so bad that you honestly cannot find anything worthwhile in it, look for a how-not-to-do-it lesson. Ask yourself, "What can I learn from this

Tips for Your Career

speaker's mistakes?" Here is an example of how one business executive profited from a poor speech:

> At a convention recently I found myself in an extremely boring seminar (on listening, ironically enough). After spending the first half-hour wishing I had never signed up, I decided to take advantage of the situation. I turned my thought, "This guy isn't teaching me how to run a seminar on listening," into a question: "What is he teaching me about how *not* to run a seminar?" While providing a negative example was not the presenter's goal, I got a useful lesson.[16]

"When life hands you a lemon, make lemonade," some wise person once advised. If you look for value or a how-*not*-to-do-it lesson in every poor speech, you will find that the sourest oratorical lemon can be turned into lemonade. "Know how to listen," the Greek writer Plutarch said 20 centuries ago, "and you will profit even from those who talk badly."

Speech Evaluations

Both evaluators and speakers profit from a speech evaluation. Evaluators gain insights into what works and what doesn't work in speechmaking. Speakers can use suggestions to improve their speaking skills.

When Evaluating

Evaluating speeches should not be limited to a public speaking class. You also can apply these techniques to speeches that you hear in your career.

Establish criteria. Before you listen to a speech, decide upon the criteria for judging it. This will keep you from omitting important elements. For classroom speeches, your instructor may give you a checklist or tell you to analyze certain features of a speech. Otherwise, you can use the "Quick Guide to Public Speaking" in Chapter 1 for your criteria.

An attentive listener takes notes and keeps her focus on the speaker.

Listen objectively.   Keep an open mind. Don't let yourself be swayed emotionally by the speaker's delivery or appearance. If, for example, a speaker sounds ill at ease and uncertain, this doesn't necessarily mean that her arguments are inferior. Don't let your own biases influence your criticism; for example, if you are strongly against gun control, but the speaker argues in favor of it, be careful to criticize the speaker's ideas fairly and objectively.

Take notes.   Jot down your observations throughout the speech. Otherwise, you will forget key items.

Concentrate on one criterion at a time.   If you try to evaluate everything at once, you will find your attention scattered too widely. Focus on one item at a time: evaluate eye contact, then gestures, and so on. If time permits, you may want to use videotape to take a second or third look at the speech.

Look for both positive and negative aspects.   Emphasize the positive (so that the speaker will continue doing what works well) as well as pointing out the negative (so that he or she can improve).

Give positive comments first.   When it comes to public speaking, most people have fragile, easily bruised egos. If you start out a critique with negative remarks, you can damage the speaker's confidence and self-esteem. Always begin by discussing his or her strengths. Point out positive attributes that might seem obvious to you but may not be obvious to the speaker. For example, "You looked poised and confident."

Couple negative comments with positive alternatives.   When you point out a flaw, immediately give a constructive alternative. For example, you can inform a speaker that he has the habit of jingling coins in his pocket, and then you can suggest an alternative: "Instead of putting your hands in your pockets, why don't you rest them on the lectern?"

In most cases, ignore nervousness.   Because people cannot prevent themselves from being jittery, don't criticize nervousness–unless you can give a useful tip. In other words, saying, "You looked tense and scared" is unhelpful, but saying, "Put your notes on the lectern so that your trembling hands don't rustle the paper" is helpful advice.

Be specific.   It is not useful for the speaker to hear generalized comments such as "You did great" or "Your delivery was poor." Be as specific as possible. Instead of saying, "You need to improve your eye contact," say, "You looked too much at the floor."

When Receiving Evaluations

To get maximum benefit from evaluations, follow these guidelines:

Don't be defensive.   Try to understand criticism and consider its merits. Don't argue or counterattack.

Seek clarification.   If an evaluator makes a comment that you don't understand, ask for an explanation.

Strive for improvement.   In your next speech, try to make corrections in problem areas. But don't feel that you must eliminate all errors or bad habits at once.

Resources for Review and Skill Building

connectpublic
speaking.com

Connect Public Speaking provides resources for study and review, including sample speech videos, an Outline Tutor, and practice tests.

Summary

Listening effectively is often a difficult task, but it can be rewarding for the person who is willing to make the effort. The guidelines for effective listening include the following:

1. Prepare yourself for the act of listening. Do whatever background reading or research that is necessary for gaining maximum understanding of the speech.

2. Be willing to put forth energy. Since listening is hard work, especially if the material is new or difficult, you must have a strong desire to listen actively and intelligently.

3. Listen analytically, focusing on main ideas and evaluating support materials.

4. Take notes, not only for a record of key points, but also as a way of keeping your mind from wandering.

5. Resist distractions, both external and internal. Use rigorous self-discipline to keep your mind concentrated on the speaker's remarks.

6. Avoid fakery. Don't pretend to be listening when in fact your mind is wandering; this kind of behavior can settle into a hard-to-break habit.

7. Give every speaker a fair chance. Don't discount a speaker because of personal appearance or the organization he or she represents.

8. Control your emotions. Don't mentally argue with a speaker: you might misunderstand what he or she is really saying.

As a listener you have three important obligations to a speaker: to avoid all forms of rudeness, to provide encouragement, and to find value in every speech. The more support you give a speaker, the better the speech will be, and the more you will profit from it.

Evaluating speeches can help you improve your own speechmaking skills. Look for both positive and negative aspects of a speech, and give specific, constructive suggestions. When you are on the receiving end of evaluations, don't be defensive. Try to understand the criticism and then make improvements.

Key Terms

hearing, *43*   listening, *43*

Review Questions

1. What is the difference between *hearing* and *listening?*

2. Name at least four problems caused by ineffective listening in business.

3. Why should a listener avoid faking attention?

4. What is the difference between listening to easy material and listening to complex material?

5. List at least two ways in which you can prepare yourself physically and intellectually to listen to a speech.

6. The text lists four types of distractions: auditory, visual, physical, and mental. Give two examples of each type.

7. What two speech elements should a listener examine analytically?

8. List three advantages of taking notes during a speech.

9. When you are a listener, how can you encourage a speaker?

10. When you evaluate a speech, how should you handle both the positive and the negative aspects that you observe?

Building Critical-Thinking Skills

1. Some psychologists characterize listening as "an act of love." To illustrate what this statement means, describe a real or imaginary conversation between two people (spouses, close friends, doctor/patient, etc.) who are truly listening to each other.

2. Science writer Judith Stone wrote, "There are two ways to approach a subject that frightens you and makes you feel stupid: you can embrace it with humility and an open mind, or you can ridicule it mercilessly." Translate this idea into advice for listeners of speeches.

Building Teamwork Skills

1. In a group, conduct this role play: One student gives an impromptu speech describing his or her classes this term, while all the other group members exhibit rude behaviors (chatting, reading a magazine, putting head on desk, solving math problems with a calculator, etc.). Then the speaker discusses how he or she felt about the rudeness. (If time permits, other group members can play the speaker's role.)

2. Working in a group, compile a list of the attributes that would describe "the ideal listener" for a speech. Then do likewise for a conversation. In what ways are the lists similar and different?

This is the kind of audience that every speaker desires—enthusiastic, attentive, and responsive. In front is Riley Woina, 14, of Plymouth, Connecticut, who is taking part in a graduation ceremony of U.S. Army Rangers at Ft. Benning, Georgia. Woina, who has cystic fibrosis, spent a week as a Ranger, thanks to the Make-a-Wish Foundation, which tries to grant the wishes of children with life-threatening medical conditions.

Reaching the Audience

OBJECTIVES

After studying this chapter, you should be able to:

1. Describe the difference between a speaker who is audience-centered and one who is not.

2. Define audience analysis and audience adaptation and state why they are important.

3. Use interviews and surveys to gain information about an audience in advance.

4. Explain how speakers can be responsive to diverse audiences.

5. Describe how speakers can adapt to varying levels of audience knowledge, attitudes, interest, and needs and desires.

6. Explain how speakers should adapt to the occasion (time limit, purpose, and size of audience).

7. Describe how a speaker can adapt to the audience during a speech.

"Care deeply about your audience" is a piece of advice that some veteran speakers give when they are asked, "What is the most important rule for public speaking?"

One speaker who has a reputation for caring deeply about his audiences is Brazilian soccer star Robson de Souza (known by his nickname Robinho), who gives presentations to student groups in Brazil and in European countries. "I enjoy talking to people," he says, "and I enjoy explaining the nuances of the most popular sport on earth." He finds out in advance the age level and sports experience of each audience—so that he doesn't talk over anyone's head.[1]

During a presentation in Germany, Robinho smiles at a listener who is asking a question.

The Audience-Centered Speaker

Some speeches are ineffective because the speaker is self-centered, focusing on "How do I look?" and "Am I doing a good job?" and "Does everyone like me?" The self-centered speaker fails to focus on the audience and their needs.

A better approach is taken by the **audience-centered speaker**—one who tries to connect with listeners and offer them a meaningful experience. If you are an audience-centered speaker, you learn everything you can about your listeners

audience-centered speaker
one who tries to establish a meaningful connection with listeners

in advance, and then you tailor your speech to their needs and interests. You look directly at the audience, speak with enthusiasm, and try to reach every listener.

Consider the experience of one speaker:

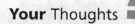

> Soheil Nasseri, a 27-year-old pianist, speaks at schools throughout New York City to try to create interest in classical music. If he were a self-centered speaker, he would start off by talking about his love for Beethoven and Brahms—and ignore the yawns and bored expressions on the faces of the young listeners. Instead, knowing that classical music is considered stuffy and "terminally uncool" by many students, Nasseri takes an audience-centered approach. He begins by talking about hip-hop (an audience favorite), and after a while, he explains how hip-hop grew out of the basic elements of classical music. Then he slowly moves into a discussion of classical music—by which time, the students are hooked. They eagerly ask questions to learn details about classical music.[2]

Nasseri demonstrates the two tasks that all audience-centered speakers should perform: (1) **analyze** the listeners to find out exactly who they are and what they know and (2) **adapt** the speech to the listeners' knowledge level and to their needs and outlooks.

You might find it helpful to know that the process of analysis and adaptation has a synonym–**customizing,** a popular strategy in the business world. If you sell customized vans, you find out what features each customer needs and then outfit the van accordingly. For a person with paralyzed legs, you provide brake controls that are operated by hand; for a carpenter, you furnish special compartments for lumber and tools; and for a rock band, you provide storage space for drums and guitars. Customizing in public speaking means tailoring a speech to fit a particular audience.

Here are some guidelines for customizing speeches.

audience analysis
collecting information about audience characteristics

adaptation
adjusting one's material and delivery to meet listeners' needs

customize
to make or alter to a customer's specifications

Prepare a separate analysis of each audience.   It is a mistake to think that if a speech works well with one group, it will surely succeed with another. Sometimes it will, but sometimes it won't.

I once delivered a speech that was received with much laughter and applause. So sweet was the success that I delivered the same speech a month later to another group. It was a dud. If I had not been so giddy with success, I would have seen that the second audience had a different educational background and a different set of attitudes. They needed a different speech.

Customize for different segments of the same audience.   Many audiences contain subgroups, with the people in each subgroup sharing the same needs and level of understanding. Try to reach all the subgroups. For example, in a speech on traveling abroad, one subgroup–young parents–may want information on recreation options for children, while another subgroup–older travelers–may want information on discounts for seniors.

Never sacrifice ethical principles.   Customizing does not mean telling listeners whatever would make them happy–regardless of truth. Many politicians–of all persuasions–tell voters that a certain program can be implemented without raising taxes, even though they know this to be untrue. An ethical speaker never lies or distorts information.

Ethical Issue

Tips for Your Career

Have you ever seen this old comedy routine on TV? A nervous young man is waiting for his blind date to appear at a prearranged spot. As he waits, he fantasizes how she will react to him. The TV camera captures the fantasies: When she approaches him, she looks at him with disappointment bordering on disgust. When he introduces himself, she laughs at his name and says it is stupid. When he suggests that they go to a particular restaurant for dinner, she ridicules his idea of good food. When he tries to make small talk, she laughs at his accent. The fantasy goes on and on, from one humiliation to another. Finally, the fantasies fade away as the real, live date appears on the scene. By now, however, the young man is so enraged that he screams at her, "Well, I didn't want to go out with you, either!" and storms away, as the startled woman stands alone, blinking her eyes in confusion.

In like fashion, some speakers indulge in fantasies of audience rejection. When they actually stand up to speak,

they act defensive, as if they *know* that everyone in the audience is going to reject them and their ideas. Their "body language"—tone of voice, facial expression, posture—is defensive, sometimes even angry and sullen. I saw one such speaker argue in favor of hunting animals for sport. He knew that some members of the audience were opposed to hunting. From start to finish, he acted as if the audience had just insulted him. "We are not sadistic people who enjoy watching animals suffer," he said angrily. Who said he was sadistic? Who said he enjoyed watching animals suffer? Like the young man waiting for his blind date, this speaker had unnecessarily worked himself into a rage.

Don't prejudge your audience. Most listeners are kind and sympathetic to speakers. Even if they reject your ideas, they usually respect you, as long as you respect them.

Instead of nurturing gloomy fantasies, try to develop a positive attitude toward every audience.

Getting Information about the Audience

A speaker's worst nightmare–being laughed at by listeners–came true for Lawrence B. Gibbs.

Speaking to an audience of 1,000 tax preparers at a convention in Las Vegas, Gibbs, who was at the time Internal Revenue Commissioner, said, "What about the gloomy predictions that this tax-filing season would drive taxpayers crazy, confuse them unmercifully, or break them financially?" *[Dramatic pause]* "It just hasn't happened, folks!"[3]

The convention hall exploded with howls of laughter. The tax preparers had just finished a tax season in which the scenario that Gibbs dismissed as nonexistent had (from their perspective) actually occurred. Regardless of whose viewpoint was accurate, Gibbs had revealed that he knew nothing about what his audience felt and believed. If he had interviewed just a few of his listeners beforehand, he could have escaped public ridicule.[4]

You can avoid this kind of blunder by finding out as much as possible about your listeners–their backgrounds and what they know and don't know. Two good ways to collect information about them are interviews and surveys.

connectpublic
speaking.com
For career and community speeches, see "Checklist for Audience and Occasion" in Supplementary Readings on *Connect Public Speaking.*

Interviews

Start with the program director (or whoever invited you to speak). Find out all that you can about listeners' knowledge level, attitudes, needs, interests, and backgrounds. Also, get details about the occasion–purpose of the event, other speakers on the program, time limit, and size of audience.

Next, ask for the names and phone numbers of a few prospective listeners and interview them–either in person or by telephone–to find out what they already know about your subject, what ideas and information they are hoping to receive from your speech, and whether any particular approach (such as visual aids) works well with this group. When you start your speech, you can thank—by name—the people you interviewed. Doing so will add to your credibility because it shows your desire to meet the needs and interests of your listeners.

Surveys

A good way to get information is to conduct a survey, using a questionnaire to poll listeners' knowledge, interests, and attitudes. A questionnaire can be handed out (in a classroom or elsewhere) or sent by e-mail or postal service.

Let's suppose you are planning a speech on food poisoning, and you want to ascertain whether your listeners know and apply good hygiene. The questionnaire in Table 4.1 shows the types of questions that can be asked:

Question 1: A simple yes/no question tells you the listeners' personal experiences. Probably all have suffered food poisoning, but if a sizable minority has not, you need to describe the pain and danger of the affliction to show that your speech is not about a trivial issue.

Question 2: A scale can probe for the *degree* of knowledge or ignorance on a subject. Do your listeners know about the upsurge of food-poisoning cases in recent years? If the scale indicates they are unaware, you should explain that cases have increased by 30 percent in the last five years—to 325,000 hospitalizations and 5,000 deaths annually.

Question 3: A multiple-choice question—a type familiar to all students—can gauge whether the listeners know basic food-safety facts. The second item is correct; all the others are commonly held myths. The listeners' answers can help you determine which myths need to be attacked in your speech. (There is no need, of course, to attack a myth if all your listeners know it is erroneous.)

Question 4: People should wash their hands in all the situations listed in this checklist. Knowing how your audience behaves can tell you which of these matters to emphasize. Note the final "Other" category. This option is often included in questionnaires to cover unforeseen responses, and it sometimes yields surprising and useful answers.

Question 5: An open-ended question—in which a person writes out a sentence or a paragraph—is useful when you need a detailed response. In this case, finding out how your listeners wash their hands will tell you whether you need to inform them of basics (removing rings, using warm water and soap, and scrubbing for a minimum of 20 seconds).

Question 6: Ranking is a handy way for listeners to show relative importance or frequency. In our food-poisoning scenario, you can find out where most of your listeners eat their food, and then concentrate on food-safety tips for those places.

Question 7: A fill-in-the-blank question is similar to the open-ended question above except that it is designed to elicit only a word or two. If most of your listeners fail to record the correct answer—refrigerator—you know that you must cover the point in your speech.

Here are some guidelines for surveys:

- Keep a questionnaire short. Most people don't have time for a long document.

connectpublicspeaking.com
To see a speaker who uses a questionnaire effectively, view the sample speech "Bicycle Helmets."

Table 4.1   Types of Survey Questions

Yes/No	1. Have you ever suffered from food poisoning? yes ☐ no ☐
Scale	2. Please mark an X on the scale to show how you rate the risk of food poisoning in the United States today as compared with five years ago. ←————————————————————————→ Much worse A bit worse About the same A bit better Much better
Multiple choice	3. Which one of the following statements about food safety is correct? ☐ Freezing destroys bacteria. ☐ Frozen foods that are thawed can be refrozen. ☐ Contaminated food always smells bad. ☐ Raw meat and poultry must be rinsed thoroughly before cooking.
Checklist	4. In which of the following situations do you regularly wash your hands? (Check all that apply.) ☐ Before preparing food ☐ Before eating a meal ☐ After using the bathroom ☐ After handling raw meat ☐ Other (Please specify):
Open-ended	5. Describe how you wash your hands:
Ranking	6. Where do you eat your meals? Rank these places in the order of frequency, from 1 (most often) to 5 (least often). ☐ School cafeteria ☐ Restaurant ☐ Home, prepared by yourself ☐ Home, prepared by someone else ☐ Snack bar (vending machines)
Fill in the blank	7. Food should be placed _____ _____ while it is marinating.

- Devise questions that yield precise answers. Instead of asking, "What do you know about food poisoning?" ask, "How long is it safe to let food sit at room temperature?"
- Before submitting a questionnaire to listeners, test it with a few friends or colleagues, who can point out any confusing questions.

Sometimes the results of a survey can be included in a speech as a point of interest. In your speech on food poisoning, for example, you can say, "According to my survey, half of you wash your hands just by quickly rinsing them. Are you aware that this method is unsafe and can lead to sickness?"

Audience Diversity

In presentations today, you are likely to see a wide diversity of listeners: men and women of different ages, races, nationalities, ethnic groups, religions, economic levels, educational backgrounds, and physical abilities. To be a successful communicator, you should welcome the opportunity to meet the needs of *all* listeners, not just those who resemble you.

Gender

The gender of your listeners may give you some clues about their social and economic situation. For example, despite the advances made by women in the workplace in recent decades, many females still receive a lower wage than male co-workers who perform the same job. A speaker trying to persuade workers to join a labor union could stress such inequities if some of the listeners are women.

Although gender can sometimes give clues, you should avoid making assumptions based on gender stereotypes. Men may become irritated by a speaker who assumes that only females are interested in issues concerning the health of babies. And women may be annoyed by a speaker who says, "For the benefit of the men in the audience, let me give some tips about buying tools for household repairs"— as if women never buy and use such tools.

Listeners can lose respect for a speaker who uses **sexist language**—that is, words that convey stereotypes about men or women. Instead of saying "the girl at the front desk," say "Ms. Martinez" or "Maria Martinez." Instead of "the best man for the job," say "the best person for the job."

sexist language
words based on gender stereotypes

Abstain from making assumptions about marriage and sexual orientation. For example, Kitty O. Locker, who teaches business communication at the Ohio State University, advises speakers to "avoid terms that assume that everyone is married or is heterosexual." Instead of announcing to employees, "You and your husband or wife are cordially invited to the company picnic," say, "You and your guest are cordially invited to the company picnic."[5]

Age

If you have a variety of ages represented in your audience, be sensitive to the interests, attitudes, and knowledge of all your listeners, giving explanations or background whenever necessary. If, for example, you are talking about a musician who is popular only with young people, you may need to give some information about her music and lifestyle for the benefit of older members of the audience.

Be careful about making generalizations concerning any age group. For an audience of elderly people, for example, you are wise to consider the fact that many people suffer hearing loss as they age, but you shouldn't jump to the conclusion that you must shout during your speech. Not all elderly people are hard of hearing, and those who do have problems might be wearing hearing aids. Investigate the needs of your particular listeners instead of relying on generalizations.

Your Thoughts **?**

A 65-year-old man is preparing a speech to high school students on the need to save money throughout one's life. What advice would you give him to enhance his chances of persuading his youthful audience?

Educational Background

Find out the educational level of your listeners. Avoid talking over their heads, using concepts or language that they cannot understand. Also avoid the other extreme: talking down to them as if they were ignorant children.

Define terms whenever necessary. Fred Ebel, past president of a Toastmasters club in Orlando, Florida, says that to one audience, "I told a joke which referred to an insect called a praying mantis. I thought everyone knew what a praying mantis was. But I was greeted by silence that would have made the dropping of a pin sound like a thunderclap. Several listeners came up to me and asked, 'What is a praying mantis?' It came as a shock to me until I realized that not everyone had taken a course in biology."[6]

Occupation

Knowing your listeners' occupational background can help you shape your remarks. Let's say you give speeches on resume padding. To a group of students, you might want to point out how one's career can be ruined if an employee is found to have lied on a resume. To a group of human resources managers, you can give tips on how to detect false information. To a group of lawyers, you can discuss legal action that can be taken against someone who has lied on a resume.

Religious Affiliation

Knowing the religious affiliations of your audience will give you some good clues about their beliefs and attitudes. Most Seventh-Day Adventists, for example, are very knowledgeable about nutrition because of the strong emphasis the denomination places on health; many Adventists are vegetarians and nondrinkers. If you are asked to speak to an Adventist group on a health-related issue, you can assume that the audience has a higher level of background knowledge on the subject than the average audience. You can therefore avoid going over basic information they already know.

Although religious background can give you clues about your audience, be cautious. You cannot assume that all members of a religious group subscribe to official doctrines and pronouncements. A denomination's hierarchy, for example, may call for a stop to the production of nuclear weapons, but the majority of the members of that denomination may not agree with their leaders' views.

Economic and Social Status

Be sensitive to the economic and social status of your listeners so that you can adapt your speech accordingly. Suppose you are going to speak in favor of food stamps for the poor. If your listeners have low incomes, most of them will probably be favorably disposed to your ideas before you even begin. You therefore might want to aim your speech at encouraging them to support political candidates who will protect the food-stamp program. If your listeners are upper-middle-class, however, many of them may be opposed to your ideas and you will have to aim your speech at winning them over to your way of thinking.

International Listeners

The world today is a "global village" of interlocking interests and economies. No matter what field you are in, you must know how to interact with clients and colleagues in many different countries. You may travel overseas for meetings and presentations, or you may give speeches in the United States to visitors from abroad or immigrants to the United States and their families. In classroom speeches, your listeners may include some international students. In these situations, many of your listeners may speak English, of course, but often their command of the language is imperfect.

Tips for Your Career

Tip 4.2 Work Closely with Interpreters

Use interpreters if there is a chance that some listeners will not hear or understand your message. For example, you might use a sign-language interpreter for deaf listeners and a foreign-language interpreter for non-English-speaking listeners. Here are some tips on using interpreters effectively:

- Because interpreters say that they stumble less and make fewer misinterpretations when they know the speaker's message in advance, provide a copy of your outline to the interpreter well before the event.

- If possible, ask him or her to rehearse with you several times, and to alert you if any elements in your speech are likely to be misunderstood.

- In your opening remarks, introduce the interpreter to the audience and express your appreciation for his or her assistance.

- When using a foreign-language interpreter, you will probably employ the popular *consecutive interpretation* method, in which you and the interpreter take turns. Say only a few sentences at a time, so that neither language group gets weary of waiting its turn. (A less-frequent method is *simultaneous interpretation,* in which your words are rendered into a separate microphone a few seconds later for listeners wearing headphones. At large international meetings, a speech may be rendered into many languages simultaneously.)

- To demonstrate your desire to connect with all listeners, learn a few words and phrases from sign language and/ or a foreign language to sprinkle into your presentation.

- Even if all listeners are using the services of a sign-language interpreter, you should still talk directly to the listeners, not to the interpreter.

Actor Nicolas Cage smiles as he speaks to reporters at a press conference in Seoul, South Korea. Assisting him is an unidentified Korean interpreter.

To meet the challenge of reaching international listeners, consider the following:

Respect taboos. Every culture has its own set of **taboos,** and violating a prohibition can undermine a speaker's credibility. Stacie Krajchir of Venice Beach,

taboo

an act, word, or object that is forbidden on grounds of morality or taste

67

California, who works around the world as a television producer, says, "I have a habit of putting my hands on my hips when I talk." In Indonesia, she was told that "when you stand that way, it's seen as a sign of rudeness or defiance."[7]

You can avoid taboos by educating yourself about a culture—a task that is not very difficult if you consult an expert, as discussed below.

connectpublic speaking.com
For an interactive exercise on nonverbal signals, visit Chapter 4 on *Connect Public Speaking*.

Thumbs-up means approval in some countries, but it's an insult in others.

Learn nonverbal signals. Nonverbal communication cues, such as eye contact and facial expression, vary from country to country. American business executives assume a person who won't look them in the eye is evasive and dishonest, but in many parts of Latin America, Asia, and Africa, keeping your eyes lowered is a sign of respect.[8] A few years ago, some Americans who were trying to negotiate a contract with Japanese executives were happy to see nods of assent throughout the meeting but were later stunned when the Japanese rejected their proposal. The Americans were unaware that in Japan a nod of assent doesn't mean agreement; it signifies only that the listener understands what is being said.[9]

Although nonverbal cues vary from culture to culture, there are some cues that are recognizable everywhere. First and foremost is the smile, which Roger Axtell, an international behavior expert, says is the most understood and most useful form of communication in the world.[10] As a Mexican-American proverb puts it: *Todos en el mundo sonreimos en la misma lengua*—"Everyone in the world smiles in the same language." (The smile discussed here is the involuntary expression that all people make when they are happy—not variations such as the embarrassed smile of someone caught in a misdeed.)

Consult experts. Even though you probably don't have time to become well versed in all the cultures in the world, you can find out what you need to know about a particular culture by consulting an expert—a business traveler or a professor who knows the culture well, or a person from the culture, such as an immigrant or an international student. In the early stages of your preparation, interview him or her for facts and insights. After you prepare your speech, conduct a trial run and ask the expert to critique your words, visual aids, and delivery. Emphasize that you want to eliminate any element that could be confusing or offensive.

You also can get tips from the Internet—by browsing at Web sites specializing in international cultures and by soliciting comments from people who live or travel in a particular country. For help in connecting to these sources, visit Connect Public Speaking (connectpublicspeaking.com), click on WEBLINKS, and explore links for this page. Books and articles also can be good sources, but make sure they are recent, because cultural information can become outdated.

Be careful with jargon and slang. Avoid using idiomatic expressions such as "cramming for an exam," "bite the bullet," and "the ball is in your court." If you must use jargon, such as "interface" or "virtual reality," explain or illustrate each term.

Maintain a serious, formal tone. Americans are accustomed to speakers using a humorous and informal approach to public speaking, but American presenters who adopt this tone with international audiences are often viewed as frivolous and disrespectful. "Most foreign audiences," says Richard Crum, senior editor for

Berlitz Translation Services in Woodland Hills, California, "expect seriousness. An important presentation can be undermined by a presenter who is joking or boastful."[11]

If possible, provide handouts covering some of your main points a day or two before a presentation.   (But don't give out lengthy material immediately before or during a meeting–for reasons to be discussed in Chapter 6.) Most nonnative speakers of English have greater comprehension when reading than when listening.[12] If they read the material beforehand, they can find out the meaning of any terms they don't understand, and when they come to the actual presentation, they will have a knowledge base that will maximize their understanding of your remarks.

Provide visual and tactile learning.   Can you use visual aids or demonstrations to illuminate your ideas? Can you provide any hands-on experiences?

America's Diverse Cultures

The same sensitivity you show toward international listeners should be extended to ethnic, racial, religious, and other groups in the United States.

Here are some suggestions.

Avoid ethnocentrism.   The belief that one's own cultural group is superior to other groups is known as **ethnocentrism.** People who are ethnocentric view the customs and standards of other groups as inferior or wrong.

In most cases, different customs are not a matter of right and wrong but of choice and tradition. In some African-American churches, listeners shout affirmative responses during a sermon, while in some other churches, listeners remain silent. One custom is not superior to the other; they are simply different.

Learn the expectations and viewpoints of different cultures and groups.   Let's say you are a manager giving an informal training talk to a group of employees and you try to encourage them to ask questions as you go along. Some of the Asian-American employees, however, never ask questions. Before you conclude that these employees are uninvolved and uninterested, keep in mind that for some Asian Americans, asking questions is considered a disrespectful challenge to the speaker's authority.

If you don't know much about the attitudes and viewpoints of an American ethnic group, interview a few representative audience members beforehand to learn about their backgrounds and needs. Also, ask for advice from associates who have had experience communicating with the kinds of listeners to whom you will be speaking.

Focus on individuality.   Although becoming informed about group differences is a worthwhile goal, treat your knowledge as possible clues, not as absolute certainties. In the example above, notice that I spoke of *some* Asian Americans–not all. If you have Asian Americans in your audience, be sensitive to possible cultural differences, but you should treat these listeners primarily as individuals who may have characteristics that do not coincide with those of other Asian Americans. In dealing with diverse groups, be sensitive to possible differences and special needs, but as much as possible, focus on the individuality of each listener.

connectpublic
speaking.com
See Video Clip 4.2, Helping Listeners Who Speak English as a Second Language.

ethnocentrism
judging other cultures as inferior to one's own culture

Never ridicule any group.   Some people think that if no members of a particular group (such as women, gays and lesbians, or minorities) are present, it is all right to make insulting jokes. It is *never* all right. Such slurs are offensive and unfunny to many men and women who don't belong to the group being ridiculed, and they will automatically lose respect for the speaker.

Listeners with Disabilities

Because of laws protecting their rights, and a growing awareness of the contributions they can make to our society, people with disabilities are increasingly active in the workplace and in their communities. To meet the special needs of these listeners, how can speakers know what accommodations to make? Scott H. Lewis, who describes himself as "a blind Toastmaster" (he's a member of a Toastmasters club in Port Angeles, Washington), has a simple answer: "Ask the disabled participant." Fearful of making a social blunder, some speakers shy away from the best source of information. Lewis says, "Persons of disability know what they need . . . and are the best and most qualified resources to consult when making reasonable accommodations."[13]

Here are some general tips for being sensitive to listeners with disabilities:

- If you ask your audience to gather around you for a demonstration, or if you involve them in an activity, be sure to encourage listeners with disabilities to participate to the greatest extent possible.
- Never treat adults with disabilities as if they were children. Don't use first names unless you are using first names with all others present. Don't speak in an exaggerated, condescending manner.
- Don't equate physical limitations with mental limitations. The fact that a listener is in a wheelchair doesn't mean that he or she has mental disabilities.
- The Easter Seals campaign gives this advice: "It's okay to offer help to a person with a disability if it seems needed, but don't overdo it or insist on helping. Always ask first."[14]
- Never grab the arm of a person with a mobility or visual impairment. Instead, offer your arm.

Now let's look at tips for specific types of disabilities.

Listeners with Mobility Impairments

- Try to remove barriers that would limit wheelchair access. Whenever there is a choice, ask the listener where he or she would like to sit–don't assume that he or she would prefer to be in the back of the room.
- Never patronize people in wheelchairs by patting them on the head or shoulder.
- Don't lean against or hang on someone's wheelchair, which is viewed by the person as part of his or her personal space.[15]

Listeners Who Are Deaf or Hearing-Impaired

- If hearing-impaired listeners must see your mouth to understand your words, try to avoid turning away. At the same time, don't put them in a spotlight by standing directly in front of them and looking at only them.

- "It is not necessary to exaggerate your words," says Deborah L. Harmon, a college counselor for students with disabilities, "although it may be appropriate to slow your rate of speech slightly when talking with people who are hearing-impaired."[16]

- Whenever possible, speakers should augment their remarks with visual aids, says Harmon. "Write technical terms on a board when first introduced" so that deaf audience members can see how the terms are spelled and thus can figure out their pronunciation.[17]

- Be aware that "people in the deaf community and culture," writes social worker Helen Sloss Luey, "tend to perceive deafness not as a disability, but as an alternate lifestyle and culture."[18]

Listeners Who Are Blind or Visually Impaired

- Talk in a normal voice. Just because a person has limited vision, don't assume that he or she has a hearing impairment, too.

- Don't pet or call a guide dog, says Harmon. Trying to play with it interferes with the performance of its duties. These animals are highly trained work dogs that will not disrupt a speech and thus don't need to be soothed or distracted by you.[19]

- Don't assume that listeners who are blind or visually impaired will not want copies of your handouts. "Even if they can't read them at the meeting," says Sharon Lynn Campbell of St. Louis, Missouri, "they may want to have them read aloud later."[20]

- If you say to a listener who is blind, "Do you see what I mean?" or a similar phrase, there is no need to become flustered or apologetic. The listener realizes that you are using a common phrase out of habit and that you intend no insult.

Audience Knowledge

Thomas Leech, a business consultant in San Diego, California, tells of a manager at an electronics firm who was asked to explain a new electronics program to a group of visiting Explorer Scouts. "He pulled two dozen visuals used for working meetings, went into great detail about technical aspects, and spoke of FLMs and MOKFLTPAC," says Leech. "He was enthusiastic, knowledgeable, and totally ineffective, since his audience was lost for about 44 of his 45 minutes."[21]

This man made a common mistake: failing to speak at the knowledge level of his listeners. To avoid this mistake, find out what your listeners know and don't know about your subject, and then adapt your remarks to their level.

So far, this sounds simple. What happens when listeners have different levels of knowledge, with some already knowing a lot, some knowing only a moderate amount, and some knowing nothing at all? Here are some tips for handling different levels.

Audiences that know a lot about the topic. Your listeners will be bored and resentful if you waste their time on information that everyone already knows. Instead, give them new ideas and concepts. Early in your speech, reassure them that you will cover new ground. For example, if you are speaking to an audience

connectpublicspeaking.com

To see a speaker who gives his audience information that he knows they lack, view Video Clip 4.1, Analyzing the Audience: "How to Make Avocado Salsa."

of advanced skiers, tell them in your introduction that you are not going to spend much time on the well-known, nearby ski resort. Instead, you will give them tips on some good out-of-the-way ski resorts that many skiers don't know about.

Audiences that know little or nothing about the topic.

- Carefully limit the number of new ideas you discuss. People cannot absorb large amounts of new information in a short period of time. If you overwhelm them with too many concepts, they will lose interest and tune you out.
  - Whenever possible, use visual aids to help the listeners grasp the more complicated concepts.
  - Use down-to-earth language; avoid technical jargon. If you feel that you must use a specialized word, be sure to explain it.
  - Repeat key ideas, using different language each time.
- Give vivid examples.

Don't assume that all your listeners know the concept of yin/yang. Find out in advance.

Mixed audiences.   What should you do if some listeners know a lot about your subject and others know nothing? Whenever possible, the solution is to start off at a simple level and add complexity as you go along. For example, if you are speaking on identity theft to a mixed audience, you can hold the attention of everyone by saying something like this: "I realize that some of you know nothing at all about this problem, while some of you have already become victims. So, to bring everyone up to speed, I want to begin by defining what identity theft is, and then I'll get into the nitty-gritty of how we can defeat the crime." Regardless of their level of knowledge, listeners usually appreciate this kind of sensitivity.

Audience Psychology

Your listeners do not see the world the same way you do, because they have lived a different life, with different experiences, different mistakes, and different successes.

To understand your listeners psychologically, assess their level of interest, attitudes, and needs and desires.

Interest Level

All speakers want to avoid boring their audiences, but how can you tell if listeners will find your material interesting? Here are some guidelines.

Assess interest in your topic.   Ask your listeners—through interviews or surveys—whether they are interested in your topic. You can have a scale, such as, "How does a speech on hunting for dinosaur fossils sound to you? _____ very interesting, _____ moderately interesting, _____ boring."

Maintain interest throughout a speech.   Once you have an interesting topic, make sure that you develop it in interesting ways—with examples, stories, and visual aids. Avoid getting bogged down in technical material that will bore the audience.

If necessary, create interest. In some cases, if your audience is not very interested in a topic before you speak, you can generate interest. One student prepared a speech on handwriting analysis, a topic that she knew—from pre-speech interviews with audience members—was considered boring. So she began her speech by saying, "Did you know that when you fill out papers for a job interview, some employers send the papers to handwriting experts who claim that they can determine whether you are honest and reliable?" Now the audience found the topic interesting because it obviously had a potential impact on their lives.

One of the best ways to generate interest is to relate your topic to the listeners' needs and desires (as will be discussed later in this chapter).

connectpublic
speaking.com
To see a speaker who fails to offer her audience new and interesting material, view Speech 5 ("Animal Helpers").

Attitudes

Attitudes are the emotional inclinations—the favorable or unfavorable predispositions—that listeners bring to a speech. Each listener's attitudes are derived from a complex inner web of values, beliefs, experiences, and biases.

Before your speech, try to determine your listeners' attitudes—negative, neutral, or positive—toward your goal, yourself as speaker, and the occasion.

attitude
a predisposition to respond favorably or unfavorably toward a person or an idea

Attitudes toward the Goal

Unfavorable.   If listeners are negative toward your goal or objective, you should design your speech either to win them over to your views or—if that is unrealistic—to move them closer to your position.

When Najuana Dorsey, a student at Georgia Southern University, planned a speech on the desirability of insects as a source of protein for poor people in impoverished countries, she knew (from a questionnaire) that her classmates had a negative attitude toward the idea of anyone eating insects. So she devised a plan to change their attitude. In the early part of her speech, she gave solid scientific data about the nutritional value of insects. Near the end, she pulled out a cricket cake and said, "The crickets are roasted, and they taste like pecans. Why don't you try just one bite?" Despite initial squeamishness, all but one of her classmates ended up eating an entire piece, finding the cake to be surprisingly delicious. On after-speech evaluation sheets, students indicated that they now agreed with Dorsey's contention that insects could help alleviate hunger in the world.[22] (See Figure 4.1.)

Neutral.   If your listeners are apathetic or neutral, try to involve them in the issue, and then win them over to your side. For example, if an audience seems unconcerned about the extinction of hundreds of species of plants every year, you can tell them of the many medicines that are derived from plants. For example, digitalis, which is derived from the leaves of the foxglove plant, is used to treat heart disease. "Who knows," you can say, "if one of the many plants that will disappear from earth this year contains an ingredient that could have saved your life someday?" What you are trying to do, of course, is show that the issue is not a faraway abstraction but a real concern that could affect listeners' own lives.

Favorable.   If your audience is favorably disposed toward your ideas, your task is to reinforce their positive views and perhaps even motivate them to take action.

Figure 4.1
When student speaker Najuana Dorsey invited her classmates at Georgia Southern University to try some cricket cake, how did they respond? See text for the answer.

For example, you might give a pep talk to members of a political party in your community, urging them to campaign on behalf of the party's candidate in an upcoming election.

Attitudes toward the Speaker

Listeners will have a negative attitude toward a speaker if they suspect that he or she is unqualified to speak on a particular subject. This skepticism can be overcome if the person introducing you states your credentials and expertise. Otherwise, you can establish your credibility yourself at the beginning of your speech. Angie Chen, a student speaker, gave a classroom speech on acupuncture. During her introduction, she revealed that she had grown up in China and had undergone acupuncture treatment herself and had watched it performed on friends and relatives. Though Chen did not claim to be a medical expert, her summary of her experiences showed that she knew a great deal about the subject.

You also can enhance your credibility by explaining how you got your information. Let's say you give a report on recovery programs for drug addicts in your community. In your introduction, it is appropriate to mention that you have read two books on the subject and interviewed a local expert on chemical dependency. This is not bragging; it is simply a way to let the audience know that your information is based on solid research.

Attitudes toward the Occasion

Sometimes listeners are grumpy because they have been ordered to attend–they are a "captive audience"–and because they think the meeting is unnecessary. With such audiences, give a lively presentation geared to their precise needs. If possible, show an awareness of their situation and your desire to help.

> One speaker had to address a group of disgruntled employees who were required to attend a 4 P.M. meeting to listen to her. At the beginning she said, "I know you'd rather be somewhere else right now, and I know you think this meeting is pointless, but let's make the best use of our time as possible. I have talked to several of you about the issues that you are grappling with, and I'd like to zero in on those issues and not waste your time. And I promise to be finished by 5." Her comments, she said, caused the listeners to drop their gloomy expressions and become receptive to her presentation.

Needs and Desires

People want to be healthy, feel secure, have friends, make money, solve problems, enjoy life, and learn interesting things–to name just a few of the many human motivations. If you can offer ways for people to satisfy their needs and desires, they will listen to you with great interest.

In a speech on animal bites, student speaker Jeanne Perl appealed to a need and a desire:

- ***Need for safety.*** Perl warned about two common ways in which people get bitten: trying to separate fighting animals and trying to help injured ones.

- ***Desire to save money.*** She recommended that anyone who is bitten should seek immediate medical care, an action that usually saves money in the long run. She explained that an untreated bite often results in an infection that requires expensive treatment later.

The more needs and desires you can help listeners satisfy, the stronger your speech.

The Occasion

Find out as much as you can about the occasion and the setting of your speech, especially when you are giving a speech in your community or at a career-related meeting. Here are some issues to ask about; pay special attention to the first one.

Time Limit

Many public occasions are marred by long-winded speakers who drone on and on, oblivious to the lateness of the hour and the restlessness of the audience. Always find out how much time has been allotted for your speech, and *never* exceed the limit. This rule applies when you are the sole speaker and especially when you are one of several speakers.

Long-winded speakers create sleepy listeners.

If four speakers on a program are supposed to speak for only 10 minutes apiece, imagine what happens when each speaks for 30 minutes. The audience becomes fatigued and inattentive.

Some speakers have absolutely no concept of time. For a 5-minute speech, some of my students talk for 20 minutes and then swear later that they could not have talked for more than 5–something must have been wrong with my stopwatch. As we will see later, practicing your speech at home and clocking yourself will help you keep within time limits. If you tend to be a talkative speaker, follow the wise speechmaking formula of President Franklin D. Roosevelt:

- Be sincere.
- Be brief.
- Be seated.

Purpose of the Occasion

A popular columnist for a large metropolitan newspaper was asked to speak at a writing workshop for college journalists. She spent over an hour talking about the celebrities she had interviewed over the years. The gossip was fascinating, but the journalists were disappointed because the stated purpose of the workshop was to provide tips on how to write lively, interesting nonfiction. The speaker gave no tips.

Find out in advance the purpose of a meeting and then make sure you give listeners what they are expecting.

Other Events on the Program

Find out all that you can about other events on a program. Are there other speakers on the agenda? If so, on what topic will they speak? It would be disconcerting to prepare a speech on the life of Martin Luther King and then discover during the ceremony that the speaker ahead of you is talking on the same subject.

Even more alarming is to come to a meeting and find out that you are not just giving a speech but also debating someone on your topic. Obviously you need to know such information in advance so that you can anticipate the other speaker's argument and prepare your rebuttal.

Audience Size

It can be unsettling to walk into a room expecting an audience of 20 but instead finding 200. Knowing the size of your audience ahead of time will help you not only to prepare yourself psychologically but also to plan your presentation. Will you need extra-large visual aids? Will you need a microphone?

It's easier to connect with your listeners if they are close to you physically. If you have relatively few listeners, and they are scattered throughout a big room or they are all clumped together in the back rows, ask them to move to the front and center. Because some listeners dislike having to move, you may have to appeal for their cooperation by saying something like, "I hate to bother you, but it will save my throat if I don't have to shout."

Your Thoughts **?**

While you are waiting to give a speech, you discover that the person speaking just before you is covering the same topic. When you stand up, what will you do and say?

Tips for Your Career

One of the most exasperating situations you can face is this: Because of circumstances beyond your control, your speech comes at the end of a long, tedious meeting when listeners are weary and yearning to leave. Often the best response is to trim your speech. As the following incident shows, the audience will be grateful:

> An all-day professional conference was supposed to end at 3:30 P.M. so that participants would have plenty of daylight for driving back to their hometowns. Unfortunately, most of the speakers on the program exceeded their time limit, and the final speaker found himself starting at 3:18. Without commenting on the insensitivity of the other speakers, he started out

by saying, "How many of you would like to leave at 3:30?" Every hand went up. "I will end at 3:30," he promised. Though it meant omitting most of his prepared remarks, the speaker kept his promise. One of the participants said later: "We appreciated his sensitivity to us and his awareness of the time. And he showed class in not lambasting the earlier speakers who stole most of his time. He showed no anger or resentment."

Here's a technique to consider: When I am invited to speak at meetings where there are several speakers, I prepare two versions of my speech—a full-length one to use if the other speakers respect their time limits and a shorter version if events dictate that I trim my remarks.

Adapting during the Speech

Adapting your speech to your audience, so important during the preparation stages, also must take place during the actual delivery of the speech. Be sensitive to your listeners' moods and reactions, and then make any appropriate adjustments that you can. Here is an example.

> Using a portable chef's stove, Lester Petchenik, a student speaker, was demonstrating how to cook green beans *amandine*. At one point he sprinkled a large amount of salt into his pan—an action that caused several members of the audience to exchange glances of surprise. Noticing this reaction, Petchenik ad-libbed, "I know it looks like I put too much salt in, but remember that I've got three pounds of green beans in this pan. In just a moment, when you taste this, you'll see that it's not too salty." (He was right.)

Try to overcome any barriers to communication. John Naber of Pasadena, California, an Olympic gold medalist in swimming, says that he once gave a speech in a room with poor acoustics. Realizing the audience would have trouble understanding him if he stayed at the lectern, he said, "I moved into the middle of the group and walked among them as I spoke."[23]

Be sensitive to the mood of the audience. Are listeners bored, drowsy, or restless? Sometimes they are listless not because your speech is boring but because of circumstances beyond your control. It is eight o'clock in the morning, for example, and you have to explain a technical process to a group of conventioneers who have stayed up partying half the night.

Try to "wake up" a listless audience. For droopy listeners, here are some techniques you can use: (1) Invite audience participation (by asking for examples of what you are talking about or by asking for a show of hands of those who agree with you). (2) Rev up your delivery (by moving about, by speaking slightly louder at certain points, or by speaking occasionally in a more dramatic tone).

Don't compromise principles to win approval.   What if, contrary to our discussion in Chapter 2, listeners' frowns mean disapproval? Should you alter your speech to make everyone happy? No, of course not. Although you should try to be sensitive to the mood of the audience, never compromise your principles or violate your personal integrity simply to win approval. Your goal in public speaking is not to make the audience like you but to communicate your ideas to them clearly and effectively.

Resources for Review and Skill Building

connectpublic speaking.com *Connect Public Speaking* provides resources for study and review, including sample speech videos, an Outline Tutor, and practice tests.

Summary

To be an effective speaker, concentrate your attention and energies on your audience, and have a strong desire to communicate your message to them. Analyze the listeners beforehand and adapt your materials and presentation to their needs and interests.

To get information about an audience, you can interview the program director or whoever invited you to speak, you can interview a few future listeners, or you can conduct a survey of your listeners.

A wide diversity of listeners—men and women of different ages, races, nationalities, ethnic groups, religions, economic levels, and physical abilities—are likely to be in your audiences.

When speaking to international audiences, learn as much as you can about the culture of the listeners. One of the best ways to learn is to consult an expert. Learn non-verbal signals, be careful with jargon and slang, and maintain a serious, formal tone. If possible, provide handouts covering some of your main points a day or two before a presentation.

Extend the same sensitivity to America's diverse cultures. Avoid ethnocentrism, the belief that one's own cultural group is superior to other groups. Learn the expectations and viewpoints of different cultures, but treat your knowledge as possible clues, not absolute certainties. As much as possible, treat listeners primarily as individuals who may have characteristics that do not coincide with those of others in their cultural group.

Try to accommodate the needs of listeners with disabilities. If you are in doubt about what they need, simply ask them. Never treat adults with disabilities as if they were children, and don't equate physical limitations with mental limitations.

Analyze and adapt your presentations to such factors as age, gender, educational levels, occupations, religious affiliations, and economic and social status.

Consider your listeners' level of knowledge about your material, their level of interest in your subject matter, their needs and desires, and their attitudes toward the goal, the speaker, and the occasion.

Analyze the occasion to gather details about the time limit, the purpose of the meeting, other events on the program, and the number of people who will attend.

Be prepared to adapt to the needs of the listeners during the speech itself. Be sensitive to the cues that indicate boredom, restlessness, or lack of understanding.

Key Terms

adaptation, *61*

attitude, *73*

audience analysis, *61*

audience-centered speaker, *60*

customize, *61*

ethnocentrism, *69*

sexist language, *65*

taboo, *67*

Review Questions

1. What is an *audience-centered* speaker?

2. What is meant by audience analysis and adaptation?

3. How can a speaker get advance information about an audience?

4. What are taboos, and why are they an important concern for a speaker?

5. Do international audiences usually prefer a presentation that is humorous and informal or one that is serious and formal? Explain your answer.

6. What is ethnocentrism?

7. Who is the best source of information about the needs of listeners with disabilities, and why?

8. What are the three elements of audience psychology that should be analyzed?

9. What guidelines should be followed for a speech to an audience that knows little or nothing about your topic?

10. What aspects of the speech occasion should you examine before giving your talk?

Building Critical-Thinking Skills

1. Several books provide ready-made speeches that readers are welcome to use as their own. Aside from the dishonesty involved, why would using such speeches be a mistake?

2. At what time of day are you normally least alert? What conditions in a room (such as temperature and noise) cause you to be inattentive? Now imagine that you are a listener in these circumstances. What would a speaker need to do to keep you awake and engaged?

Building Teamwork Skills

1. Work with a group to create a questionnaire aimed at finding out where an audience stands concerning one of these issues: (a) Should "vicious" breeds of dogs such as pit bulls be outlawed? (b) Should the legal drinking age be changed? (c) Should pain sufferers seek relief by means of acupuncture? Use all the types of questions shown in Table 4.1.

2. In a group, create a list of 10 examples of American slang or jargon that might be misunderstood by visiting physicians from Hong Kong who speak British English.

A public speaking class can give you an opportunity to explore topics you normally would not have time to investigate. This photo, which shows caretaker Steffi Krueger playing with polar bear cub Flocke (German for snowflake) at a zoo in Nuremberg, Germany, appeared in a magazine story about the campaign by zoos to save polar bears from extinction. The story fascinated student speaker David Johnson, who decided to do research and give a speech on why polar bears are endangered.

Selecting Topic, Purpose, and Central Idea

OBJECTIVES

After studying this chapter, you should be able to:

1. Select appropriate and interesting speech topics.

2. Specify the general purpose of a speech.

3. Develop a clear, concise specific purpose statement for every speech you prepare.

4. Develop a clear, coherent central idea for every speech you prepare.

5. Understand how the specific purpose and the central idea fit into the overall design of a speech.

After volunteering as a teacher at an orphanage in Africa one summer, Tim Leaton, a student at Virginia Tech, had no trouble choosing a topic for a class speech. He told his classmates about the poverty—and the hope—that he had seen in the lives of the children at the orphanage, and he showed video clips that he had made with his camcorder. He urged each listener to sponsor a child and donate money to the orphanage.[1]

From the standpoint of public speaking, Leaton did two noteworthy things. First, he spoke on a topic that he cared a great deal about. Second, he focused on a clear message. Listeners had no doubt about what he was asking them to do.

Virginia Tech student Tim Leaton displays the camcorder he used in Africa.

Leaton's approach may sound easy and obvious, but some speakers—on campus and beyond—fail to speak on topics they are passionate about, and they end up boring the audience. Other speakers are enthusiastic about their topics, but they fail to have clear objectives. They meander and roam, causing listeners to become irritated and confused.

To help you avoid these mistakes, the first half of this chapter shows how to choose a good topic, and the second half explains how to develop clear objectives, using three valuable tools—general purpose, specific purpose, and central idea.

Selecting a Topic

For some of the speeches that you will give during your lifetime, your topic will be chosen by someone else. Your boss, for example, tells you to give a talk to your fellow employees on a new policy.

In most public speaking classes, in contrast, students are permitted to choose their own topics. Given such freedom, some students spend days walking around with a dark cloud over their heads, moaning to friends, "I have to give a speech next week and I can't think of a *thing* to speak on." Don't let yourself get stuck at this stage. Choose your topic far in advance, because you will need to spend a great deal of time and energy on researching, outlining, and practicing. If you delay choosing a topic, you may find yourself without enough time to prepare the speech adequately.

While you are taking this course, keep a notepad handy and jot down ideas for topics as they come to you so that you will have a stockpile from which to draw. In the weeks ahead, you can add to your list as you come up with more ideas.

Here are some important points to bear in mind as you look for a topic.

connectpublic speaking.com
For hundreds of sample topics, see Topic Helper.

Select a Topic You Care About

Has anything ever happened to you that was so exciting or interesting or infuriating you could hardly wait to tell your friends about it? That's the way you should feel about your speech topic. It should be something you care about, something you are eager to communicate to others. Are you thrilled by the sport of water skiing? Speak on how to water ski. Are you angry over the rising number of car thefts in your community? Speak on how to foil car thieves.

Enthusiasm is contagious; if you are excited, some of your excitement will spread to your listeners. If you are not excited about your topic, you are likely to do a lackluster job of preparing the speech, and when you deliver it, you will probably come across as dull and unconvincing.

Select a Topic You Can Master

A nightmare scenario: You give a speech on a subject about which you know very little. In the question-and-answer period, some listeners (who know the subject well) ridicule your lack of understanding, and they point out your omissions and errors.

This nightmare happened to me once in college, and it has happened to other speakers, but it need not happen to you. Make things easy for yourself. Speak on a subject with which you are already thoroughly familiar—or about which you can learn through research.

Here are several ways to probe for topics about which you know a lot (or can learn).

Personal Experiences

If you are permitted to choose your own topic, start your search with the subject on which you are the world's foremost expert—your own life.

"But my life isn't very interesting or exciting," you might say. Not so. Maybe you are not an international celebrity, but there are dozens of aspects of your

connectpublic
speaking.com

To see a topic chosen to satisfy the speaker's intellectual curiosity, view Video Clip 5.1, Choosing a Topic: "Humanoid Robots."

life that could make interesting speeches. Here are some examples, all involving students:

- After a friend was defrauded by a student-loan scam, Christina Morales researched the crime and told classmates how to find honest, reliable lenders for student loans.
- Michael Kaplan demonstrated how to make a thin crepe (pancake) filled with spinach, cheese, and tomato.
- Rachel Keller gave a classroom speech on the joys of rising into the sky in a hot-air balloon.

These students were *ordinary* people who chose to speak on *ordinary* aspects of their lives, but their speeches turned out the way all good speeches should turn out—interesting. When you are searching for a topic, start by looking for interesting experiences in your own life.

To help you assess your interests, you can create a personal inventory, using the categories shown in Figure 5.1 (which is an example of how one student, Lisa Lorenzo, used the technique). After you have filled in the inventory, go back and analyze the list for possible speech topics. You may want to ask a friend or an instructor to help you.

All the items in Lorenzo's inventory are potentially good speech topics. The best one would be whichever she is most eager to share with the audience.

Exploring Interests

Can you identify a topic that intrigues you—a topic that you have always wanted to know more about? If you choose such a topic, you not only get a subject that is fun to research but also gain a stockpile of new and interesting information. Your topic might even influence the direction of your life, as this example shows:

A college classroom speech on volcanoes changed the course of Jonathan Castro's life

> In a freshman public-speaking class at Humboldt State University in California, Jonathan Castro chose a topic that he had always wanted to investigate—volcanoes. Preparing and delivering the speech ignited a passionate interest that led Castro to choose volcanology as his life's work. After graduating from Humboldt, he earned a Ph.D. in geology at the University of Oregon, and today he is a volcano specialist at Oberlin College.[2]

Even if it doesn't change the course of your life, an intriguing topic can yield benefits. One student had always wanted to know the safest options for investing in the stock market. She researched and gave a speech on the subject, and a year later, she used the information to make her own investments.

Brainstorming

brainstorming
generating many ideas quickly and uncritically

If the suggestions already discussed don't yield a topic, try **brainstorming** (so called because it is supposed to create intellectual thunder and lightning). In brainstorming, you write down whatever pops into your mind. For example, if you start off with the word *helicopter,* the next word that floats into your mind might be *rescue* and then the next word might be *emergencies,* and so on. Don't censor any words. Don't apply any critical evaluation. Simply write whatever comes into your mind. Nothing is too silly or bizarre to put down.

Using a sheet of paper (with categories such as those in Figure 5.2), jot down words as they come to your mind. When you finish brainstorming, analyze your list for possible topics. Don't discard any possibility until you have chosen a topic.

```
Name: ___Lisa Lorenzo___

               Personal Inventory

Jot down as much information about yourself
as you can in the categories below.

Work experience (past and present)
     Crime lab technician
     Free-lance photographer


Special skills or knowledge
     Photography
     Fingerprinting
     Crime evidence analysis

Pastimes (hobbies, sports, recreation)
     Photographing sports events
     Softball
     Volleyball
     Bicycle riding

Travel
     Spain
     Portugal
     Italy

Unusual experiences
     Took pictures at Super Bowl
     Bicycled over 300 miles in Europe


School interests (academic and extracurricular)
     Law enforcement
     Photography for school paper


Concerns or beliefs (politics, society, family, etc.)
     Gangs are outgunning police.
     Spouse abuse must be stopped.
     More bike lanes should be established on highways.
```

Figure 5.1
A personal inventory, as filled in by one student.

Figure 5.2 shows one student's brainstorming notes. Under most categories, the student's brainstorming was fairly straightforward. It is easy to see his train of thought. But under "Social Problems," he made some interesting jumps (which is okay; writing down whatever comes to mind is the way brainstorming works). He started with aggressive drivers, a serious problem today. This led him to jot down "highway safety," perhaps because aggressive drivers sometimes cause accidents. This idea led to "air bags," and then his mind jumped to alternatives to automobile transportation–"commuter trains" and "bicycle lanes." His final entry is "pedestrian deaths," a growing problem on urban streets. Any of the ideas in this list could be developed into a strong speech.

You may be wondering why you should put all this down on paper. Why not just let all your ideas float around in your mind? The advantage of writing your

connectpublic
speaking.com
For printable copies of both the Personal Inventory and the Brainstorming Guide, see the Supplementary Readings.

Figure 5.2
One student's entries on a brainstorming guide.

Brainstorming Guide

People	Music
Tom Cruise	rock bands
Brad Pitt	drums
Angelina Jolie	synthesizers
Charlize Theron	Korg
Halle Berry	Kurzweil

Places	Sports
Caribbean	snowboarding
Bahamas	skiing
Barbados	ski patrol
Virgin Islands	Alpine skiing
Cuba	ice flying

Things	Current Events
wedding ring	immigration
diamond	deportation
pearl	farm workers
ruby	migrant children
sapphire	abuse of immigrants

Health	Social Problems
diabetes	aggressive drivers
obesity	highway safety
diet	air bags
low-fat	commuter trains
diet pills	bicycle lanes
food safety	pedestrian deaths

thoughts down is that you end up with a document that can be analyzed. Seeing words on a page helps you focus your thinking.

Exploring the Internet

A quick and enjoyable way to find topics is to search on the Internet. Here are some good sites:

- **Pathfinders** (ipl.org/div/pf)
- **Yahoo! News** (news.yahoo.com/topics)
- **Librarians' Index to the Internet** (lii.org)

For updates and other links, visit Connect Public Speaking (connectpublicspeaking. com), click on WEBLINKS, and explore links for this page.

Choose a Topic That Will Interest the Audience

To engage your audience, choose a topic that is timely, worthwhile, and interesting. A talk on why people need to take vacations would be dull and obvious—everyone already knows why. Instead, give a lively presentation on scuba diving in the Caribbean or backpacking in the Rockies.

Don't try to convince listeners of what they already believe. (As the old saying goes, "Don't preach to the converted.") Advocating the value of a college education to a college class is wasted effort. If everyone in the audience didn't already agree, they wouldn't be where they are today.

"I'm excited about my topic," some students say, "but I'm afraid the audience will be bored. How can I know?" Most listeners are bored by speeches that give them no personal enrichment. Their attitude is "What's in it for me?" To see things from their perspective, imagine a typical listener approaching you five minutes before your presentation and saying, "I'm trying to decide whether to stay for your talk. What do I stand to gain by listening to you?" If you realize that you couldn't make a compelling case, change your topic.

This doesn't mean that you must show listeners a dollar-and-cents gain, such as how to make money on the stock market. Perhaps their payoff is purely intellectual–a glimpse into a fascinating subject, such as how filmmakers use computers to "morph" (gradually transform) a human face into that of a werewolf. A speech like this would satisfy the human desire to understand behind-the-scenes tricks–a rewarding payoff. But if the only thing that listeners are offered is a dry and obvious explanation of why computers are popular, they will be bored.

Two other ways to determine whether a topic is boring or interesting: (1) Consult your instructor for his or her suggestions. (2) Several weeks before your talk, distribute a questionnaire to members of the audience to find out how interested they would be in several potential speech topics. For each topic, provide a scale for them to check, ranging from "very interesting" to "moderately interesting" to "not very interesting."

Your Thoughts

Regarding the topic "investing in the stock market," how could you make it interesting to an audience of college students? How could you make it boring?

Narrow the Topic

Once you find a topic, you often need to narrow it. Suppose that you want to give a speech on weather; 5 minutes–or 20–is not enough time to adequately cover such a broad topic. How about limiting yourself to just storms? Again, 5 minutes would be too short to do justice to the topic. How about one type of storm–thunderstorms? This subject perhaps could be handled in a 5-minute speech, but it would be advisable to narrow the topic down even more–to one aspect of the subject: "how to avoid being struck by lightning."

Narrowing a topic helps you control your material. It prevents you from wandering in a huge territory: you are able to focus on one small piece of ground. Instead of talking on the vast subject of elections, you might limit yourself to explaining how some states conduct voting via the Internet.

Ask yourself this question: Is my topic one that can be adequately and comfortably discussed in 5 minutes (or whatever your time limit is)? If the honest answer is no, you can keep the topic, but you must narrow the focus.

Here are some examples of broad topics that can be narrowed:

Too broad: Native Americans
Narrowed: Shapes, colors, and legends in Pueblo pottery
Too broad: Prisons
Narrowed: Gangs in federal and state prisons
Too broad: Birds
Narrowed: How migrating birds navigate

connectpublic
speaking.com
For handy guidelines, see "Checklist for Preparing and Delivering a Speech."

An important way to narrow your topic is to formulate a specific purpose, which will be discussed later in this chapter. First, let's take a look at your general purpose.

The General Purpose

general purpose
the broad objective of a speech

Establishing a **general purpose** for your speech will help you bring your topic under control. Most speeches have one of the following purposes:

- To inform
- To persuade
- To entertain

Speeches may have other purposes—to inspire, to stimulate, to introduce, to create goodwill, and so on—but these three are the most common.

To Inform

In an informative speech, you are concerned about giving new information to your listeners. You can define a concept (such as intellectual property); explain a situation (how overdosages of vitamin pills cause health problems); demonstrate a process (the correct way to cross-country ski); or describe a person, a place, an object, or an event (a volcanic eruption).

Your main concern in this kind of speech is to have your audience understand and remember new information. You are in effect a teacher—not a preacher, a salesperson, or a debater. Here is a sampling of topics for informative speeches:

connectpublic
speaking.com
For a sample
informative speech,
view the speech video
"Wedding Crashers."

- The possible causes of autism
- Traditional West African drumming and dancing
- How the airplane was invented
- Growing vegetables in an organic garden

To Persuade

Your aim in a persuasive speech is to convince the listeners to come over to your side, to adopt your point of view. You want to *change* them in one or both of these ways:

connectpublic
speaking.com
For a sample
persuasive speech,
view "The Deadliest
Natural Disaster."

1. *Change their minds.* You try, for example, to persuade them that television cameras should be barred from courtrooms.

2. *Change their behavior.* You try to bring about a transformation in either a positive or a negative direction; that is, you try to get your listeners either to *start* doing something they normally don't do (such as using seat belts) or to *stop* doing something they normally do (such as sprinkling salt on their food).

Here are some examples of topics for persuasive speeches.

- The dumping of garbage and toxic chemicals into the world's oceans should be stopped.
- A parent who reneges on child-support payments should be forced to pay or be sent to prison.
- State and local governments should increase the number of bicycle pathways built along abandoned railroad rights-of-way.
- Couples should not go into debt for any purchase except a home.

To Entertain

An entertaining speech is aimed at amusing or diverting your audience. It is light, fun, relaxing.

Some students mistakenly think that an entertaining speech is a series of jokes. Although jokes are an obvious component of many entertaining speeches, you can amuse or divert your audience just as easily with other types of material: stories, anecdotes, quotations, examples, and descriptions. (For more details, see Chapter 10.)

Here are some examples of topics for entertaining speeches:

- People who regret winning a lottery
- My life with a parrot named Alex
- The five most outrageous excuses for absenteeism at work
- Being an "extra" in a Hollywood movie

Topic for an entertaining speech: "TV commercials in the 1950s were unintentionally hilarious."

The Specific Purpose

After you have chosen a topic and determined your general purpose, your next step is to formulate a **specific purpose,** stating exactly what you want to accomplish in your speech. Here is an example:

Topic: Foodborne illnesses
General Purpose: To inform
Specific Purpose: To tell my listeners how to protect themselves from foodborne illnesses

specific purpose
the precise goal that a speaker wants to achieve

Later, when you create a speech outline, the statement of your specific purpose will occupy a key position at the top of the outline, but it is not a statement that you actually say in your speech. Rather, it is a tool used for planning.

Devising a specific purpose forces you to put your ideas into sharp focus so that you don't wander aimlessly in your speech and lose your audience.

If you were to choose a topic such as protection of the environment, and then did nothing to bring it into sharp focus, you might make the mistake of cramming too many different issues into one speech. How about protecting national parks? This is more manageable, especially if you emphasized just one specific park:

Topic: Preserving Yosemite National Park
General Purpose: To persuade
Specific Purpose: To persuade my audience to support steps to reverse overcrowding and neglect in Yosemite National Park

Now you have a sharp focus for your speech. You have limited yourself to a topic that can be covered adequately in a short speech.

Here are some guidelines for formulating a specific purpose statement.

Begin the Statement with an Infinitive

An **infinitive** is a verb preceded by *to*—for example, *to write, to read.* By beginning your purpose statement with an infinitive, you clearly state your intent.

infinitive
a verb form beginning with "to"

Your Thoughts

The best way to write a love letter, the Swiss-French philosopher Jean Jacques Rousseau said, is to begin without knowing what you are going to say. This may be a good formula for a love letter, but would it be wise for speechmaking? Explain your answer.

Poor: Pyramids in Egypt

Better: To explain to my audience how the pyramids in Egypt were constructed

For informative speeches, your purpose statement can start with such infinitives as "to explain," "to show," and "to demonstrate." For persuasive speeches, your purpose statement can start with infinitives such as "to convince," "to prove," and "to get the audience to believe."

Include a Reference to Your Audience

Your specific purpose statement should refer to your audience. For instance, "To convince my listeners that . . ." This may seem like a minor matter, but it serves to remind you that your goal is not just to stand up and talk but also to communicate your ideas to real flesh-and-blood human beings.

Poor: To explain how some employers are using psychological tests to determine whether prospective employees are honest

Better: To explain to my listeners how some employers are using psychological tests to determine whether prospective employees are honest

Limit the Statement to One Major Idea

Resist the temptation to cover several big ideas in a single speech. Limit your specific purpose statement to only one idea.

Poor: To persuade the audience to support efforts to halt the destruction of rain forests in Central and South America, and to demand higher standards of water purity in the United States

Better: To persuade the audience to support efforts to halt the destruction of rain forests in Central and South America

In the first example, the speaker tries to cover two major ideas in one speech. Although it is true that both themes pertain to the environment, they are not closely related and should be handled in separate speeches.

Make Your Statement as Precise as Possible

Strive to formulate a statement that is clear and precise.

Poor: To help my audience brighten their relationships

Better: To explain to my listeners three techniques people can use to communicate more effectively with loved ones

Your Thoughts

"Telling about my first cruise vacation." How could you improve this statement of a specific purpose?

The first statement is fuzzy and unfocused. What is meant by "to help"? What is meant by "brighten"? And what kind of relationships are to be discussed: marital, social, business? The second statement is one possible improvement.

Tips for Your Career

Make Sure You Can Achieve Your Objective in the Time Allotted

Don't try to cover too much in one speech. It is better to choose a small area of knowledge that can be developed adequately than to select a huge area that can be covered only sketchily.

> *Poor:* To tell my audience about endangered species
>
> *Better:* To convince my audience that international action should be taken to prevent poachers from slaughtering elephants

The first statement is much too broad for a speech; you would need several hours to cover the subject. The second statement narrows the topic so that it can be covered easily in a short speech.

Don't Be Too Technical

You have probably sat through a speech or lecture that was too technical or complicated for you to understand. Don't repeat this mistake when you stand at the lectern.

> *Poor:* To explain to my listeners the chemical composition of vegetable oils
>
> *Better:* To explain to my audience how to choose the right vegetable oil for cooking different kinds of food

The first statement is too technical for the average audience. Many listeners would find the explanation tedious and over their heads. The second statement focuses on valuable information that people can use in their own kitchens.

The Central Idea

In a college class, a counselor from an alcohol rehabilitation center spoke on alcoholism, giving many statistics, anecdotes, and research findings. I did not hear the speech, but afterward, I overheard some of the listeners arguing about it. Several contended that the speaker's message was "Drink moderately–don't abuse alcohol," while others thought the speaker was saying, "Abstain from alcohol completely." Still others said they were confused–they didn't know what the speaker was driving at.

If this happens to you–if you give a speech and people later wonder or debate exactly what point you were trying to make–you have failed to accomplish your most important task: to communicate your **central idea.**

central idea
the key concept of a speech

The central idea is the core message of your speech expressed in one sentence. It is the same as the *thesis sentence, controlling statement,* or *core idea*–terms you may have encountered in English courses. If you were forced to boil your entire speech down to one sentence, what would you say? *That* is your central idea. If, one month after you have given your speech, the audience remembers only one thing, what should it be? *That* is your central idea.

As we will see in later chapters, the central idea is a vital ingredient in your outline for a speech. In fact, it *controls* your entire speech: everything you say in your speech should develop, explain, illustrate, or prove the central idea. Everything? Yes, everything–all your facts, anecdotes, statistics, and quotations.

If you are unclear in your own mind about your central idea, you will be like the counselor who caused such confusion: Listeners will leave your speech wondering, "What in the world was that speaker driving at?"

Devising the Central Idea

Let's imagine that you decide to give a speech on why governments should spend money to send powerful radio signals into outer space. The specific purpose statement of your speech might look like this:

connectpublic speaking.com
For a sample central idea, view Video Clip 5.2, "The Folly of Crash Diets."

Specific Purpose: To persuade my listeners to support government funding of radio transmissions into outer space

How are you going to persuade your audience? Can you simply say, "Folks, please support radio transmissions into outer space"? No, because merely stating your position isn't likely to sway your listeners. They might say to themselves, "I don't want my tax dollars being spent on some harebrained scheme to beam radio signals into the sky." To convince them, you need to sell the audience on a central idea that, if believed, might cause them to support your position:

Central Idea: Most scientists agree that radio transmissions are the best means for making contact with extraterrestrial civilizations (if any exist).

If you can sell this idea, you will probably succeed in your specific purpose: To persuade the listeners to support public funding of radio transmissions. They will be persuaded because the central idea is so intriguing: Most people like the notion of communication with aliens from faraway planets, and if most scientists back the idea, it cannot be considered far-out and impractical. "Yes," the listeners will say, "let's spend some of our tax dollars to explore the universe."

After you decide upon a central idea, your task in preparing the rest of the speech is to find materials–such as examples, statistics, and quotations–to explain and prove the central idea. In this case, you would need to explain the technology and cite the testimony of eminent scientists who support radio transmissions into space.

Some students have trouble distinguishing between the specific purpose and the central idea. Is there any significant difference? Yes. The specific purpose is written from your point of view—it is what *you* set out to accomplish. The central idea is written entirely from the listeners' point of view—it is the message *they* go away with.

The central idea of one speech: "Gardening relieves stress."

To learn to distinguish between the specific purpose and the central idea, study the examples in Table 5.1.

In planning your speech, write the specific purpose statement first—before you start gathering material. In many cases, you will be able to write the central idea immediately afterward. Sometimes, however, you may need to postpone formulating the central idea until you have completed your research. Imagine that you are preparing a speech on the use of steroids by athletes and bodybuilders. From watching news on television, you know that coaches and health experts are warning people not to use steroids, and you feel certain that your investigation will confirm this view. So you start off with a specific purpose statement like this:

Specific Purpose: To inform my audience of the health risks of using steroids for developing muscles

You haven't done any research yet, so you can't really write a central idea. But after you spend a few days in the library, studying articles on steroids, you become able to create your central idea:

Central Idea: Individuals who chronically use steroids risk kidney and liver damage, as well as serious mental disorders.

Now that you have a clear statement of the key idea of your speech, your task will be to show the audience that what you say about steroids is true by citing statistics, case studies, and the testimony of experts.

Table 5.1 How Topics Can Be Developed

Topic	General Purpose	Specific Purpose	Central Idea
Space junk	To inform	To inform my audience about the dangers of "space junk" (dead satellites and bits of expended rocket stages) that orbits the earth	The 9,000+ pieces of debris that orbit the earth threaten commercial and scientific satellites.
Buying a car	To persuade	To persuade my audience to avoid high-pressure sales tactics when buying a car	By comparing prices and using reputable car guides, consumers can avoid being "taken for a ride" by car salespeople.
Driving tests	To entertain	To amuse my audience with the true story of my abysmal failure to pass my driving test	Taking the test for a driver's license is a scary and sometimes disastrous event.
Rosa Parks	To inspire	To uplift my listeners by describing Rosa Parks's courageous defiance of segregation laws in 1955	By going to jail for the cause of freedom and justice, Rosa Parks was a major influence in persuading America to move away from racial discrimination.

Guidelines for the Central Idea

1. **Every speech should have only one central idea.**   Why not two? Or three? Because you are doing well if you can fully illuminate one big idea in a speech. If you try to handle more than one, you run the risk of overwhelming the listeners with more information than they can absorb.

2. **Put the central idea on paper.**   It is important that you actually write down your central idea rather than have some vague notion floating around in your mind. Writing it down gives you a clear sense of the direction your speech will take.

3. **Limit the central idea to a single sentence.**   Whenever theatrical producer David Belasco was approached by people with an idea for a play, he would hand them his business card and ask them to write their concept on the back. If they protested that they needed more space, he would say, "Then you don't have a clear idea."[3]

4. **Make an assertion rather than an announcement or a statement of fact.**   A common mistake is to formulate the central idea as a mere announcement:

> *Ineffective:*   I will discuss robots as surgeons. *(This is a good topic, but what idea does the speaker want to communicate?)*

Another mistake is to put forth nothing more than a statement of fact:

> *Ineffective:*   Several operations at Johns Hopkins Medical Center have been performed by surgeons using robots. *(This is interesting, but it is just a fact—a piece of information that can be included in the speech but does not stand alone as an overarching theme.)*

Now let's turn to a better version—one that makes an assertion:

> *Effective:*   Robots are valuable assistants in surgery because they can perform repetitive actions with great precision and no fatigue. *(This is a good central idea because it asserts a worthwhile point that can be developed in a speech.)*

5. **Let the central idea determine the content of the entire speech.**   As you prepare your outline, evaluate every potential item in light of the central idea. Does Fact A help explain the central idea? If yes, keep it. If no, throw it out. Does Statistic B help prove the central idea? If yes, keep it. If no, throw it out.

Let's assume that you want to give a talk on the following:

> *Topic:*   Daytime use of headlights
>
> *General Purpose:*   To persuade

Next you write down what you want to accomplish with your audience:

> *Specific Purpose:*   To persuade my audience to turn on their low-beam headlights while driving during the day

To carry out your specific purpose, you need to plant one key idea in the minds of your listeners:

> *Central Idea:*   Driving with low-beam headlights on during the day is a simple way for drivers to reduce the risk of traffic accidents.

Now you have your speech in a nutshell. As you decide what to put in the speech, let the central idea control the process. Let's say, for example, that you find an interesting story about how headlights became a standard feature on cars.

Fascinating, but does it relate to the central idea? No, so discard it. Next, you discover some research showing a 20 percent drop in car accidents in two foreign countries after low-beam lights during the day were required by law. Does this support your central idea? Yes, so include it.

Overview of Speech Design

How do the items discussed in this chapter fit into the overall design of a speech? If you look at Figure 5.3, which is an overview of a typical plan for a speech, you will see this chapter's items listed in the top ellipse, labeled "Objectives." These items–general

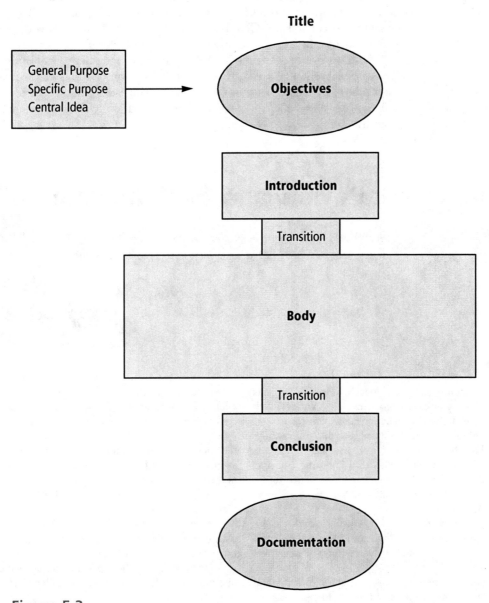

Figure 5.3

An overview of a typical plan for a speech. "Objectives" are explained in this chapter. The other terms will be covered in Chapters 7–9.

purpose, specific purpose, and central idea—are planning tools to help you create a coherent speech. They are *not* the opening words of your speech. The bottom ellipse, "Documentation," is also a planning tool and does not represent the final words of a speech. The actual speech that you deliver is shown in the rectangles.

Don't make the mistake of assuming that a speaker should create the rectangles from top to bottom, in the order in which they appear. For reasons that will be obvious later, it makes sense to work on the body first, and then tackle the introduction and the conclusion.

Here is a preview of the next seven chapters, as we learn how to build a speech that is as solid as a brick building. First we will look at how to find raw materials and produce strong bricks (Chapter 9). Next we will examine how to sort and organize the bricks—in the body of the speech (Chapter 7) and the introduction and conclusion (Chapter 8). Finally, we will discuss how to put our best bricks together to create a coherent structure (Chapter 9).

All this work may seem wasteful of your time and energy, but in the long run, it pays rich dividends. It channels your thinking and prevents you from scattering your efforts across too wide a field. It helps you fashion an orderly, understandable speech, increasing the chances that you will enlighten, rather than confuse, your listeners.

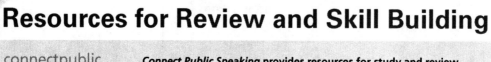

Resources for Review and Skill Building

connectpublic speaking.com

Connect Public Speaking provides resources for study and review, including sample speech videos, an Outline Tutor, and practice tests.

Summary

In choosing a topic for your speech, think of subjects (1) about which you care a great deal, (2) about which you know a lot (either now or after you complete your research), and (3) that your audience will find interesting.

In looking for topics, start with yourself. What personal experiences might yield an interesting speech? If you want to go outside your own life, explore topics that intrigue you—subjects about which you have always wanted to know more.

Other methods for finding a topic include brainstorming (writing down ideas that come to your mind) and exploring Internet sites that list subjects for college papers and speeches.

After you choose a topic, decide upon your general purpose in speaking (such as to inform, to persuade, or to entertain) and then formulate your specific purpose—exactly what you hope to accomplish in the speech. Follow these guidelines: (1) Begin the statement with an infinitive. (2) Include a reference to your audience. (3) Limit the statement to one major idea. (4) Make your statement as precise as possible. (5) Make sure you can achieve your objective in the time allotted. (6) Don't be too technical.

Next, write out your central idea: the one key idea that you want your audience to remember even if they forget everything else in the speech. Make sure the central idea is phrased as an assertion rather than an announcement or a statement of fact.

In the long run, these preliminary steps will help you organize your ideas in a coherent, understandable form.

Key Terms

brainstorming, *84*

central idea, *92*

general purpose, *88*

infinitive, *89*

specific purpose, *89*

Review Questions

1. When a speaker is enthusiastic about his or her ideas, how do listeners usually react?

2. How does brainstorming work?

3. What are the characteristics of speeches that listeners find boring?

4. List three *general* purposes for speeches.

5. Are jokes required for an entertaining speech? Explain your answer.

6. List the six criteria discussed in this chapter for writing a specific purpose statement.

7. What is the central idea of a speech?

8. What is the difference between the specific purpose and the central idea?

9. Give an example of an infinitive.

10. What are hidden purposes, and how should you handle them?

Building Critical-Thinking Skills

1. Narrow down the following broad subjects to specific, manageable topics:

    a. Outdoor recreation

    b. Musical groups

    c. Illegal drugs

    d. Saving money

    e. Cloning

2. All but one of these specific purpose statements are either inappropriate for a brief classroom speech or incorrectly written.

    Name the good one, and rewrite the bad ones so that they conform to the guidelines in this chapter:

    a. To inform my audience of the basics of quantum inelastic scattering and photodissociation code

    b. To inform my listeners about creativity on the job, getting raises, and being an effective manager

    c. To explain to my audience how to perform basic yoga exercises

    d. How persons with disabilities can fight back against job discrimination

    e. Immigration since 1800

    f. To persuade my audience to be careful

Building Teamwork Skills

1. Beforehand, each group member should list five potential speech topics. In your group, evaluate each topic: Is it interesting and appropriate for a classroom speech?

2. In a group, brainstorm topics that would be boring or inappropriate for speeches in your class. Choose one person to write down the topics. Remember that no one should criticize or analyze during the brainstorming session. Afterward, the group (or the class) can discuss each choice (Does everyone agree? Why is the topic inappropriate?).

3. Follow the instructions for item 2, except brainstorm topics that would be interesting and appropriate for speeches in your class.

In a ceremony in Los Angeles, Actress Cameron Diaz presents a human rights award to Carlos Rojas (pictured rear), who uses video to monitor and document human rights abuses against indigenous and peasant communities in Mexico's southern states. The slide illustrates two guidelines for visual aids: (1) make sure a visual is large enough to be seen clearly by every listener, and (2) choose images over words whenever possible.

Presentation Aids

OUTLINE

OBJECTIVES

After studying this chapter, you should be able to:

1. Explain at least seven advantages of using visual aids in a speech.
2. Describe the types of visual aids.
3. Describe the media for visual aids.
4. Prepare appropriate visual aids.
5. Present visual aids effectively.
6. Appeal to channels other than visual.

Imagine how hard it would be to describe an observation robot, using only words (Figure 6.1). Fortunately for General Peter Schoomaker, U.S. Army chief of staff, when he gave a presentation to the Senate Armed Services Committee, he was able to supplement his words by demonstrating how the robot worked and how it transmitted images from a remote location.

Visuals are powerful tools for informing and persuading. Because most people have grown up with television and therefore are conditioned to learn via imagery, visual aids are considered a vital part of most business, technical, and professional presentations today. The attitude throughout society is: "Don't just tell me; show me."

While this chapter concentrates on the visual channel of communication, we will also discuss other channels—hearing, smell, taste, touch, and physical activity—which can be useful in reaching your listeners.

Figure 6.1
Visual aids are powerful tools in a speaker's arsenal.

Advantages of Visual Aids

While *verbal* supports (discussed in the preceding chapter) are important for explaining and illustrating your ideas, you also should look for *visual* support. Let's examine some reasons for using visual aids.

1.   **Visual aids can make ideas clear and understandable.**   Your listeners can quickly grasp how to jump-start a car if you display a drawing that shows where to connect battery cables.

2.   **Visual aids can make a speech more interesting.**   In a speech on pollution, a chemist showed color slides of gargoyles and statues in Europe that had been eaten away by acid rain. The slides added a lively, provocative element to a technical subject.

3.   **Visual aids can help an audience remember facts and details.**
Research shows that oral information alone is not as effective as oral information coupled with visual aids.[1] Imagine that you give the same speech (on how to create a spreadsheet on a computer) to two different groups. To the first group, you use only words; to the second group, you use words plus visuals. If the audiences are tested a week later, the second group will score far higher in comprehension.[2]

4.   **Visual aids can make long, complicated explanations unnecessary.**
In medical schools, professors use close-up slides and videotapes to teach surgical procedures. The visuals show exactly where and how to make an incision, sparing the professor from having to give a tedious verbal explanation.

5.   **Visual aids can help prove a point.**   If a prosecuter shows the jury a surveillance video in which the defendant is seen robbing a store, the jury can be easily convinced of the defendant's guilt.

6.   **Visual aids can add to your credibility.**   Researchers have found that presenters who use good visual aids are rated by listeners as more persuasive and credible than presenters who use no visuals.
But a note of warning: If listeners think that visual aids are poor, their confidence in the speaker declines. In other words, if you can't use a good visual, don't use any at all.[3]

7.   **Visual aids enhance communication with people who speak English as a second language.**   As more and more audiences include professionals and businesspeople from other countries, international students, immigrants, and others whose command of English is imperfect, visual aids have become a crucial way to overcome language limitations.

Your Thoughts

Using a good visual bolsters a speaker's credibility. Why do you think that listeners react in this way?

Types of Visual Aids

In this section, we will look at various types of visual aids. As you select aids for your speeches, be flexible. Public speaking instructor Linda Larson of Mesa Community College advises her students to think of "tools" instead of "visual aids." In various jobs, not every tool works. For example, not every job needs a hammer. In a particular speech, a PowerPoint slide may be the wrong tool, while a handout may be the perfect tool.[4]

Figure 6.2

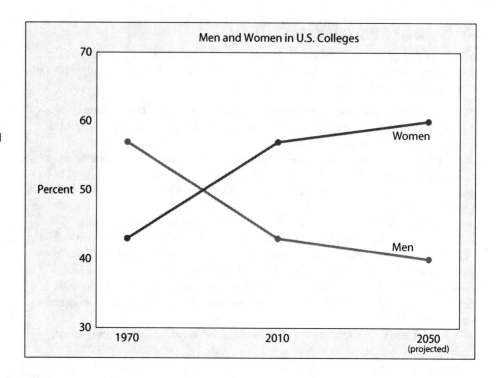

Figure 6.2

Sample Line Graph
In 1970 in the United States, 43 percent of college students were women. Today they have surpassed men and are expected to reach 60 percent by 2050.

line graph
a visual consisting of lines (charted on a grid) that show trends

bar graph
a visual that contrasts two or more sets of data by means of parallel rectangles of varying lengths

pie graph
a circle showing a given whole that is divided into component wedges

pictorial graph
a visual that dramatizes statistical data by means of pictorial forms

information chart
text material arranged as a series of key points

table
numbers or words arranged systematically in rows and columns

Graphs

Graphs help audiences understand and retain statistical data. The **line graph,** which is widely used in textbooks, uses a horizontal and a vertical scale to show trends and the relationship between two variables, such as percent and years in Figure 6.2.

A **bar graph** consists of horizontal or vertical bars that contrast two or more variables, as in Figure 6.3. A bar graph can effectively display a great deal of data in a clear, easily comprehended manner.

A **pie graph** is a circle representing 100 percent and divided into segments of various sizes (see Figure 6.4). A pie graph in a speech should have no more than 7 or 8 wedges. (If necessary, several small segments can be lumped together into an "all others" category.) If you see a 20-piece pie graph in a book, resist the temptation to use it in a speech. While such a graph is fine in a book because readers can scrutinize it as long as they wish, it would be hard to decipher in a presentation.

Of all graphs, a **pictorial graph** is perhaps the easiest to read, because it visually translates information into a picture that can be grasped instantly. Figure 6.5 is an example of a pictorial graph.

Charts

Charts provide information in a compact, easily digested form. An **information chart,** also called a *list of key ideas,* is a convenient way of presenting main points or steps in a process. Figure 6.6 shows a good format for presenting a list.

An information chart can sometimes take the form of a **table,** in which information is presented in rows and columns. Figure 6.7 shows how easy it can be to understand a table.

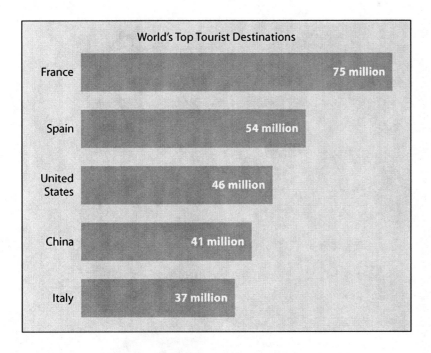

Figure 6.3
Sample Bar Graph
This bar graph shows the average annual tourist arrivals at the world's most popular destinations.

Note of caution: Most instructors dislike a speech that is nothing more than a recitation of a lengthy list. One student's entire speech was a list of 42 lucrative careers–a lazy way of doing a speech.

Drawings and Photos

Drawings make good visual aids because they can illustrate points that would be hard to explain in words. One kind of drawing that is highly effective is a map. By sketching a map yourself, you can include only those features that are pertinent to your speech. If you were speaking about the major rivers of America, for example, you could outline the boundaries of the United States and then draw heavy blue lines for the rivers, leaving out extraneous details, such as cities. Figure 6.8 shows a map.

Because photographs have a high degree of realism, they are excellent for proving points. Lawyers, for example, often use photographs of the scene of an accident to argue a case. In a speech, you should not use a photograph unless it can be enlarged so that everyone can see it clearly.

connectpublic
speaking.com

See Video Clip 6.3, Using a Photograph: "Humanoid Robots."

Figure 6.4
Sample Pie Graph
Of the millions of dollars that retail stores lose each year from theft, employees account for 68 percent and shoplifters account for 32 percent.

Figure 6.5
Sample Pictorial Graph
When the speaker explains that each image represents 400 wolves, the audience can quickly visualize the comeback of the gray wolf, an endangered species that had an estimated 400 survivors in 1965. Thanks to protection mandated by federal law, the gray wolf population has climbed to 3,200.

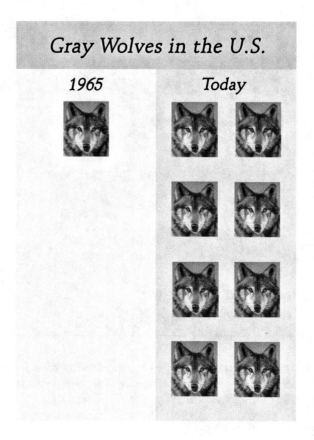

Video and Animation

With video, you can transport your audience to any corner of the world. To give listeners a glimpse of the rich spectacle of Mexican weddings, student speaker Victor Treviño showed a video of ritual, music, and dance at the wedding celebration of his sister in Guadalajara.

Figure 6.6
Sample Information Chart
An information chart (or list of key ideas) can be presented on PowerPoint slides, posters, or transparencies. If possible, display only one item at a time so that listeners stay with you and don't read ahead.

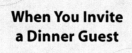

When You Invite a Dinner Guest

1. Ask about food preferences

2. Any food allergies?

3. Any special dietary needs?

Most Popular Baby Names

Decade	Girl	Boy
2000s	Emily	Jacob
1990s	Jessica	Michael
1980s	Jessica	Michael
1970s	Jennifer	Michael
1960s	Lisa	Michael
1950s	Mary	James

Figure 6.7
Sample Table
A table is an effective type of information chart. This table shows the most popular names chosen for girls and boys in America during six decades.

If you videotape an interview as part of your research, you may be able to use some excerpts in your speech. Student speaker Adrienne Shields interviewed a bank official on how crooks steal from ATMs (automated teller machines). In her speech, Shields played video segments of the official as he demonstrated the machine's vulnerabilities. The video was much more effective than a verbal description alone would have been.

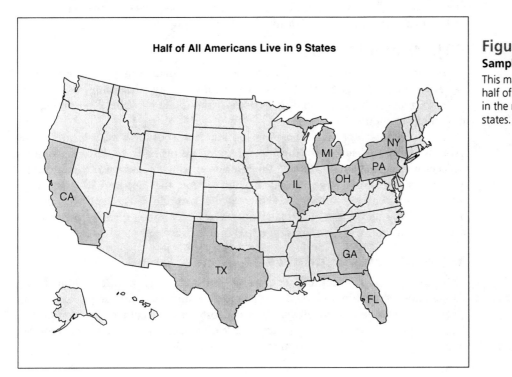

Half of All Americans Live in 9 States

Figure 6.8
Sample Map
This map illustrates that half of all Americans live in the nine most populous states.

Tips for Your Career

Animation—a sequence of drawings (such as diagrams or cartoons)—can be used in a PowerPoint presentation or video to clarify points. In courtroom trials, for example, lawyers often use animated drawings to re-create a car accident and help the jury understand what happened.

Audio and video gimmicks are incorporated into PowerPoint and can sometimes be used effectively, but Bill Howard, senior executive editor of *PC Magazine*, advises: "Go easy on the fly-in, swivel, wipe, zoom, laser text, and similar PowerPoint special effects. They get old in a hurry." For example, one presenter used the audio "gunshot" effect as each word was flashed in sequence on the screen. One irritated listener said later, "I felt like I was on a firing range."[5]

Objects and Models

Three-dimensional objects make good visual aids, provided they are large enough for everyone in the audience to see. You could display such things as a blood-pressure gauge, a hibachi, handmade pottery, mountain-climbing equipment, and musical instruments.

A model is a representation of an object. One speaker used a model of the great pyramids to discuss how the ancient Egyptians probably built them. Another speaker used a homemade "lung," the interior of which consisted of clean cotton. When cigarette smoke was sucked through a tube, the lung turned from white to a sickening yellow-brown. One advantage of a model is that you can move it around. If you had a model airplane, for example, you could show principles of aerodynamics more easily than if you had only a drawing of a plane.

Yourself and Volunteers

Using yourself as a visual aid, you can demonstrate yoga positions, judo holds, karate chops, stretching exercises, relaxation techniques, ballet steps, and tennis strokes. You can don native attire, historical costumes, or scuba-diving equipment. One student came to class dressed and made up as a clown to give a speech on her part-time job as a clown for children's birthday parties.

Volunteers can enhance some speeches. You could use a friend, for example, to illustrate self-defense methods against an attacker. (For a classroom speech, be sure to get permission from your instructor before using a volunteer.)

Make sure you line up volunteers far in advance of speech day and, if necessary, practice with them to make sure they perform smoothly. Have substitutes lined up in case the scheduled volunteers fail to appear. Give instructions in advance so that volunteers know when to stand, when to sit, and so on. You don't want your volunteers to become a distraction by standing around when they are not needed.

PowerPoint Slides

Microsoft PowerPoint is a presentation program that permits you to create and show slides containing artwork, text information, animation, and audiovisuals.

Use a PowerPoint slide when you need to illustrate, explain, or enhance a key point in your speech. Make each slide attractive and simple. Choose graphics whenever possible, and use only small amounts of text.

The Basic Steps

To get maximum benefit from PowerPoint, take these steps:

1. **Create your outline before you even think about using Power-Point.**   Your slides should *not* be your speech. In other words, don't collect a bunch of photos and then give a speech that just adds narration to the photos. PowerPoint slides should be aids–helpers–for the key ideas that you have already created in your outline.
2. **Look at your outline and ask, "Do I need visuals to highlight or explain any of my key points?"**   Some points will not need visuals, but others may require them so that the audience will understand and remember what you are trying to say.
3. **For points that need visual support, decide which type of visual would be most effective.**   Options include photos, drawings, graphs, charts, lists of key ideas, or other visuals discussed in this chapter.
4. **Create your slides.**   Make them appealing and simple. (See the appendix at the end of this chapter for guidelines.)
5. **Practice in the room where you will be presenting.**   Rehearse with all of the equipment several times so that you don't fumble during the actual speech. If possible, have a friend give a critique. Check your slides from the back row. If any words or graphics are hard to see, revise them before speech day.
6. **Give your speech, making sure that you–not the slides–are the dominant presence in the room.**   Letting PowerPoint become the "star of the show," some speakers stand shyly in the shadows, stare at the screen, and narrate what appears on the slides. They are letting technology upstage a live, dynamic human being. You can avoid this mistake by boldly seizing your role as the primary communicator. Stand as close as possible to your listeners, and try to stay connected to them. Keep the room partially lit so that the audience can see your face. Focus all of your energy on reaching the listeners. Look at them–not the screen.

The Basic Steps in Action

Let's take another look at the steps we just discussed and use them in a scenario.

For more information on how to use PowerPoint effectively, see the appendix

Step 1: Create your outline before you even think about using PowerPoint.

The topic for your speech is "The Power of Friendliness in the Business World." You examine several new research studies, including one by the *Harvard Business Review,* which show that friendliness can translate into extra money and advancement in most careers.[6] You create your outline, with carefully selected main points and support material.

Step 2: Look at your outline and ask, "Do I need visuals to highlight or explain any of my key points?"

You see three ideas that can use some visual support to help the audience remember them. For our scenario, let's focus on just one. You plan to tell your listeners about research by Dr. Michael Lynn, a professor at Cornell University, who discovered that when servers in restaurants gave diners a big, friendly smile, their tips were–on average–140 percent larger than their tips when they gave a small, weak smile.[7] Since statistics are often hard to remember, you decide that it would be helpful for the audience to see this information on a slide.

Step 3: For points that need visual support, decide which type of visual would be most effective.

You decide to use text for the words "big smile" and the statistic "140 percent." (Additional words are unneeded because you will supply all the details orally.) Though not essential, a photo would brighten the slide and make it more interesting, so you search on the Internet and find a photo of a smiling server.

Step 4: Create your slides.

In the PowerPoint program, you create a simple, readable slide with the photo and the key words. The result is Figure 6.9.

Figure 6.9
According to a Cornell University researcher, servers in restaurants who give diners a big, friendly smile receive a tip that is 140 percent larger—on average—than if they give a small, weak smile.

Step 5: Practice in the room where you will be presenting	A week before your speech, you go to the classroom and run through several rehearsals, using all the equipment until you are proficient with it. A friend sits in the back row and gives you a critique. She suggests that one slide needs larger print for visibility. Later, you revise the slide.
Step 6: Give your speech, making sure that you—not the slides—are the dominant presence in the room..	You stay at center stage throughout your speech, focusing your attention and energy on the audience. Because you have only a few slides, the screen at the front of the room stays blank most of the time. When you display a slide, you continue to look at the audience. After discussing it, you blank the screen (press "B" on a keyboard or "A/V Mute" on a remote control) until you are ready to discuss the next slide.

"How to Avoid 'Death by PowerPoint'" at the end of this chapter and PowerPoint tutorials at connectpublicspeaking.com.

Multimedia from the Internet

On the Internet, you can find photos, drawings, maps, charts, videos, and audio clips on a vast variety of subjects.

Is it legal to download these items without getting permission? For classroom speeches, yes. Copyright restrictions do not apply, because you are engaged in noncommercial, educational, one-time use of materials. For many business and professional presentations, however, you need to seek permission.

More and more student speakers are using clips from commercial videos and online sources such as YouTube (see Figure 6.10). A video clip should be brief, and it should contain no material that might offend any audience member. Avoid choosing a clip that has only a weak connection to your topic. (One student played an amusing YouTube clip on canine misadventures, but it was irrelevant to his topic—spaying and neutering pets.)

To find multimedia materials on the Internet, use search engines such as Google Image Search (images.google.com), Yahoo (images.search.yahoo.com), and Google Video (video.google.com).

To download a video, consult the host Web site for instructions. For example, YouTube (youtube.com) has a clip demonstrating how to download. To download an image, follow these steps:

1. On most computers, position the mouse pointer over the image, click the right-hand mouse button, and choose "Save Image As" from the menu.
2. As you save the image, designate a location for storage, such as your computer's hard drive, a CD, or a USB flash drive.

There is one possible complication: Most of the free, downloadable images on Web sites have **low resolution,** which means they are sharp and clear only at small sizes. This may not be a problem if you are using the images for PowerPoint or for a small illustration in a handout. But you can't use "low-res" for anything that requires enlargement, such as posters or visual presenters, because they would be

connectpublic speaking.com
See Video Clip 6.1, Internet Graphics: "Is Your Boss Spying on You?"

Your Thoughts ?

What are the advantages and the disadvantages of using a video clip from YouTube (the popular video sharing Web site)?

low resolution
lacking fine detail

Figure 6.10
A video clip on the injuries (including paralysis) caused by backyard trampolines can be effective in a classroom speech if it is brief and drives home the speaker's points.

high resolution
possessing great detail

thumbnail
reduced image

fuzzy and indistinct. Instead you would need **high-resolution** images, which are sharp and clear at both small and large sizes. (If you are not sure whether an image has high or low resolution, import it into a word-processing program, enlarge it to 8 × 10 inches, and print it. If it comes out muddy and distorted, it's low resolution; if it's crisp and clear, it's high resolution.)

Some images on Web sites are **thumbnails**—tiny images with very low resolution. Often you can click on a thumbnail to display a bigger version, which is a better choice for reproduction. Although the bigger version may not have high resolution, at least it will have more resolution than the thumbnail.

Media for Visual Aids

The types of visual aids we have just discussed—charts, graphs, and so on—can be conveyed to the audience through a variety of media.

Multimedia Projectors and TVs

Now the most popular technology for presentations, multimedia projectors can project a large array of audiovisuals—text slides, photos, drawings, animation, video clips, and DVD movies—onto a screen. They are usually linked to desktop or laptop computers, but some units need only a memory card.

Depending on the brightness of the screen and the strength of the machine's projection, you may need to dim the lights in a room, especially if you want to convey the full richness of a photo or a video.

An alternative to a projector is a large-screen TV linked to a computer. Some presenters use two or more TVs placed at different vantage points in a large room. Some TV screens are very bright, making it unnecessary to dim lights in a room.

Boards

Two types of presentation boards are whiteboards (well known for multicolored, "dry erase" pens) and chalkboards (less and less used because of chalk dust, which causes breathing problems for some people). Either type of board makes a good tool for visual aids if you have complex drawings that require constant insertions and erasures–for example, if you are diagramming plays for a soccer team.

Boards have some disadvantages. If you put your visual–a graph, say–on a board during your speech, you have to turn your back on the audience; while you're drawing, their attention drifts away from you, and you may find it hard to regain it. Would it be a good idea to put your graph on the board before the speech begins? No, because the audience would be distracted by it; they would scrutinize it before you are ready to talk about it. (It would do no good to say, "Don't pay any attention to this until I get to it." Such a request would make the graph all the more interesting–and therefore distracting.) There is one possible solution: cover the part of the board on which you have written. But this can be awkward. You would have to find something large enough to do the job without being distracting. Another problem is that speakers preceding you might also be planning to use the board, and they might have to erase your visual aid.

Because of the limitations of boards, some instructors forbid their use in a classroom speech, so be sure to find out your instructor's policy.

Posters

You can put many kinds of visual aids–such as graphs, drawings, and charts–on posters. They do the same work as boards, but they are usually neater and more visually appealing.

In the age of PowerPoint, posters are not outdated–they are widely used. In courtrooms, for example, many attorneys prefer posters to PowerPoint because posters can be placed on easels and kept on display for long periods, enabling jury members to glance at them whenever they need to refresh their memories. In some cases, jurors are allowed to take the posters into the deliberation room. (Normally you shouldn't keep posters on display after you've discussed them, but this situation is an exception to the rule.)

connectpublic
speaking.com
See Video Clip 6.2,
Using a Poster: "Too
Much of a Good
Thing."

Make sure there is a reliable place to put your posters. If you prop them against a chalkboard or tape them on a wall, they may fall to the floor during the middle of the speech. Using thumbtacks might work if a corkboard or some other suitable place for tacking is available. One technique is to pile your posters on a desk and hold them up one at a time, being sure to hold them steady. Another method is to put your poster on an easel (which your school's audiovisual department may be able to provide). Even with an easel, however, some posters tend to curl and resist standing up straight. To prevent this, tape a second poster or a piece of cardboard to the back of your poster. (*Tip:* An even better solution to the problem of curling is to buy poster stocks that are sturdier than the standard stock sold at drugstores. Office-supply and craft stores have *foamboards*. Though more expensive than standard poster stock, these materials will not sag or curl.)

Flip Charts

A **flip chart** is a giant writing pad whose pages are glued or wired together at the top. It can be mounted on an easel. When you are through with each page, you can tear it off or flip it over the back of the easel.

flip chart
a large book consisting
of blank sheets (hinged
at the top) that can be
flipped over to present
information sequentially

You can prepare the visuals on each page in advance, or you can "halfway" prepare them—that is, lightly pencil in your sheets at home; then during the speech, with a heavy marker, trace over the lines. With some flip charts, the paper may be so thin that ink will seep to the next page, so you may need to leave a blank page between each drawn-on sheet.

Be aware that some instructors disapprove of student speakers writing on a flip chart during a speech.

Handouts

handout
material distributed to an audience as part of a speaker's presentation

Despite the availability of high-tech tools, one of the most popular formats used in business and professional presentations is the paper **handout.** It is easy to explain the enduring popularity of handouts: they are easy to prepare, can be updated quickly at the last moment, and provide a permanent document that listeners can take with them when they leave a presentation.

Though handouts are popular, they are often misused. I have witnessed the following fiasco dozens of times: A presenter distributes stacks of handouts at the beginning of a talk. While he or she discusses each handout, the room is filled with the sound of rustling papers, as the listeners race ahead, reading material the presenter has not yet reached, ignoring or only half-listening to what he or she is saying. (Some speakers try to solve this problem by imploring the audience to stay with them and not read ahead, but this is futile; humans are naturally curious, and their eyes cannot resist reading.)

Giving listeners text-heavy handouts during a speech is a sure way to lose them.

Because listeners study the pages instead of paying attention to the speaker, handouts are banned in some public speaking classes. Even if your instructor permits them, they are usually unsuitable during a classroom speech because distributing them eats up time and creates a distraction.

The best use of handouts—especially lengthy, complex documents—is to give them *after* the question-and-answer period so that listeners can take them to office or home for further study and review. (For classroom speeches, check with your instructor; he or she may prefer that you wait until the end of the class period; if you give out material at the end of your speech, students might read it instead of listening to the next speaker.)

One exception to the preceding advice: for informal presentations in career and community settings, it is permissible to distribute a handout during a presentation if it is short and simple—a one-page document with an easy-to-understand graphic or a *small* amount of text. In such situations, follow these guidelines: (1) Never distribute a handout until you are ready to talk about it—a premature handout grows stale. (2) Avoid talking about a handout while you are distributing copies. Wait until every listener has a copy before you start your explanation.

Visual Presenters

visual presenter
a device capable of producing images of both two- and three-dimensional objects

A **visual presenter,** also known as a document camera or ELMO (the name of a leading manufacturer), is a camera mounted on a stand and pointed at a platform below (see Figure 6.11). What the camera sees is shown on a TV or video monitor, or projected onto a screen by means of a digital projector. Visual presenters can show two-dimensional items such as photos and diagrams, and they also can show three-dimensional objects such as jewelry. A zoom feature permits very small items, such as a coin, to be enlarged for easy viewing.

Figure 6.11
A visual presenter can convert a photo to a digital image that can be displayed in a large size on a screen or a TV.

Visual presenters are popular because they are easy to use, and a speaker can make last-minute changes. Unfortunately, they are often used in a clumsy fashion that makes the speaker look like a fumbler who has lost eye contact with the audience. Here is what can happen:

> Some speakers bring a book or magazine that contains an illustration, but when they try to use the visual presenter, they have trouble holding the material in place, they spend a lot of time positioning the illustration correctly, and they waste time zooming in and out. When they finally get the illustration in position, two more problems may emerge: (1) the illustration may be bordered by extraneous material that is distracting and (2) if it is printed on glossy paper, it may be obscured by glare.

To use a visual presenter skillfully, follow these guidelines:

1. Discard an illustration if it's not crisp and clear. If you have a dark, blurry snapshot, using a visual presenter will not improve its appearance. It will show up on the screen as a dark, blurry picture, and the audience will be displeased. Find a replacement or do without.

2. If possible, use an assistant to handle the presentation of material. This frees you to look at your audience and not waste time in positioning items.

3. Several days beforehand, rehearse the speech in the actual room where the speech will be given. If you are using an assistant, have him or her practice using the equipment and displaying the visuals at the appropriate times.

4. When using books and magazines, frame your illustrations by using stick-on slips to mask all extraneous material.

5. Minimize glare by making sure that a page lies flat. If necessary, you or your assistant can press down on the area surrounding the illustration to ensure flatness.

6. Immediately before your speech, adjust the camera's zoom feature so that you have the correct setting. Remember that a preceding speaker might have used a setting that is wrong for your needs.

Overhead Transparencies

transparency
clear sheets on which visuals are drawn or printed, and then viewed by light shining from an overhead projector

Overhead projectors are illuminated boxes that project images from **transparencies** (clear sheets of acetate) onto a screen. Transparencies are inexpensive and simple to produce.

To create a transparency, you can write directly on the acetate sheet with color pens (you must use a pen especially designed for overheads) or you can make a master copy on plain white paper and use an office copier or your own printer to make the transparency. Whether you use a copier or a printer, be aware that you need a special kind of acetate that won't melt inside the machine. Your college's audiovisual department may be able to help you produce transparencies for a small fee, or a quick-print shop in your community can make transparencies from your master copy.

Preparing Visual Aids

Here are some guidelines for planning and creating your visual aids.

Choose Visuals That Truly Support Your Speech

Before using a visual, ask yourself: Will it help clarify or illustrate an important idea in my speech? If the honest answer is no, discard it. Your job is not to dazzle people with pretty colors on a screen or to impress them with your creative artwork. A beautiful drawing of an airplane in flight, for example, would not contribute much to a speech on touring the castles of Europe.

Your Thoughts ?

Regarding visual aids, trial attorney Joe Jamail says, "If you use too many pictures and make it like a circus or going to a matinee, jurors will think you think they're stupid." What advice would you give attorneys for using visual aids in the courtroom?

Prepare and Practice Far in Advance

Practice using your visuals as you rehearse your speech. If you will be using unfamiliar equipment, rehearsals will help prevent fumbling or faltering during your speech.

Don't create a visual—such as a diagram on a whiteboard—while you are actually giving your speech: few people can write or draw effectively while speaking to an audience. Make them far in advance so that they are not sloppy and unpolished.

Choose the Appropriate Number of Visuals

A common mistake is to display a large number of boring slides. For this reason, some speech coaches recommend that you use only three or four slides in a speech. Some supervisors forbid employees from using more than three. Although such rules might improve some speeches, they are too rigid to apply to all. The best rule is this: use a visual whenever it can make a key point more interesting, understandable, and memorable. Some speeches (such as a eulogy) may need no visuals at all. Some may need only one, while others may need more than a dozen.

Before speech day, practice in front of classmates or colleagues and ask their advice on which visuals, if any, should be eliminated.

While deciding how many visuals to use, here is an important consideration: When listeners complain about too many visuals, they are usually referring to slides or posters that are densely packed with text. They rarely complain about the number of visuals if all of them are exciting, easy-to-grasp photos and illustrations.

Figure 6.12
This sign grabs the attention of passing motorists and gives key information quickly. It is a good model for a visual aid in a speech—simple, informative, and inviting.

Make Visual Aids Simple and Clear

Make each visual aid so simple that your listeners can quickly grasp its meaning—either at a glance or after minimal explanation by you. Avoid complexity. Too much information can confuse or overwhelm the listeners.

A good model for a public speaker is an outdoor sign. As you walk or drive past it, the sign must snare your attention and convey a brief message—in just a few seconds. See Figure 6.12 for an example. A speech is a bit different because you have more than just a few seconds, but the key principles used by sign designers are worth applying to visuals in a speech:

1. Use graphics instead of words whenever possible.
2. If you must use words, use only a few.

Sometimes you might see a wonderful graphic in a book. Will it translate into a wonderful graphic in a speech? Not necessarily. Some visual aids in books are jampacked with fascinating details; they are suitable in a book because the reader has ample time to analyze them, but they're too complex for a speech.

In visuals such as graphs, make all labels horizontal. (In a textbook, many labels are vertical because readers of a book can turn the visual sideways, but listeners should not be forced to twist their necks to read vertical lettering.) You need not label every part of your visual, since you are there to explain the aid.

If you are displaying a multidimensional object, be sure to turn it during your talk so that everyone can see all sides of it.

Tips for Your Career

Aim for Back-Row Comprehension

I once saw a government official display a poster to an audience of over 300 people, but only the people in the first few rows were close enough to be able to read the words and decipher the charts on the poster.

Ridiculous? Yes, but this mistake is made in countless meeting rooms throughout the world every day. Many business and professional people say that the most frequent audiovisual mistake made by presenters is using graphics that are difficult or impossible for everyone in the audience to see.

The best way to achieve comprehension by everyone is to design every visual aid for the back row. *If all lettering and details cannot be seen easily and comfortably by a person in the rear of the room, don't use the visual.*

To help you meet the needs of the people in the back row, here are some guidelines.

Make letters, numbers, and graphics much larger than you think necessary.   Be on the safe side. I've never heard anyone complain about visuals being too large.

Use thick, bold strokes.   Whether you are creating by hand or using a computer, you need big, bold, thick strokes for lettering and graphics. Thin strokes tend to be weak and hard to see:

Thin strokes   **Thick strokes**

Make enlargements.   You can magnify a too-small visual by using video, visual presenters, PowerPoint slides, or posters. Here are some of the easiest options:

- A camcorder with a zoom lens can be used to make a close-up videotape of a snapshot, a drawing, or a small object such as jewelry. A blank videotape is inexpensive and can be erased and used later for other purposes.
- To turn a photo or drawing into a PowerPoint slide, you can have the item scanned and converted into a digital file. Try the media center on your campus or visit a digital-imaging store in your community.
- If you have access to a visual presenter such as ELMO, you can easily enlarge both two- and three-dimensional items. For example, a speaker can demonstrate the chemical changes taking place in a small test tube, while the enlargement on a TV or a wall screen ensures that everyone in the audience can see the results clearly.

Test the visibility of your visuals.   Before the day of your speech, go to the room where you will be speaking, display your visual aid in the front of the room, and sit in the back row to determine whether you can see it clearly. (Even better, have a friend sit in the back row to pass judgment.) If your visual cannot be seen with crystal clearness from the back row, discard it and create another (or simply don't use one).

Presenting Visual Aids

Here are some tips for using visual aids effectively in your speeches.

Choose the Best Time to Show Visuals

Many speakers undermine their speech's effectiveness by showing visual aids at inappropriate times. Here are several guidelines.

Don't display a visual before your speech begins.   If visual aids are in plain sight before you start, you deprive your speech of an element of drama and freshness. There are exceptions, of course, as when you must set up items for a demonstration on a table in front of the room.

Display a visual whenever the audience needs help in understanding a point.   One speaker gave a talk on rock formations in caves but waited until the end to show photos illustrating his points. During the body of the speech, listeners were mystified and frustrated: What do these rock formations look like? Though he ultimately showed pictures, his listeners would have experienced a much greater understanding of the subject matter if he had displayed the images as he went along.

If listener comprehension is unharmed, it is acceptable to delay.   In some cases, you may want to withhold a visual or a demonstration to build suspense. In a speech on how to use Tae Kwon Do karate techniques to break objects, Lee Wentz stood in front of a cement block as he spoke, waiting until the end to demonstrate the actual breaking of the block with one hand. This built suspense—the audience wondered whether he would succeed. (He did, and the listeners applauded.)

Never Circulate Visual Aids among the Audience

Some people try to solve the problem of a too-small visual aid (such as a piece of jewelry) by passing it around the room, but this is a mistake. People will look at the visual instead of listening to the speaker. And there's likely to be distraction, perhaps even whispered comments, as it is being passed from one person to another. Some speakers walk from listener to listener to give each person a close-up view of the visual aid. This is also a poor technique; the listeners who are not seeing the visual may get bored or distracted, and they may start whispering comments to their friends. Moreover, the listeners who are looking at the aid may ask questions that mean nothing to the rest of the audience. In a case like this, the speaker can easily lose the audience's attention and interest.

One way to solve the problem of a too-small object is to leave it in the front of the room and invite the audience to see it *after* the speech. This strategy is acceptable unless listeners need to see the aid during your speech to understand what you are talking about. In this case, the best solution is to create an enlarged image of the object, which you display during the speech, and then permit listeners to take a look at the real object after the speech.

Tips for Your Career

When they need to show steps in a process, some speakers invite the audience to come to the front of the room and gather around a table. One speaker did this so that everyone could see him making garnishes out of vegetables (a tomato was transformed into a "rose"). If you are considering this approach, here are three guidelines: (1) Use the technique only with small audiences. (2) Make sure no disabled listeners are excluded from participating. (3) Get your instructor's permission before trying this in a classroom speech.

Remove Physical Barriers

Right before a speech, move any objects or furniture that might block the view of some listeners. If you're using equipment such as a projector, make sure it doesn't obstruct anyone's vision. If, despite your best efforts, some listeners will be blocked from seeing your visuals, ask them (before you start your introduction) to shift their chairs or move to a different part of the room.

Make Sure Listeners Get Maximum Benefit from Visuals

Don't rush through your visuals. A common mistake is for speakers to display a visual for a moment and then remove it from view. To these speakers, the visual is simple and obvious (they have seen it so many times, they are tired of it), but they should realize that it is brand-new to the listeners, who need time to study and absorb the contents.

Discuss each visual aid. But, you might say, can't listeners see and figure out for themselves? In some cases, yes, but by discussing each visual as you display it, you guarantee that listeners stay in step with you.

For a complex visual, don't wave your hand in the general direction of the aid and assume that the audience will know which feature you are pointing out. Be precise. Point to the specific part that you are discussing. For pointing, use a finger, a pen, or an extendable pointer. To avoid twisting your body, use the hand nearer the aid.

Don't Let Visuals Distract from Your Message

Visuals should never distract your audience from what you are saying. Here are some tips.

Show one visual at a time.   If you display five posters, neatly lined up on a chalk tray, your listeners will scrutinize the fourth poster while you are talking about the first. To keep the eyes and minds of your listeners focused on your remarks, show a visual, discuss it fully, put it away, and then display your next visual. There is one exception to this rule: if you have a visual aid that can provide a simple, undistracting backdrop or evoke a mood, you may leave it on display during the entire speech. One speaker kept a bouquet of flowers on the front table through-out her speech on gardening; the flowers provided a pleasing complement to her remarks.

Blank the screen.   If you have an interval between PowerPoint slides, blank the screen by pressing "B" on a keyboard or "A/V Mute" on a remote control.

Beware of using animals or children as visuals.   Exotic pets and cute kids can easily draw the attention of your listeners away from your ideas, so use them care-fully, if at all. One speaker brought in a ferret to demonstrate what great pets they make. The only trouble was that the ferret acted up during the speech, causing the audience to laugh at its antics rather than listen to the speech. Some instructors dis-approve of using animals in speeches, so be sure to get permission before bringing an animal into the classroom.

Don't Talk to Your Visual Aid

Many speakers are so intent on explaining a visual aid that they spend most of their time talking to it instead of to the audience. You should stand next to your aid and face the audience during most of your discussion. Look at the aid only in two situations: (1) When you introduce it, look at it for several seconds–this is long enough to draw the listeners' attention toward it. (2) Whenever you want to direct the audience's attention to a particular segment, look at the aid for one or two sec-onds as you point out the special feature.

Use Progressive Revelation

Whenever possible, use **progressive revelation**–that is, reveal only one part or item at a time. If, for example, you are discussing three sections of a sculpture, you can keep the entire piece covered at the beginning, and then unveil one section at a time. Progressive revelation creates suspense, making the listeners curious about what comes next, and it prevents them from reading or studying ahead of you. A variation of this technique, called the "build," is used in PowerPoint to reveal parts of a slide–for example, a pie chart can be shown one piece at a time. Likewise, bullet points can be displayed one point at a time.

progressive revelation
piece-by-piece unveiling of a visual

Plan for Emergencies

With visual aids, there is always a chance of a foul-up, so you should plan carefully how you will handle any problems that might arise. Before you use any electronic media, talk with your instructor or the program chairperson to make arrangements (for darkening the room, getting an extension cord, and so on). Always check out the location of your speech in advance. Is there an electrical outlet nearby? If not, can you get an extension cord? Can the room be darkened for PowerPoint slides? Is there a place to put your posters? Is there a whiteboard or a chalkboard?

Be prepared for the unexpected, such as sudden malfunctioning of a computer or a multimedia projector. Some disasters can be mitigated by advance planning. For example, carry a backup CD of your PowerPoint presentation and have paper copies of your PowerPoint slides for quick distribution. If equipment breaks down and cannot be fixed quickly, continue with your speech as best you can. Try to keep your poise and sense of humor.

Appealing to Other Channels

While the visual channel of communication is powerful, don't overlook other channels—hearing, taste, smell, touch, and physical activity—which can be effective avenues for reaching your audience.

Hearing

In almost all presentations, the sense of hearing is paramount, since you use your voice to convey words and meaning. (See Chapter 10 for tips on language and voice.) In addition, you can supply audio aids. For example, to accompany a visual presentation on dolphins, marine biologist Jennifer Novak played an audio clip of the clicks, whistles, and other sounds that dolphins use to communicate with one another.

The Internet has a rich variety of audio sources. For example, National Public Radio (npr.org) provides audio clips and podcasts that you can download to a desktop computer or MP3 device and then play during a presentation. (Some speakers insert their clips into PowerPoint presentations.) Here is a sampling of NPR downloads:

- Music and comments by the Latin jazz drummer Poncho Sanchez
- Interviews with ex-smokers who share their secrets for quitting the habit
- The lilting sounds of Irish accents in Dublin

Taste and Smell

Known as the chemical senses, taste and smell are closely related channels. Floral designer Charlene Worley gave a speech on how flowers provide not only messages of love and consolation but also medicine and food. At the end of her talk, she invited the audience to sniff a bouquet she had created. She also appealed to the sense of taste by serving crackers on which she had spread jam made from violets.

In culinary demonstrations, smelling a savory dish as it is prepared can stimulate appetite and interest, and tasting it can help the audience decide whether it is worthwhile.

Many business and professional presentations are held in rooms with a side table that provides beverages and snacks. This courtesy is more than simply satisfying people's hunger and thirst. Experienced presenters have discovered that

A culinary class involves seeing, hearing, smelling, tasting, touching, and physical activity.

the aroma of fresh coffee and the savor of tasty food can put an audience in a receptive mood and make it easier to inform or persuade. (Many real estate agents know that the smell of coffee evokes childhood memories of a pleasant home where breakfast is being prepared, so they arrange to have a pot of coffee brewing as they enter a house with a client to help make the house seem like a home.)

Touch and Physical Activity

Wishing to disprove the notion that snakes have slimy skin, herpetologist Jeanne Goldberg invited listeners to come forward and stroke the nonpoisonous king snake she was holding. Many listeners were surprised to find the skin dry and firm, with a texture like glass beads tightly strung together.

For learning new skills, the sense of touch is often coupled with physical activity. You need touch and muscular movement to apply first aid, draw a map, or perform a card trick. To persuade people to buy a product, some presenters give an audience hands-on experience. For example, one laptop computer sold well because sales representatives put laptops in front of listeners and invited them to try out the keyboard's pleasing responsiveness. In some situations, presenters provide physical activity by passing out pads and pens and inviting listeners to take notes during the presentation.

Using Multiple Channels

How many channels should you use? Some speeches (such as inspirational talks) do not require a variety of channels, but in many situations (such as teaching new material), the more you can use, the greater the likelihood that your listeners will understand and remember the information.[8]

In some cases, you can appeal to all the major channels in a single presentation. For example, in a culinary class, students can *see* the process as it is demonstrated, *hear* the explanations, *smell* the aromas, *taste* the delicacies, and use *touch* and *physical activity* as they practice making a dish.

Resources for Review and Skill Building

Summary

Presentation aids—which can involve vision, hearing, smell, taste, touch, and physical activity—enrich and enliven a speech. The most popular type, visual aids, can make your ideas clear and understandable; make your speech more interesting and memorable; help an audience remember facts and details; make long, complicated explanations unnecessary; help prove a point; add to your credibility; and enhance communication with people who speak English as a second language.

The major types of visual aids include graphs, charts, drawings, photos, videos, animations, objects, models, yourself, volunteers, PowerPoint slides, and multimedia from the Internet.

They can be conveyed to the audience through various media: multimedia projectors, TVs, boards, posters, flip charts, handouts, visual presenters, and overhead transparencies.

Guidelines for preparing visual aids: (1) Choose visual aids that truly support your speech. (2) Prepare and practice far in advance. (3) Choose the appropriate number of visuals. (4) Make your aids as simple and clear as possible. (5) Aim for comprehension by everyone, including the people in the back row.

Tips for presenting visual aids: (1) Decide on the best time to show visuals. (2) Never circulate a visual aid among the audience. (3) Remove physical barriers so that everyone has an unimpeded view. (4) Make sure listeners get the maximum benefit from each visual. (5) Make sure

the aids don't distract from your message. (6) Don't talk to your aids. (7) Use progressive revelation. (8) Plan how you would handle equipment failure and other emergencies.

Although visuals are the most popular form of presentation aids, the other channels of communication—hearing, taste, smell, touch, and physical activity—can be quite effective. Whenever possible, use several channels to maximize listener understanding and retention.

Key Terms

bar graph, *168*

flip chart, *177*

handout, *178*

high resolution, *176*

information chart, *168*

line graph, *168*

low resolution, *175*

pictorial graph, *168*

pie graph, *168*

progressive revelation, *185*

table, *168*

thumbnail, *176*

transparency, *180*

visual presenter, *178*

Review Questions

1. List at least six types of visual aids.
2. List at least five media for presenting visual aids.
3. What is progressive revelation?
4. A *list of key ideas* is another name for which kind of chart?
5. Is it legal to use graphics from the Internet in a student speech in the classroom? Explain your answer.
6. The text recommends that you "aim for back-row comprehension." What does this mean and why is the advice necessary?

7. How can speakers test the visibility of their visuals?
8. Is it always a mistake for a speaker to wait until the conclusion of a presentation to show a visual or perform a demonstration? Explain your answer.
9. Why would it be a mistake to circulate a small photograph during your speech?
10. Explain three options that a speaker can take to magnify a too-small visual.

Building Critical-Thinking Skills

1. "Some pictures may be worth a thousand words, but a picture of a thousand words isn't worth much," says corporate executive Don Keough. Explain what this means in terms of oral presentations.
2. At one Web site devoted to communication, public speakers are advised to distribute thought-provoking handouts at the beginning of a speech so that "if members of the audience get bored during the speech, they will have something interesting to read." Do you agree with this advice? Defend your position.

Building Teamwork Skills

1. Working in a group, create a scenario in which a sales representative gives a presentation that appeals to all five senses.
2. In a group, create an outdoor sign that violates the rules of this chapter. Then create a new sign that corrects all the mistakes.

Appendix

How to Avoid "Death by PowerPoint"

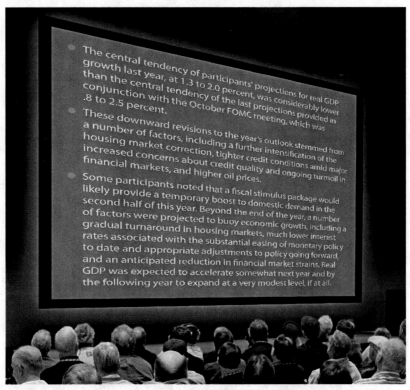

Imagine sitting in this audience as the speaker reads every word to you. Now imagine one hour of seeing 25 more slides just like this, all of them read to you. By the end of the presentation, you will be weary and bored.

This torment is known in the business and professional world as "Death by PowerPoint."[1] According to *Industry Week,* "PowerPoint presentations have drugged more people than all the sleeping pills in history."[2]

Every day, in every part of the world, thousands of speakers display slides like the one above. The problem is not the PowerPoint software—it's the speakers. Why do they inflict so much misery? One reason is that they are self-centered instead of audience-centered.

If you focus primarily on yourself and your own convenience, PowerPoint seems like an easy way to create a speech. All you have to do is dump your information onto slides and read the material aloud. You don't even have to look at your audience.

If you are audience-centered, on the other hand, you will ask yourself, "How can I help my listeners understand and remember my key points?" If you decide that PowerPoint can help you to reach your goal, you will make sure that your slides are interesting and easy-to-grasp. During the presentation, instead of hiding behind the technology, you will occupy center stage. You will look directly at your listeners and stay connected to them.

On the following pages are six rules to help you avoid inflicting death by PowerPoint. For additional tips, visit connectpublicspeaking.com.

Problem

Don't make the mistake of thinking that every presentation should have PowerPoint. Imagine that you have compelling stories to tell about the plight of the people of Darfur. For such an anguished topic, a slide like this would undermine the emotional intensity of the speech.

Darfur Tragedy

- **Eviction**

- **Hunger**

- **Genocide**

Solution

When student speaker Dawit Kebede of Ethiopia addressed an audience of students and professors at Goshen College in Indiana, he used no PowerPoint. He spoke on the horrors of genocide in Darfur, painting pictures with words—vivid images more powerful than PowerPoint slides like the one above.

Rule 2: Choose images over text (when possible)

Sometimes firefighters deliberately start fires

They choose old homes that had been destined for demolition

- Test equipment
- Practice skills

Problem

Text slides are sometimes needed to help listeners remember key details, but in this case, text is unnecessary because the information can be easily understood in spoken form. Listeners would prefer to hear your comments than read a text slide.

Solution

Display a photo while sharing your information. The slide makes your spoken words more engaging and memorable.

Using images also demonstrates to listeners that you care enough about them to do the extra work of locating interesting visuals.

Rule 3: Use text sparingly

Problem

You make a huge blunder if you display large blocks of text, which are boring and fatiguing.

You make a second blunder if you read the text aloud—a common practice that one executive calls "a form of torture that should be banned by international law."

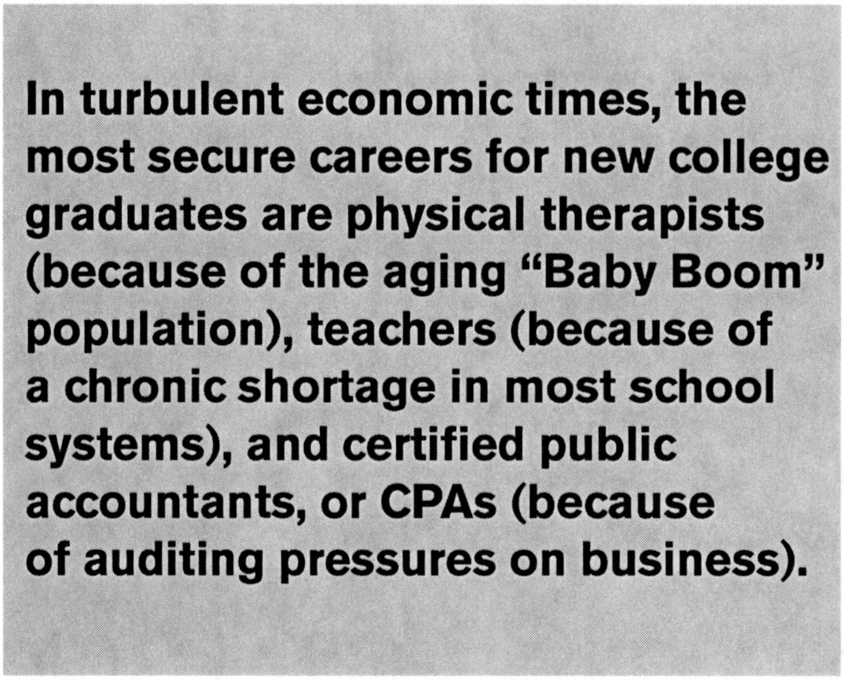

In turbulent economic times, the most secure careers for new college graduates are physical therapists (because of the aging "Baby Boom" population), teachers (because of a chronic shortage in most school systems), and certified public accountants, or CPAs (because of auditing pressures on business).

Solution

In this slide, text is okay because you want to help listeners remember the three professions. Only a small amount of text is needed because you will elaborate with spoken words.

What about all the empty space on this slide? Is that bad? No, the space makes the key words stand out— and it makes the slide more inviting to the eye.

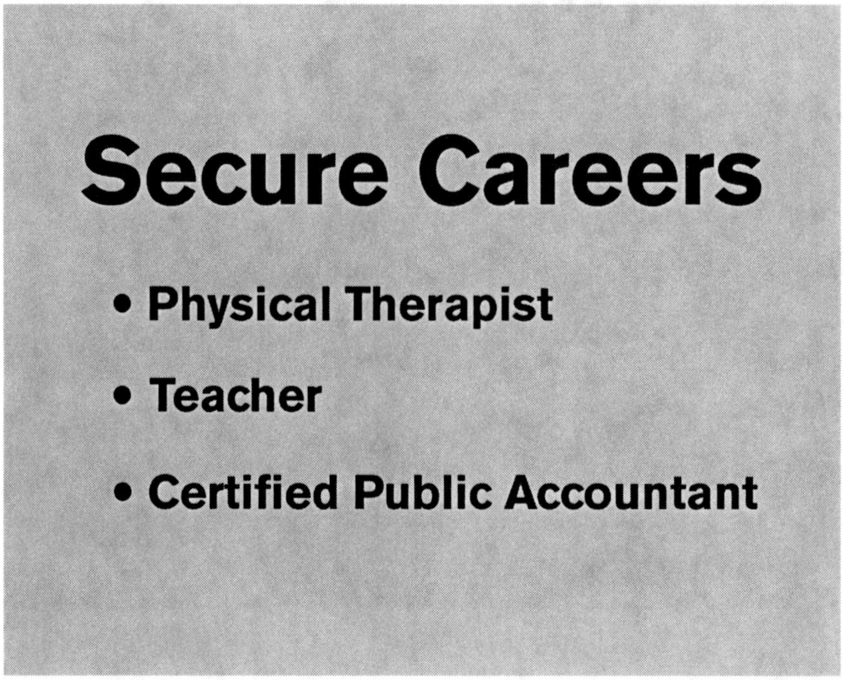

Secure Careers

- **Physical Therapist**

- **Teacher**

- **Certified Public Accountant**

Rule 4: Format text for easy reading

Bad Typography

- OVERUSE *of* FANCY fonts *and different* **CO ORS**

- **Emphasizing with *italics* and <u>underlining</u>**

- **TOO MANY WORDS THAT USE ALL CAPITAL LETTERS**

Problem
This slide hinders easy reading because (1) it uses too many different typefaces and colors, (2) it emphasizes with italics and underlining, and (3) it has too many words in all capital letters.

Good Typography

- **Simple, readable font**

- **Color and bold for emphasis**

- **All capitals only for headings**

Solution
Choose a typeface that is simple and easy to read, and avoid a lot of different colors. To emphasize a word or phrase, use a contrasting color or bold print, but avoid italics and underlining (which may be fine for printed material but impede readability on-screen). Use all capital words only for headings—excessive use is tiring to the eyes and hard to read.

Rule 5: Use care in placing text on images

Problem

Text on top of an image can be acceptable if it is superimposed with care. This slide, however, makes four mistakes: (1) There is too much text. (2) The text obstructs the image. (3) The typeface is not bold enough. (4) The color of the text blends with the underlying image.

Solution

This version uses a small amount of text, which is positioned to avoid obstructing the main view. The words are easy to read because a bold typeface has been chosen and printed in contrasting white.

Aim for contrast. When an image is dark, choose text that is white or another light color. When an image is light, choose text that is black or a dark color.

Rule 6: Avoid visual clutter

Problem

This slide has too many small images and too many messages. Your listeners might fail to follow what you are saying because their eyes are roving over the slide.

Some speakers try to solve the problem by using a "build"– displaying the first element, then adding the second, and so on. Though this is an improvement, you still end up with visual clutter.

Solution

Create six slides, one for each idea. On each slide, the image is large and there is no clutter.

Does this approach add to the length of the presentation? No. Showing six simple slides should take no more time than showing one cluttered slide.

When paleontologist Paul Sereno gives speeches on a newly discovered dinosaur named Nigersaurus taqueti, he begins by discussing the head and then moves back toward the tail. By arranging his description from head to tail, he is using the *spatial* (physical space) pattern, one of the organizational schemes discussed in this chapter.

The Body of the Speech

OBJECTIVES

After studying this chapter, you should be able to:

1. Explain the importance of skillfully organizing the body of the speech.

2. Create the body of a speech by using a central idea to develop main points.

3. Identify and use five patterns of organization: chronological, spatial, cause–effect, problem–solution, and topical.

4. Identify and use four types of transitional devices: bridges, internal summaries, signposts, and spotlights.

5. Simplify the process of organizing speech material.

Preparing a TV report and preparing a speech are very much

alike, say veteran news reporters. In both cases, you must organize your material in a clear, logical manner so that the audience is not confused.

To arrange his material, Richard Engel, who spent over five years covering the Iraq War for NBC News, uses two methods: the *chronological* pattern (narrating a sequence of events from beginning to end) and the *problem–solution* pattern (explaining a problem and then examining possible solutions). These two patterns are among the organizational techniques we will discuss in this chapter.

Before proceeding, let's look at where we stand in the speech-preparation process. In previous chapters, we discussed finding and developing materials such as statistics, examples, and visual aids. Now our task is to organize. We must take all our materials—our bricks and mortar—and put them together to build a solid, coherent structure. This chapter will focus on organizing the body of a speech, Chapter 8 on creating introductions and conclusions, and Chapter 9 on putting all the parts together in an outline.

To avoid confusing viewers, TV reporters such as NBC News correspondent Richard Engel arrange their reports in logical patterns.

The Importance of Organization

A well-organized speech has vast advantages over a poorly organized one:

1. A well-organized speech is easier to understand. Wesley J. Smith, a former judge at a small-claims court in Los Angeles, says, "The most effective cases I heard involved people who presented their side of the issue as if they were telling a story. Their cases were organized logically, with a beginning, a middle, and an end. That not only kept my interest but helped me quickly understand the issues."[1]

2. A well-organized speech is easier for the audience to remember. In an experiment with a list of endangered species, one group of students memorized list A in Figure 7.1 and another group memorized list B. When tested two weeks later, the students who had learned list A recalled 56 percent of the terms, while the students who had learned list B recalled 81 percent.[2]

List B is easier to remember because items are grouped in meaningful clusters. In a good speech, you should apply the same principle: Group your ideas in meaningful clusters that are easy to comprehend and recall.

3. A well-organized speech is more likely to be believed. Studies show that if you present a poorly organized speech, your listeners will find you less believable at the end than they did at the beginning of the speech.[3] If your speech is well-organized, however, you will come across as someone who is in full command of the facts, and therefore believable.

Creating the Body

A speech works best if it is divided into three well-developed sections: introduction, body, and conclusion. Does this mean that you should begin by working on the introduction? Not necessarily. Many experienced speakers find it easier

List A	List B	
Indian python	**Mammals**	
Cheetah	Polar bear	Gorilla
Great white shark	Cheetah	Gray wolf
Gorilla		
Hawksbill turtle	**Birds**	
Hawaiian crow	California condor	Hawaiian crow
Gray wolf	Shore plover	Whooping crane
California condor		
Common sturgeon	**Reptiles**	
Polar bear	American crocodile	Indian python
Whooping crane	Hawksbill turtle	Painted terrapin
Giant catfish		
Shore plover	**Fish**	
Painted terrapin	Giant catfish	Cutthroat trout
Cutthroat trout	Great white shark	Common sturgeon
American crocodile		

Figure 7.1
A list of endangered species is shown in two formats. Because it is organized in logical clusters, list B is easier to memorize and retain than list A.

to prepare the body first and then prepare the introduction. If you stop to think about it, this makes sense: How can you introduce the body until you know its full nature?

Let's look at a good technique for creating the body.

To create the body of a speech, start with your *specific purpose,* which is the goal of your speech, and your *central idea,* which is the key concept that you want to get across to your audience. (If you are unsure about these terms, please review Chapter 5 before proceeding in this chapter.)

Suppose you hear a news report about a charity that has been ripping off donors, and you decide to devote your next speech to charity fraud. After reading articles and conducting interviews, you come up with the following purpose statement:

Specific Purpose: To persuade my audience to be cautious in donating to charity

Next, ask yourself, "What is my essential message? What big idea do I want to leave in the minds of my listeners?" The answer is your central idea. Here is one possibility:

Central Idea: Before donating to a charity, make sure it is honest.

This central idea is your speech boiled down to one sentence. It is what you want your listeners to remember if they forget everything else.

The next step is to ask yourself this question: "How can I get my audience to understand and accept my central idea?"

main points
key assertions made by a speaker to develop his or her central idea

The best way to get the central idea across to your audience is to implant in their minds a few **main points** that are based on the central idea. In our charities example, here are three main points that could be made:

I. Some charities give only a tiny sum to the needy.
II. These charities channel most of their money to salaries and gifts for staff members.
III. Potential donors should look for warnings posted on the Internet by watchdog groups that monitor charities.

The first and second main points focus on the problem (charity rip-offs), and the third main point provides a solution (investigation on the Internet).

By themselves the main points are not sufficient. Listeners would want more information, so you need to develop each main point with support materials such as narratives, examples, and statistics. For instance, if your listeners heard main point I, they would say, "Well, okay, can you give some examples?" Here are a couple of examples you could use:

- The *New York Times* reported that one man set up a charity to help wounded veterans, raising more than $168 million in two years. But he gave only 25 percent to help vets.[4]
- The *Knoxville News-Sentinel* revealed that a local charity called "A Child's Dream" raised $3 million to grant the wishes of sick and dying children, but only 3 percent of the funds were actually given to children.[5]

For the second main point, you could describe the lavish lifestyles of the owners of rip-off charities. For the third main point, you could discuss Web sites that post lists of fraudulent charities. At the end of your speech, you could give all

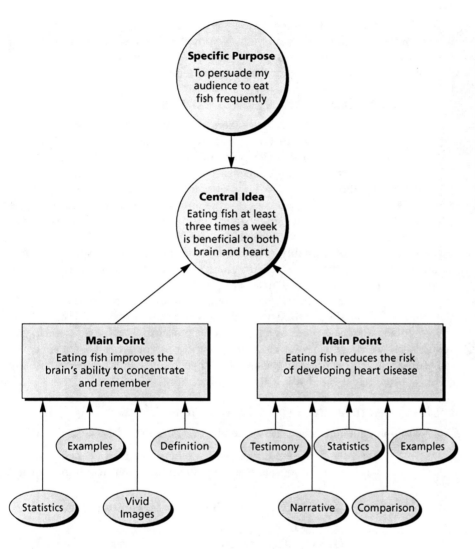

Figure 7.2
Speech preparation should start with a specific purpose and a central idea. Then the central idea is developed by two or three (or occasionally four) main points, which in turn are strengthened by a variety of support materials, such as examples and statistics.

listeners a handout containing the Web addresses so that they could pursue their own investigations later.

To see an overview of the process we have just discussed, take a look at Figure 7.2, which shows the key elements of a speech aimed at persuading listeners to eat fish frequently. The specific purpose leads to the central idea, which is sustained by two main points. The main points are not likely to be believed by the audience unless they are supported by solid information such as statistics and testimony from experts. For example, the speaker could cite clinical tests by reliable medical researchers that demonstrate the value of omega-3 acids (found in fish) for the brain and the heart.

Devising Main Points

"Do I need more than one main point?" some students ask. Yes. If you have only one main point to develop your central idea, you have a weak structure, like a bridge that has only one pillar to hold it up. If you provide only one main point,

connectpublic
speaking.com
For handy guidelines, see "Checklist for Preparing and Delivering a Speech."

your listeners have only *one* reason to believe your central idea. If you give them two or three main points, you multiply your chances of convincing them.

"How many main points should I have?" you may be asking. To answer this and other questions, let's examine some guidelines for refining main points.

Limit the Number of Main Points

A common mistake of public speakers is to cram too many points into a speech. They do this because they are approaching the speech from their own viewpoint and not from the viewpoint of the listeners. If you ask yourself, "How much information can I squeeze into the five minutes allotted?" you are approaching the speech from your own viewpoint. To approach from the audience's viewpoint, you should ask, "How much information can the audience comfortably pay attention to, understand, and remember?" Audiences simply cannot absorb too much new information. You should know this from your own experience; you can probably recall many speakers (including some teachers) who overwhelmed you with a barrage of ideas, facts, and figures. Don't be reluctant to cut and trim your material.

Exactly how many main points should you have? In a short speech (5 to 10 minutes), you should limit yourself to two or three (or occasionally four) main points. That is as much as an audience can absorb. In a longer speech, you could have as many as five main points, but most experienced speakers cover only two or three, regardless of the length of their speech. It is a rare—and usually ineffective—veteran speaker who attempts six or more.

Having 3 main points is better than having 10.

Restrict Each Main Point to a Single Idea

Each main point should focus on just one idea. Consider the following:

Poor: I. Some employees who are diagnosed with cancer lose their jobs, and some of them lose their health-insurance coverage.

Better: I. Some employees who are diagnosed with cancer lose their jobs.

            II. Some lose their health-insurance coverage.

The first set makes the mistake of covering two issues; the second set splits the material into two distinct points.

Avoid Announcements

Your Thoughts **?**

Most public speaking experts recommend that you use complete sentences to create your central idea and main points. Why do you think this advice is given?

Rather than simply announce a topic, each main point should make an assertion, a forthright declaration of the idea that you want to convey. Imagine that you create the following:

Poor: I'll talk about hot-dog headaches.

What about it? What's your point? You have done nothing but announce your topic.

Better: Sodium nitrites contained in hot dogs cause many people to suffer headaches.

Now you have made a point—a clear assertion of what you are driving at.

Customize Points for Each Audience

As you play with ideas in your search for main points, ask yourself, "What main points would work best with this particular audience?" If you tailor your speech to each audience's needs and desires, you may end up using different main points with different audiences.

Let's say you plan to give speeches in your community aimed at persuading people to take up nature photography as a hobby. If you talk to a group of college students, you can anticipate that they will raise an objection: photography is too expensive. So you create a main point—"Photography is not out of reach for people with modest incomes"—and devote a good portion of your speech to giving specific examples and prices. If, however, you speak to an audience of wealthy individuals who could easily afford any kind of camera, this point may be unnecessary.

Another potential main point is that nature photography teaches a person to see the world with fresh eyes—to find "splendor in the grass," the visual glories that abound in nature for those who develop keen perception. This would be a good point to make with an audience of urban dwellers who rarely explore the outdoors. But if your audience is a birdwatchers' society, this point is probably unnecessary; these people have already trained their eyes to detect nature's nuances.

Use Parallel Language Whenever Possible

Parallel language means that you use the same grammatical forms throughout a sentence or a paragraph. Read the following sentence aloud: "Joe enjoys hunting, fishing, and to camp." There is nothing wrong with the sentence grammatically, but it doesn't sound as pleasant to the ear as this version: "Joe enjoys hunting, fishing, and camping." Rather than the discord of *-ing, -ing,* plus *to,* our ears prefer the rhythm of *-ing, -ing, -ing,* as in the second sentence.

parallel language
equivalent grammatical forms to express equivalent ideas

Suppose that you started with the following:

Specific Purpose: To persuade my audience to swim for exercise

Central Idea: Swimming is an ideal exercise because it dissipates nervous tension, avoids injuries, and builds endurance.

Now decide which of the following sets of main points would be more effective:

First Set: I. You can work off a lot of nervous tension while swimming.

II. Muscle and bone injuries, common with other sports, are not a problem with swimming.

III. Swimming builds endurance.

Second Set: I. Swimming dissipates nervous tension.

II. Swimming avoids muscle and bone injuries.

III. Swimming builds endurance.

Just as parallel lines are pleasing to the eye, parallel language is pleasing to the ear.

The second set is preferable because it follows a parallel grammatical form throughout (the noun *swimming* followed by a verb). This consistent arrangement may not be practical in every speech, but you should strive for parallelism whenever possible.

Organizing Main Points

Main points should be organized in a logical, easy-to-follow pattern. Five of the most popular patterns used by speakers are chronological, spatial, cause–effect, problem–solution, and topical.

Chronological Pattern

chronological pattern
an arrangement of information in a time sequence

In the **chronological pattern,** you arrange your main points in a *time* sequence—what occurs first, what occurs second, and so on. If, for example, you are describing a process, you can use the chronological pattern to show the step-by-step progression. For an illustration, see Figure 7.3.

The chronological pattern is a logical choice for a speech dealing with periods of time in history. If, for example, you were speaking on the history of immigration in the United States, you could divide your subject into centuries, from the seventeenth to the twenty-first.

If you were speaking on the life of a person, you might divide your speech according to the stages of life, as in the following example:

Specific Purpose: To inform my listeners of the heroism of Harriet Tubman, a leading 19th-century abolitionist

Central Idea: Harriet Tubman was a courageous woman who escaped from slavery and then returned to the South to rescue others.

Main Points:

(Childhood)   I. Born a slave on a plantation in Maryland, Tubman suffered many whippings while growing up.

(Youth)   II. She escaped to freedom by using the Underground Railroad.

(Adulthood)   III. Wearing various disguises, Tubman smuggled over 300 slaves to safe havens from 1850 to 1860.

Spatial Pattern

spatial pattern
an arrangement of information in terms of physical space, such as top to bottom

In the **spatial pattern,** you organize items according to the way in which they relate to each other in *physical space*—top to bottom, left to right, north to south, inside to outside, and so on. If you were speaking on the solar system, for example, you could discuss the sun first, then move outward in space to Mercury, Venus, Earth,

Figure 7.3
Chronological Pattern
The process of treating a bee sting is a chronological pattern (or time sequence)—what to do first, second, and third.

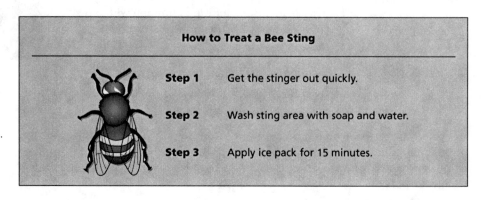

How to Treat a Bee Sting	
Step 1	Get the stinger out quickly.
Step 2	Wash sting area with soap and water.
Step 3	Apply ice pack for 15 minutes.

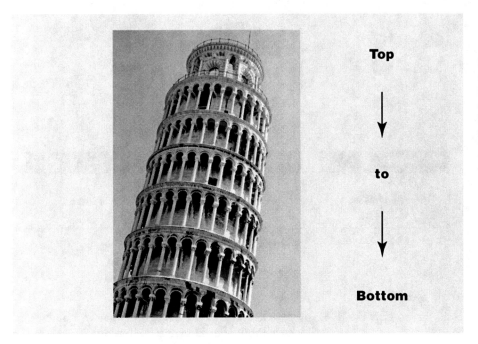

Figure 7.4
Spatial Pattern
For a discussion of the Leaning Tower of Pisa, a speaker could use the spatial (physical space) pattern, progressing from top to bottom. (Or the tower could be discussed from bottom to top.)

Mars, and so on. Here is an example in which the speaker divides a car into space-related sections:

Specific Purpose: To tell my audience how to inspect a used car before deciding whether to buy it

Central Idea: If you examine a used car carefully and critically, you can avoid buying a "lemon."

Main Points: I. Inspect the condition of the body of the car.

II. Inspect the condition of the motor.

III. Inspect the condition of the interior.

For an example of the spatial pattern as used from top to bottom, see Figure 7.4.

Cause–Effect Pattern

In some speeches, you are concerned with why something happens or happened—a cause-and-effect relationship. For example, some people refuse to ride in elevators because they have an inordinate fear of closed spaces. Their claustrophobia is the *cause* and their refusal to ride in elevators is the *effect*. For an illustration of a **cause–effect pattern** in a speech, see Figure 7.5.

Sometimes it is more effective to start with the effects and then analyze the causes, as in this case:

Specific Purpose: To explain to my listeners why many people are unable to get bank loans for a new car or house

Central Idea: If you are denied a loan for a new car or house, it could be because you have been incorrectly branded as a poor credit risk by credit-rating companies.

connectpublic
speaking.com
To review organizational patterns, do the interactive exercise in Chapter 7 on *Connect Public Speaking*.

cause–effect pattern
a scheme that links outcomes (effects) and the reasons for them (causes)

Figure 7.5
Cause–Effect Pattern
For a speech about
insufficient sleep, a
speaker could show
a cause-and-effect
relationship.

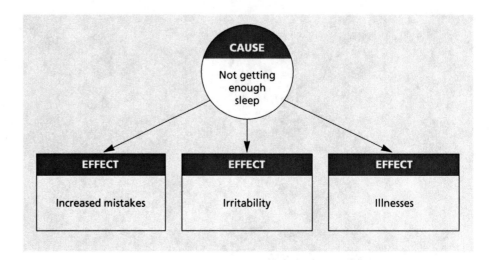

Main Points:

(Effect)   I. Many people are barred from getting loans for a new car or house without ever knowing the reason.

(Cause)   II. The credit-rating companies that keep computerized files on 90 percent of Americans frequently make mistakes without the consumer ever knowing.

In this case, putting the effect first is good strategy because it makes the listeners receptive to the rest of the speech—they are curious to know what caused the situation.

Problem–Solution Pattern

**problem–solution
pattern**
an arrangement of
information that explores
a problem and then offers
a solution

A much-used device for persuasive speeches is the **problem–solution pattern,** which divides a speech into two main sections: a problem and its solution. Here is an example:

Specific Purpose: To persuade my audience to support "pet therapy" for lonely elderly people in nursing homes

Central Idea: Contact with a pet can decrease the loneliness and improve the physical and emotional health of elderly people in nursing homes.

Main Points:

(Problem)   I. Many elderly people in nursing homes are lonely and depressed—emotional states that harm their physical health.

(Solution)   II. Researchers have discovered that contact with a pet improves the elderly person's physical and emotional health.

This pattern has the advantage of simplicity. You convince the listeners that a particular problem exists, and then you tell them how it can be solved. See Figure 7.6 .

Figure 7.6
Problem–Solution Pattern

A speech on air pollution could explain the problem (harmful emissions from coal-burning plants) and offer a solution (clean energy from wind turbines).

Topical Pattern

In the **topical pattern,** you divide your central idea into components or categories, using logic and common sense as your guides.

Thus, a speech on the symphonic orchestra could be divided into three sections: string instruments, wind instruments, and percussion instruments. A speech on job interviews could be divided into three types of interviews: personal, video, and computer. See Figure 7.7 for another example.

Here is a portion of an outline that illustrates the topical pattern:

topical pattern
a division of a topic into components, types, or reasons

Specific Purpose: To inform my audience of the two kinds of sleep that all people experience

Central Idea: The two kinds of sleep that all people experience at alternating times during the night are NREM (non-rapid-eye-movement) sleep and REM (rapid-eye-movement) sleep.

Serif	Sans-Serif	Script
A	A	*A*

Figure 7.7
Topical Pattern

A speech on typefaces could be divided into an explanation of three major styles. Serif letters have lines or curves projecting from the end of a letterform, while sans-serif letters do not have finishing strokes. Script letters simulate fancy handwriting.

Main Points: I. NREM (non-rapid-eye-movement) sleep is the period in which a person does very little dreaming.

II. REM (rapid-eye-movement) sleep is the period in which a person usually dreams.

statement-of-reasons pattern
a variation of the topical pattern in which a speaker gives reasons for an idea

A variation of the topical pattern is sometimes called the **statement-of-reasons pattern.** The speaker subdivides an idea by showing reasons for it, as in the following example:

Specific Purpose: To persuade my listeners that telephone companies should use alternatives to cellular phone towers

Central Idea: Telephone companies should be required to place their cellular antennas on buildings and trees rather than on freestanding towers.

Main Points:
(First reason) I. Cellular phone towers are huge and ugly.
(Second reason) II. Cellular telephone antennas work as effectively on church steeples, tall trees, and high buildings as they do on freestanding towers.
(Third reason) III. Steeples, trees, and buildings are easily available because many churches, landowners, and businesses desire the fees that telephone companies pay for antenna placement.

Your Thoughts **?**

Which pattern would a speaker probably choose for a speech on how society's obsession with thinness has led to unhealthy weight-loss methods and eating disorders?

Note of caution: Some students make the mistake of thinking that the topical pattern is a formless bag into which anything can be dumped. Though you have a great deal of liberty to organize your points in whatever order you choose, you still must apply logic—by, for example, arranging your points from least important to most important, or separating your material into three major subdivisions.

Selecting Support Materials

In the preceding sections, we concentrated on main points, but main points by themselves are not enough for the body of a speech. You also need support materials—such as examples, narratives, testimony, and statistics—to develop and amplify your main points. Support materials help your audience to understand and remember main points.

To see how support materials can be developed for main points, let's take a look at an outline of the body of a speech by student speaker Wendy Trujillo, who uses the statement-of-reasons pattern to give two reasons why cotton swabs should never be used for cleaning ears.[6] The introduction and the conclusion for this speech are printed in Chapter 8.

General Purpose: To persuade
Specific Purpose: To persuade my audience to avoid using cotton swabs in their ears
Central Idea: For cleaning ears, cotton swabs are dangerous and ineffective.

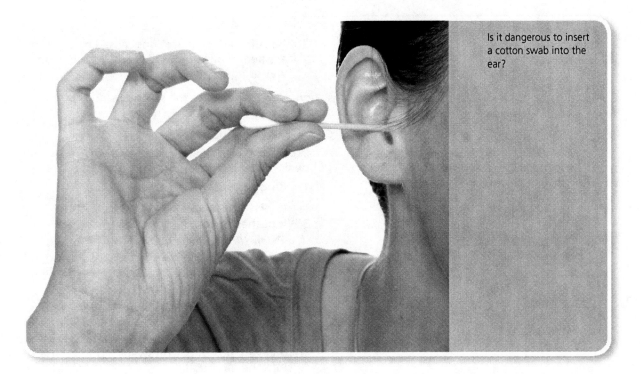

Is it dangerous to insert a cotton swab into the ear?

BODY

I. Cotton swabs can cause injury.

   A. Cotton swabs send more people to the hospital than razor blades or shavers.

      1. Over 400,000 Americans visit hospital emergency departments for ear injuries each year. (Centers for Disease Control and Prevention)

      2. Most of the injuries are caused by cotton swabs.

      3. These injuries can impair hearing.

   B. Some ear injuries are severe.

      1. New York Giants football player Chase Blackburn nearly ruptured his eardrum in the locker room while cleaning his ear with a cotton swab.

      2. He fell to the floor, bleeding, and lost his hearing for a few weeks

   C. In a few cases using cotton swabs leads to death.

      1. Daniel St. Pierre of Montreal, Canada, died in March, 2007.

Commentary

The body has two main points, each giving a reason to avoid swabs.

*Trujillo cites **statistics** from a trustworthy source.*

*A **narrative** (or story) helps the audience to visualize the risks involved.*

*The speaker gives an **example** to support her point.*

(continued)

2. He suffered complications caused by the accidental piercing of his eardrum while he was using a cotton swab.

(*Transition:* Now let's turn to the second reason for not using swabs on your ears.)

II. Cotton swabs are ineffective.

*An **analogy** between a swab and a broom helps to show the futility of using swabs to clean ears.*

A. Experts say that cleaning your ears with a cotton swab is like using a broom on a dirt floor.
1. It just moves things around.
2. It doesn't really get rid of most of the gunk.
3. It pushes the gunk further down the ear canal, where it can create a problem.

*An expert's **testimony** bolsters the speaker's argument.*

B. If you have a lot of earwax or some object lodged in your ear, a physician is far more effective than a swab. (Ear specialist Dr. Cynthia Steele)
1. A physician has safe techniques, equipment, and liquids.
2. Dr. Steele shows patients the warning label on every box of cotton swabs: "Do not insert into the ear canal."

If possible, distribute your supporting materials evenly. In other words, don't put all your support under point I and leave nothing to bolster point II. This does not mean, however, that you should mechanically place the same number of supporting points under every main point. You have to consider *quality* as well as *quantity*. A single powerful anecdote may be all that is required to illustrate one point, whereas five minor supports may be needed for another point.

When you are trying to decide how many supporting points to place underneath a main point, use this rule of thumb: Have enough supporting points to adequately explain or bolster the main point, but not so many that you become tedious and repetitious.

Supplying Transitions

transition
an expression that links ideas and shows the relationship between them

Words, phrases, or sentences that show logical connections between ideas or thoughts are called **transitions.** They help the listeners stay with you as you move from one part of your speech to the next. To get an idea of how transitions work, take a look at two paragraphs, the first of which has no transitions:

Poor: Olive oil is used extensively in Mediterranean cooking. It never became popular in Latin America. Olive trees can grow in Mexico and coastal regions of South America. The colonial rulers in Spain did not want anyone competing against Spain's farmers. They banned the production of olive oil in Latin America. The oil had to be imported. It was very expensive.

Now let's add transitions (shown in bold print):

Better: Olive oil is used extensively in Mediterranean cooking. **However,** it never became popular in Latin America. Olive trees can grow in Mexico and coastal regions of South America, **but** the colonial rulers in Spain did not want anyone competing against Spain's farmers, **so** they banned the production of olive oil in Latin America. The oil had to be imported **and therefore** was very expensive.

 connectpublic speaking.com See Video Clip 7.1, Providing Transitions: "Too Much of a Good Thing."

The transitions obviously make the second paragraph superior.

In a speech, transitions clarify the relationship between your ideas, thereby making them easy to comprehend. They serve as signals to help the listeners follow your train of thought. Here is a sampling of the many transitional words or phrases in the English language:

- To signal addition: *and, also, furthermore, moreover, in addition*
- To signal time: *soon, then, later, afterward, meanwhile*
- To signal contrast: *however, but, yet, nevertheless, instead, meanwhile, although*
- To signal examples: *for example, to illustrate, for instance*
- To signal conclusions: *in summary, therefore, consequently, as a result*
- To signal concession: *although it is true that, of course, granted*

Your Thoughts ?

In a speech, transitions must be more prominent than they are in a book. Why?

In public speaking, special types of transitions can be employed to help your listener follow your remarks. Let us look at four of them: bridges, internal summaries, signposts, and spotlights.

Bridges

In crossing a bridge, a person goes from one piece of land to another. In giving a speech, the speaker can build **bridges** to tell the listeners of the terrain they are leaving behind and the terrain they are about to enter.

bridge
a transitional device that links what went before with the next part of a speech

Imagine that you had the following as your first main point in a speech on workplace violence:

I. Violence in the workplace has increased in recent years.

You give examples and statistics to back up this point, and now you are ready for your second main point:

II. Workplace violence can be reduced if managers and employees are trained in conflict resolution.

How can you go from point I to point II? You could simply finish with point I and begin point II, but that would be too abrupt. It would fail to give the listeners time to change mental gears. A smoother way is to refer back to the first main point at the same time you are pointing forward to the second:

Although workplace violence has increased dramatically, the situation is not hopeless. There is a way to reduce the number of incidents—a way that has proven successful in many companies throughout the world.

In a speech, a bridge takes listeners smoothly from one idea to another.

This is a successful bridge because it smoothly and gracefully takes your listeners from point I to point II. It also has the virtue of stimulating their curiosity about the next part of the speech.

Tips for Your Career

Internal Summaries

internal summary
a concise review of material covered during the body of a speech

At the end of a baseball game, announcers always give a summary of the game. But during the game itself, they occasionally give a summary of what has taken place up to the present moment ("We're in the middle of the fifth inning; Detroit is leading Milwaukee 4 to 3 on a grand-slam homer by . . ."). Though this summary is designed primarily for the viewers who have tuned in late, it is also appreciated by the fans who have been watching the entire game, because it gives them a feeling of security and confidence–a sense of knowing the "main facts." You can achieve the same effect in a speech. During the body of a speech, when you finish an important section, you may want to spend a few moments summarizing your ideas so that they are clear and understandable. This device, called an **internal summary,** is especially helpful if you have been discussing ideas that are complicated or abstract. An internal summary can be combined with a bridge to make an excellent transition, as follows:

> [*Internal summary*] By now I hope I've convinced you that all animal bites should be reported to a doctor or health official immediately because of the possibility of rabies. [*bridge*] While you're waiting for an ambulance or for an examination by a doctor, there is one other important thing you should do.

Signposts

signpost
an explicit statement of the place that a speaker has reached

Just as signposts on a road tell motorists their location, **signposts** in a speech tell listeners where they are or where they are headed. If you gave a speech on how to treat a cold, you could say, "Here are three things you should do the next time you catch a cold." Then the audience would find it easy to follow your points if you said, "First, you should . . . Second, you should . . . Third, you should . . ." Using these signposts is much more effective than linking your points by saying, "Also . . ." or "Another point is . . ."

Spotlights

Spotlights are transitional devices that alert the listeners that something important will soon appear. Here are some examples:

- Now we come to the most important thing I have to tell you.
- What I'm going to explain now will help you understand the rest of the speech.
- If you take with you only one idea from this speech . . .

Spotlights can build up anticipation: "And now I come to an idea that can mean extra money in your pocket . . ." Or: "If you want to feel healthier and happier, listen to the advice of Dr. Julia Brunswick . . ."

When you choose transitional devices, remember that your listeners are totally unfamiliar with your speech, so try to put yourself in their shoes at each juncture. Ask yourself, "How can I lead the listener from one point to another in a way that is logical and smooth?"

Simplifying the Process

Organizing bits and pieces of material into a coherent, logical speech can be a difficult task, but it can be simplified if you use the following method:

1. **Survey all your material.** Bring together and examine your personal observations, interview notes, research notes, and visual aids.
2. **Choose an organizational method.** Three options are recommended:

   - **Computers.** Most word processing programs permit split screens, so that you can have notes in one window and an outline in another, making it easy to look over your notes and transform them into items for your outline.
   - **Stick-on slips.** This method uses file folders of different colors, with a different-colored folder for each major part of the speech. Stick-on slips (such as the 3M Post-it™ slips) are placed inside the folders.
   - **Cards.** This method is similar to the stick-on slips, except that index cards are used. The cards can be kept together by a rubber band or stored in a file folder.

All three options give you flexibility. You can easily move items around, add extra material, and delete unimportant points. Items can be spread out–stick-on slips in file folders, computer entries on a screen, and cards on a tabletop. This procedure lets you see the "big picture"–the overall architecture of your speech.

3. **Limit each note to just one idea.** To make the method work effectively, *you must use a separate slip, card, or computer entry for each point*. This will make it easy to move items around.
4. **Experiment with different sequences.** Try several ways of arranging your material until you find a good sequence, a smooth flow that will be easy for the audience to follow. Marcia Yudkin, a business trainer from Boston, uses the card system, but her advice can be applied to stick-on slips and computer screens as well:

> Sit in a comfortable chair and shuffle those ideas, asking yourself questions like, "What if I start with this, and move on to this, then this . . . ?" You're looking for a smooth, natural flow from each point to the next. Some sort of sequence

will eventually emerge from this exercise. Don't get perturbed if you end up with extra cards that refuse to fit in; any leftover material might be perfect for the question-and-answer period after your speech, or for another presentation.[7]

5. Transfer your material to a formal outline.   Once you have your information arranged, it's a good idea to transfer it to a formal outline—as a way to gain control over it and to test its strength and continuity. Your instructor may have a required format for the outline. If not, I suggest you use the format shown in Chapter 9.

Resources for Review and Skill Building

connectpublic
speaking.com

Connect Public Speaking provides resources for study and review, including sample speech videos, an Outline Tutor, and practice tests.

Summary

A well-organized speech is more understandable, credible, and memorable than a poorly organized one.

The body of the speech should be organized with two or three (occasionally four) main points that develop the central idea of the speech. Some guidelines for main points: (1) Restrict each main point to a single idea. (2) Avoid announcements. (3) Customize points for each audience. (4) Use parallel language whenever possible.

Arrange the main points in a logical pattern, such as *chronological,* in which main points are placed in a time sequence; *spatial,* in which items are arranged in terms of physical space; *cause–effect,* in which causes and effects are juxtaposed; *problem–solution,* in which a problem is explained and a solution offered; or *topical,* in which a central idea is divided into components.

Next, select support materials to back up the main points, and then supply transitions to help the listeners stay with you as you move from one part of your speech to the next. Common types of transitions are bridges, internal summaries, signposts, and spotlights.

To simplify the task of organizing material, use one of these three options: stick-on slips, computers, and cards. Put one item on each slip, computer entry, or card so that you can easily add, delete, and rearrange your material.

Key Terms

Review Questions

1. How many main points should you have in a speech?
2. How many ideas should be represented in each main point?
3. What is meant by the advice to "customize points for each audience"?
4. Which pattern of organization would be best suited for a speech on the solar system?
5. Which pattern of organization would be ideal for a speech on food contamination and how the problem can be corrected?
6. Which pattern of organization would be best suited for a speech on the three major reasons why businesses declare bankruptcy?
7. Why are transitions important in a speech?
8. In terms of speech organization, what is an internal summary?
9. Describe the transitional device called *bridge*.
10. Describe the transitional device called *spotlight*.

Building Critical-Thinking Skills

1. Which organizational pattern is used in the following:

   Specific Purpose: To inform my listeners how to soundproof a room

   Central Idea: A room can be insulated so that sounds do not penetrate.

   Main Points:

   (Top)   I. The ceiling can be covered by acoustic tile and a tapestry to block sounds from above.

   (Middle)   II. The walls can be covered with ceiling-to-floor tapestries (and heavy, lined drapes for windows) to block noise from outside.

   (Bottom)   III. The floor can be covered with acoustic padding and wall-to-wall carpet to block sounds from below.

2. Which organizational pattern is used in the following:

   Specific Purpose: To tell my listeners how to revive a person who is in danger of drowning

   Central Idea: To revive a person who is in danger of drowning, you should follow three simple procedures.

   Main Points:

   (First)   I. With the victim on his or her back, tilt the head back so that the chin juts upward.

   (Second)   II. Give mouth-to-mouth resuscitation until the victim breathes regularly again.

   (Third)   III. Place the victim on his or her stomach with the head facing sideways.

Building Teamwork Skills

1. Working in a group, examine the following scrambled statements and decide which is the central idea and which are the main points. (One item below is a central idea and the other two are main points to develop the central idea.) Discuss what kinds of support materials would be needed under each main point.

   a. Many U.S. companies that have instituted the 30-hour workweek report higher job satisfaction and performance with no loss of profits.

   b. A 6-hour day/30-hour workweek should be the standard for full-time employees in the United States.

   c. All Western European countries have fewer working hours than the United States.

2. In a group, discuss which organizational pattern would be most effective for the following speech topics.

   a. Why most fatal car accidents occur

   b. Three types of working dogs

   c. How to gift wrap a present

   d. Stalking—and what can be done to stop it

   e. The Amazon River

To unveil "the world's thinnest notebook computer," Apple CEO Steve Jobs shows images of the MacBook Air being pulled out of a standard manila office envelope. According to *Wired* magazine, the images elicited a "chorus of ooh's and aah's" from the thousands of listeners at Mac World Expo in San Francisco. A visual aid like this is an effective way to grab audience attention and interest at the beginning of a speech.

Introductions
and Conclusions

chapter 8

OUTLINE

Introductions
Gain Attention and Interest
Orient the Audience
Guidelines for Introductions

Conclusions
Signal the End
Summarize Key Ideas

Reinforce the Central Idea with a Clincher
Guidelines for Conclusions

Sample Introduction and Conclusion

OBJECTIVES

After studying this chapter, you should be able to:

1. Formulate effective attention material for the introductions of your speeches.

2. Formulate effective orienting material for the introductions of your speeches.

3. Create effective conclusions for your speeches.

Courtroom battles are like dramas, with three distinct parts:

- Beginning (opening statement)
- Middle (examination of evidence)
- End (closing argument)

While all three parts are important, most attorneys say that their opening and closing statements to the jury usually determine whether they win or lose a case.[1] "When you first talk to the jury, you've got to make a favorable impression and win their empathy immediately," says Michelle Roberts, a defense attorney in Washington, D.C. Later, near the end of the trial, "your closing argument must be powerful and persuasive."[2]

In speeches outside the courtroom, the stakes are rarely so high: no one will be forced to go to prison or pay a million dollars in damages if the introduction and the conclusion are weak. Nevertheless, these two parts have great importance. If you don't have a lively introduction, you can lose your audience. "People have remote controls in their heads today," says Myrna Marofsky, an Eden Prairie, Minnesota, business executive. "If you don't catch their interest, they just click you off."[3] And a conclusion that is weak or clumsy can mar the effectiveness of what otherwise might have been a good speech.

Prosecutor Amy Haddix presents her closing arguments in a second-degree murder trial in San Francisco. (She won the case.) For Haddix and other attorneys, their opening and closing remarks to a jury often determine whether they win or lose a case.

Introductions

The introduction to your speech has two main goals: first, to capture and hold your audience's attention and interest, and second, to prepare your audience intellectually and psychologically for the body of the speech. Let's examine each goal in greater detail.

Gain Attention and Interest

If you were sitting in an audience, would you want to listen to a speech that begins with: "I'd like to talk to you today about the fishing industry"?

The subject sounds dull. You might say to yourself, "Who cares?" and let your attention drift to something else.

Now imagine that you were sitting in the audience when student speaker Julie O'Mara began a speech with these words:

> Good news, bad news.
>
> The good news: Scientists estimate that the oceans of the world contain as many as 30 million species of animals, and most of them have not yet been discovered.
>
> Now the bad news: Half of these creatures may soon become extinct because of overfishing in the sea.[4]

Hearing this information about overfishing, you would have a hard time turning your attention away. O'Mara's technique was to use alarming statistics as an attention-grabber.

An attention-grabber is needed because of an unfortunate fact: audiences don't automatically give every speaker their full, respectful attention. As you begin a speech, you may find that some listeners are engaged in whispered conversations with their neighbors (and they don't necessarily stop in midsentence when you start speaking); some are looking at you but their minds are far away, floating in a daydream or enmeshed in a personal problem. So your task is clear: grab their attention when you start talking.

But grabbing their attention is not enough: your introduction must also make listeners want to hear the rest of your speech. Some speakers grab attention by telling a joke, but a joke creates no interest in the rest of the speech. In O'Mara's speech, her provocative opener made the typical listener want to learn more: "How can we stop mass extinction in the seas?"

In this book, "grabbers" are called **attention material,** which should always be the first part of your introduction. In the following section, we will examine some of the more common varieties. Sometimes two or more grabbers can be combined.

Relate a Story

Telling a story is one of the most effective ways to begin a speech, because people love to listen to narrative accounts. Cynthia Wray of Western Carolina University began a speech with this story:

> A few years ago, over 100 third-graders were on a field trip at Chicago's O'Hare International Airport. Suddenly, an 87-year-old man lost control of his car and slammed into the group. One child was killed, and 67 children and 10 adults were injured.[5]

Your Thoughts ?

In several elementary schools in recent years, visiting speakers have grabbed the attention of students by staging a fake invasion of gun-toting terrorists. Why do you think most educators have denounced this strategy?

attention material
the part of the introduction designed to capture audience interest

connectpublic
speaking.com
To see a speaker who tells an interesting story, view Video Clip 8.1.

Wray went on to argue that older drivers should be tested frequently and denied a license if found to be impaired. As Wray demonstrates, a story should always provide an easy and natural entry into the rest of the speech.

hypothetical illustration
an imaginary scenario that illuminates a point

Besides the real-life story, you can use a **hypothetical illustration,** as demonstrated by Jerome David Smith, an attorney, who used the following hypothetical illustration in a speech:

> One day you become angry over the nasty pollution of a river near your home, so you sit down and write a letter to the editor of your local newspaper. The letter is a scathing attack on a corporation that you believe is responsible for ruining the river. Two weeks later, you get a letter from the corporation's attorney informing you that you are being sued for $100,000 for "harming the reputation, prestige, and credibility of the corporation." Does this sound incredible? Can this happen in a country that celebrates freedom of speech? Yes, it can happen . . .

In the rest of his speech, he explained how lawsuits have become a way for companies and public officials to retaliate against criticism.

Ask a Question

Asking a question can be an effective way to intrigue your listeners and encourage them to think about your subject matter as you discuss it. There are two kinds of questions that you can use as attention material: the rhetorical question and the overt-response question.

rhetorical question
a question asked solely to stimulate interest and not to elicit a reply

With a **rhetorical question,** you don't want or expect the listeners to answer overtly by raising their hands or responding out loud. Instead, you want to trigger their curiosity by challenging them to think about your topic. For example:

> With powerful radio signals being beamed into outer space at this very moment, is there any realistic chance that during our lifetime we human beings will establish radio contact with other civilizations in the universe?

Not only does such a question catch the attention of the listeners, but it also makes them want to hear more. It entices them into listening to your speech for the answer to the question.

This PowerPoint slide was used by a student speaker as an attention-getter. The correct answer is "d", Canada, which provides 19 percent of imported oil. Saudi Arabia is second with 15 percent.

The top provider of oil for the U.S. is

a. Saudi Arabia
b. Iraq
c. Iran
d. Canada

With an **overt-response question,** you want the audience to reply by raising their hands or answering out loud. For example, student speaker Meredith Bollinger began a speech by asking:

> There is only one Olympic sport in which men and women compete against each other head to head in direct confrontation. Which sport am I talking about?

One listener guessed water polo–wrong. Another guessed softball–wrong. Another guessed synchronized swimming–wrong. Finally, Bollinger gave the correct answer: equestrian (horseback) competition.

Here are some pitfalls to avoid when asking questions.

Avoid questions that can fizzle.   One college student began a speech by asking, "How many of you are familiar with Future Farmers of America?" Everyone raised a hand, so the speaker looked foolish as he continued, "Today I'd like to inform you about what FFA is." Before you choose a question, imagine the answers you might get from the audience. Could they cause embarrassment or awkwardness?

When you ask questions, don't drag out the suspense.   If listeners are forced to guess and guess until the right answer is found, they may become exasperated, wishing that the speaker would get to the point.

Never ask embarrassing or personal questions.   Avoid such questions as "How many of you have ever tried cocaine?" or "How many of you use an underarm deodorant every day?" An audience would rightfully resent such questions as intrusions into their private lives.

Never divide your audience into opposing camps by asking "loaded" questions.   An example of a loaded question: "How many of you are smart enough to realize that capital punishment is an absolute necessity in a society based on law and order?" By phrasing your question in this way, you insult those who disagree with you.

When asking overt-response questions, don't expect universal participation.   With some overt-response questions, you can try to get every member of the audience to participate, but this can be very risky, especially if you poll the audience in this way: "How many of you favor the death penalty? Raise your hands. Okay . . . Now, how many of you are opposed to the death penalty? Okay, thanks . . . How many of you are undecided or unsure?" What if 3 people raised their hands for the first question, 5 for the second question, 10 for the third–but the remaining 67 people never raised their hands? When this happens, and it often does, it is a major embarrassment for the speaker. Sometimes audiences are in a passive or even grumpy mood; this is especially true with "captive" audiences–that is, audiences that are required (at work or at school) to listen to a speech. In such a case, refrain from asking questions that require the participation of the entire audience.

Make sure the audience understands whether you are asking a rhetorical question or an overt-response question.   If you ask, "How long will Americans continue to tolerate shoddy products?" the audience knows you are not expecting someone to answer, "Five years." It is clearly a rhetorical question. But suppose you ask a question like this: "How many of you have ever gone swimming in the ocean?" The listeners may be confused about whether you want them to raise their hands.

overt-response question
a question asked to elicit a direct, immediate reply

Make it clear. If you want a show of hands, say so at the beginning: "I'd like to see a show of hands, please: How many of you have ever gone swimming in the ocean?" Alerting them in advance not only helps them know what you want but also makes them pay special attention to the question, since they know that you are expecting them to respond.

Make a Provocative Statement

An opening remark that shocks, surprises, or intrigues your listeners can certainly grab attention. (Just make sure the statement is not one that would offend or alienate the audience.) Student speaker Vanessa Sullivan began a speech on human cloning with this statement:

> I have seen a human clone with my own eyes. And so have you.

Then she explained:

> Richard Lewontin, professor of biology at Harvard University, says that about 30 human genetic clones appear every day in the United States. You and I know them as identical twins. Dr. Lewontin says that "identical twins are genetically more identical than a cloned organism is to its donor."[6]

Sullivan went on to argue that despite important ethical problems, cloning is not as far from human experience as many people think.

Cite a Quotation

A quotation can provide a lively beginning for a speech. In a speech on showing respect, student speaker Blake Painter began by saying:

> The American poet Maya Angelou once said, "If you have only one smile in you, give it to the people you love. Don't be surly at home, then go out in the street and start grinning 'Good morning' at total strangers."

Quotations usually work best when they are short. Don't use a quotation that is so long that the listeners lose track of where the quotation ends and your remarks begin. The best way to indicate that you have finished quoting is to pause at the end of the quotation. The pause acts as an oral punctuation device, signaling the end of one thought and the beginning of another.

Arouse Curiosity

An effective attention-getter is one that piques the curiosity of the audience. Brenda Johnson, a chef, began a speech by saying:

> I am addicted to a drug. I have been addicted to it for many years now. I feel like I need it to make it through the day. If I don't get this drug, my head aches. I'm nervous, irritable, and I begin to tremble. It's true—I am addicted.

Having aroused the curiosity of her listeners, Johnson continued:

> I am addicted to caffeine. Most people don't realize that caffeine is a drug—and that it is very addictive. It is present not only in coffee and tea and soft drinks but also in many legal drugs such as weight-control pills and pain relievers.

Johnson spent the rest of the speech giving details about caffeine and how listeners could reduce their intake.

connectpublic speaking.com
To see a speaker who cites a quotation, view Video Clip 8.2.

connectpublic speaking.com
To see a speaker who arouses curiosity, see Video Clip 8.3.

Provide a Visual Aid or Demonstration

Any of the visual aids we discussed in Chapter 6 could be used to introduce a speech, but you must be sure that while the aids get the audience's attention, they also are relevant to the main points of your speech. One student showed slides of sunbathers on a beach to begin a talk on sharks. Though there was a logical link (sometimes sunbathers who go into the water must worry about sharks), the connection was too weak to justify using these particular slides. In a case like this, it would be better to show a slide of a ferocious shark while describing a shark attack.

A demonstration can make an effective opener. Working with a friend, one student gave a demonstration of how to fight off an attacker, and then talked on martial arts. If you want to give a demonstration, get permission from your instructor beforehand. *One note of caution:* Never do anything that might upset the listeners. Holding a revolver and firing a blank to start off a speech on gun control or suicide would upset some people and put them out of a receptive mood.

Give an Incentive to Listen

At the beginning of a speech, many listeners have an attitude that can be summed up in these two questions: "What's in it for me? Why should I pay attention to this speech?" Such people need to be given an incentive to listen to the entire speech. So, whenever possible, state explicitly why the listeners will benefit by hearing you out. It is not enough to simply say, "My speech is very important." You must *show* them how your topic relates to their personal lives and their own best interests. If, for example, you were giving a talk on cardiopulmonary resuscitation (CPR), you could say, "All of you may someday have a friend or loved one collapse from a heart attack right in front of your eyes. If you know CPR, you might be able to save that person's life." Now each person in the audience sees clearly that your speech is important to his or her personal life.

If you tell listeners you will explain how to avoid food poisoning, they have an incentive to listen carefully.

Orient the Audience

Once you have snared the interest of your listeners by means of the attention material, you should go into the second part of your introduction, the **orienting material,** which gives an orientation—a clear sense of what your speech is about, and any other information that the audience may need in order to understand and absorb your ideas. The orienting material is a road map that makes it easy for the listeners to stay with you on the journey of your speech and not get lost and confused.

orienting material
the part of the introduction that gives listeners the information they need to fully understand and believe the rest of the speech

The orienting material does more than prepare the listeners intellectually for your speech; it also prepares them psychologically. It reassures them that you are well-prepared, purposeful, and considerate of their needs and interests. It shows them you are someone they can trust.

The three most common ways to orient the audience are (1) give background information, (2) establish your credibility, and (3) preview the body of the speech. They are listed in this order because number 3 is usually delivered last, as a prelude to the body.

Do you need all three options in every speech? For classroom speeches, follow your instructor's guidelines. For some career speeches, you may not need the first two. The best advice is to use an option if it will promote audience understanding and acceptance.

Give Background Information

Part of your orienting material can be devoted to giving background information—definitions, explanations, and so on—to help your listeners understand your speech. In a speech on the Boston-to-Washington megalopolis, Vandana Shastri used her orienting material to define the term:

> A megalopolis is a region made up of several cities and their suburbs which sprawl into each other. The biggest megalopolis in the United States is a densely populated, 500-mile-long corridor that starts in Boston and goes southward through Connecticut, New York City, northern New Jersey, Philadelphia, Wilmington (Delaware), Baltimore, and then ends in the Washington, D.C., suburbs of northern Virginia.

Sometimes it helps the audience if you explain the boundaries of your speech. For example, assume that you are giving a speech on the notion that criminals should make restitution to their victims. If you are not careful, many people in your audience will reject your argument immediately by saying to themselves, "Restitution, baloney! How can a murderer make restitution to his victim?" So in your orienting material, you head off such objections by saying, "In this speech, I will talk about criminals making restitution to their victims, but I'm only talking about nonviolent criminals such as swindlers, embezzlers, and bad-check writers. I'm not talking about rapists and murderers." By showing the boundaries of your subject, you increase the chances that the audience will listen with open minds.

Establish Your Credibility

No one expects you to be the world's authority on your subject, but you can increase your audience's chances of accepting your ideas if you establish your **credibility**—that is, give some credentials or reasons why you are qualified to speak on the subject. When student speaker Randy Stepp talked on how to escape a burning building, he enhanced his credibility by mentioning that he was a volunteer firefighter in a rural community and had fought many fires.

credibility
audience perception of a speaker as believable, trustworthy, and competent

Some people shy away from giving their credentials or background because they think that doing so would make them seem boastful and arrogant. This concern is unfounded if you provide facts about yourself in a modest, tactful manner. In other words, if you are speaking on air pollution, say something like "I'm a chemist and I've analyzed in my lab the content of the air that we breathe in this community" instead of "I'm a professional chemist, so I know more about air pollution than anybody else in this room."

For information that does not come from your personal experience, you could cite your sources in the orienting material. For example, one speaker said, "The information I am giving you today comes from a book by David E. Hoffman entitled *The Oligarchs: Wealth & Power in the New Russia.*"

Note: Mentioning your sources in the orienting material is just one of two options for citing sources. See Tip 12.2 in the next chapter. Before choosing an option, find out your instructor's preference.

In some speeches, you should tell the audience your connection to the topic—why you are speaking on that particular subject. For example, "I am speaking on defective automobile tires because my sister was seriously hurt in an accident that was caused by bad tires."

In a speech on horses, revealing your experience as a show jumper enhances your credibility.

Confess any conflict of interest or bias. For example, "I am urging you to use Ask-an-Expert.com for Internet searches because I think it's the best expert site, but I should tell you that I get paid for being one of their experts."

Preview the Body of the Speech

Have you ever had trouble listening to a speech or lecture because the information seemed jumbled and disconnected and you couldn't grasp the significance of example A and statistic B? An important way to avoid this problem is for the speaker to give the listeners a **preview** of the body of the speech.

preview
a preliminary look at the highlights of a speech

To help you see the value of a preview, consider this analogy: Suppose I give you a sack containing the 400 pieces of a jigsaw puzzle and ask you to complete the puzzle. You will have a hard time because you lack a sense of how the puzzle is supposed to look when finished. Now imagine that I hand you a full-color picture of what the puzzle looks like when it is completely assembled–a panoramic view. Will your task be easier now? Yes, because the pieces "make sense"–you instantly recognize that a light blue piece belongs to the sky in the upper part of the picture, a dark brown piece is part of a tree on the left side, and so on.

A speech is just like the puzzle. If you fail to give a preview, you are giving out bits of information–pieces of the puzzle–without providing listeners with any clues as to how they all fit together. If you do give a preview, you are providing your listeners with a panoramic view of the speech. Then, as you progress through the body, you give details–the pieces of the puzzle–and the listeners are able to fit them into a logical, coherent picture in their minds.

A preview gives the big picture. As you speak, listeners can place the pieces.

Your instructor may have specific requirements for what you must put in your preview. In general, and unless he or she advises you otherwise, I recommend that you include your central idea or your main points or both.

1.   **State the central idea.**   Your audience can listen intelligently to your speech if you stress your central idea in the orienting material. For example, "Acid rain is killing all the trees on our highest peaks in the East. To prove this, I will give you evidence from leading scientists."

In a speech on losing weight, Mary E. McNair, a nurse, stated her central idea in this way:

> Fad and crash diets can actually backfire, causing a person in the long run to gain more weight than was originally lost.

This helped the audience listen with "the right set of ears." They knew to pay attention to what she had to say about the counterproductive effects of fad and crash diets.

2.   **State the main points.**   In most speeches, listeners appreciate being given a brief preview of your main points. For example, Barbara LeBlanc said,

> I believe that passive-solar heating should be used in every home—for two reasons: First, it's easy to adapt your house to passive solar. Second, the energy from passive solar is absolutely free. Let me explain what I'm talking about.

By stating the main points, LeBlanc not only helped the audience listen intelligently but also gave them an incentive to listen: She mentioned the possibility of saving money.

Tips for Your Career

Tip 8.1 Use an "Icebreaker" to Start Off a Community Speech

You have probably noticed that many speakers at business and professional meetings start off by saying something like this: "I'm glad to have a chance to speak to you today." They are giving an *icebreaker*—a polite little prologue to "break the ice" before getting into their speech.

In outline form, here is how an introduction with an icebreaker would look:

I. Icebreaker
II. Attention Material
III. Orienting Material

When you give speeches in the community, an icebreaker is helpful because it eases your nervous tension and it lets the audience get accustomed to your voice. You don't need an icebreaker for classroom speeches because your audience has already settled down and is ready to listen. (Besides, most instructors would disapprove of using one.)

I don't like "Hello, how are you?" as an icebreaker. It sounds too breezy and flip. It leaves a question as to whether the speaker wants the audience to roar a response like "Fine, thank you!" It is much better to say, "I appreciate the opportunity to speak to you tonight." But, you might object, phrases like this have been used so often, they are meaningless. Yes, they are. They are clichés. Nevertheless, they are valuable aids to smooth social relationships. When you engage in small talk with your friends, you use sentences like "Hi, how are you?" Such expressions are trite, but they are necessary because they lubricate the wheels of human discourse.

In addition to expressing appreciation for the invitation to speak, you can include a thank-you to the person who introduced you or a reference to the occasion ("I'm delighted to take part in the celebration of Martin Luther King's birthday"). Some speakers also use the icebreaker to formally greet the audience. This custom, however, has fallen out of fashion. In the old days, orators would begin speeches like this: "Madame President, Distinguished Members of the Paradox Society, Honored Guests, Ladies and Gentlemen, Greetings!" Such introductions are used today only in formal, traditional settings, such as a college commencement. In most of the speeches you will give in your life, a flowery greeting would sound pompous.

A note of caution: An icebreaker should be very brief—just a sentence or two. If you are too slow getting into the attention material of your introduction, you may cause some listeners to tune you out.

Giving a preview by stating the central idea and the main points reassures the listeners that you are not going to ramble. In other words, you give the audience a message that says, loud and clear, "I'm well-prepared; I know exactly what I'm going to say; I'm not going to waste your time."

Guidelines for Introductions

connectpublic
speaking.com

For an interactive exercise on introductions, see Chapter 8 on *Connect Public Speaking*.

Here are some points to keep in mind for introductions.

1. Don't prepare your introduction first. When you prepare a speech, what usually works best is to complete the body of the speech and *then* work on your introduction. Once you have developed your main points, you are in a stronger position to decide how to introduce them.

2. Make your introduction simple and easy to follow, but avoid making it too brief. Your audience needs time to get into the groove of your speech. If the introduction is too short, it may go by too fast for the listeners to absorb. That is why effective joke tellers stretch out their introduction to give the listeners time to get "into" the joke.

If the idea of stretching out an introduction sounds wrong to you, it is probably because you have been taught in English classes to write concisely. While it is a sin in English composition to stretch out essays, it is a virtue to do so with a speech's introduction that might otherwise be too abrupt for an audience.

   A note of caution: Don't let this tip cause you to go to the opposite extreme—being tedious and long-winded. Be brief, but not too brief. If you are unsure about whether you have achieved a happy medium, deliver your speech to relatives or friends and then ask them if they thought your introduction was too long or too short.

3. Make sure that your introduction has a direct and obvious tie-in with the body of the speech.   A common mistake is for speakers to give an introduction that has a weak or dubious link with the rest of the speech. This kind of introduction can be annoying and confusing to the listeners.

4. Never apologize.   You weaken your speech and hurt your credibility if you say things like "I didn't have much time to prepare" or "This may be too technical for you" or "I'm sorry I didn't draw a diagram."

Your Thoughts **?**

What advice would you give a speaker who begins by saying, "I know this speech is going to bore you"?

Conclusions

When movies are made, the producers spend a lot of time and energy on getting a "perfect" ending because they know that if the ending is unsatisfying, the viewers will tend to downgrade the film as a whole. As with the movies, the ending of a speech can either add to or subtract from the audience's opinion of the entire speech. So it is worthwhile to spend a lot of time working on your conclusion.

   In your conclusion, you should do three important things: (1) signal the end of the speech to satisfy the audience's psychological need for a sense of completion, (2) summarize the key ideas of the speech, and (3) reinforce the central idea with a clincher. Let us discuss these points in greater detail.

Signal the End

Imagine that you are listening to your favorite song on the radio and letting your mind float freely with the music. Then suddenly, before the song is finished, the disc jockey cuts in with a commercial or a news bulletin. You missed only the last 10 seconds of the song, but you feel annoyed. Why? Because most people need to experience a sense of completion.

   In listening to a speech, we have the same need for a sense of finality. We don't like an abrupt halt—we like to hear a conclusion that is psychologically satisfying.

   To give listeners a satisfying finale, provide signals that the end is approaching. These signals can be verbal or nonverbal or both.

A good conclusion wraps up a speech and leaves a memorable impression.

Verbal signals.   You can openly announce that you are coming to your conclusion by saying, "So, in conclusion, I'd like to say . . . ," or "Let me end by saying . . . ," or "Let me remind you of the three major points I've been trying to explain today."

Nonverbal signals.   Two nonverbal cues are subtle but important: (1) say your conclusion with a tone of dramatic finality and (2) subtly intensify your facial expression and gestures. These cues should come naturally to you, since you have seen numerous speakers use them in your lifetime. If you feel unsure of yourself, practice your conclusion in front of a mirror or, better yet, in front of a friend (who can give you feedback). You also can say it in front of a camcorder and play it back to check whether you have the appropriate tone of finality in your voice.

Summarize Key Ideas

Because listening is often a difficult mental task, some people in the audience might get drowsy or inattentive toward the end of your speech. But when you signal that you are about to finish, listeners usually perk up. If they know they can rest soon, they are better able to stay alert for a few more minutes. Like runners near the finish line, they can bring forth an extra burst of energy.

This mental alertness of your listeners gives you a good opportunity to drive home your message one more time. One of the best ways to do this is to summarize your key ideas. There is a formula for giving a speech that has been around for over 100 years. Sometimes it is attributed to a spellbinding country preacher, sometimes to a savvy Irish politician. The true originator will probably never be known, but the formula is worth heeding:

> Tell 'em what you're going to tell 'em.
> Tell 'em.
> Then tell 'em what you told 'em.

The first sentence refers to the introduction, the second to the body, and the third to a summary in the conclusion. The summary gives you a chance to restate the central idea or the main points or both.

If you are like a lot of people, you may say, "Why do I need to repeat my message? Isn't this overkill?" No, research shows that restating your main points increases the likelihood that the listeners will remember them.[7]

A summary should be brief, as in this recap of the body of a speech about preventing car theft:

> So remember, you can prevent your car from being stolen if you follow these guidelines: Always park in a well-lighted area. Always remove your key from the ignition. Always close all windows and lock all doors.

Listeners don't mind hearing this kind of information again; it helps them retain it.

Reinforce the Central Idea with a Clincher

clincher
a final statement in a speech that drives home the key concept of the speech

In addition to providing a summary, close your speech with a **clincher** that reinforces the central idea–a finale that drives home the main theme of your entire speech.

Public speakers are like carpenters driving a nail into a floor, says Edward L. Friedman. They begin with a few preliminary taps in the introduction to get the speech started right. As they get into the body of the speech, they deliver one hammer blow after another to drive the nail into its proper place with carefully executed strokes. Then, in conclusion, they execute a powerful, clinching blow.[8]

Use a clincher that is memorable, that leaves a lasting impression with the listener. You can find clinchers by using some of the techniques mentioned earlier in this chapter for the introduction (such as a rhetorical question or a visual aid), or by using some of the following techniques.

Cite a Quotation

A good quotation can dramatize and reinforce a speaker's central idea. After urging her audience always to buckle their seat belts, one speaker said,

> I would like to close with a quotation from Laura Valdez, an emergency medicine technician in California, who said, "I have driven my ambulance to hundreds of traffic accidents. I have found many people already dead, but I have yet to unbuckle the seat belt of a dead person."

At the end of a speech on why citizens should fight social ills rather than succumb to despair, Richard Kern said:

> Let me leave you with the words of Eleanor Roosevelt: "It is better to light one candle than to curse the darkness."

Eye contact is important at the end of your speech, so if you use a quotation, practice it so that you can say it while looking at the audience, with only occasional glances at your notes.

Issue an Appeal or a Challenge

In a persuasive speech, you can end by making an appeal or issuing a challenge to the audience. If you are trying to persuade the listeners to donate blood, you can end by saying:

> Next week the bloodmobile will be on campus. I call upon each of you to spend a few minutes donating your blood so that others may live.

One speaker tried to convince her audience to make out a will, and in her conclusion she issued a challenge:

> The simple task of writing a will can protect your family and give you peace of mind. It is a sad fact that three out of four Americans will die without a will. Are you going to be one of them? I hope not. Why don't you write your will before you go to bed tonight?

Give an Illustration

An illustration is a popular way to reinforce the central idea of a speech. In a speech urging classmates to avoid Internet gambling, one student speaker concluded with a true story:

> In his entire life, college senior Mark Scott had never gambled until one night, when he got an e-mail that said, "Congratulations, Mark, you won $100." Scott was intrigued, and he clicked on the gambling site and began playing blackjack. After an hour, $175 of his money was gone. Three months later, he had run up a $9,000 gambling debt on his credit card.

Refer to the Introduction

Using the conclusion to hearken back to something said in the introduction is an effective way to wrap up your speech. One way to do this is to answer a question asked at the beginning of a speech. Student speaker Daniel Hirata asked in his introduction, "Should we permit job discrimination on the basis of a person's weight?" In his conclusion, Hirata repeated the question and answered it:

> Should we allow job discrimination against overweight people? From what I've said today, I hope you'll agree that the answer is no. To deny a person a job

connectpublic speaking.com
To see a speaker who cites a quotation, view Video Clip 8.4.

connectpublic speaking.com
To view a speaker who closes with an illustration, see Video Clip 8.5.

connectpublic speaking.com
To see a speaker who refers to the introduction, view Video Clip 8.6.

simply because he or she is overweight is as wrong as to deny a person a job because of skin color or ethnic background.

Guidelines for Conclusions

There are four pitfalls to avoid in conclusions.

1.   Don't drag out the ending.   Some speakers fail to prepare a conclusion in advance. When they reach what should be the end of their remarks, they cannot think of a graceful way to wrap things up, so they keep on talking. Other speakers signal the end of their speech (by saying something like "So, in closing, let me say . . ."), but then they drone on and on. This gives false hope to the listeners. When they see that the speaker is not keeping the promise, they feel deceived and become restless.

2.   Don't end weakly.   If you close with a statement such as "I guess that's about all I've got to say," and your voice is nonchalant and unenthusiastic, you encourage your listeners to downgrade your entire speech. End with confidence.

3.   Don't end apologetically.   There is no need to say: "That just about does it. I'm sorry I didn't have more time to prepare . . . ," or: "That's it, folks. I guess I should have looked up more facts on . . ." Apologies make you look incompetent. Besides, some people may not have noticed anything wrong with your speech or your delivery; you may have done better than you realized, so why apologize?

4.   Never bring in new main points.   It is okay to use fresh material in your conclusion; in fact, it is a good idea to do so, as long as the material does not constitute a new main point. Let's say you have given your audience three well-explained techniques for losing weight. It would be a mistake to end by saying, "Oh, yes, and another technique is . . ." This would drag out your speech. On the other hand, it would be acceptable to end with a brief comment about the 10 pounds you lost because you used the techniques discussed in the body of the speech.

Sample Introduction and Conclusion

In the previous chapter, we looked at the body of a speech on cotton swabs. Now let's see how Wendy Trujillo developed an introduction and a conclusion for her speech.[9]

Danger in the Bathroom

General Purpose:	To persuade
Specific Purpose:	To persuade my audience to avoid using cotton swabs in their ears
Central Idea:	For cleaning ears, cotton swabs are dangerous and ineffective.

INTRODUCTION

I. Attention Material
   A. Which item in a typical bathroom sends more people to the hospital emergency department than any other?
      1. Is it razor blades . . . scissors . . . hair dryers?
      2. No, none of these.
   B. The correct answer is cotton swabs, which many people use to clean their ears.

Trujillo opens with a question that is designed to capture the listeners' attention and interest.

II. Orienting Material
   A. Today I would like to show you why you should never put cotton swabs into your ear.
   B. Reason number one: They are dangerous.
   C. Reason number two: They are ineffective.

To give listeners a clear road map of her speech, the speaker states her central idea and main points.

[The body of the speech, which appears in Chapter 7, uses the statement-of-reasons pattern.]

CONCLUSION

I. Summary
   A. We have discussed two reasons why you should never use cotton swabs for cleaning your ears.
   B. First, you risk injury.
   C. Second, you are using a device that is worthless for truly cleaning ears.

Trujillo gives a brief summary of the key information of the speech.

II. Clincher
   A. Dr. George Alexiades of the New York Eye and Ear Infirmary has treated hundreds of people who punctured their eardrums with cotton swabs.
   B. He has some good advice: "Never put anything in your ear smaller than your elbow."

The speaker closes with a humorous quotation that underscores her central idea.

Resources for Review and Skill Building

Summary

Much of the success of a speech depends on how well the speaker handles the introduction and the conclusion. The introduction consists of two parts: attention material, which gains listeners' attention and interest, and orienting material, which gives the audience the information they need to listen intelligently to the rest of the speech.

For attention material, you can use one or more of the following techniques: tell a story, ask a question, make a provocative statement, cite a quotation, arouse curiosity, provide a visual aid or demonstration, and provide the audience with an incentive to listen.

For orienting material, you have three options: give background information, such as definitions; establish your credibility on your topic; and preview the body of the speech (by stating the central idea, the main points, or both).

The introduction should have a direct and obvious tie-in with the body of the speech. Avoid apologies and a too-brief introduction.

The conclusion of your speech should signal the end, summarize your key ideas, and reinforce the central idea with a clincher. A clincher may be an appeal or a challenge, an illustration, a reference to the introduction, or any of the techniques mentioned for attention material (such as a rhetorical question).

Avoid conclusions that are weak, apologetic, or drawn-out. While fresh material may be used, never bring in new main points.

Key Terms

attention material, *219*

clincher, *228*

credibility, *224*

hypothetical illustration, *220*

orienting material, *223*

overt-response question, *221*

preview, *225*

rhetorical question, *220*

Review Questions

1. Why is it necessary to have attention material at the beginning of a speech?
2. What is the purpose of the orienting material in the speech introduction?
3. What is a rhetorical question?
4. What is an overt-response question?
5. How can you give listeners an incentive to listen to a speech?
6. What is credibility?
7. In what way does a preview of main points reassure the audience?
8. Why is it a mistake to end a speech abruptly?
9. What is a clincher?
10. Why should you restate your main points in the conclusion?

Building Critical-Thinking Skills

1. What advice would you give a speaker who says, in the introduction, "This speech may be too technical for you."

2. Create a rhetorical question concerning the destruction of the Central American rain forest.

Building Teamwork Skills

1. In a group, brainstorm possible attention-getters to introduce speeches on
   a. world famine
   b. burglar alarm systems
   c. vacationing in France
   d. overcoming fatigue
   e. finding an honest car repair shop

2. Working in a group, discuss how listeners react when they hear speakers make these apologies:
   a. "I didn't have much time to prepare."
   b. "I'm not much of a speaker."
   c. "I know this is a boring topic."
   d. "I had wanted to show you some PowerPoint slides."
   e. "That last speech is a tough act to follow."
   f. "I hate public speaking."
   g. "I'm really nervous."

As Colombian pop star Shakira gives a speech in Barranquilla, Colombia, she holds speaking notes in her left hand to help herself stay on track and remember key points.

chapter 6

Outlining
the Speech

OUTLINE

OBJECTIVES

After studying this chapter, you
should be able to:

1. Understand the importance of developing an
   outline for a speech.

2. Create a coherent outline for a speech.

3. Create effective speaking notes based on
   your outline.

Architect Santiago Calatrava of Spain has designed some of the world's most interesting and provocative buildings. He plans every building in meticulous detail, using a blueprint to show builders the exact layout and specifications.

Calatrava is also known as an eloquent speaker. In one speech, for example, he said, "Architecture is the greatest of all the arts because it embraces all the others—music, painting, and sculpture." In planning his speeches, Calatrava finds that a valuable tool is an outline, which he says is similar to an architectural blueprint because it creates a global, coherent preview, enabling you to detect flaws.[1]

Many other public speakers (and writers) extol the virtues of an outline, which helps them to organize their thoughts into a logical sequence and to see which points are irrelevant, improperly placed, or poorly developed. It prevents them from rambling.[2]

Outlining is the culmination of the process we began describing many chapters ago—the process of gaining control of our subject matter. Up to this point, we have talked about formulating objectives (Chapter 5), gathering and developing materials (Chapter 6), and then organizing them in the body (Chapter 7) and the introduction and conclusion (Chapter 8). Now we will discuss how to put all these elements together in outline form.

Because some students have trouble understanding how an outline fits into the overall process of speechmaking, I created Figure 9.1. This flowchart shows your next three steps: First, create an outline; second, use the outline to prepare speaking notes; and third, use the speaking notes to deliver the speech. The first two steps will be covered in this chapter; the third step, delivering the speech, will be discussed in Chapter 10. (For your classroom speeches, your instructor may have different guidelines. You should, of course, follow his or her rules.)

Spanish architect Santiago Calatrava explains his design of the Turning Torso apartment tower in Sweden. The 54-floor building turns 90 degrees around its own axis. Calatrava got the idea from seeing a sculpture of the human body in a twisting motion.

Step 1 Create an Outline

This is a slice from a student's outline. An outline is the basic structure of a speaker's ideas in streamlined form. It is not a word-for-word script. A detailed outline (like this one) is used only for preparation. It is not taken to the lectern.

Outline

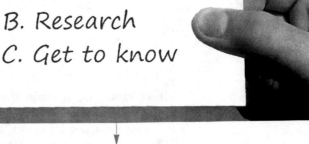

I. Avoid choosing the wrong dog.
A. Never buy on a whim.
B. Research to find the right breed for you.
C. Get to know a dog before adoption.

Step 2 Prepare Speaking Notes

The speaker prepares brief notes—derived from his outline—to be used in practicing and delivering the speech. These notes contain only a few key words—just enough to jog his memory. By using brief notes instead of his outline, he avoids the mistake of reading a speech.

Speaker's notes

I. Wrong dog
A. Never – whim
B. Research
C. Get to know

Step 3 Deliver the Speech

When he delivers the speech, the speaker talks in a natural, conversational manner, glancing at his note cards occasionally to remind himself of his next point.

Speaker's actual words

Do you want to avoid choosing a dog that just isn't right for you? Never buy a dog on the spur of the moment because it's cute. Instead spend time researching the different breeds until you find the best match for your . . .

Figure 9.1
The outline-to-speech process has three steps.

Guidelines for Outlining

Instead of using an outline, why not just write out the entire speech? For one thing, a word-for-word script would create a sea of material that might overwhelm you. Even worse, you might be tempted to read the script, a method that could put the audience to sleep.

An outline is better than a script because it shows the basic structure of your ideas in a streamlined form. It also helps you to see the relationship between ideas.

In essence, outlining is a commonsense way of arranging information in a logical pattern. The Federal Bureau of Investigation's Crime Index, for example, can be broken down into two broad categories:

FBI Crime Index

I. Violent crimes
II. Property crimes
   We could then break down each category into specific types of crimes:

I. Violent crimes
   A. Murder
   B. Rape
   C. Robbery
   D. Aggravated assault
II. Property crimes
   A. Burglary
   B. Larceny-theft
   C. Motor vehicle theft
   D. Arson

connectpublic
speaking.com
For help in outlining your material, use the Outline Tutor.

If we wanted to, we could divide items A, B, C, and D into subcategories. For example, we could break murder down into categories of weapons used, with one category for guns, one for knives, and so on.

The next section offers instructions for formatting your outlines.

Choose an Outline Format

The two most popular formats for outlines are the *topic outline* and the *complete-sentence outline.* Find out if your instructor prefers or requires one or the other. Some instructors and professional speakers recommend using both methods—the topic format in the early stages of preparation (when you are struggling to impose order on your material) and the complete-sentence format in the later stages (when you are refining and polishing your ideas).

Topic Outline

topic outline
a systematic arrangement of ideas, using words and phrases for headings and subheadings

In a **topic outline,** you express your ideas in key words or phrases. The advantage of this format is that it is quicker and easier to prepare than a complete-sentence outline. The FBI Crime Index outline above is a topic outline. Also see the topic outline in Figure 9.2.

Topic Outline	Complete-Sentence Outline
Pre-employment Screening	Pre-employment Screening
I. Presenting self	I. Presenting yourself to a potential employer gives you a chance to highlight your qualifications for a job.
A. Job interview	A. A job interview can show your enthusiasm and commitment.
B. Résumé	B. A résumé summarizes your experience, education, and skills.
II. Testing	II. Testing is used by employers to eliminate unqualified or high-risk applicants.
A. Skills tests	A. Skills tests determine if you have the aptitudes and abilities needed for the job.
B. Physical exams	B. Physical exams determine whether your health will allow you to fulfill the duties of the job.
C. Drug tests	C. Drug tests screen for illegal substances such as cocaine and marijuana.

Figure 9.2
Some speakers use both forms of outlines: the topic outline for early drafts, the complete-sentence outline for refinements.

Complete-Sentence Outline

In the **complete-sentence outline,** all your main points and subpoints are expressed in complete sentences (see Figure 9.2). Unless your instructor tells you otherwise, I recommend that you use complete sentences for your final outline. Here is why: (1) Writing complete sentences forces you to clarify and sharpen your thinking. You are able to go beyond fuzzy, generalized notions and create whole, fully developed ideas. (2) If another person (such as an instructor) helps you with your outline, complete sentences will be easier for him or her to understand than mere phrases, thus enabling that person to give you the best possible critique.

complete-sentence outline
a systematic arrangement of ideas, using complete sentences for headings and subheadings

All the sample outlines in the rest of this book, including the one featured later in this chapter, use the complete-sentence format.

Note of caution: The complete-sentence outline is not your speech written out exactly as you will present it. Rather, it is a representation of your key ideas; the actual speech should elaborate on these ideas. This means that your actual speech will contain many more words than the outline. See Figure 9.1 for an example.

Use Standard Subdivisions

In the standard system of subdividing, you mark your main points with roman numerals (I, II, III, etc.); indent the next level of supporting materials underneath and mark with capital letters (A, B, C, etc.); then go to arabic numerals (1, 2, 3);

Tips for Your Career

We have discussed why you should never exceed your time limit, but what should you do when no time limit is set—that is, when you are invited to speak for as long as you like? The best advice is this: Be brief. Keep it short.

How brief should you be?

- For a short presentation, aim for 5 to 7 minutes—a popular length, especially when several speakers are sharing the podium. *Videomaker*, a magazine for producers of commercial videos, says that the best length for a training video is about 7 minutes. If it's any longer, "people begin to squirm, perhaps because 7 minutes is the length of time between commercials on TV."

- For longer speeches, such as after-dinner addresses, I recommend no more than 20 minutes.

Audiences today prefer—and are getting—shorter and shorter speeches, possibly because television has conditioned people to assimilate only short bursts of material. The demand for brevity is even being voiced in America's churches, which once featured sermons lasting well over an hour. Most ministers today preach for no more than 30 minutes. Donald Macleod, who teaches sermon preparation at Princeton Theological Seminary, tells his seminarians that 18 minutes is the maximum time for an effective sermon.

Whenever you are in doubt about length, remember that if one must err, it is better to err on the side of brevity. If, when you finish a speech, the listeners are still hungering for more wisdom from your mouth, no harm is done. They will probably invite you to come back and speak again. But if you speak so long that they become bored, weary, and sleepy, they will resent you for wasting their time.

---

then to small letters (a, b, c); and if you need to go further, use parentheses with numbers and letters. Here is the standard form:

I. Major division
II. Major division
   A. First-level subdivision
   B. First-level subdivision
      1. Second-level subdivision
      2. Second-level subdivision
         a. Third-level subdivision
         b. Third-level subdivision
            (1) Fourth-level subdivision
            (2) Fourth-level subdivision
   C. First-level subdivision

Notice that each time you subdivide a point, you indent. For most speeches, you will not need to use as many subdivisions as illustrated here.

Avoid Single Subdivisions

Each heading should have at least two subdivisions or none at all. In other words, for every heading marked "A," there should be at least a "B." For every "1" there should be a "2." The reason is obvious: how can you divide something and end up with only one part? If you divide an orange, you must end up with at least two pieces. If you end up with only one, you have not really divided the orange. One problem that arises is how to show on an outline a single example for a particular point. Below is the *wrong* way to handle the problem:

A. Many counterfeiters are turning to items other than paper money.
   1. Counterfeit credit cards now outnumber counterfeit bills.

B. . . .

This is wrong because item "A" cannot logically be divided into just one piece. There are two ways to correct the problem. One way is simply to eliminate the single item and combine it with the heading above:

A. Many counterfeiters are turning to items other than paper money: Counterfeit credit cards now outnumber counterfeit bills.

B. . . .

Another way to handle the problem is not to number the item but simply to identify it in the outline as "example":

A. Many counterfeiters are turning to items other than paper money. Example: Counterfeit credit cards now outnumber counterfeit bills.

B. . . .

Parts of the Outline

The parts of the outline discussed below are keyed to the sample outline presented in the next section. Your instructor may have requirements for your outline that deviate somewhat from the description in these pages. (See Figure 9.3 for a schematic overview of a typical outline.)

1.   Title.   Your outline should have a title, but you *do not actually say it in your speech.* In other words, don't begin your speech by saying, "How to Lose Weight Permanently" or "The title of my speech is 'How to Lose Weight Permanently.'"

If you should not say the title, why have one? For classroom speeches, your instructor may want you to write one simply to give you experience in devising titles. For some out-of-class speeches, a title may be requested so that your speech can be publicized in advance. A catchy title might entice people to come to hear you.

Your title should be brief and descriptive; that is, it should give a clear idea of what your speech is about. For example, "The Increase in Cheerleader Injuries" is a short and helpful guide. If you want an attractive, catchy title, you can use a colorful phrase coupled with a descriptive subtitle– "Nothing to Cheer About: The Increase in Cheerleader Injuries." Here are some other examples:

• Czech It Out! Why You Should Visit Prague

• Are You Being Ripped Off? How to Find an Honest Mechanic

• Ouch! What to Do When a Bee Stings You

2.   Purposes and central idea.   Having your general purpose, specific purpose, and central idea listed on your outline will help you bring into sharp focus the main points and supporting materials.

Your Thoughts ?

On an Internet discussion forum, a student wanted to entice as many people as possible to read his argument for the vegetarian diet, so he used this title: "How to Make a Million Dollars." Is this a blunder or a clever strategy?

SNAKES ON A PLANE

Intriguing titles draw attention to movies—and to speeches.

Figure 9.3
This is an overview of a typical outline. Although this outline shows three main points, a speech may have two or, occasionally, four.

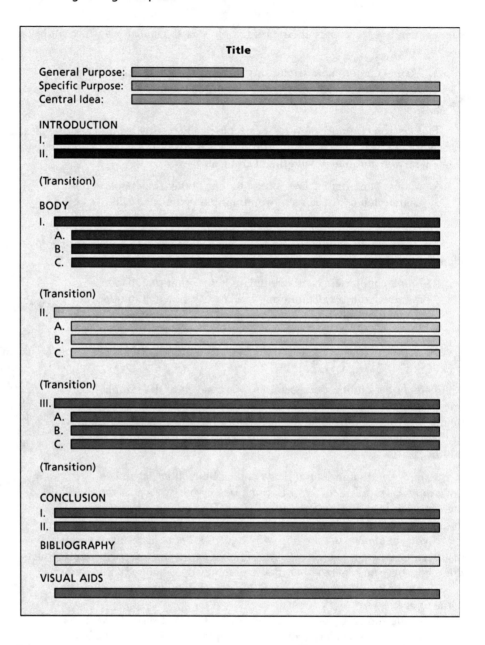

connectpublic
speaking.com
To test your
knowledge of
outline parts, do the
interactive exercise in
Chapter 6.

3.   **Introduction and conclusion.**   The introduction and the conclusion are so vitally important in a speech that they deserve special attention and care. Both sections should have their own numbering sequence, independent of the body of the speech.

4.   **Body.**   In the body of the outline, each main point should be identified by roman numerals. The body has its own numbering sequence, independent of the introduction and conclusion. In other words, the first main point of the body is given roman numeral I.

5.   **Transitions.**   The transitional devices we discussed in Chapter 7 should be inserted in the outline at appropriate places. They are labeled and placed in parentheses, but they are not included in the numbering system of the outline.

Tips for Your Career

You strengthen your credibility with your listeners if you tell them where you got your information. But it would be boring if you read aloud your bibliography. How, then, can you cite sources without bogging down the speech?

Here are two options, which can be used singly or in combination. (For classroom speeches, seek your instructor's guidance on which option to use.)

1. Reveal the key data about your sources as you proceed through the body of your speech.

You could preface new points by saying something like "According to an article in the latest issue of *Communication Education* . . ." or "Writing in *American Heritage* magazine, historian Christine Gibson says . . ."

2. Cite sources in the orienting material of the introduction.

For example, one speaker said, "The information I am giving you today comes from an article by Margaret Zackowitz entitled 'Royal City of the Maya' in *National Geographic* magazine, and from the Web site of the Mexico Tourism Board."

In some situations, you can list your sources on a handout that is provided to listeners at the end of a speech.

While transitional devices should be placed wherever they are needed to help the listener, make sure you have them in at least three crucial places: (1) between the introduction and the body of the speech, (2) between each of the main points, and (3) between the body of the speech and the conclusion.

6. **Bibliography.**   At the end of the outline, place a list of the sources–such as books, magazines, and interviews–that you used in preparing the speech. Give standard bibliographical data in alphabetical order. Check with your instructor to see if he or she wants you to use a special format.

The bibliography is useful not only as a list of sources for your instructor but also as a record if you ever give the speech again and need to return to your sources to refresh your memory or to find additional information.

7. **Visual aids.**   If you plan to use visual aids, give a brief description of them. This will enable the instructor to advise you on whether the visual aids are effective.

Sample Outline with Commentary

Below is an outline for a speech called "Four-Day Work Week–Pros and Cons" by Felipe Dieppa. The video of the speech can be viewed at www.connectpublic speaking.com. In addition, a transcript of the speech is printed at the end of this chapter.

Although the following outline uses the complete-sentence format, your instructor may prefer that you create a topic outline (which we discussed a few pages earlier). In this case, use the same system as here except write words or phrases instead of full sentences.

The speaker's outline uses the topical pattern, dividing the subject into two parts–the case for the four-day work week and the case against it.

The Four-Day Work Week–Pros and Cons

Commentary

Purposes and central idea should appear at the top of the outline to help the speaker stay on target.

General Purpose: To inform

Specific Purpose: To explain to my listeners the pros and cons of the four-day, 10-hour work week

Central Idea: Proponents of the four-day work week say it saves time and money, while opponents stress weariness and scheduling problems.

INTRODUCTION

The introduction has its own label and numbering sequence.

The speaker grabs attention with a provocative question.

I. Attention Material
   A. At work, which would you prefer—8 hours a day or 10 hours?
   B. The traditional work week is 5 days, 8 hours.
   C. Recently some employers have converted to 4 days, 10 hours. (Show poster.) [Figure 9.4]
   D. Either way, the total is 40 hours.

II. Orienting Material

Giving the central idea provides a good preview of the body of the speech.

   A. Advocates say the 4-day week saves money and gives employees a 3-day weekend.
   B. Opponents say long days lead to mistakes and scheduling difficulties.
   C. I am neutral and will discuss both sides.

Transitions are placed in parentheses and are not part of the numbering system.

(*Transition:* Let's begin with the pros.)

BODY

Roman numerals are used for main points.

I. Advocates have strong arguments for the 4-day week.
   A. With one less day of driving, you save money on gas.
      1. Birmingham, AL, switched from 5 days to 4.

Figure 9.4
This poster helps the speaker introduce the topic to the audience.

**4 days
10 hours**

    2. Mayor Larry Langford says employees save $100,000 in gas annually.

B. If you work 4 days, you get a 3-day weekend.

    1. You can have more relaxation time with family and friends.

    2. You can shop and do errands that are hard to do during a work week.

C. You can be happier and more productive.

    1. Employees at software company 37 Signals get a 3-day weekend and return Monday refreshed and happy.

    2. They work very hard during the week so that they won't have to return to the 5-day system.

D. Some companies have switched to the 4-day week to save money.

    1. Wabash National makes trailers in Lafayette, IN.

    2. The 4-day schedule saves on energy bills, janitorial services, and security costs.

E. In 2008, Utah became the first state to set up a 4-day work week.

    1. It was mandatory for all of its 17,000 employees.

    2. The conversion has saved Utah $3 million annually.

(*Transition:* Now let's look at the other side.)

II. Opponents have strong arguments *against* the idea.

A. Working 10 hours can cause weariness, which can lead to mistakes and accidents.

    1. Studies show: the longer you work, the greater the chance of accidents. (*Los Angeles Times*)

    2. Long hours for surgeons, truck drivers, and airline pilots can lead to fatal accidents.

    3. Some companies switched to 10-hour days in the 1970s during an energy crisis, but later switched back to 8 hours.

        a. Chris Stiehl of San Diego worked for a pharmaceutical company that adopted 10-hour days.

        b. "The company experienced an uptick in accidents late in the day" because "people were tired and less careful."

        c. When the crisis eased, the company returned to 8 hours—and accidents decreased.

Under each main point, subpoints are marked with capital letters.

Sub-subpoints are marked with arabic numerals (1, 2, 3).

Each level of subordination is shown by indention.

Transitions are needed between main points.

Audiences like to know the source of information—in this case, a leading newspaper.

Complete sentences are used to make sure all material is clear and well-developed.

Even though complete sentences are used, this outline is not a script to be read aloud. It is just a skeleton of key points. In the speech itself, the speaker expands on the points, using additional words in a conversational-style delivery.

(*continued*)

B. Working 10 hours can cause a decrease in productivity.
  1. An insurance agent posted a message on an Internet discussion forum.
  2. "My brain gets tired," she said, "and I just coast the last two or three hours."
C. Long days can cause problems for some families.
  1. Some parents have trouble fitting in tasks like taking kids to after-school events, preparing dinner, and helping with homework.
  2. Some parents have trouble arranging day care for late in the day.

The final transition prepares the audience for the conclusion.

(*Transition:* Let's sum up.)

The conclusion has its own label and numbering system.

The speaker summarizes the main points.

CONCLUSION

I. Summary
  A. The pros of a 4-day work week are money savings and a 3-day weekend.
  B. The cons are weariness and mistakes and problems with scheduling.
II. Clincher

The speaker's finale uses an interesting anecdote to highlight the pros and cons.

  A. This issue doesn't have easy answers.
  B. My friends all say they prefer a 4-day work week.
  C. But then I ask if they favor it for surgeons, truck drivers, and airline pilots.
  D. Their response: No way!

BIBLIOGRAPHY

The bibliography lists all sources used to prepare the speech.

Sources are listed alphabetically.

Gardner, Marilyn. "Firms Squeeze the Workweek." *Christian Science Monitor* 28 July 2008: 14. Print.

Johnson, Tory, CEO, Women for Hire. Interview on ABC's *Good Morning America.* 15 Aug. 2008. Television.

"Shorter Work Weeks." *Signal vs. Noise*, Weblog of 37 Signals, 20 May 2008. Web. 19 Aug. 2008. <http://www.37signals.com>.

"State Workers: Thank God It's Thursday." Wolters Kluwer Law & Business, 8 July 2008. Web. 19 Aug. 2008. <http://hr.cch.com/news>.

Weikel, Dan. "Over the Long Haul, Fatigue Kills." *Los Angeles Times* 24 Apr. 2005: A1+. Print.

Visual aids should be listed so that the instructor can give guidance.

VISUAL AIDS

Poster showing these words: 4 days/10 hrs.

Speaking Notes

After you have devised an outline, what do you do with it? Do you use it to practice your speech? No. Do you take it with you to the lectern to assist you in the delivery of your speech? No. You use the outline only for *organizing* your ideas. When it comes to *practicing* and then *delivering* the speech, you should use brief **speaking notes** that are based on the outline.

Speaking from brief notes is a good technique because it enables you to look at your audience most of the time, occasionally glancing down to pick up your next point. It encourages you to speak naturally and conversationally.

How about using no notes at all? Would that be even better? No, without notes, you might forget important points, and you might fail to present your ideas in a logical, easy-to-follow sequence.

Notes bolster your sense of security. Even if you are in full command of the content of your speech, you feel more confident and self-assured knowing that you have notes as a safety net to rescue you if your mind goes blank and you fail to recall your next point.

By the way, some people have the idea that using notes is a sign of mental weakness or a lack of self-confidence, but this belief is unfounded. Most good speakers use them without losing the respect of an audience. After all, your notes represent a kind of compliment to your listeners. They show that you care enough about the occasion to spend time getting your best thoughts together in a coherent form. The kind of speaker that audiences *do* look down on is the windbag who stands up without notes and rambles on and on without tying things together.

Guidelines for Preparing Notes

As you read these guidelines, you may want to refer to the sample speaking notes in Figure 9.5.

- Make indentions in your speaking notes that correspond to those in your outline. This will reinforce the structure of the speech in your mind. Some speakers use checkboxes and dashes to signal points; others use the same numbering system that they used in their outline.

- Use only one side of a sheet of paper or note card because you might forget to turn the paper or card over.

- Write down only the minimum number of words or phrases necessary to trigger your memory. If you have too many words written down, you may overlook some key ideas, or you may spend too much time looking at the notes instead of at the audience. Exceptions to this rule are long quotations or statistics that you need to write out in full for the sake of accuracy.

- Write words in large letters that are neat and legible so that you have no trouble seeing them when you glance down during a speech.

- Include cues for effective delivery, such as "SHOW POSTER" and "PAUSE" (see the sample notes in Figure 9.5). Write them in a bright color so that they stand out. (By the way, some speakers find it helpful to use a variety of coded colors on their notes—for example, black for main points, green for support materials, blue for transitions, and red for delivery cues.)

- For speaking, use the same set of notes you used while rehearsing so that you will be thoroughly familiar with the location of items on your prompts.

speaking notes
brief reminders of the points a speaker plans to cover during a speech

connectpublic
speaking.com
For handy guidelines, see "Checklist for Preparing and Delivering a Speech."

Figure 9.5

Here are samples of note cards for the speech about the four-day work week. Only the first two cards are shown.

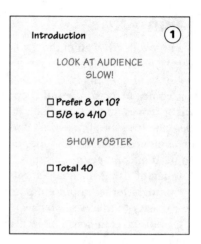

Cues remind the speaker to look at the audience and speak slowly during the introduction.

For reminders, red ink is effective.

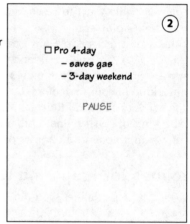

Each card is numbered so that if the speaker accidentally drops or scrambles the cards, they can be put back into order very easily.

Only a few key words are used to jog the speaker's memory.

I once practiced with a set of notes on which I penciled in so many editing marks that I made a fresh set of notes right before I delivered the speech. This turned out to be a mistake because the notes were so new that some of the key words failed to trigger my memory quickly, causing me to falter at several points. I should have stayed with the original notes. Even though they were filled with arrows and insertions and deletions, I knew them intimately; I had a strong mental picture of where each point was located. The new notes, in contrast, had not yet "burned" their image in my brain.

- Don't put your notes on the lectern in advance of your speech. A janitor might think they are trash and toss them out, or a previous speaker might accidentally scoop them up and walk off with them.

Options for Notes

Your instructor may require you to use one particular kind of note system, but if you have a choice, consider using one of these three popular methods.

Option 1: Use Note Cards

Your speaking notes can be put on note cards, as shown in Figure 9.5.

Note cards (especially the 3″ × 5″ size) are compact and rather inconspicuous, and they are easy to hold (especially if there is no lectern on which to place notes). The small size of the card forces you to write just a few key words rather than long sentences that you might be tempted to read aloud verbatim. If you use cards, be sure to number each one in case you drop or scramble them and need to reassemble them quickly.

Option 2: Use a Full Sheet of Paper

If you use a full sheet of paper, you can have the notes for your entire speech spread out in front of you. There are, however, several disadvantages: (1) Because a whole sheet of paper is a large writing surface, many speakers succumb to the temptation to put down copious notes. This hurts them in speech-making because they end up spending too much time looking at their notes and too little time making eye contact with the audience. (2) A full sheet of paper can cause a speaker's eyes to glide over key points because the "map" is so large. (3) If a sheet is brought to the room rolled up, it can curl up on the lectern, much to the speaker's dismay. (4) If a sheet is handheld because no lectern is available, it tends to shake and rustle, distracting listeners. (5) It is harder to make corrections on paper than on note cards. With paper, you may have to rewrite all your notes, whereas with note cards, you can simply delete the card containing the undesired section and write your corrected version on a fresh card.

If you have access to a lectern, you can use several 8.5″ × 11″ sheets in a clever way: put notes only on the top one-third of a sheet, leaving the bottom two-thirds blank. This will help your eye contact because you can glance at your notes without having to bow your head to see notes at the bottom of the page.

A final tip: To avoid the distraction of turning a page over when you have finished with it, simply slide it to the other side of the lectern.

Note cards are effective, but this speaker should have left one hand free for gesturing.

Option 3: Use Visual Aids as Prompts

A popular technique is to use your visual aids (such as PowerPoint slides or posters) as the equivalent of note cards. The visuals jog your memory on what to say next.

This system "allows you to walk around the room, projecting greater confidence than you would if you remained riveted, eyes-to-paper, behind a lectern," according to media consultants Mike Edelhart and Carol Ellison.[3]

If you use this strategy, avoid using a visual aid that is primarily a cue for yourself and has no value for the audience. In other words, design a visual aid for audience enlightenment, not for speaker convenience. Take a look at the notes in Figure 9.5. They are fine on note cards, but if they were displayed on a slide, they would be cryptic to the audience.

The options just discussed do not have to be used exclusively. They can be combined. For example, you could use note cards for part of a speech and visuals as prompts for another part.

Controlling Your Material

While preparing your outline, don't let your material become like an octopus whose tentacles ensnare you and tie you up. You must control your material, rather than letting your material control you. Here are four things you can do to make sure that you stay in control.

1. **Revise your outline and speaking notes whenever they need alterations.**   Some students mistakenly view an outline as a device that plants their feet in concrete; once they have written an outline, they think that they are stuck with it–even if they yearn to make changes. An outline should be treated as a flexible aid that can be altered as you see fit.

2. **Test your outline.**   One of the reasons for creating an outline is to *test* your material to see if it is well-organized, logical, and sufficient. Here are some questions that you should ask yourself as you analyze your outline (in your career, you can ask colleagues to critique your outline, using the same questions):

- Does the introduction provoke interest and give sufficient orienting material?
- Do I preview the central idea and/or main points?
- Do the main points explain or prove my central idea?
- Are the main points organized logically?
- Is there enough support material for each main point? Is there too much?
- Do I have smooth transitions between introduction and body, between main points, and between body and conclusion?
- Have I eliminated extraneous material that doesn't truly relate to my central idea?
- Does my conclusion summarize the main points and reinforce the central idea?
- Is my conclusion strong and effective?

3. **Revise for continuity.**   Often an outline looks good on paper, but when you make your speaking notes and start practicing, you find that some parts are disharmonious, clumsy, or illogical. A speech needs a graceful flow, carrying the audience smoothly from one point to another. If your speech lacks this smooth flow, alter the outline and speaking notes until you achieve a continuity with which you are comfortable. (If you practice in front of friends, ask them to point out parts that are awkward or confusing.)

4. **Make deletions if you are in danger of exceeding your time limit.**   After you make your speaking notes, practice delivering your speech while timing yourself. If the speech exceeds the time limit (set by your instructor or by the people who invited you to speak), go back to your outline and speaking notes and trim them. Deleting material can be painful, especially if you have worked hard to get a particular example or statistic. But it *must* be done, even if you exceed the limit by only five minutes.

Your Thoughts ?

If you practice in front of friends, why is it better to say "Tell me the parts that need improvement" instead of "Tell me if you like this"?

connectpublic speaking.com
View this speech as it was delivered.

Sample Speech as Presented

Earlier we examined the outline and sample notes for Felipe Dieppa's speech about the four-day work week. To view a video of the speech, visit www.connectpublicspeaking.com. A transcript is printed below. Notice that the wording of the actual speech is not identical to that of the outline. The reason is that Felipe Dieppa delivers the speech extemporaneously, guided by brief speaking notes.

The Four-Day Work Week–Pros and Cons

If you have a full-time job, would you rather work 8 hours a day – or 10?

Ever since World War II, the typical work week has consisted of 5 days a week for 8 hours a day – for a total of 40 hours. But in recent years, some companies, schools, and some government agencies have converted to a different work week [*Speaker shows poster in Figure 9.4.*] – 4 days for 10 hours a day. That's a total of 40 hours, of course.

Is the new system better? Some people say it's superior because it helps save time and money. On the other hand, opponents of the idea say that a 10-hour day creates problems with fatigue and scheduling.

Now I am not here to argue for or against. I just want to lay out the pros and the cons, and then you can decide for yourself.

Let's start with the pros. People who argue in favor of the four-day work week have a strong case. They point out that employees save money on gas by traveling to and from work one less day. The mayor of Birmingham, Alabama, Larry Langford, says that after his city switched from five days to four, city employees saved $100,000 on gas each year.

Working only four days a week also means that you have a three-day weekend. You have more time to relax, take trips, go out with your family and friends. You have more time to run other errands that are harder to do during the work week.

Many employees say that a four-day work week makes them happier and more productive. A manager at 37 Signals, a software company in Chicago, says that a 3-day weekend means that employees come back on Monday feeling more relaxed and refreshed. And they work harder and more efficiently during the work week because they don't want to go back to the old system.

Some employers have switched to the four-day system, not only to help employees save money on gas, but to save money for the business or agency. For example, Wabash National, a trailer making company in Lafayette, Indiana, only has their plant open for four days a week to save money on energy bills, janitorial services, and security costs.

The first state to have a mandatory four-day work week for state employees was Utah. That was in 2008. That change affected 17,000 employees. Utah officials estimated the conversion saves the state $3 million a year.

So far, the four-day work week sounds great, but let's look at the other side of the debate. There are strong arguments *against* the four-day work week. A 10-hour day can be very fatiguing, and can cause you to create more mistakes and accidents. *The Los Angeles Times* studied federal accident reports, and concluded that the longer you work, the more problems you can make. When it comes to surgeons and truck drivers and airline pilots, those mistakes can lead to fatal accidents.

In the 1970s there was an energy crisis that caused some companies to convert to the four-day week, but most of these companies eventually shifted back to the five-day week. Why? Chris Stiehl of San Diego gives an insight. He says he was working as an industrial engineer in a pharmaceutical company in the 1970s. After adopting 10-hour days, he says, the company experienced an uptick in accidents. People were tired and less careful. After the gas crisis waned, the company returned to 8 hours a day and the number of accidents dropped.

The 10-hour workday can cause a drop in productivity as well. For example, on an Internet discussion forum, one woman who worked at an insurance agency, said, "My brain gets tired, and I just coast the last two or three hours."

The four-day work week causes family problems as well. On Monday through Thursday, parents have a hard time fulfilling their responsibilities–taking kids to sports and school activities, preparing a family dinner, helping with homework. Sometimes it's hard to arrange for day care so late in the day.

Now let's review. We've seen that some people like the four-day work week because it gives them an extra day, gives them a longer weekend. But opponents say that the shorter work week can lead to fatigue and mistakes and scheduling problems.

This is a tough issue that doesn't have an easy answer. I spent the last week asking my friends which one they would prefer, and when I asked, they all said they prefer the four-day work week. Now when I asked if they preferred longer shifts for people like surgeons, truck drivers and airline pilots, everyone said, No way!

For three other complete outlines and transcripts of speeches, see the samples at the end of Chapters 11, 12, and 13.

Resources for Review and Skill Building

connectpublic
speaking.com

Connect Public Speaking provides resources for study and review, including sample speech videos, an Outline Tutor, and practice tests.

Summary

An outline is as important to a speechmaker as a blueprint is to a builder: the outline provides a detailed plan to help the speaker organize thoughts into a logical sequence and to make sure nothing important is left out.

Two popular types are the topic outline, which uses words and phrases for headings, and the complete-sentence outline, which uses entirely written-out headings. Some speakers use both forms: the topic outline for early drafts and the complete-sentence outline for refinements.

The parts of the outline include title, purposes, central idea, introduction, body, conclusion, transitions, bibliography, and visual aids.

After you complete your outline, prepare speaking notes based on it. You have three options: note cards, a full sheet of paper, or speaking notes displayed as a visual aid. Whichever you choose, avoid writing too many words because when you use notes in a speech, you want to be able to glance down quickly and retrieve just enough words to jog your memory.

Through all these stages, control your material by revising your outline and speaking notes whenever they need alterations. Test the strength of your outline, and revise for continuity—a smooth, logical flow from one part to another. Finally, make deletions if you are in danger of exceeding your time limit.

Key Terms

complete-sentence outline, *239*   speaking notes, *247*   topic outline, *238*

Review Questions

1. Why is an outline recommended for all speeches?

2. What is a topic outline?

3. What are the advantages of using complete sentences in an outline?

4. What are the parts of an outline?

5. The text says that the title of an outline should not be spoken in the speech. Why, then, should you have one?

6. Why should each subdivision of an outline have at least two parts?

7. What are the advantages of using cards for speaking notes?

8. What are the disadvantages of using a full sheet of paper for speaking notes?

9. You are advised to "revise for continuity." What does this mean?

10. What are the advantages of using visual aids as prompts?

Building Critical-Thinking Skills

1. Sort out the following items and place them into a coherent topic outline. In addition to a title, the scrambled list includes four major headings, with three subheadings under each.

   Scrabble, Cameras, Recipes, Ornamentals, Photography, Paintball, Gardening, Digital Imagery, Kitchenware, Annuals, Stoves, Hobbies & Interests, Cooking, Darkroom, Bingo, Perennials, Games

2. Transform the topic outline in the next column into a complete-sentence outline. Create a central idea for the outline.

Research

   I. Library

      A. Printed material

      B. Electronic databases

      C. Audiovisuals

  II. Personal

      A. Experiences

      B. Interviews

      C. Surveys

Building Teamwork Skills

1. Working in a group, create a central idea and a topic outline on one of the following topics. Put each item on a separate index card or slip of paper so that the group can experiment with different sequences. Your outline should have at least three major headings, each of which has at least three subheadings.

   a. automobile drivers

   b. fast food

   c. leisure-time activities

   d. good health

2. In a group, create a *complete-sentence* outline on how to study effectively. Include a central idea, at least three major headings, and at least four tips under each heading.

When Chicago Bears coach Lovie Smith speaks in Miami, Florida, on the eve of Super Bowl XLI, he demonstrates good delivery techniques by looking directly at his listeners and using gestures. Note that he has dressed up—an important way to show respect for the audience and the occasion.

Delivering the Speech

OBJECTIVES

After studying this chapter, you should be able to:

1. Explain the four methods of delivery.

2. Practice and deliver an extemporaneous speech.

3. Use effective vocal techniques in a speech.

4. Demonstrate effective nonverbal communication in a speech.

5. Conduct a question-and-answer period in a manner that encourages audience participation.

6. Utilize productive methods in practicing a speech.

Although Michelle Kwan had skated in front of millions of

people as a world champion figure skater, she was very nervous when she gave her first speech after being appointed by the U.S. State Department as a goodwill ambassador for the United States.

She began her talk in a choked, hesitant voice, she stumbled over her words a few times, she inserted a number of "uh's" into her remarks, her hands were fidgety and trembling, and she looked down at the lectern too often.

After a few minutes, however, a remarkable change occurred. She stopped shaking and stumbling. She looked straight at her audience. Her hands moved with strong gestures. She spoke smoothly and confidently.

How did Kwan change from shaky to polished? "I learned in skating," she said, "if you fall, you quickly get up and keep going." She was determined to succeed, she said, because she wanted to reach every listener with her message—"All of us are alike, and we need to live in peace."

Since that first speech, she has taken her message to audiences in China, Russia, and many other countries, and she has gained a reputation as an effective speaker who creates a strong bond with her listeners.[1]

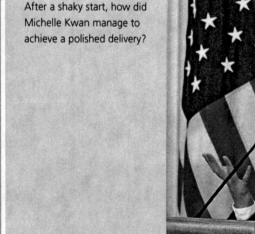

After a shaky start, how did Michelle Kwan manage to achieve a polished delivery?

The Key to Good Delivery

The preceding story about Michelle Kwan exemplifies an important point: *The key to good delivery is a strong desire to communicate with the audience.* Though Kwan started out shaky, she had a burning desire to communicate with the audience, and before long she was unconsciously using good delivery techniques.

Your Thoughts

Is perfect delivery necessary for a speech to be considered highly successful? Defend your answer.

I have seen this phenomenon many times: Speakers who care deeply about conveying their ideas to the audience almost always do an adequate job with their delivery–even if they lack professional polish and training. R. T. Kingman, a General Motors executive, says that if you know what you want to say and if you want everybody in the room to understand your message, "all the other things like looking people in the eye and using good gestures will just come naturally."[2]

I am emphasizing the speaker's desire to communicate so that you can put the ideas of this chapter into proper perspective. The dozens of tips about delivery in the pages that follow are important, and you should study them carefully. But bear in mind that a strong desire to communicate with your audience gives you the power to deliver a speech with energy and effectiveness.

Methods of Speaking

Four basic speaking methods are used by public speakers today: memorization, manuscript, impromptu, and extemporaneous.

Memorization

A few speakers memorize an entire speech and then deliver it without a script or notes. Memorizing is a bad idea for most speakers, however, because of the following liabilities:

- You are forced to spend an enormous amount of time in committing the speech to memory.
- At some point in your speech, you might suddenly forget what comes next. This could cause you to panic. Once derailed, you might be unable to get back on track.
- Even if you remembered your entire speech, you would be speaking from your memory, not from your heart. This could cause you to sound remote and lifeless–more like a robot than a human being.

Memorizing does have one advantage: it lets you figure out your *exact* wording ahead of time. But this gain in precision fails to outweigh the disadvantages. I don't recommend this method.

Manuscript

Some speakers put their entire speech word for word on a **manuscript,** which they read aloud to the audience. In most cases, this is a poor method. Although a few people can read a text effectively, most speakers lack spontaneity and enthusiasm. They fail to look at the audience, fail to speak with adequate expression, and often read too quickly.

manuscript method
delivery of a speech by reading a script

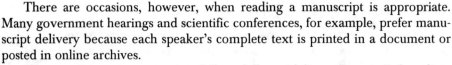

There are occasions, however, when reading a manuscript is appropriate. Many government hearings and scientific conferences, for example, prefer manuscript delivery because each speaker's complete text is printed in a document or posted in online archives.

If you must use a manuscript, follow these guidelines: For ease of reading, print the document in large letters and leave generous spacing between lines. Use a yellow highlighter to mark key words and phrases. Underline words that need to be spoken with extra emphasis. Insert slanting lines to indicate pauses. Practice reading the document many times until you are thoroughly familiar with it.

If you are well-rehearsed, you should be able to look at your audience frequently and make gestures. Because you are using a method that is often boring, try to inject vigor and variety into your voice. Above all else, don't race through the manuscript.

One danger of using a manuscript is failure to look at the audience.

impromptu method
speaking with little or no preparation

Impromptu

Speaking **impromptu** means speaking on the spur of the moment—with no opportunity for extensive preparation. For example, without warning you are asked to give a talk to your fellow employees about your recent conference in Detroit. Or during a meeting, you are asked to explain a new procedure in your department.

Because you have to respond immediately, impromptu speaking can be stressful. Just remind yourself that your listeners realize you are speaking off the cuff—they are not expecting a polished masterpiece. Here are some guidelines for impromptu success:

Decide your conclusion first.   Knowing how you will finish can prevent a long, drawn-out ending or a weak comment like "Well, I guess that's it."

Organize your speech.   You can use an organizational pattern from earlier chapters—for example, the problem-solution pattern—or you might consider one of the ready-made patterns shown in Table 10.1. These patterns are used by experienced speakers to quickly structure impromptu speeches.

Let's explore one of the methods by imagining that you work for an accounting firm that has a standard 9-to-5 schedule, and you want to recommend staggered hours. At a staff meeting, you are asked to make your case. Having only a few moments to prepare, you decide to use the PREP template (Table 10.1). Here is a streamlined version of your remarks:

Position—"I believe that all employees will be happier and more productive if they are permitted to work 11-to-7 for one day a week."

Reason—"With our present 9-to-5 system, many important services are unavailable to us."

Example—"For example, we have no chance to renew a driver's license because the state license office is open only on weekdays, 9-to-5."

Position—"Giving us one 11-to-7 day per week will improve morale because we will be able to meet both professional and personal responsibilities."

Table 10.1
Patterns for Impromptu Speeches

Point-Support-Conclusion

- **Point** (State your point of view—that is, your key idea or objective.)
- **Support** (Give examples, stories, or other support material to explain or prove the point.)
- **Conclusion** (End with a restatement of the point and/or an appeal to action.)

PREP Method

- **Position** (State your position on the topic.)
- **Reason** (State your reason for taking the position.)
- **Example** (Give an example that helps to illuminate or explain your reasoning.)
- **Position** (Summarize and repeat your position.)

Past-Present-Future

- **Point** (State your key point.)
- **Past** (Discuss what happened in the past.)
- **Present** (Talk about what is occurring today.)
- **Future** (Predict what will or could happen in the future.)
- **Point** (Drive home your key point.)

Don't rush.   Speak at a steady, calm rate. At the beginning, and at various intervals, pause for a few seconds to collect your thoughts.

Whenever possible, link your remarks to those of other speakers.   When you take a statement made by a previous speaker and build upon it, you connect with your audience and hold their attention.

Don't feign knowledge.   If you are asked to comment on a matter about which you know nothing, simply say, "I don't know." Don't try to "wing it." Some speakers think that admitting ignorance will hurt their credibility, but the opposite is often true: if you fail to admit your ignorance and try to hide it behind a smokescreen of verbal ramblings, you can look insincere and foolish. In some situations you can say, "I don't know the answer to that, but I'll look into it and get back to you as soon as I can."

Be brief.   Some impromptu speakers talk too long, repeating the same ideas or dwelling on irrelevant matters. They usually do so because they are afraid they are omitting something important, or because they lack a graceful way of closing the speech. Rambling on and on is a certain way to weaken a speech.

Try to foresee situations where you are likely to be called upon to speak impromptu.   Plan what you will say. For example, driving back from a workshop, rehearse in your mind what you will say if the boss asks you to make a little presentation to your colleagues about what you learned.

Extemporaneous

The **extemporaneous method** is the most popular style of speaking in the United States today. The idea is to sound as if you are speaking spontaneously, but instead of giving the clumsy, faltering speech that many off-the-cuff speakers give,

extemporaneous method
delivery of a speech from notes, following extensive preparation and rehearsal

you present a beautifully organized, well-developed speech that you have spent many hours preparing and practicing.

In extemporaneous speaking, you speak from notes, but these notes are not a word-for-word script. Instead, they contain only your basic ideas, expressed in a few key words. When you speak, therefore, you make up the exact words as you go along. You glance at your notes occasionally to remind yourself of your next point, but most of the time you look at the listeners, speaking to them in a natural, conversational tone of voice.

This conversational tone is valued in a speech because it is the easiest kind for an audience to listen to, understand, and remember. When you speak conversationally, you are speaking directly, warmly, sincerely. Your manner is as close as possible to the way you talk to your best friends: Your voice is full of life and color; your words are fresh and vital.

Speaking extemporaneously permits flexibility because you can easily make adjustments to meet the needs of an audience. If, for example, you see that some listeners don't understand a point, you can restate your message in different words. If you are the last speaker of the evening at a banquet and you sense that your audience is about to go to sleep because of the long-winded speakers who preceded you, you can shorten your speech by cutting out minor points.

Despite its advantages, the extemporaneous method can be disastrous if used incorrectly. Here are some common scenarios:

- In a three-point speech, Speaker A looks at his notes, states the first point, and then elaborates on it at great length. He loses track of time—until he finally notices a clock and gallops through the remaining points, confusing the audience.
- Speaker B has notes with key points, but she talks on and on about *all* the points. This causes her to go 20 minutes over her time limit, much to the annoyance of her listeners.
- Speaker C works from carefully crafted notes, but because he has not practiced the speech, his delivery is hesitant and ragged.

To avoid such mistakes, you must spend a lot of time preparing an outline and notes, and then rehearsing your speech, using a clock to make sure you are not ad-libbing too much.

connectpublic speaking.com To contrast effective and ineffective delivery, view "Animal Helpers"—"Needs Improvement Version" and "Improved Version."

Voice

Some people think that to be an excellent speaker, you must have a golden voice, rich and resonant, that enthralls listeners. This is not true. Some of the greatest orators in history had imperfect voices. Abraham Lincoln's voice was described by his contemporaries as "thin, high-pitched, shrill, not musical, and . . . disagreeable"[3] and Winston Churchill "stammered and even had a slight lisp."[4] It is nice to have a rich, resonant voice, but other characteristics of the human voice are more important—volume, clarity, and expressiveness. Let's examine all three.

Volume

The larger the room, the louder you have to speak. You can tell if your volume is loud enough by observing the people in the back. Are they leaning forward with quizzical expressions as they strain to hear your words? Then obviously you need

Tips for Your Career

Tip 10.1   It's Okay to Cry

When one of my students, Sarah Mowery, was showing me her outline for a speech on drowsy driving, she told me that she planned to eliminate a photo and story about a close friend who had died after falling asleep at the wheel.

"But why?" I said. "That would be the most powerful part of your speech."

"I'm afraid I'd break down and cry," she replied.

I convinced her to keep the photo and story in the speech, and I told her a technique that I have used successfully when I deliver a eulogy at a funeral: As part of your preparation, accept the fact that you might be overcome with emotion. Have a handkerchief or tissue in your pocket or even in your hand. Tell yourself that tears are appropriate and that the audience will be sympathetic. Just making these preparations may be all that is necessary—I have never had to actually use my handkerchief.

In Mowery's situation (a classroom speech), the audience would not be expecting deep emotion, so I recommended that she hold a tissue in her hand and say, "Now I am going to tell you a sad story. I hope I can tell it without crying, but if I do cry, I am sure you will understand." Mowery followed this advice, and she ended up not crying at all.

But if she had cried, so what? The death of a close friend is a good reason to cry. Don't be afraid to show emotions. Listeners are very understanding, and some of them may join you in shedding tears.

One note of caution: Don't let tears cause you to end your speech prematurely. Pause, pull yourself together, and continue.

Jim Fordice, son of former Mississippi Governor Kirk Fordice, pauses in his eulogy to his father to wipe away tears. Fordice wisely kept a box of tissues nearby.

to speak louder. You may have to raise your voice to overcome noises, such as the chatter of people in a hallway or the clatter of dishes during a banquet.

Speaking loudly enough for all to hear does not mean shouting. It means *projecting* your voice a bit beyond its normal range. If you have never spoken to a large group or if your instructor tells you that you have problems in projecting your voice, practice with a friend. Find an empty classroom, have your friend sit in the back row, and practice speaking with extra force—not shouting—so that your friend can hear you easily.

If you will be using a microphone, go to the meeting site early and spend a few minutes testing it. Adjust it to your height. If someone readjusts it during the ceremonies, spend a few moments getting it just right for you. Your audience will not mind the slight delay. Position it so that you can forget that it is there. This frees you to speak naturally, without having to bend over or lean forward.

When you speak into a mike, your voice will sound better if your mouth is 6 to 12 inches away. And remember this: You don't need to raise your voice. In fact, says professional speaker Arnold "Nick" Carter, "the invention of the microphone made it possible for me to speak to 18,000 people with a whisper."[5]

Clarity

Spoken English is sometimes radically different from written English, as this news item demonstrates:

> One group of English-speaking Japanese who moved to the United States as employees of Toyota had to enroll in a special course to learn that "Jeat yet?" means "Did you eat yet?" and that "Cannahepya?" means "Can I help you?" Their English classes in Japan had failed to prepare them for "Waddayathink?" (What do you think?), "Watchadoin?" (What are you doing?), and "Dunno" (I don't know).[6]

articulation
the act of producing vocal sounds

For many speakers of English, **articulation**—the production of speech sounds by our vocal organs—is lazy and weak, especially in daily conversations. We slur sounds, drop syllables, and mumble words. While poor articulation may not hurt us in conversation as long as our friends understand what we are saying, it can hinder communication in a speech, especially if English is a second language for some of our listeners. We need to enunciate our words crisply and precisely to make sure that everything we say is intelligible.

If you tend to slur words, you can improve your speech by reading poems or essays aloud 15 minutes a day for three weeks. Say the words with exaggerated emphasis, and move your mouth and tongue vigorously. Enunciate consonants firmly and make vowel sounds last longer than normal. In real situations, you should not exaggerate in this way, but the practice will help you avoid the pitfalls of slurring and mumbling.

pronunciation
correct way of speaking a word

While poor articulation stems from sloppy habits, poor **pronunciation** is a matter of not knowing the correct way to say a word. Examine the common pronunciation mistakes listed in Table 10.2 .[7]

Be careful using words that you have picked up from books but have never heard pronounced. One student had read about the Sioux Indians but had never heard the tribal name pronounced—he called them the *sigh-ox*. Another common slip is to confuse words that sound alike. For example, one student said that a man and woman contemplating marriage should make sure they are compatible before they say their *vowels*. (One listener couldn't resist asking, at the

	Incorrect	Correct
across	uh-crost	uh-cross
athlete	ath-uh-lete	ath-lete
burglar	burg-you-lur	burg-lur
chef	tchef	shef
chic	chick	sheek
drowned	drown-did	drownd
electoral	e-lec-tor-ee-al	e-lec-tur-al
environment	en-vire-uh-ment	en-vi-run-ment
et cetera	ek-cetera	et-cetera
evening	eve-uh-ning	eve-ning
grievous	greev-ee-us	greev-us
height	hithe	hite
hundred	hun-derd	hun-dred
library	li-berry	li-brar-y
mischievous	miss-chee-vee-us	miss-chuh-vus
nuclear	nu-cu-lar	nu-cle-ar
perspiration	press-pi-ra-tion	per-spi-ra-tion
picture	pitch-er	pick-shur
pretty	pur-tee	prit-ee
professor	pur-fess-ur	pruh-fess-ur
quiet	quite	kwy-it
realtor	reel-uh-tor	re-ul-tor
recognize	reck-uh-nize	rec-og-nize
relevant	rev-uh-lant	rel-uh-vant
strength	strenth	strength

Table 10.2
Common Pronunciation Mistakes

end of the speech, whether consonants were also important for marriage.) You can avoid such mistakes by practicing a speech in front of friends or colleagues and asking them to flag errors.

Expressiveness

A dynamic speaker has a voice that is warm and expressive, producing a rich variety of sounds. Let's examine five basic elements of expressiveness.

Pitch and Intonation

The highness or lowness of your voice is called **pitch.** The ups and downs of pitch—called **intonation** patterns—give our language its distinctive melody. Consider the following sentence: "I believe in love." Say it in a variety of ways— with sincerity, with sarcasm, with humor, with puzzlement. Each time you say it, you are using a different intonation pattern.

pitch
the highness or lowness of a sound

intonation
the use of changing pitch to convey meaning

In conversation, almost everyone uses a variety of intonation patterns and emphasizes particular words, but in public speaking, some speakers fail to use any variety at all. Instead, they speak in a monotone—a dull, flat drone that will put many listeners to sleep. Even worse, they run the risk of appearing insincere. They may say something dramatic like "This crime is a terrible tragedy for America," but say it in such a flat way that the audience thinks they don't really mean it.

An absence of intonation also means that some words fail to receive the emphasis they deserve. For example, take a sentence like this: "Mr. Smith made $600,000 last year, while Mr. Jones made $6,000." A speaker who talks in a monotone will say the two figures as if there were no difference between $600,000 and $6,000. But to help listeners hear the disparity, the speaker should let his or her voice place heavy emphasis on the $600,000.

Loudness and Softness

Besides using the proper volume so that everyone in the audience can hear you, you can raise or lower your voice for dramatic effect or to emphasize a point. Try saying the following out loud:

> *(Soft:)* "Should we give in to the kidnappers' demands? *(Switch to loud:)* NEVER!"

Did you notice that raising your voice for the last word conveys that you truly mean what you say? Now try another selection out loud:

> *(Start softly and make your voice grow louder as you near the end of this sentence:)* Edwin Arlington Robinson's character Richard Cory had everything that a man could want—good looks, lots of money, popularity. *(Now make your voice switch to soft:)* But he went home one night and put a bullet through his head.

Changing from loud to soft helps the listeners *feel* the tragic discrepancy between Richard Cory's outward appearance and his inner reality.

Rate of Speaking

How quickly or slowly should you speak? It all depends on the situation. If you are describing a thrilling high-speed police chase, a rapid rate is appropriate, but if you are explaining a technical, hard-to-understand concept, a slow pace is preferred.

One of the biggest mistakes inexperienced speakers make is speaking too fast. It is especially important that you speak at a deliberate rate during your introduction. Have you ever noticed how TV dramas start? They don't divulge important details of the story until you are three or four minutes into the show. One obvious reason for this is to have mercy on late-arriving viewers, but the main reason is to give you a chance to "tune in" to the story and meet the characters. If too much action takes place in the first minute, you are unable to absorb the story. Likewise, when you are a speaker, you need to give your audience a chance to "tune in" to you, to get accustomed to your voice and subject matter. If you race through your introduction, they may become lost and confused.

Speaking at a deliberate, unhurried pace helps you come across as someone who is confident and in control, as someone who cares about whether the listeners understand.

Pauses

When you read printed material, you have punctuation marks to help you make sense out of your reading. In a speech, there are no punctuation marks, so listeners must rely on your oral cues to guide them. One of these cues is the pause, which lets your listeners know when you have finished one thought and are ready to go to the next. Audiences appreciate a pause; it gives them time to digest what you have said.

A pause before an important idea or the climax of a story can be effective in creating suspense. For example, student speaker Stephanie Johnson told of an adventure she had while camping:

> It was late at night when I finally crawled into my sleeping bag. The fire had died down, but the moon cast a faint, spooky light on our campsite. I must have been asleep a couple of hours when I suddenly woke up. Something was brushing up against my sleeping bag. My heart started pounding like crazy. I peeked out of the slit I had left for air. Do you know what I saw? *[pause]*

By pausing at this point, Johnson had the audience on the edge of their chairs. What was it? A bear? A human intruder? After a few moments of dramatic tension, she ended the suspense: "By the light of the moon, I could see a dark little animal with a distinctive white stripe. *[pause]* It was a skunk."

A pause also can be used to emphasize an important statement. It is a way of saying, "Let this sink in." Notice how Yvette Ortiz, a political science professor, used pauses in a speech on community service:

> When I am tempted to reject those ignorant fools who disagree with me, I remind myself of the words of novelist Peter De Vries: "We are not primarily put on this earth to see through one another, *[pause]* but to see one another through." *[pause]*[8]

In some speeches, you may find yourself pausing not because you want to but because you have forgotten what you were planning to say next and you need to glance at your notes. Or you may pause while searching your mind for the right word. Such a pause seems like an eternity, so you are tempted to use **verbal fillers** such as "uh," "er," or "um." Instead, remain silent, and don't worry that your silence is a "mistake." A few such pauses can show the audience that you are conscientious speaker who is concerned about using the most precise words possible.

verbal fillers
vocalized pauses in which a speaker inserts sounds such as "uh"

Conversational Quality

Some inexperienced speakers give their speeches in a dull, plodding voice. Yet five minutes afterward, chatting with their friends in the hall, they speak with animation and warmth.

They need to bring that same conversational quality into their speeches. How can this be done? How can a person sound as lively and as "real" when talking to 30 people as when chatting with a friend? Here are two suggestions:

1. Treat your audience not as a blur of faces but as a collection of individuals.   Here's a mental ploy you can use: at the beginning of a speech, look at one or two individuals in different parts of the room and act as if you are talking to them personally. You should avoid staring, of course, but looking at each face briefly will help you develop a conversational attitude. As the speech goes on, add other faces to your "conversation."

connectpublic
speaking.com
View Video Clip 10.2,
Conversational Style
of Speaking: "How
to Make Avocado
Salsa."

2. Be yourself—but somewhat intensified.　To speak to an audience with the same natural, conversational tone you use with your friends, you must speak with greater energy and forcefulness. We are not talking now about projecting your voice so that the people can hear you but, rather, about *intensifying* the emotional tones and the vibrancy of your voice. How can you do this? Here are two ways:

First, let your natural enthusiasm show. If you have chosen a topic wisely, you are speaking on something you care about and want to communicate. When you stand in front of your audience, don't hold yourself back; let your voice convey all the enthusiasm that you feel inside. Many speakers are afraid they will look or sound ridiculous if they get involved with their subject. "I'll come on too strong," they say. But the truth is that your audience will appreciate your energy and zest. Think back to the speakers you have heard: Didn't you respond best to those who were alive and enthusiastic?

Second, practice loosening up. Some novice speakers sound and look stiff because they simply have had no practice in loosening up. Here is something you can try: Find a private location. For subject matter, you can practice a speech you are working on, recite poetry, read from a magazine, or simply ad-lib. Whatever words you use, say them dramatically. Ham it up. Be theatrical. Act as if you are running for president and you are trying to persuade an audience of 10,000 people to vote for you. Or act as if you are giving a poetry reading to 500 of your most enthusiastic fans. You will not speak so dramatically to a real audience, of course, but the practice in "letting go" will help you break out of your normal reserve. It will help you learn to be yourself, to convey your natural enthusiasm.

Nonverbal Communication

nonverbal communication
transmission of messages without words

Nonverbal communication consists of the messages that you send without words—what you convey with your eyes, facial expression, posture, body movement, and the characteristics of your voice (as discussed in the preceding section).

To be credible to your audience, your nonverbal communication must be synchronized with your words. If you say, "I'm very happy to be here," but your eyes are cast downward and your face is glum, your audience will think that you are not being honest. *Whenever there is a discrepancy between "body language" and words, listeners will believe the nonverbal signals instead of the verbal message.*[9]

We don't know their words, but what does their "body language" say?

To get your nonverbal signals synchronized with your words, show enthusiasm (with your eyes, facial expression, posture, and tone of voice) as you speak. But you may be asking, "What if I don't really feel happy and confident? I can't lie with my body, can I?" This is a good question, because there are times when you don't want to speak or don't feel like standing up in front of a group. At times like these, what should you do?

Pretend. Yes, pretend to be confident in yourself and in your ideas. Pretend to be glad to appear before your audience. Pretend to be enthusiastic. But, you may ask, isn't this phony? Isn't this forcing the body to tell a lie? Yes, but we often must simulate cheerfulness and animation: a crucial job interview, a conference with the boss, an important date with someone we love. By *acting* as if we are confident, poised, and enthusiastic, we often find that after a few minutes, the pretense gives way to reality. We truly become confident, poised, and enthusiastic.

Consider the comedians and talk-show hosts who appear night after night on TV. Do you think they are always "up"? No. Like you and me, they have their bad days. Nevertheless, they force themselves to perform and pretend to be enthusiastic. After about 60 seconds, most of them report, the pretense gives way to reality and they truly *are* enthusiastic. (*A word of advice:* If this transformation fails to happen to you—if you don't feel enthusiastic after a few minutes—you should continue to pretend.)

How can you make your body "lie" for you? By knowing and using the signals that the body sends out to show confidence and energy. The following discussion of the major nonverbal aspects of public speaking will help you become aware of these signals.

Personal Appearance

Your audience will size up your personal appearance and start forming opinions about you even before you open your mouth to begin your speech. You should be clean, well-groomed, and attractively dressed.

Janet Stone and Jane Bachner, who conduct workshops for women executives, have some good advice for both men and women:

> As a general rule of thumb, find out what the audience will be wearing and then wear something yourself that is just a trifle dressier than their clothes. The idea is to establish yourself as "The Speaker," to set yourself slightly apart from the crowd . . .[10]

Dressing up carefully is a compliment to the audience, sending a nonverbal message: You are important to me—so important that I dressed up a bit to show my respect for you.

Don't wear anything that distracts or diminishes communication. Baseball caps tend to hinder eye contact, and to some listeners, they suggest disrespect. A T-shirt with a ribald or controversial slogan printed on the front may direct attention away from the speech itself, and it may offend some members of the audience.

Some students have trouble accepting the idea of dressing up. Isn't it true, they say, that people should be judged by their character and not by their clothes? Yes, but in the real world, you *are* judged by what you wear. In the words of one magazine article title: "What You Wear Is Almost as Important as What You Say."[11] This is an exaggeration, of course, but the point is important: How you dress does make a difference.

Your Thoughts

What nonverbal message is given by a person who goes to a funeral dressed in a T-shirt and jeans?

Eye Contact

Look at your audience 95 percent of the time. Good eye contact is important because: (1) It creates an important bond of communication and rapport between you and your listeners. It is, in the words of Jack Valenti, former president of the Motion Picture Association of America, a "figurative handshake."[12] (2) It shows your sincerity. We distrust people who won't look at us openly and candidly. (3) It enables you to get audience feedback. For example, did a number of listeners look puzzled when you made your last statement? Then you obviously confused them; you need to explain your point in a different way.

The biggest spoiler of good eye contact is looking at your notes too much—a mistake that is usually made for these two reasons: (1) You are unprepared. This can be corrected by rehearsing your speech so many times that you need only glance at your notes to remind yourself of what comes next. (2) You are nervous.

Some speakers are well-prepared and don't really need to look at their notes very often, but they are so nervous that they scrutinize their notes to gain security and avoid the audience. One way to correct this is to put reminders, in giant red letters, on your notes–LOOK AT AUDIENCE–to nudge you out of this habit.

Another killer of eye contact is handouts. As we discussed in Chapter 6, you should never distribute a handout during a speech unless it is simple and short. If you give listeners an eight-page packet during your speech, you will lose eye communication.

Eye contact is more than glancing at the audience from time to time. It is more than mechanically moving your head from side to side like an oscillating fan. For a large audience, the best technique is to have a "conversation" with three or four people in different parts of the room (so that you seem to be giving your attention to the entire audience). For a small audience, look at *every* listener. Professional speaker Danny Cox uses a technique called "locking" whenever he speaks to a small gathering:

> I learned something once from a piano player. I couldn't believe how she held an audience in a cocktail bar. It was so quiet in there you couldn't believe it. I realized one night what she was doing. She was looking at each person and as soon as she made eye contact with them, she smiled at them. And then moved on to the next one, and smiled. She was "locking" everybody in. This is a good technique in public speaking—very simple, too.[13]

Facial Expressions

Let your face express whatever emotion is appropriate during your speech. One student told me he was planning to speak on how to perform under pressure; his primary example was the thrilling moment in high school when he kicked the winning field goal in the final seconds of a championship football game. As he talked to me, his face was suffused with excitement. But when he got up in front of the class and told the same story, his face was blank. Gone was the joy; gone was the exhilaration. Without expression, he weakened the impact of the story.

Whatever your subject matter might be, your face should be animated. "Animation," says speech consultant Dorothy Sarnoff, "is the greatest cosmetic you can use, and it doesn't cost a cent. Animation is energy in the face. . . . It's action that comes not only through the eyes, but around the mouth and the whole face. It tells the listener you're glad to be right where you are–at the lectern, around a conference table or across a desk."[14] How can you make your face animated? By choosing a subject you care about, by having a strong desire to communicate your message to your listeners, and by delivering your speech with energy and enthusiasm.

Posture

posture
the position of your body
as you sit or stand

Good **posture** conveys confidence. Stand up straight, with your weight equally distributed on your feet so that you appear stable and assured. Avoid two common pitfalls–slouching and drooping at one extreme, and being rigid and tense at the other extreme. Your goal should be relaxed alertness–in other words, be relaxed but not *too* relaxed.

If you are speaking at a lectern, here are some things *not* to do: Don't lean on it. Don't slouch to one side of it. Don't prop your feet on its base. Don't rock back and forth with it.

Tips for Your Career

Experienced speakers disagree about whether a lectern should be used for career and community speeches. Some say that a lectern gives the speaker dignity and is a convenient stand for notes, especially on formal occasions such as an awards ceremony or a funeral. Others object that a lectern creates a physical barrier. "I don't want anything coming between me and my audience," a politician told me. British speech consultant Cristina Stuart says, "I am 5'2" and some lecterns are 4'0" high, so how can I be a powerful speaker if my listeners can only see my head peeping over the edge?" Her advice: "Even if you are over six feet tall, try to stand to one side of the lectern so that you can refer to your notes and your listeners can see all of your body."

Here is a technique that has become popular: using the lectern as "home base," walk a few paces to the left or right of it each time you make a point. In other words, glance at the notes on the lectern to remind yourself of the point you want to make, move away from the lectern a few paces, make the point, then walk back to the lectern to pick up your next point.

If a lectern is movable, some speakers remove it and simply hold their note cards in one hand (leaving the other hand free for gesturing). For a large audience, if the lectern is unmovable and has a stationary microphone, says Stuart, "you have no choice but to stand behind it. Stand on a box if you are short so that your upper body can be seen."

With some audiences, you can arrange for a remote or mobile microphone so that you can move away from the lectern.

Some speakers like to sit on the edge of a desk to deliver a speech. This posture is fine for one-hour classroom lectures because the speaker gets a chance to relax, and his or her body language conveys openness and informality. But for short speeches, especially the kind you are expected to deliver in a public speaking class, stand up. This will help to make you alert and enthusiastic.

Movement

You don't have to stand in one place throughout your speech. Movement gives your body a chance to dissipate nervous energy. It also can be used to recapture your listeners' attention if they are getting bored or tired; an animated speaker is easier to follow than an unanimated speaker who stays frozen in one spot.

You can use movement to emphasize a transition from one point to the next. (For example, walk a few steps to the left of the lectern as you say, "Now that we have examined the problem, let's discuss the solution.") You can move *toward* your listeners when you plead for an immediate response (for example, "Please donate five dollars to help find a cure for cystic fibrosis").

Make sure that all movements are purposeful and confident—not random and nervous. If you pace like a tiger in a cage, your audience will be distracted and even annoyed. Don't sway back and forth; don't rock on your heels. In short, make your movements add to your speech, rather than subtract from it.

Using Notes

For classroom speeches, your instructor will tell you whether you may use notes. For speeches in your career, the note system that was explained in Chapter 9 is highly recommended.

Most professional speakers use cards or sheets of paper, and they have different ways of using them. Speakers who use a lectern place their notes in a stack on the lectern and consult one at a time, or they spread notes out so that several are

connectpublic
speaking.com
View Video Clip 10.3,
Speaking with Notes:
"Humanoid Robots.

visible at a time. Speakers who don't use a lectern prefer to hold their notes in one hand while gesturing with the other.

Whatever system you use, remember our earlier warning: *Use notes sparingly.* Look at your audience 95 percent of the time.

Gestures

Making gestures with your hands and arms can add power to your words, and cause you to look animated and engaged. Except in a few cases (discussed below), gestures should be natural and unplanned. They should occur spontaneously and be in harmony with what you are saying.

At all times, have at least one hand free to make gestures. To help yourself abide by this rule: (1) Don't grip the lectern with your hands. (2) Don't clutch your notes with both hands. (3) Don't stuff both hands into your pockets.

If you use a lectern, don't let it hide your gestures. Some speakers rest their hands on the lectern and make tiny, flickering gestures that can be sensed but not seen by the audience. This makes the speaker look tentative and unsure.

When you make gestures, use all of your arm, advises British speech consultant Cristina Stuart:

Don't tuck in your elbows to your waist or make jerky, half-hearted, meaningless gestures. I remember a tall woman in one of my courses who, through shyness, stood hunched up, making tiny movements with her hands. We advised her to

Your Thoughts **?**

Italians tend to use big gestures, and they gesture more frequently than the typical American. Should an American speaker try to imitate the style of Italian speakers? Defend your answer.

Gustavo Kuerten of Brazil announces his retirement in São Paulo after a career as one of the world's top professional tennis players. Note his delivery techniques: he looks at his audience, he has good posture, and he holds a microphone with one hand while using the other hand to gesture.

stand tall, make eye contact, and use her arms to express her enthusiasm. The result was startling—she became regal and was very impressive. Without even opening her mouth, she looked like a self-confident, interesting speaker.[15]

Some speeches call for lots of gestures; some call for few or none. If you were describing your battle to catch a huge fish, you would find your hands and arms constantly in motion; if you were giving a funeral eulogy, you might not make any gestures at all.

While most gestures should occur naturally, there are a few occasions when it is appropriate to plan and rehearse them. If you have three major points to make, you can practice holding up the correct number of fingers. If you are discussing two contrasting ideas, you can hold up one hand when you say, "On the one hand . . ." and then hold up your other when you say, "On the other hand . . ."

connectpublic
speaking.com
To see a speaker who
uses gestures well,
view "How to Hide
Valuables."

The larger the audience, the more sweeping your gestures should be. Evangelists and political leaders who use broad, expansive arm movements in addressing multitudes in giant stadiums are doing so for a good reason: they are able to establish a bond with people who are hundreds of yards away. Small gestures would be lost in the vastness of the arena.

Some students worry too much about gestures. If you are the kind of person who simply does not gesture a great deal, don't be dismayed. Just be sure to keep at least one hand free so that if a gesture wells up, you will be able to make it naturally and forcefully.

One final note about your hands: make sure they do nothing to distract the audience. Don't let them jingle keys, riffle note cards, fiddle with jewelry, adjust clothes, smooth your hair, rub your chin, or scratch any part of your body.

Beginning and Ending

First impressions are important, especially in a speech, where "you have only one chance to make a first impression," as one IBM executive told me. You make this first impression as you walk to the front and as you say your first few words.

When you rise from your seat, avoid sighing or groaning. Walk forward with an air of confidence. Avoid the mistake of rushing forward and starting to speak even before you get to the front. Listeners need time to get settled for your speech, clear their minds of other things, and tune in to you.

When you face your audience, pause a few seconds. Don't say a word–just stand in silence. Some inexperienced speakers are terrified by this silence; they think it makes them look too frozen with fear to speak. If you have this concern, relax. A brief period of silence is an effective technique that all good speakers use. It is a punctuation device, separating what went before from what is to come–your speech. It creates drama, giving the audience a sense of anticipation. In some cases, you may need to wait longer than a few seconds. If you are speaking at a community meeting, for example, and people are arriving late, it is best to wait until the noise created by the latecomers has settled down. Or if many members of the audience are chatting with one another, simply stand and wait until you have their attention.

During these opening moments of silence, you have a chance to make sure your notes are in order and to review once again what you will say in your introduction. The next step is very important. Before you say a word, give your audience a friendly, confident look (if possible and appropriate, smile) and then, continuing to look at your listeners instead of at your notes, say your first few sentences. You

Tips for Your Career

Tip 10.3   Deal with Distractions in a Direct but Good-Humored Manner

In classroom speeches, you should have an attentive, courteous audience, but at some point in your career, you may encounter an audience that contains listeners who chat among themselves while you are trying to speak, distracting other listeners.

Professional speakers stress that you should *not* ignore disturbances. Confront these listeners, but do so in a calm, friendly, good-humored manner.

One technique is to simply stop your speech and look directly at the rude listeners (Try to look friendly and not irritated.) This is often all it takes to cause the persons to stop talking. Sometimes people sitting near the offenders will pick up on your cue and help you out by turning and saying, "shh."

Professional speaker Rosita Perez of Brandon, Florida, says that you may lose the respect of your entire audience if you ignore the talkative few. "Confront them *kindly*," she advises. "Say, 'It seems to me you must have a lot of catching up to do with your friends. I wonder if you would visit outside so I can continue?'" In most such cases, the listeners will stay in the room and give the speaker respectful silence for the rest of the speech.

Speech consultant Sandy Linver says that with a large audience,

> I take the trouble to gently zero in on . . . the chatterers and pull them back in. I say something like, "Are you with me?". . . If it's a small group, side conversations often are important to the subject at hand, so it is important not to ignore them. If I were speaking at a business meeting of 15 people or so, I might say to the 3 people talking among themselves, "That looks as if it might be important. Would you like to share it with the group?" Often they are discussing something I have said that needs clarification or elaboration, and the whole group benefits when they are encouraged to speak up.

A crying baby and a cell phone are a double distraction.

Some speeches are marred by the incessant crying of a baby. Actor and orator Steve Allen once handled this situation by saying, "As the father of four sons I've more than once been in the position of the parents of that child. Personally I could go on even if there were several children crying at the same time, but I know that most people are too distracted by that sort of thing to concentrate on what is being said. So if you wouldn't mind taking the child out—at least until he stops crying—I'm sure the rest of our audience would appreciate it." This remark, says Allen, prompted applause from the audience and "gracious cooperation from the parents."

Some speeches are marred by listeners with electronic devices. For advice on how to handle these situations, see Tip 3.3, "Confront Electronic Rudeness," in Chapter 3.

should have practiced your introduction thoroughly so that you can say it without looking down at your notes. It is important to establish eye contact at this point. By looking at the listeners directly, your body language is saying, "I'm talking to you–I'm not up here just going through the motions of making a speech. I want to communicate. I want to reach out to you."

While first impressions are vital, final impressions are also important. Your conclusion should be well-rehearsed (though not memorized) so that you can say it without looking at your notes. At the end of your speech, pause a few moments, look at your audience, and say, "I wonder what questions you have" or "I'll be happy to answer your questions now." Avoid gathering up your papers and leaning toward your seat—this sends a nonverbal message: "Please don't ask me any questions."

The Question-and-Answer Period

The question-and-answer period enables listeners to get clarification and further information about your topic. In classroom speeches, it usually involves only a small percentage of the total time spent in front of the audience, but in some career presentations—such as selling a product—it is the longest and most important part.

Many listeners are so accustomed to listener–speaker interaction that they will interrupt during a speech to ask questions. In some technical presentations or classroom lectures, such interruptions may be appropriate and acceptable, but in other speeches, they are a nuisance. The continuity of the speaker's remarks is broken because listeners are prematurely asking questions that will be answered later in the speech. If you feel that your speech would be marred by interruptions, you should announce (in the orienting material of your introduction), "I know many of you will have questions. I'd like to ask you to hold them until I finish my presentation and then I'll be happy to try to answer them."

Why is the Q & A period considered vital in many presentations?

Don't feel defeated if you are not asked any questions. It could mean that you have covered everything so well that the listeners truly have nothing to ask.

Here are some guidelines:

Planning

- Find out ahead of time if the person planning the program will want or permit a question-and-answer period, and, if so, how much time will be allotted.
- Plan for the question-and-answer period by jotting down all the questions that might come from the audience and decide how you would answer them. Also discuss your speech with a few friends or associates and ask them to prepare a list of possible questions.

Fielding Questions

- Give the audience time to ask their questions. Some speakers impatiently wait 3 seconds, and then dash back to their seats. They don't really give the audience a fair chance. When you ask for questions, pause for as long as 10 seconds. If you get the feeling that no questions at all will be asked, you can say, "Thank you," and then sit down. But if you sense that the audience is simply shy, you can break the ice by saying, "One question that I am often asked is . . ." In some community and career contexts, you may want to involve listeners by asking *them* a question; for example, "What do *you* think of my proposal?"
- While a person is asking a question, look directly at him or her, but as you give your answer, look at the entire audience.

- In a large room, when a question is asked, repeat it for the benefit of listeners who may not have been able to hear it. Repeating it also gives you time to frame your answer. If a question is unclear to you, ask the listener to clarify it.

- Be consistent in how you respond. If you reward some questions with "That's a good question" or "I'm glad you asked that," the listeners who receive no praise may feel as if their questions have been judged inferior. Reward all questions—or none.

- If you don't know the answer to a question, say so. Your listeners will not think less of you. They *will* think less of you if you try to fake expertise. In some cases, you can ask the audience for help: "I don't know the answer; can anyone help us out?"

Handling Problems

- If a listener points out an inaccuracy or an omission in your material, don't be defensive. If the listener's point seems to have merit, say so. You can say something like "You may be right—that statistic could be outdated. I'll have to check it. Thanks." Such an approach is not only honest—it gains respect from listeners.

- Don't let any listener hog the question-and-answer period. If a person persists in asking one question after another or launches into a long monologue, it is your responsibility to intervene. You can say something like "Let's give others a chance to ask questions; if we have time later, I'll get back to you" or "Why don't you and I talk about this in greater detail after the meeting?"

- Decline to answer questions that are not appropriate for a discussion in front of the entire audience—for example, questions that are too personal or that require a long, technical explanation that would bore most of the listeners. You can politely explain your reasons; for example, "That's a little too personal—I'd rather not go into that," or "I'm afraid it would take up too much time to go into the details right now." In some cases, you might tell the questioner to see you afterward for a one-on-one discussion.

Ending the Session

- Don't let the question-and-answer period drag on. If you have been allotted an hour, say, for both your speech and the Q & A period, end the session promptly at the end of an hour—even if some listeners still have questions. If you sense that some listeners would like to continue the session, you can say, "I'm stopping now because I promised I would take up only one hour of your time. However, if any of you would like to stay afterwards, you can move to the seats here at the front and we'll continue our discussion."

- At the end of the Q & A session, provide a conclusion. No, not the conclusion you have already given in your speech, but a brief wrap-up—to give a sense of closure and provide one last look at your message. For example: "Thank you for letting me talk to you today about the need to get a flu shot every year. With flu season approaching, I hope each of you will get a flu shot as soon as possible."

Practice

After you have written your outline and made notes based on it (as discussed in Chapter 9), you should spend a great deal of time rehearsing your speech. Practice, practice, practice—it's a crucial step that some inexperienced speakers leave out. Practice makes you look and sound fluent, smooth, and spontaneous. Practice bolsters your confidence, giving you a sense of mastery and competence.

Here are some tips:

- Start early. If you wait until the eve of your speech, you will not have enough time to develop and polish your delivery.

- Practice going through your entire speech at least four times. Spread your practice sessions over several days, because having time intervals between sessions will cause you to make greater progress.

- "Practice ideas, not words" is a popular saying in Toastmasters clubs. In other words, learn your speech point by point, not word for word. Remember that your goal in extemporaneous speaking is not to memorize or read a speech. Every time you say your speech (whether in practice or in delivery to an audience), the wording should be a bit different. The ideas will be the same, but not the exact words.

- Time yourself. If your speech exceeds the time limit set by your instructor or by the group that invited you, go back to your outline and notes and trim them down.

- During most of your practice sessions, go all the way through the speech. Don't stop if you hit a problem; you can work it out later. Going all the way through helps you see whether your ideas fit together snugly, and whether your transitions from point to point are smooth.

- Some speakers find it helpful to practice in front of a mirror or to use a video camcorder or an audiotape recorder. Whether or not you use one of these techniques, you should practice at least once in front of a *live* audience—friends or relatives who can give you a candid appraisal. Don't say, "Tell me how I do on this," because your evaluators will probably say, "Good job—I liked the speech," to avoid hurting your feelings. Instead give them a specific assignment: "Please note at least three positive things and at least three things that need improvement." Now your listeners have an assignment that they know will not hurt your feelings, and you are likely to get some helpful feedback.

- Some speakers find it helpful to make a trial run in the very room in which they will give the speech. This would be an especially good idea if you have visual aids and equipment.

- In addition to practicing the entire speech, devote special practice time to your beginning and your ending—two parts that should be smooth and effective.

- Be sure that you don't put too many words on your notes. Have just the bare minimum necessary to jog your memory. Practice from the actual notes that you will use in the speech. Don't make a clean set right before the speech; the old, marked-up notes are more reliable because you're familiar with them from your practice sessions.

Time yourself in practice. If you are in danger of exceeding the time limit, trim your speech.

connectpublic
speaking.com
Read the article "Can You Practice Too Much?" in the Supplementary Readings.

Resources for Review and Skill Building

Connect Public Speaking provides resources for study and review, including sample speech videos, an Outline Tutor, and practice tests.

Summary

The key to good delivery is a strong desire to communicate with the audience. Speakers who concentrate on getting their ideas across to their listeners usually find themselves using good delivery techniques.

There are four methods of delivering a speech: memorization, manuscript, impromptu, and extemporaneous. Of the four, extemporaneous is the most popular and usually the most effective, because the speaker delivers a well-prepared, well-rehearsed speech in a lively, conversational manner.

In delivering a speech, your voice should be loud enough for everyone to hear, your words should be spoken clearly so that they are easily understood, and your voice should be expressive so that you sound interesting and lively.

Nonverbal communication is the message you give with your body by means of personal appearance, eye contact, facial expressions, posture, movement, and gestures. All these elements should convey confidence and a positive regard for the audience. Of special importance is eye contact. You should look at your listeners during 95 percent of your speech to maintain a bond of communication and rapport with them and to monitor their feedback.

The question-and-answer period enables listeners to get clarification and further information. Anticipate what questions may be asked and prepare your answers accordingly. Try not to be defensive if you are challenged by a listener, and be prepared to say "I don't know" if you don't have an answer—in other words, don't try to fake expertise.

Practice is a vital part in the success of your speech. You should practice the entire speech over and over again—until you can deliver it with power and confidence.

Key Terms

articulation, *280*	manuscript method, *275*	pronunciation, *280*
extemporaneous method, *277*	nonverbal communication, *284*	verbal fillers, *283*
impromptu method, *276*	pitch, *281*	
intonation, *281*	posture, *286*	

Review Questions

1. What are the disadvantages of impromptu, manuscript, and memorized speeches?

2. What ingredient is essential for the success of an extemporaneous speech?

3. Why is it a serious mistake to speak too rapidly at the beginning of a speech?

4. What are the characteristics of good eye contact?

5. What can speakers do with their hands to make sure that they are free for gesturing?

6. Why should a speech be learned and practiced point by point, instead of word for word?

7. What form of visual aids can cause you to lose eye contact with your audience?

8. How many times should a speaker practice going through the entire speech?

9. How should you handle a listener who casts doubt on some of your facts and figures?

10. If there is a discrepancy between your words and your nonverbal behavior, which will the audience believe?

Building Critical-Thinking Skills

1. "If a man takes off his sunglasses, I can hear him better," says writer Hugh Prather. Explain the meaning of this statement in terms of public speaking.

2. Tennis coaches observe a phenomenon called "analysis equals paralysis." Players become so fixated on holding the racket correctly and swinging properly that they miss the ball. What lessons could public speakers draw from this phenomenon?

Building Teamwork Skills

1. In a group, create a list of six attributes of good delivery that are of utmost importance to group members when they are in an audience. Taking a vote, rank the attributes in order of importance. Then discuss why the top two attributes are more important than the others.

2. To practice impromptu speaking, members of a group should take turns playing the role of candidate in a job interview, while the rest of the group act as interviewers. Make the interview as realistic as possible, with serious questions and answers. After each candidate is interviewed, the group should give a brief critique of his or her verbal and nonverbal responses.

Katrina Bartlett, an art conservation graduate student at Buffalo State College (New York), explains how she restored early 20th-century paintings of Nora Barnacle and her husband, author James Joyce. In her presentation, Bartlett used the chronological pattern, telling what she did first, what she did second, and so on.

Speaking to Inform

OUTLINE

Goals of Informative Speaking

Types of Informative Speeches
Definition Speech
Description Speech
Process Speech
Explanation Speech

Guidelines for Informative Speaking
Relate the Speech to the Listeners' Self-Interest
Make Information Interesting

Avoid Information Overload
Tailor Information for Each Audience
Use the Familiar to Explain the Unfamiliar
Help Listeners Remember Key Information

Sample Informative Speech
The Outline with Commentary
The Speech as Delivered

OBJECTIVES

After studying this chapter, you should be able to:

1. Prepare an informative speech.
2. Identify four types of informative speeches.
3. Explain how to make information interesting.
4. Explain how to help listeners understand and remember key information.

Chinese calligraphy can be taught using a simple tried-and-true formula:

1. Demonstrate the correct steps.
2. Have the learners try out the steps as you observe and correct any miscues.
3. Encourage the learners to practice, practice, practice.[1]

This formula is one of many techniques that you can use when you engage in informative speaking, a rewarding form of human communication. On topics such as "why some people become addicted to chocolate," you can enlighten your audience. On topics such as "how to improve photos with image-enhancing software," you can enrich the lives of your listeners. On topics such as "how to shut out distractions when you drive," you can even save lives.

In this chapter, we will look at four types of informative speeches and then discuss guidelines to help you create informative speeches that are clear, interesting, and memorable.

A father in Taipei teaches his son to write "Spring" in traditional Chinese calligraphy.

Goals of Informative Speaking

When you give an informative speech, your task is to be a teacher—not a persuader, or an advocate, or a salesperson. Think of yourself as a reporter who gives facts, instead of a debater who makes arguments or a pundit who offers opinions. You have three major objectives:

1. **Convey fresh information.** Provide as much new material as possible.
2. **Make your material interesting.** Use supports such as examples, stories, and visual aids.
3. **Help listeners remember important points.** Make your ideas clear and easily grasped. Repeat—in a graceful manner—key information.

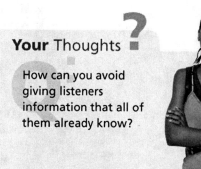

Your Thoughts **?**

How can you avoid giving listeners information that all of them already know?

Types of Informative Speeches

Informative speeches can be categorized in many ways, but in this chapter we will concentrate on four of the most popular types: definition, description, process, and explanation.

Definition Speech

Do you know what *synesthesia* is? Most people don't, so let me give you a dictionary definition: "a condition in which one type of stimulation evokes the sensation of another."

Still not sure what I'm talking about? Here are some elaborations.[2]

- Neurologist Richard Cytowič says that two people out of every million experience a mingling of senses, so that they may taste a shape, hear a color, or see a sound. "Music, for example, is not just a sound and a melody, but it's like a visual fireworks that they see in front of them . . . rather than in the mind's eye."

- A woman named Kristen tastes words, and often the spelling affects the flavor. "Lori," for example, tastes like a pencil eraser, while "Laurie" tastes lemony.

- People who experience synesthesia, says Cytowič, are not crazy, but as children they often fear that they are, and they hide their sensitivity. Carol Steen, a New York artist, recalls, "When I was about 7, I was walking back from elementary school with a classmate, and we must have been learning how to write. I said that the letter 'A' was a wonderful shade of pink, and she was quiet, and then she looked at me and said, 'You're weird.' And I didn't say another word until I was 20."

These examples and quotations constitute an **extended definition,** one that is richer and more meaningful than a dictionary explanation. That is what a **definition speech** is all about—giving an extended definition of a concept so that the listeners get a full, richly detailed picture of its meaning. While a dictionary definition would settle lightly on the listeners' brains and probably

Definition Speech topic: Gambling addiction.

extended definition
a rich, full elaboration of the meaning of a term

definition speech
an oral presentation that gives an extended definition of a concept

vanish overnight, an extended definition is likely to stick firmly. Here are some sample specific purpose statements for definition speeches:

- To define for my audience "financial bubbles" in the world's economy
- To define for my listeners "trolls" who operate on the Internet
- To define for my audience a "Pyrrhic victory" in business and politics

connectpublic **speaking.com**
For hundreds of sample topics, see the Topic Helper.

Any of the support materials that we discussed earlier (such as narratives, examples, vivid images, and statistics) can be applied to defining a topic. In a speech on iatrogenic injuries, Rosharna Hazel of Morgan State University in Maryland defined the term as "any injury caused by medical treatment" and then elaborated by giving two examples and some troubling statistics from a prestigious source.[3]

- Willie King of Baltimore was scheduled to have his right leg amputated below the knee, but during surgery, the surgeon incorrectly amputated his left leg instead.
- A woman named Martha entered a New York hospital to receive one of her last chemotherapy treatments in an apparently successful battle against cancer. She was given the wrong drug, however, and died a few days later.
- According to a study at Harvard University School of Public Health, "1.3 million Americans may suffer unexpected, disabling injuries in hospitals each year, and 198,000 may die as a result."

Sometimes the best way to define a topic is to compare or contrast it with a similar item. If you were trying to define what constitutes child abuse, for example, it would be helpful to contrast abuse with firm but loving discipline.

Description Speech

description speech
an oral presentation that describes a person, place, object, or event

A **description speech** paints a vivid picture of a person, a place, an object, or an event. As with all speeches, a description speech should make a point—and not be merely a list of facts or observations. Here are some specific purpose statements for description speeches:

- To describe to my listeners the Gulf Stream in the Atlantic Ocean
- To describe for my audience the "marijuana mansions" that drug dealers use in suburbs
- To describe to my audience the highlights of the life of civil rights leader Rosa Parks

Description Speech topic: Russian Easter eggs.

If you were describing an object or a place, you might want to use the *spatial* pattern of organization. Here is an example of the spatial pattern as used in an outline describing New Zealand. The speaker travels from south to north.

Specific Purpose:	To describe to my listeners the geographical variety of New Zealand
Central Idea:	The two-island nation of New Zealand has more scenic variety than any other country on earth.
Main Points:	I. The South Island—colder because it is closer to the South Pole—reminds visitors of Norway.

A. The Southern Alps, with snowcapped peaks over 10,000 feet, extend the entire length of the island.
B. Fjords, streams, and lakes are unspoiled and breathtakingly beautiful.

II. The North Island is like a compact version of the best of Europe and Asia.
  A. The cities suggest the elegance of Italy.
  B. The mountains and vineyards remind one of France.
  C. Active volcanoes look like those found in the Philippines.
  D. In the northernmost parts, the beaches and lush, tropical forests seem like Hawaii.

connectpublic speaking.com
For help in outlining your material, use the computerized Outline Tutor.

Describing a person, living or dead, can make a fascinating speech. You might want to use the *chronological* pattern; in a speech on United Farm Workers co-founder Dolores Huerta, for example, you could discuss the major events of her life in the order in which they occurred. Or you might prefer to use the *topical* pattern, emphasizing three major features of Huerta's career:

Specific Purpose: To describe to my audience the life and accomplishments of Dolores Huerta

Central Idea: Dolores Huerta is one of the most influential labor leaders in United States history.

Main Points: I. As co-founder of the United Farm Workers union, Huerta struggled to improve working conditions for migrant farmworkers.
  II. She is credited with introducing to the United States the idea of boycotting as a nonviolent tactic.
  III. Though Huerta practiced nonviolence, she endured much suffering.
    A. She was arrested more than 20 times.
    B. In 1988 she was nearly killed by baton-swinging police officers who smashed two ribs and ruptured her spleen.

Process Speech

A **process speech** covers the steps or stages by which something is done or made. There are two kinds of process speeches. In the first kind, you show the listeners how to *perform* a process so that they can actually use the skills later. (This is sometimes called a *demonstration* speech.) Here are some examples of specific purpose statements for this kind of speech:

process speech
an oral presentation that analyzes how to do something or how something works

- To demonstrate to my audience how to perform daily exercises to avoid and relieve back pain
- To show my listeners how to make low-fat pumpkin bread
- To teach my audience how to transform discarded CDs and DVDs into useful objects

In the second kind of process speech, you provide information on "how something is done" or "how something works." Your goal is to tell about a process—not

connectpublic
speaking.com
For a sample
demonstration
speech, view "How
to Make Avocado
Salsa."

so that listeners can perform it themselves, but so that they can understand it. For example, let's say that you outline the steps by which counterfeiters print bogus money. You are showing these steps to satisfy the listeners' intellectual curiosity and also to teach them how to spot a counterfeit bill, not so that they can perform the job themselves. Here are some samples of specific purpose statements for this kind of speech:

- To inform my audience of the process used to train horses to race in the Kentucky Derby
- To outline for my listeners the steps that astronomers take to find new stars in the universe
- To inform my audience of the process used by crime investigators to find and test DNA evidence

Here are some guidelines for preparing a process speech.

Use visual aids.   In some speeches, you can use a live demonstration. For instance, if you wanted to show how to treat a burn, you could use a volunteer and demonstrate the correct steps. In other speeches, PowerPoint slides and video are effective. For example, a student speaker told how to change a flat tire, using a video (with the sound off) to illustrate the steps in the process.

Involve the audience in physical activity whenever possible.   If you involve the audience in a physical activity, you capitalize on more than just the listeners' sense of hearing and seeing; you also bring in touch and movement. There is an ancient Chinese proverb that says:

- I hear—and I forget.
- I see—and I remember.
- I do—and I understand.

The wisdom of this saying has been confirmed by psychologists, who have found that of the three main channels for learning new information, the auditory is weakest, the visual is stronger, and physical action is strongest of all. The best approach is to bring all three together. For example, if you were telling how to do stretching exercises, you could discuss the techniques (auditory) as you give a demonstration (visual); then you could have each listener stand and perform the exercises (physical action). Some audience involvement can be accomplished while the listeners remain in their chairs; for example, if you are speaking on sign language, you can have the listeners practice the hand signals as you teach them.

Notes of caution: (1) Get your instructor's approval before you include physical activity in a speech. (2) Don't use an activity if it is likely to cause listeners to get so involved that they ignore you. (3) Don't ask listeners to do something that would be embarrassing or awkward for some of them.

Proceed slowly.   Always bear in mind that much of what you say may be new to the listeners. If you are giving instruction about how to make leather belts, for example, you may be describing activities that are so easy for you that you could perform them blindfolded, but they may be completely foreign to some members of the audience. That's why you should talk slowly and repeat key ideas if necessary. Give listeners ample time to absorb your points and form mental images.

Figure 11.1
To show the steps in making a YouTube video, Garrett Roth used PowerPoint slides, including this image (from a video on how to take care of pet snakes). See text for more details.

Give warning of difficult steps.   When you are ready to discuss especially difficult steps, use transitions to give the listeners a warning. For example, "The next step is a little tricky." Or: "This next step is the hardest one of all." This alerts the listeners that they need to pay extra special attention.

Student speaker Garrett Roth presented a process speech on how to make a YouTube video. Using the chronological pattern, he displayed PowerPoint slides (including Figure 11.1) to illustrate the steps. Here is the outline for the body of the speech, with each main point devoted to a different step in the process:

Specific Purpose: To show my listeners how to make a video for YouTube

Central Idea: Making a YouTube video is easy if you follow three simple steps.

Main Points:

(1st Step)   I. Film your video.
  A. Use a camcorder or any other device that captures video.
  B. Make sure audio quality is high.
   1. Have participants speak up.
   2. They can raise their voices without shouting.

(2nd Step)   II. Edit the video.
  A. Download to your computer's video-editing program.
  B. Delete unwanted footage.
  C. Make the length less than 10 minutes.

(3rd Step)   III. Post the video on YouTube.
  A. Register for a free account.
  B. Click on "Upload Videos."
  C. Create a title and tags so that people can easily find the video.

If you look closely, you will see that Roth's outline really has more than three steps. There are a lot of minor steps underneath the three major steps. Did he make a mistake in not listing all these steps as main points? No, treating all steps as equal might have caused the audience to feel overwhelmed by technical details. By dividing his speech into three major sections, he makes the material more manageable—easier to grasp and remember.

Explanation Speech

An **explanation speech** (sometimes called an oral report or a lecture) involves explaining a concept or a situation to the audience. For this type of speech, you often must conduct in-depth research, using books, articles, and interviews, rather than relying on your own experiences.

Here are examples of specific purpose statements for explanation speeches:

- To explain to the audience why works of art are highly prized as financial investments
- To inform my listeners of the reasons for the near extinction of mountain gorillas
- To explain to the audience the pros and cons of the Electoral College

connectpublic
speaking.com
To see an explanation speech, view "Humanoid Robots."

Explanation Speech topic: Why most people don't vote in local elections.

For organizing an explanation speech, you can use any of the popular patterns (topical, chronological, spatial). One arrangement that is especially effective is the *statement-of-reasons* pattern, which lists reasons for a situation or an event. Student speaker Melissa Greenbaum uses this pattern in a speech on stolen cars. Here is the essence of her outline:

Specific Purpose: To inform my listeners of the reasons why old cars are stolen more frequently than new cars

Central Idea: The most frequently stolen cars in North America are Toyotas and Hondas that are about 10 years old.

Main Points:
(1st Reason)   I. Stealing an old car is more profitable than stealing a new car because of the high demand for old-car parts.
(2nd Reason)   II. New cars are harder to break into because of sophisticated security devices.
(3rd Reason)   III. Old-car owners are less careful about locking up their vehicles.

In her speech, Greenbaum developed each reason with examples and statistics.

Another pattern is the *fallacy–fact* pattern, which also can be called *myth-reality*. In this pattern, the speaker cites popular fallacies and then presents facts that refute them. Student speaker Bob Metzger used this pattern to refute three popular misconceptions about nutrition:

Specific Purpose: To give my audience accurate information to overcome three common misconceptions about nutrition

Central Idea: Eggs, spicy foods, and frozen vegetables do not deserve their bad nutritional reputation.

Main Points:
(Fallacy)   I. "Eggs are bad for you" is a fallacy.

(Facts)   A. Eggs get a "bad rap" because they are high in cholesterol, but what's important is the level of cholesterol in the blood, not in the food.

B. Saturated fat is what causes high cholesterol levels in the blood.

C. Eggs are low in saturated fat, so they do not make a significant contribution to high cholesterol levels in the blood.

(Fallacy) II. "Spicy food is bad for the stomach" is a fallacy.

(Facts)   A. Medical studies of healthy persons who eat spice-rich Mexican and Indian foods found no damage or irritation in the protective lining of the stomach.

B. In a medical experiment in India, the stomach ulcers of patients who were fed spicy foods healed at the same rate as those of patients who were fed a bland diet.

(Fallacy) III. "Frozen vegetables are not as nutritious as fresh" is a fallacy.

(Facts)   A. Quick freezing preserves all nutrients.

B. In fact, if fresh vegetables have been sitting on the produce aisle for too long, frozen vegetables are better.

Guidelines for Informative Speaking

In informative speaking, strive to make your message clear, interesting, and memorable. You can achieve this goal by applying the principles that we have covered so far in this book, plus the following guidelines.

Relate the Speech to the Listeners' Self-Interest

Many listeners approach a speech with an attitude of: "Why should I care? Why should I pay attention? What's in it for me?" The best motivator in a speech, therefore, is something that has an impact on their lives.[4]

Let's say you are planning to give a process speech showing listeners how to clean their computers. How do you think your listeners will react when they discover what your topic is?

"B-o-r-ing!" they will probably say to themselves. "Why should I pay attention to this stuff?"

Your best strategy, therefore, is to appeal to their self-interest:

Imagine you sit at your computer all weekend working on a big research paper. You are almost through when suddenly your computer fails. Not only does it fail, but it deletes your entire report. To make matters worse, the technician who repairs your computer charges you $250.

This could happen to you if you don't clean and maintain your computer. Today I'd like to show you some easy steps you can take to safeguard your computer files and avoid repair bills.

Now your listeners see that your information can have an impact on their own lives. They should perk up and listen carefully.

connectpublic
speaking.com
To see a speaker relate a speech to the listeners' self-interest, view video clip 11.1.

Make Information Interesting

The most important element in an effective speech, says nationally known TV and radio reporter Nina Totenberg, is "interesting information."[5]

Many speeches are boring because the speakers deal primarily with *generalities,* which tend to be dull and vague. To make a speech lively, use generalities sparingly, and each time a generality is offered, follow it with lots of *specifics,* such as examples and ancedotes.

Student speaker Catalina Garcia gave an informative speech on mystery shoppers—people who are hired to pose as customers to evaluate the quality of a company's service and products. She began by asking her audience to look at an ad for mystery shopping [Figure 11.2] and said, "Sounds like an exciting job, doesn't it?" Then she made this generalized statement:

> But as I read articles and interviewed people on the Internet, I discovered that for most mystery shoppers, the job is far from glamorous—it's a lot of hard work for low pay.

Garcia followed her generality with lots of specifics, including these:

- "Pamela Whitaker of Louisville, Kentucky, thought she would dine at fancy restaurants with her husband. Instead, she worked for a fast-food chain. She would visit one restaurant after another. First she would inspect the restroom. Then she would order food and take it out to her car. She would eat a few bites of a burger and fries and throw the food away. Then she would fill out her evaluation of cleanliness, friendliness, and the taste and temperature of the food. She said the job was boring, and she was paid

Tips for Your Career

Tip 11.1 For Long Presentations, Plan a Variety of Activities

Your boss asks you to conduct a three-hour workshop, scheduled for a Friday afternoon, to explain important procedures to a group of new employees. What do you do? Do you spend the entire three hours talking? No, not unless you want to put the group to sleep.

For long presentations, provide a variety of activities to keep your audience awake and attentive. Here are some suggested activities.

1. INVITE AUDIENCE PARTICIPATION.

At various intervals, or even throughout the entire presentation, encourage listeners to ask questions or make comments. By letting them take an active role, instead of sitting passively for three hours, you invigorate them and prevent them from daydreaming.

2. USE VISUAL AIDS WHENEVER POSSIBLE.

Visuals provide variety and sparkle, and they can clarify and reinforce key points.

3. GIVE COFFEE OR "STRETCH" BREAKS AT VARIOUS INTERVALS.

A good rule of thumb for marathon sessions is to give a 15-minute break after every 45-minute period, even if the audience does not seem tired. In other words, don't wait until fatigue sets in. If you wait until the audience is nodding, you might lose their interest for the rest of the day. When you give a break, always announce the time for reassembly; when that time arrives, politely but firmly remind any stragglers that it is time to return to their seats. If you don't remind them, you will find that a 15-minute coffee break can stretch to 30 minutes.

4. CALL ON PEOPLE AT RANDOM.

If your presentation is in the form of a lecture, you can use the teachers' technique of calling on people at random to answer questions. This causes every listener to perk up because he or she is thinking, "I'd better pay attention because my name might be called next, and I don't want to be caught daydreaming." Call the person's name *after* you ask the question. (If you call the name before the question, everyone in the audience except the designated person might breathe a sigh of relief and fail to pay close attention to the question.)

5. ENCOURAGE LISTENERS TO TAKE NOTES.

Some speakers pass out complimentary pens and pads at the beginning of their presentations in the hope that the listeners will use them to write down key points. There is, of course, a side benefit: Taking notes helps the listeners to stay alert and listen intelligently.

---

only $7 per visit. She was reimbursed for the food she bought, but not for gas and car expenses."

- "Ed Mancini, who lives in New Jersey, worked as a mystery shopper for an office supply chain. The worst part of the job involved employees who ignored him because they were busy chatting with co-workers. He said, 'I would stand near them looking bewildered and clearly needing help.' He knew that when he filed his report, the employees would be fired. He said, 'I guess they deserved it, but I hated being a snitch.' Mancini also said he hated the tedious paperwork and the low pay. He got $18 per visit, but he traveled a lot–it turned out he was actually making only $5 per hour. After a few months, he quit."

Garcia's speech was interesting because she chose lively examples and stories. She also used a valuable strategy: before she delivered her speech, she tested her content with friends and relatives, asking them to tell her which items were interesting and which were boring. (For more on testing your material, see Tip 10.1 in Chapter 7.)

223

Avoid Information Overload

Give details, but not too many. You don't want to bore your audience with a tedious overload. "The secret of being tiresome," the French philosopher Voltaire said, "is in telling everything." Edit your material: instead of giving all 14 examples that you have compiled for a point, cite just 2 or 3.

When my students moan about all the wonderful material they must leave out, I offer a simple solution: put it on a handout or a DVD that listeners can pick up after the speech and take with them.

Tailor Information for Each Audience

A common mistake is to assume that your listeners possess the same knowledge that you possess. You may know that the Earth revolves around the Sun, but one in five adult Americans thinks that the Sun revolves around the Earth.[6] One in seven adults can't find the United States on a world map.[7] Many college students think that Islam is the dominant religion in South America.[8]

Even at elite universities, you can't make assumptions about listener knowledge. Michael Ranney, a cognitive scientist at the University of California, Berkeley, reports that students in one of his classes (who should have known that the U.S. population is about 305 million) estimated that California has 1 billion people (instead of 36.5 million).[9]

Find out in advance what your audience knows and doesn't know on your topic, and then adapt your information accordingly. Whenever necessary, define words, explain concepts, and give background information.

What should you do when your audience is mixed—that is, some know certain concepts already and some don't? How can you give explanations in a way that does not insult the intelligence of the listeners who already know the material? In some cases, you can give information in a casual, unobtrusive way. For example, let's say you are planning in your speech to cite a quotation by Adolf Hitler. Most college students know who Hitler was, but some do not. To inform the latter without insulting the intelligence of the former, you can say something like this: "In the 1920s, long before Adolf Hitler rose to power in Germany and long before he launched the German nation into World War II, he made the following prophetic statement . . ." An indirect approach like this permits you to sneak in a lot of background information.

In other cases, you may need to be straightforward in giving definitions or explanations. For example, if you need to define *recession* for a speech on economic cycles, do so directly and clearly. Knowledgeable listeners will not be offended by a quick definition as long as most of your speech supplies them with new material; in fact, they probably will welcome a chance to confirm the accuracy of their own understanding of the term.

Use the Familiar to Explain the Unfamiliar

When an Israeli leader toured the United States to drum up support for increased military aid to Israel, Dorothy Sarnoff, an American consultant, was hired to help him prepare his speeches. She gave him the following advice:

> If you describe Israel at its narrowest point by saying, "Israel is so narrow that we can be [easily] attacked," the Americans won't get it . . . Instead say, "Israel is so narrow that if you were driving on a[n] [American-style] highway, it would take you only twenty minutes to get from one side of Israel to the other."[10]

Sarnoff's advice was sound. When you want to explain or describe something that is unfamiliar to your audience, relate it to something that is familiar. Use comparisons, contrasts, and analogies. If, for example, you point out that divers in Acapulco, Mexico, astound tourists by diving into water from rocks 118 feet high, that statistic does not have much impact, unless you point out that a 118-foot plunge is equal to a dive from the roof of an 11-story building.

Similarly, to give listeners a mental picture of what the inside of a tornado is like, Dale Higgins said: "A tornado's funnel is like the vortex you see when you let water go down a drain." Since everyone has seen the swirling action of water going down a drain, the comparison helped the audience visualize a tornado's vortex.

Help Listeners Remember Key Information

To make sure that your audience retains important details, use the following techniques.

Repetition. Present key ideas and words several times.

Presentation aids. Use the sensory channels we discussed in Chapter 6—visual, hearing, taste, smell, touch, and physical activity.

Memory aids. Provide listeners with shortcuts to remembering. Here are some samples:

- In financial news reports, you often hear the terms "bull market" and "bear market." One term means that stock values are trending upward; the other means that values are trending downward. To help listeners distinguish between the two, you could tell them that "bull market" signifies an upward movement and ask them to visualize a bull's horns, which point upward. (See Figure 11.3.)

Figure 11.3
This famous statue of a bull in New York City's financial district holds a key to remembering the meaning of the term "bull market." See text for details.

- In the United States, the color blue is often associated with one major political party and red with the other (red states vs. blue states). But which color goes with which party? The Republican party is red, so just remember that Republican starts with an "R," the same letter that starts red. That leaves blue for the Democratic party.

- Acronyms are handy. For years students have recalled the names of the Great Lakes by using the word HOMES, each letter of which stands for a lake: Huron, Ontario, Michigan, Erie, and Superior. If you are speaking on how to treat injuries such as ankle sprains, you can help listeners remember the four steps of first aid by providing the acronym RICE, which stands for rest, ice, compression, and elevation.

Your Thoughts **?**

It is important to avoid overdosing on the fat-soluble vitamins K, A, D, and E. Create a memory aid to help an audience remember them.

Sample Informative Speech

Natalia Payne delivered a speech on a dangerous type of climbing. To view a video of the speech, visit connectpublicspeaking.com. Below is the outline, followed by a transcript of the actual speech. The speaker uses the topical pattern, devoting the first main point to one climber and the second main point to another climber.

The Outline with Commentary

One Slip–and You're Dead

Commentary

This speech gives an extended definition—one that goes beyond a mere dictionary definition.

General Purpose:	To inform
Specific Purpose:	To define for my listeners the extreme sport called "free solo climbing"
Central Idea:	Free solo climbing, the most extreme of all the extreme sports, means that a person climbs a cliff or mountain without ropes or any assistance.

INTRODUCTION

A dramatic photo grabs the attention and interest of the audience.

I. Attention Material
   A. Almost all climbers use ropes and safety gear.
   B. A handful use no equipment or assistance. (Show photo.) [See Figure 11.4.]

II. Orienting Material
   A. This is called "free solo climbing."
   B. It is the most extreme of extreme sports.

Figure 11.4
Free solo climbers use no ropes and safety gear.

    1.   One slip and you're dead.
    2.   Several free solo climbers have died in recent years.
  C. To define the sport, I will tell you about two famous climbers.

(*Transition:* Let's start with our first climber.)

Listeners appreciate receiving background information and a preview of the body of the speech.

BODY

I. Steph Davis of Moab, Utah, is one of the most courageous climbers in the world.
  A. Here is one of the scariest photos I've ever seen. (Show photo.) [See Figure 11.5.]
    1.   She is over 1,000 feet up a cliff, the Diamond on Longs Peak in Colorado.
    2.   She is not using ropes or safety gear.
    3.   She is using chalk (to keep her hands dry) and sticky shoes.

(*continued*)

Figure 11.5
Steph Davis conquers a sheer cliff, relying only on her climbing skills, sticky shoes, and a bag of chalk to keep her hands dry.

The speaker anticipates that the audience will want to know, Why?

Note the effective use of contrast (between the climber's sheltered childhood and her daring adult life).

B. Why does she climb free solo?
1. "Because I love it."
2. She craves the exhilaration and the freedom from daily concerns.
C. Growing up, she was not athletic.
1. She practiced piano and flute, read books, and did homework.
2. During lunch at the University of Maryland one day, a guy invited her to go rock climbing.

    3. She had never heard of rock climbing, but she skipped her calculus class to go.

    4. That first climb caused a lifetime obsession with climbing.

    5. She worked as a waitress to support herself.

D. Steph Davis is not crazy.

    1. After reading her book *High Infatuation* and exchanging e-mails, I concluded she is normal and sane.

    2. When I asked if she has any fear, she revealed she has public speaking fears.

        a. While showing slides and videos, she is afraid of technical problems.

        b. "Technology is very scary."

By taking the trouble to contact Steph Davis, the speaker comes up with a fascinating revelation.

(*Transition:* Let's talk about the second climber.)

II. Michael Reardon of Southern California may have been the greatest of all free solo climbers. (Show photo.) [See Figure 11.6.]

A. Overcoming his childhood fear of heights, he climbed some of the world's most dangerous mountains.

B. He carried only a bag of chalk and an iPod filled with Kid Rock and Hank Williams Jr.

Specific details add richness and interest to the speech.

C. Some climbers thought he had a death wish.

    1. Michael laughed at the idea.

    2. "Nothing else makes me feel so alive."

D. He would put himself into a trance.

    1. He saw only the 8 feet around him.

    2. "It's like being in a giant, 8-foot eggshell."

Brief, apt quotations add pizzazz.

    3. "It's a way to zone out the rest of the world and put all of your focus on the next move."

E. Michael believed free solo is a lot easier than using ropes and gear.

    1. You're not weighed down by equipment.

    2. Unfortunately, a climber cannot control two factors.

Without being heavy-handed and boring, the speaker weaves a lot of information into the fabric of the speech.

        a. Loose rocks and rain can cause you to slip and fall.

        b. These factors apparently caused all of the deaths of free solo climbers.

F. Michael claimed to be super-careful.

    1. He had no shame in walking away from a climb.

(*continued*)

Figure 11.6
Michael Reardon always said he would never die while climbing.

2. He wouldn't climb if rain threatened or his mind was not in the right place.

G. He predicted he would never die while climbing.

1. He was right—he died in a freak accident in Ireland in 2007.

2. Having finished a climb up and down a cliff, he waited on a ledge for the tide to go out.

3. A rogue wave swept him out to sea.

4. His body was never recovered.

H. I was unable to find statistics on the number of free solo climbers and the fatality total.

(*Transition:* Let's summarize.)

A narrative (or story) is one of the best ways to hold the attention and interest of an audience.

CONCLUSION

I. Summary

A. Free solo climbing is dangerous.

B. There are no ropes or safety equipment.

The central idea is repeated.

II. Clincher

    A. Steph Davis and Michael Reardon are not necessarily models for the rest of us to imitate.

    B. But they do demonstrate the amazing feats that some humans can achieve.

The speaker provides a graceful finale.

BIBLIOGRAPHY

Becher, Bill. "Free-Solo Climber Prefers the Unencumbered Ascent." *New York Times* 18 Nov. 2006: D7. Print.

Davis, Steph. Message to the speaker. 12 July 2008. E-mail.

Davis, Steph. *High Infatuation: A Climber's Guide to Love and Gravity.* Seattle: The Mountaineers Books, 2007. Print.

McLellan, Dennis. "Michael Reardon, 42; Free Solo Rock Climber Is Swept Away by Rogue Wave." *Los Angeles Times* 19 July 2007: B8. Print.

High-quality sources are used.

VISUAL AIDS

Photo of a free solo climber

Photo of Steph Davis

Photo of Michael Reardon

PowerPoint slides help the audience understand free solo climbing.

The Speech as Delivered

Here is a transcript of the speech as delivered by Natalia Payne.

connectpublic
speaking.com
View Natalia Payne's
speech on video.

One Slip–and You're Dead

Most people who climb cliffs or mountains use ropes and safety gear, but there are some climbers who climb without any equipment and without any assistance from other people. [*Speaker shows photo in Figure 11.4.*]

What they are doing is known as "free solo climbing." Of all the extreme sports, it is perhaps the most extreme, the most dangerous. One wrong move—and it's all over. There's no safety net. And for this reason, several free solo climbers have died over the last few years. Now I would like to give you a picture of what this sport is all about by discussing two famous climbers.

Let's look at our first climber. Steph Davis of Moab, Utah, is considered one of the most daring free solo climbers in the world. [*Speaker shows photo in Figure 11.5.*] This is one of the scariest pictures I've ever seen. Steph Davis is 1,000 feet up the side of a sheer cliff known as the Diamond on Longs Peak in Colorado. She has no ropes, no safety gear. She is relying entirely on her climbing skills, her sticky shoes, and a container of chalk to keep her hands dry.

When Steph Davis is asked why she climbs, she says, "Because I love it." She loves the exhilaration, and she loves the freedom from everyday worries.

Growing up, she was not an athlete or an outdoors-type person. She spent all of her time practicing piano and flute, reading, and doing her homework. When she was a student at the University of Maryland, her life changed. One day she was sitting outside the cafeteria eating her lunch, and a guy started talking to her, and he invited her to go rock climbing. She says she had never even heard of rock climbing, but she agreed to skip her freshman calculus class and go with him. And this first experience of climbing triggered an obsession. She decided to spend the rest of her life climbing, and she supported herself with jobs as a waitress.

Is Steph Davis crazy? I don't think so. I read her book *High Infatuation* and I exchanged e-mails with her a few weeks ago. She seems normal to me. I asked her if she has any fears. She said yes. In fact, believe it or not, she has public speaking fears. She gets very nervous when she has to show slides and video, and there's some kind of technical glitch. She says, "Technology is very scary."

Now let's turn to our second climber. Michael Reardon of Southern California is perhaps the greatest free solo climber of all time. [*Speaker shows photo in Figure 11.6.*] Although he was actually afraid of heights as a child, he has climbed some of the most dangerous cliffs and mountains in the world.

He climbed with nothing but a bag of chalk and an iPod loaded with Kid Rock and Hank Williams Jr. Some climbers say that he had a death wish, but Michael would always laugh at that suggestion. He would say, "Nothing else makes me feel so alive."

He said that he put himself in a mental trance so that he saw only the 8 feet directly around him. He said it was "like being in a giant, 8-foot eggshell. It's a way to zone out the rest of the world and put all your focus on the next move."

Michael claimed that free solo climbing was a lot easier than climbing with ropes and safety gear because you're not weighted down and bothered by all that equipment. I can see his point, but a climber has no control over two factors—loose rocks and sudden rain, which can make it easy to slip and fall. These two factors are believed to be the causes of all the deaths of free solo climbers.

But Michael insisted that he was extremely careful. He said he felt no shame in walking away from a climb—if dark clouds threatened rain, or if he felt that his mind wasn't in the right place.

And because he was so careful, Michael always said that he would never die climbing. He was right. He died in a freak accident off the coast of Ireland in 2007. He had finished climbing up and down a cliff, and he was standing on a ledge at the bottom of the cliff, waiting for the tide to go out so that he could walk across to another piece of land, when a rogue wave hit him and swept him out to sea. His body was never found.

By the way, I could not find any statistics on how many solo climbers there are and how many have died.

To sum up what we have covered: I've tried to show you what free solo climbing involves—dangerous climbing without ropes and without safety gear. It is one of the most extreme of the extreme sports.

And Steph Davis and Michael Reardon are not people who most of us would want to imitate, but they do show us the incredible feats that some human beings are capable of achieving.

For other informative speeches, see Chapter 9, and videos at connectpublicspeaking.com.

Resources for Review and Skill Building

Summary

The goals of informative speaking are to convey fresh information, make material interesting, and help listeners remember key points. Four types of informative speeches were discussed in this chapter:

- *Definition* speeches give an extended definition of a concept so that listeners get a full, richly detailed picture of its meaning.
- *Description* speeches paint a vivid picture of a person, a place, an object, or an event.
- *Process* speeches explain the steps or stages by which something is done or made.

- *Explanation* speeches involve explaining a concept or a situation to the audience.

In developing an informative speech, keep these guidelines in mind: (1) Relate the speech to the listeners' self-interest, if at all possible. Show them explicitly the connection between your material and their personal lives. (2) Make the information interesting by going beyond generalities to give lots of specifics, such as examples and anecdotes. (3) Avoid information overload. (4) Tailor information for each audience. (5) Use the familiar to explain the unfamiliar. (6) Help listeners remember key information.

Key Terms

definition speech, *299*

description speech, *300*

explanation speech, *304*

extended definition, *299*

process speech, *301*

Review Questions

1. What is an extended definition? Why is it preferable in a speech to a dictionary definition?

2. Which two organizational patterns would be most appropriate for a speech on the life and achievements of astronaut Sally Ride?

3. What are the two kinds of process speeches?

4. In a process speech, at what point should you give listeners a warning?

5. Which organizational pattern would be most appropriate for a speech aimed at dispelling misconceptions about wolves?

6. Why is it important to relate a speech, if possible, to the listeners' self-interest?

7. Why is the issue of generalities versus specifics an important matter in informative speaking?

8. What should you do if some members of an audience know the meaning of a term but others do not?

9. A speaker says, "The lungs of a heavy smoker look like charred meat." What principle of informative speaking is the speaker using?

10. "ASAP" is an example of what kind of memory aid?

Building Critical-Thinking Skills

1. A student who wanted to teach his classmates how to perform CPR (cardiopulmonary resuscitation) began his speech by asking, "How many of you know CPR?" Everyone raised a hand. What error did the speaker make?

2. A handout from a dog-obedience class says, "Training a well-behaved dog takes time and practice.

The more repetitions you do on a regular basis, the quicker your dog will understand. However, do not bore him. Keep your training sessions fun and interesting." Do you think this advice would apply to training humans? Justify your answer.

Building Teamwork Skills

1. If improperly developed, the topics below can be boring. In a group, brainstorm ways that each topic could be made interesting.

    a. Teaching methods

    b. Citizenship

    c. Transportation

2. The text advises that you relate a topic to listeners' self-interest. In a group, brainstorm how the following topics can be presented in a way that would satisfy a listener's attitude of "What's in it for me?"

    a. Social Security

    b. Rain forest destruction

    c. Secret video surveillance of employees

    d. Solar energy

    e. Homeless people

Anna Stitt, an accounting major at Carroll College in Montana, warms up her horse, Dakota. She and five classmates wanted to form the school's first rodeo team, and they achieved their goal by doing a lot of persuading. They made a presentation to student leaders to gain approval for the team, and then they gave speeches on campus and in the community to raise funds to equip the team for competition against other colleges.

Speaking to Persuade

OBJECTIVES

After studying this chapter, you
should be able to:

1. Prepare a persuasive speech.
2. Identify two major types of persuasive
   speeches.

3. Identify four patterns for organizing a
   persuasive speech.

Embarrassing photos and inappropriate comments placed by students on the Internet today can hurt them later when they apply for a job.

That's the warning that attorney Janet Judge of Portland, Maine, delivers to college students in speeches across the country. She displays samples of students' Internet postings that would look bad to a prospective employer, and she demonstrates how easy it is for employers to gain access to supposedly private sites (such as Facebook and MySpace).

Judge's goal is to persuade students to keep their Internet image untarnished, and evidently she is very successful. Administrators at several colleges have reported that after she spoke on their campus, many students went to their computers and eliminated photos and comments that could hurt them in the future.[1]

Attorney Janet Judge is highly successful in persuading college students to maintain an unblemished image on the Internet.

persuasion
the process of influencing, changing, or reinforcing listeners' ideas, attitudes, beliefs, or behaviors

The success of Janet Judge demonstrates the power of **persuasion**—influencing, changing, or reinforcing what people think, believe, or do. In a persuasive speech, you act as an advocate, a person who argues on behalf of an idea or a cause.

At first glance, persuasive speeches look like informative speeches, but that's because a persuasive speech must contain background information before you can make your case. The basic difference is that an informative speech is aimed at reporting, while a persuasive speech is aimed at winning audience assent.

To illustrate the two types of speeches, let's take the topic of solar-powered cars. For an informative speech, you would just give the facts—how the car works, how much the battery pack costs, and so on. For a persuasive speech, you would give some of the same facts, but you also would try to convince listeners that a solar-powered car is superior to a gasoline-powered vehicle and to persuade them to buy and drive a solar car.

In this chapter, we will examine types of persuasive speeches and how you can organize them. In the next chapter, we will look at persuasive strategies.

Goals of Persuasive Speaking

Three key goals in persuasive speaking are:

1. **Win over your listeners.** In some cases, you may hope that an audience will adopt your view. For example, one student tried to convince her listeners that the moon will become a tourist destination within 50 years. In other cases, you may want to spur the audience to take action. For example, in a speech on contaminated food, a student asked his listeners to call federal lawmakers to urge them to increase the number of inspections of imported food.

2. **Know your subject thoroughly.** You will have little chance of persuading listeners if you are not perceived as knowledgeable and competent on your topic. Develop as much expertise as possible by doing careful, extensive research.

3. **Maintain a high standard of ethical behavior.** Avoid any degree of manipulation and deceit. Use supports (such as examples and visual aids) that are accurate and truthful, and be forthright in revealing to the audience your true goals and motives. Don't exaggerate or use half-truths.

Your Thoughts **?**

Is it acceptable for speakers to pretend to be "just giving the facts" when they are secretly trying to sway the audience to accept a certain belief? Defend your answer.

Ethical Issue

Types of Persuasive Speeches

Persuasive speeches can be categorized according to two objectives: (1) to influence thinking and (2) to motivate action. Sometimes these categories overlap; for example, you often have to influence thinking before you can motivate action.

Speech to Influence Thinking

The **speech to influence thinking** is an effort to convince people to adopt your position on a particular subject. (If some listeners agree with your ideas even before you speak, your job is to reinforce what they already think.)

speech to influence thinking
an oral presentation aimed at winning intellectual assent for a concept or proposition

Here are some sample specific purpose statements for this kind of speech:

- To convince my audience that a paid sabbatical (extended time off) for employees is a good way for companies to avoid job burnout and low morale

- To convince my audience that child geniuses should be permitted to enroll in college classes

- To convince my listeners that immigrants continue to enrich American society and business life

speech of refutation
an oral counterargument against a concept or proposition put forth by others

A subcategory of the speech to influence thinking is the **speech of refutation,** in which your main goal is to knock down arguments or ideas that you believe are false. You may want to attack what another speaker has said, or you may want to refute popularly held ideas or beliefs that you think are false.

Here are some sample specific purpose statements for speeches of refutation:

- To persuade my audience to reject the widespread belief that everyone needs to consume eight glasses of water per day

- To convince listeners to reject the idea that tornadoes are incapable of striking large cities

- To persuade my audience to disbelieve claims by so-called psychics that they are able to predict future events

connectpublic
speaking.com
View videos of
persuasive speeches.

Refuting an argument is easier when you are dealing with facts than when you are dealing with deeply held beliefs. Suppose, for example, that you want to demolish the idea that brown sugar is more natural and therefore healthier than white sugar. You can refute this idea by citing nutrition experts who say that brown sugar offers no nutritional advantages because it is simply white sugar with small amounts of molasses or burnt sugar added for coloring. Since this assertion involves verifiable chemical facts, your persuasive task is easy. But suppose that you wanted to persuade an audience to reject the belief that children should be reared by their parents; instead, you argue, children should be reared by communes like the kibbutzim in Israel. Though you may win some respect for the value of your idea, you are highly unlikely to demolish the deeply held belief that children should grow up under the wings of their parents. Such core beliefs are extremely difficult to change.

Speech to Motivate Action

speech to motivate action
an oral presentation that tries to impel listeners to take action

Like the speech to influence thinking, the **speech to motivate action** tries to win people over to your way of thinking, but it also attempts one of the most challenging tasks of persuasion: getting people to take action. Your goal is to get listeners to respond in one or more of these ways: *start* a behavior (start taking first aid lessons), *continue* a behavior (continue donating blood), or *stop* a behavior (stop smoking).

Here are some sample specific purpose statements for speeches to motivate action:

- To persuade my listeners to sign a petition aimed at requiring drivers over 75 to be retested each year for their driver's license

- To persuade my audience to stop overspending on their credit card accounts

- To persuade my listeners to start a digital scrapbook of memories and images

Speech to Motivate Action: Do exercises to prevent back pain.

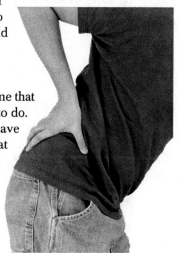

Sometimes you want prompt action from your listeners ("Please vote for my candidate in today's election"); at other times, you simply want them to respond at any appropriate point in the future ("Whenever you see a child riding a bike, please slow down and drive very cautiously").

Here are some suggestions for getting action.

Ask for the precise action that you want.   Don't just "give the facts" and assume that your listeners will know what action to take. Say *exactly* what you want them to do.

If you are speaking on the need for children in poor countries to have computers in their schools, don't be content to praise a nonprofit charity that is sending computers overseas and hope that your listeners will someday make a donation. Instead, urge them to donate at least $25 by the end of the day. (You can supply a Web address or a phone number for an easy credit card contribution.)

Late in his life, Henry Ford, founder of the Ford Motor Company, was chatting with an insurance agent whom he had known for many years. The agent, puzzled and hurt by the fact that Ford had never given him any business, finally asked, "Why didn't you ever buy insurance from me?"

Ford replied, "You never asked me."[2]

Countless speakers, says Dr. Jerry Tarver of the University of Richmond, "are reluctant to 'ask for the sale.' They appear to have a naive faith that if audiences are given some pertinent facts and a few exhortations, all will be well. These speakers fail to realize that when conditions are right, conviction can be turned into action."[3]

Whenever possible, get a response before listeners leave the room.   Often a speaker gets listeners fired up over an issue and asks them to go home and write an e-mail to the appropriate agencies. Listeners leave the room determined to write that e-mail, but unfortunately very few ever do. Everyone has good intentions, but life is busy and there are urgent personal matters to be taken care of. After a couple of weeks, the vows are forgotten.

To avoid this problem, try to get an immediate response. Even a small, token action is better than none at all. You can say, "On your way out, please sign the petition on the table at the rear of the room." Even better, if time permits, is to circulate the petition for them to sign before they stand up to leave.

Researchers have verified that if you persuade a person to take a positive step, you increase that person's commitment to your cause.[4] He or she now has made an investment of time and energy. If opponents try to persuade the person to believe the opposite of what you have espoused, he or she will be highly resistant to change (unless, of course, there is some compelling counterargument). Why? Because human beings feel a strong need to be consistent.[5] Going over to the other side would be inconsistent with an action such as signing your petition.

Let's examine some on-the-spot responses that can help strengthen your listeners' support of your position.

connectpublic
speaking.com
For hundreds of sample topics, see Topic Helper.

- **Phone calls.** Although cell phones should not be turned on during a speech, some speakers *at the end of a presentation* ask listeners to pull out their phones.

In 2008, as destructive Hurricane Gustav approached the coast of Louisiana and Texas, a speaker at a student rally at the University of Louisiana at Lafayette ended her plea for volunteer assistance by displaying the phone number of the Red Cross voice mail hotline on a large screen and urging listeners to get out their cell phones and call immediately to offer their help and donations. The room was filled with the sound of students making calls.[6]

- **Petition.** Some people feel that petitions have become a cliché, and besides, public officials just dump them in the trash. I disagree. If a senator gets petitions with 500 signatures from the folks back home, he or she sits up and pays attention–these are 500 potential voters. Lawmakers and officeholders often switch their positions after receiving a big stack of petitions. Even if officials don't respond as you wish, getting signatures on a petition is never a futile gesture, because you have increased the listeners' commitment to your idea.

- **Show of hands.** "Studies show that something as simple as having people raise their hands is more likely to get long-range results than depending, as too many speakers do, on mere mental assent," says Dr. Jerry Tarver.[7] Ask for a show of hands only when you're sure that most listeners will be eager and unembarrassed to make a public commitment.

- **Sign-up sheet.** For some future activity such as volunteer work, you can ask people to write down their names and e-mail addresses. This strategy can be effective because even if their enthusiasm cools, most people will honor their promise to help when called upon later.

Don't pressure listeners.   No matter how much you want audience action, don't browbeat, manipulate, or beg. Don't single out and embarrass those listeners who decline to take action. Listeners who feel pressured might become so resentful that they will decline to support your cause simply out of spite.

Patterns of Organization

Organizing a speech effectively can enhance your persuasiveness. While any of the organizational patterns we studied in Chapter 7 can be used, four patterns are especially strong in persuasive speeches: the motivated sequence, the problem–solution pattern, the statement-of-reasons pattern, and the comparative-advantages pattern.

Motivated Sequence

motivated sequence
a series of steps designed to propel a listener toward accepting the speaker's proposition

The **motivated sequence** is an effective approach to persuasion that was developed by Professor Alan H. Monroe.[8] The pattern is especially useful when you want to sell a product or service, or when you want to mobilize listeners to take a specific action (vote for your candidate, pick up litter). It has the virtue of being suitable for any type of audience–unaware, hostile, apathetic, neutral, or favorable. There are five steps in this pattern:

1. **Attention.** Grab the audience's attention at the beginning of your introduction, as discussed in Chapter 8.
2. **Need.** Show your audience that there is a serious problem that needs action.

Table 12.1   **Example of the Motivated Sequence**

1. Attention

(Grab the listeners' attention.)

"Sea turtles could become extinct within 15 years. This is not just an issue of losing a beautiful creature. Extinction would hurt humans, as well."

2. Need

(Describe a problem that needs action.)

"This photo shows a sea grass bed on the ocean floor— necessary for the survival of many species of fish. Sea turtles graze on sea grass, keeping the blades short (as shown here). If the turtles become extinct, the blades will grow tall, and sea grass beds will become a jungle that is unhealthy for fish. This will lead to the extinction of many types of fish that we eat."

3. Satisfaction

(Satisfy the need by presenting a solution.)

"Sea turtles spend most of their lives in the ocean, except when females go ashore to lay eggs on beaches. Sadly, the vast majority of eggs and hatchlings are eaten by animals or poached by humans. The solution is for volunteers to protect the turtles by patrolling assigned sections of beaches, nest-sitting at night, and carrying new hatchlings safely to the ocean."

4. Visualization
(Help the audience visualize the results.)

"If we get enough volunteers to protect them, sea turtles will survive and swim with fish in the ocean. The turtles will maintain the health of the sea grass beds, and the fish will provide sustenance for human beings."

5. Action
(Request audience action.)

"In Florida, turtle patrol volunteer Pam Yates prepares to release a hatchling into the sea. I urge you to join Pam in helping to save turtles. You have two options: You can do volunteer work at beaches in America or in countries like Costa Rica. Or, if you can't travel, you can 'adopt a nest' and send money to help support the volunteers on the beaches. I will give you a list of volunteer websites."

3. **Satisfaction.** Satisfy the need by presenting a solution, and show how your solution works.

4. **Visualization.** Paint a picture of results. Your scenario can be *positive:* help listeners visualize the good things that will happen when your solution is put into effect. Or it can be *negative:* show them the bad results if your solution is rejected.

5. **Action.** Request action from the listeners. Be specific: "Sign this petition" or "Write your legislators today—here are their addresses" or "You can volunteer in Room 211 this afternoon."

Table 12.1 gives an example of how the steps work.[9] While these steps seem simple enough, some students have trouble knowing how to fit the sequence into a speech outline. To clarify the matter, I have annotated the partial outline below to demonstrate how one speaker placed the steps of the motivated sequence at logical places.

INTRODUCTION

I. Did you know that you can experience eye problems if you stare too long at the screens of your electronic devices?

II. Text-messaging devices like BlackBerry are the worst, but you can also suffer from staring at a computer screen.

Attention
(Grab the listeners' attention.)

BODY

I. "Computer vision syndrome" afflicts millions of Americans who stare at a screen for long periods of time.

 A. Symptoms include dry, irritated eyes, head-aches, sensitivity to light, and blurred vision, according to Dr. Kent Daum, associate pro-fessor of optometry at the University of Alabama–Birmingham.

 B. The syndrome can cause long-term deterioration of visual acuity.

Need
(Describe a problem that needs action.)

II. Doctors recommend a simple solution—the 20/20/20 rule.

 A. "Every 20 minutes, take a 20-second break and focus on something 20 feet away," says Dr. Jeffrey Anshel of Encinitas, California, who is a consultant on visual ergonomics for American Airlines.

 B. The simple technique not only rests your eyes, but it also keeps them moist and prevents them from "locking into a close-up."

Satisfaction
(Satisfy the need by presenting a solution.)

III. The 20/20/20 rule is effective.

 A. Dr. Amy Greer of Dallas, Texas, recommended the rule to patients who were suffering from headaches and eyestrain caused by staring at small screens.

 B. All of the patients who tried the technique said that it eliminated their problems.

Visualization
(Help the audience visualize the results.)

CONCLUSION

I. Prolonged staring at a screen can cause "computer vision syndrome," with symptoms such as blurred vision, dry and irritated eyes, and headaches.

II. The solution is simple: Every 20 minutes, take a 20-second break and focus on something 20 feet away.

 A. I challenge all of you to follow the 20/20/20 rule.

 B. Your eyes will thank you.

Action
(Request audience action.)

For another speech that uses the motivated sequence, see the sample outline and transcript at the end of this chapter.

Problem–Solution Pattern

For many audiences, the most persuasive approach is the **problem–solution pattern.** You show that a problem exists, and then you present the solution. This pattern is especially effective when listeners either don't know about the problem or don't know how serious it is. Here is the partial outline of a student speech by Adam Cohen:

Specific Purpose:	To convince my audience to support tougher enforcement of child-labor laws
Central Idea:	Stronger enforcement of child-labor laws would reduce the number of deaths and injuries involving children and teenagers.

Main Points:

(Problem)   I.   Many children and teenagers are killed or maimed because they are illegally working at jobs that are supposed to be filled by adults.

  A. One child or teenager is killed on the job every five days in the United States.

  B. About 210,000 are injured annually, with 70,000 hurt badly enough to need emergency-room treatment.

  C. Some employers use underage workers for dangerous jobs such as roofing, mining, logging, meat slicing, and construction.

(Solution)   II.   The federal government should enforce the child-labor laws that already exist.

  A. Unlike the present situation, in which no one ever goes to jail for breaking child-labor laws, federal prosecuters should seek criminal indictments in cases involving serious danger.

  B. Unlike the present situation, in which the government routinely waives fines for violations, the government should assess a maximum fine of $40,000 for each violation.

Your Thoughts **?**

TV commercials for headache remedies often use the problem-solution pattern. Why do you think this pattern is chosen?

In the speech itself, under the first main point, Cohen related news accounts of child-labor tragedies to show the audience that the problem was more serious than most people realized. Under the second main point, he gave specific examples of how enforcement should be carried out.

Tips for Your Career

If you own a restaurant and you want to persuade your servers to respond in a friendly manner toward obnoxious customers, you can give them examples of how to treat diners, you can urge them to be friendly, you can show training films. But none of these techniques will be as effective as having your employees engage in role play. One person plays the role of the crabby complainer ("There's too much dressing on this salad!") while a server acts out the correct response (saying, with a smile, "I am so sorry—let me bring you another salad"). After each server's performance, give a critique and, if anything is wrong, ask him or her to try again.

According to research studies, role play is a powerful way to modify behavior. If possible, make a video of a session. All participants can view the video and discuss strengths they see, as well as areas that need improvement.

Statement-of-Reasons Pattern

The **statement-of-reasons pattern,** a variation of the topical pattern (which we discussed in Chapter 7), gives reasons for the speaker's argument. It can be used for any persuasive speech, but it is especially useful when the audience leans toward your position but needs some justification for that leaning. In one community speech, Glenda O'Neill, an emergency-medicine physician, knew (from a questionnaire) that her listeners were suspicious of pharmaceutical drugs sold on the Internet by overseas companies but were unaware of the full extent of the dangers. So her task was to give them reasons for avoiding the drugs. Here is the essence of her outline:

statement-of-reasons pattern
a variation of the topical pattern in which a speaker gives reasons for an idea

Statement-of-Reasons Pattern: 3 reasons why you should keep your pet from getting overweight

Specific Purpose: To persuade my listeners to reject unregulated medications sold on the Internet

Central Idea: Unregulated medications that can be ordered on the Internet from overseas companies are often ineffective and dangerous.

Main Points:

(1st Reason)   I. Some Internet medications contain little or none of the advertised active ingredients.

(2nd Reason)   II. Some Internet medications may create adverse interaction with other drugs.

(3rd Reason)   III. Some Internet medications may worsen a patient's condition, even causing death.

In her speech, O'Neill developed each reason with examples and statistics.

Comparative-Advantages Pattern

When listeners already agree with you that a problem exists but aren't sure which solution is best, you can use the **comparative-advantages pattern** to show that your recommended solution is superior to others. Let's say that your listeners agree with you that criminals must be punished but don't know whether prison is the best choice or whether some alternative sentence (such as

comparative-advantages pattern
an organizational scheme that shows the superiority of one concept or approach over another

Tips for Your Career

Tip 12.2 View Persuasion as a Long-Term Process

Persuasion in your career often requires a long time—weeks, months, or even years. Many successful persuaders treat their task as an ongoing process aimed at influencing people and nudging them toward a goal, rather than a one-shot event aimed at a quick decision.

At first glance, this tip may seem to contradict what was discussed earlier in the chapter: the need to directly ask your audience to take action. But there really is no contradiction. Asking the audience to take prompt action is appropriate in many situations, such as urging an audience to vote for your political candidate. In other situations, however, you may be interacting with people over a span of time, and a one-time appeal may be less effective than long-term efforts that gradually move people toward a desired decision. For example, let's say you take a new job, and you want to convince your superiors to let you do most of your work from home. If you make a blunt request for this accommodation, you might get turned down. Using a gradual approach, however, you could occasionally do some projects in your home office as a way of demonstrating that you are capable of working productively at home. A year later, your superiors might be so impressed with your performance that they grant your request.

Successful long-term persuaders in the business world are good listeners who learn all they can about their clients, and then work in friendly collaboration. Imagine that a real estate agent meets a young couple who are in the market for a new house. Instead of pressing for a quick sale, the agent would be wise to get to know the couple and truly listen to their needs. She should show many different houses, making notes on which features the couple likes and dislikes. After a long process, the agent should be able to match the couple with a house that truly satisfies their needs. This approach not only is ethical, but also reaps a long-term benefit: the couple will tell their friends about the wonderful agent who is not pushy but takes time to really listen and is patient in finding the right home for her clients.

Whether you succeed or fail in persuasion often comes down to one key question: Are you trustworthy? Before people will buy your ideas, products, or services, they want to know whether they can trust you to guide them in the right direction. Proving your reliability may take time—another reason why long-term influence is often more effective than short-term argument.

---

probation, home confinement, or community service) would be better. If you feel that the latter is the preferred option, you can use the comparative-advantages pattern:

Specific Purpose: To persuade my audience that nonviolent offenders should be given alternative sentences instead of being sent to prison

Central Idea: An alternative sentence for nonviolent offenders is more beneficial to society and the offenders themselves than a prison sentence would be.

Main Points:

(1st Advantage) I. An alternative sentence costs taxpayers about $27,000 less per offender each year than a prison term.

(2nd Advantage) II. Alternative sentences prevent offenders from learning criminal skills in prison and coming out embittered against society.

(3rd Advantage) III. Alternative sentences make it easier for offenders to get jobs because they don't carry the stigma of being an ex-con.

Each main point shows the superiority of alternative sentences over prison sentences.

Sample Persuasive Speech

Using the motivated sequence, Nicole Sudhaus argues for a creative use of jail inmates. To view a video of the speech, visit connectpublicspeaking.com. Below is the outline of the speech, which is accompanied by a commentary. Note the discussion of the five steps of the motivated sequence. Following the outline is a transcript of the speech.

The Outline with Commentary

Inmates and Tomatoes

General Purpose:	To persuade	***Commentary***
Specific Purpose:	To persuade my listeners to support garden projects in city and county jails	
Central Idea:	Inmates can be recruited to grow fruits and vegetables for low-income families.	

INTRODUCTION

I. Attention Material
   A. In city and county jails, most inmates have nothing to do. (Show photo.) [See Figure 12.1.]
   B. Why don't we recruit these inmates for work that will contribute to society?

II. Orienting Material
   A. Inmates can grow fruits and vegetables.
   B. The food can be donated to low-income families.

*The **attention** step of the motivated sequence has an intriguing photo and question.*

(Transition: First, let's discuss inner cities.)

BODY

I. Low-income citizens have the poorest health of any group, with high rates of diabetes and obesity.
   A. Poor diet is one reason.
      1. There is plenty of food.
      2. But often it's not best kind. (Dr. Adam Drewnowski, Univ. of Washington)

*For the **need** step, the speaker explains a problem.*

Citing an expert enhances credibility.

(continued)

Figure 12.1
Is doing nothing the best
use of inmates' time?

B. Part of the problem is lack of fresh produce.
    1. Most low-income people lack access to supermarkets.
    2. They are limited to small neighborhood stores.
        a. The stores can't pay for shipments of fresh fruits and vegetables.
        b. They mainly stock canned goods and high-calorie junk food.
    3. Parents would prefer fresh produce but lack time and energy to travel to suburban supermarkets.

(*Transition:* Now let's talk about jails.)

*The **satisfaction** step presents a solution to the problem.*

II. Food can be grown by inmates at city and county jails and donated to low-income families.
     A. Urban farms and gardens can be set up in a jail complex, even on rooftops.
     B. There are an estimated 800,000 inmates in city and county jails in the U.S. (Dept. of Justice)
         1. Instead of doing nothing, they could be growing food.
         2. Their work could be done year-round.
         3. In winter, plastic greenhouses could be used.

(*Transition:* Has anyone ever tried this idea?)

*The **visualization** step reveals that the speaker's proposal has been tried—with success—in three cities.*

III. The San Francisco County Jail, Chicago's Cook County Jail, and New York City's Rikers Island Prison have had success with urban farms.
      A. At the Cook County Jail, a daily sight is about 200 inmates pulling weeds, watering plants, and harvesting crops.

1. Crops include fruits like strawberries and raspberries and vegetables like tomatoes and carrots. (Show photo.) [See Figure 12.2.]

2. The food goes to the low-income people and homeless shelters.

3. Jail official Ed Simmons: Inmates learn to cooperate with each other.

   a. They appreciate a chance to help feed hungry children.

   b. "They tell me they'll put up with the bugs and the hard work as long as they're helping the babies and the kids."

   When a source states an idea in colorful language, it is effective to quote verbatim rather than paraphrase.

4. Inmates gain skills that can help them land jobs later in gardening, farming, and landscaping. (Illinois agricultural educator Ron Wolford)

B. Gardens will not turn inmates into perfect humans, but San Francisco County Jail reports amazing results.

   1. "Our Garden Project is a tremendously effective crime-prevention program." (San Francisco County Sheriff Mike Hennessey)

   In the outline, the names of sources are placed in parentheses, but in the actual speech, they will be woven into the fabric of the speaker's remarks.

   2. The recidivism rate (how many return to jail within two years) is good.

   3. Of the non-project inmates, 55 percent return to jail, while of the project inmates, only 24 percent return.

C. I have a petition for you to sign.

   *In the **action** step, the speaker spells out exactly how listeners can help.*

   1. It will urge our city and county leaders to set up a garden project.

   2. The plan would not solve all our problems with crime and hunger, but it would help to improve people's lives.

(*Transition:* Let's review.)

Figure 12.2
Inmates can harvest fresh vegetables for low-income families.

(*continued*)

CONCLUSION

I. Summary

   A. Garden projects in city and county jails can give inmates a chance to make a worthwhile contribution to society.

   B. They would be donating fresh fruits and vegetables to low-income families.

II. Clincher

   A. You can play a part in establishing a garden project in our city and county jails.

   B. Please sign my petition.

Although action has been requested earlier, it is effective to repeat the appeal in the conclusion.

BIBLIOGRAPHY

The speaker relies on high-quality, authoritative sources.

"Cook County Sheriff's Garden: A Patch of Paradise." University of Illinois Extension in Urban Illinois, n.d. Web. 6 Aug. 2008.

Drewnowski, Adam. "Obesity and the Food Environment: Dietary Energy Density and Diet Costs." *American Journal of Preventive Medicine* 27.3 (2004): 154–162. Print.

Hennessey, Mike (Sheriff of San Francisco County). Message to the speaker. 5 Aug. 2008. E-mail.

"Jail Statistics." Bureau of Justice Statistics, U.S. Department of Justice, July 2008. Web. 6 Aug. 2008.

Van Veenhuizen, René. *Cities Farming for the Future: Urban Agriculture for Green and Productive Cities.* Ottawa, Canada: International Development Research Centre, 2006. Print.

VISUAL AIDS

Photo of a prisoner behind bars

Photo of garden tomatoes

The Speech as Delivered

Here is a transcript of the speech by Nicole Sudhaus. Notice that she uses the ideas of the outline without using the exact wording. In an extemporaneous speech, a speaker does not read or memorize a speech but speaks from brief notes.

Inmates and Tomatoes

If you go to a typical city or county jail, this is what you'll see [*The speaker shows the photo in Figure 12.1.*]—inmates with nothing much to do. What if we could put those inmates to work, doing something that'll make a contribution to society?

connectpublic speaking.com
View the video of this speech.

Today I am proposing that we arrange for inmates to grow fruits and vegetables in gardens and urban farms, and then the produce can be given to families who live in low-income neighborhoods.

Before I go into detail about what the inmates can do, let's take a look at what's going on in our nation's inner cities.

People in low-income neighborhoods have the poorest health out of any group in our society. They have high rates of obesity and diabetes. Part of the reason for their poor health is a poor diet. Dr. Adam Drewnowski of the University of Washington says that low-income people get plenty of food, but often it's not the best kind of food.

One aspect of this problem is a lack of fresh produce. Most low-income people don't have access to a large grocery store where it has a vast array of fresh produce. They have to rely on small neighborhood stores that can't afford to ship in fresh fruits and vegetables. Instead they can offer canned goods and high-calorie foods such as potato chips and sodas. Parents who have been interviewed say that they'd like to be able to buy fresh tomatoes and greens and so on but they don't have the time or the money to hop on a bus and go out to the suburbs to find a supermarket.

Here is where the jails come into play. Let me give you details on how inmates in city and county jails can grow food that can be given to the low-income families.

Urban farms and gardens can be created near or inside a jail complex, including on rooftops. On any given day, there are an estimated 800,000 inmates in city and county jails in the United States, according to the U.S. Department of Justice. Instead of just sitting around, these inmates could be working to grow food. And they could work throughout the year. In the winter, plants could be grown in plastic greenhouses that are inexpensive and easy to install and maintain.

Has this idea been tried out anywhere?

Yes, three urban jails have already tried this idea with great success—the San Francisco County Jail, the Cook County Jail in Chicago, and Rikers Island Prison in New York City. Let's take a look at the Cook County Jail for a moment. On a typical day, there can be about 200 inmates found pulling weeds, watering plants, and harvesting crops. [*The speaker shows the photo in Figure 12.2.*] These crops include fruits (such as strawberries and raspberries) and vegetables (such as peas, tomatoes, peppers, carrots, sweet potatoes, cabbage, lettuce, and collard greens).

The food is then given to Chicago's low-income families and to homeless shelters. Ed Simmons, an official at the jail, says that inmates learn how to cooperate with one another, and they appreciate the opportunity to help feed hungry children. Quote: "They tell me they'll put up with the bugs and the hard work as long as they're helping the babies and the kids." Ron Wolford, an agricultural educator in Illinois, says that the experience can help inmates find jobs in gardening, farming, and landscaping.

Now a garden project won't transform all inmates into perfect human beings, but the results in the San Francisco County jail are amazing. San

Special Techniques

How to Use Leave-Behinds

When you complete a persuasive speech in your career and you sit down, don't make the mistake of thinking that your persuasive task is finished.

"No matter how impressed and convinced the people in that room are when you're through," says computer consultant Jim Seymour of Austin, Texas, "your message hasn't finally clicked until they've taken it back to their staff, superiors, engineers, sales forces, or other constituencies. If you expect them to be even half as persuasive as you were—and to get it right when they retell your story for you!—you need to arm them with the tools they need to make your case persuasively."

These tools can be provided in "leave-behinds"—materials that are distributed at the end of your question-and-answer period. Make sure each listener receives a set. Leave-behinds may include:

1. *Summary.* A condensation of your key information will help listeners recall your points later, and it will provide a good abstract for those who could not attend. The summary must be brief—no more than one page.

2. *Memory aids.* A popular technique is to provide cards that can be slipped into a wallet or purse for future reference. Figure 12.A shows a sample card.

3. *Graphics.* Copies of key charts, diagrams, and tables provide visual support.

4. *New points.* If your time limit prevents you from covering all the points you want to discuss, you can focus on just a few points in the speech and cover the others on a leave-behind.

5. *Sources and Web links.* For listeners who want to pursue your subject further, provide a CD (or a piece of paper) giving your sources and relevant Web links.

6. *Samples and multimedia.* A sample product is a tangible reminder of your message. Videos on DVD or CD can provide bonus material in an enjoyable format.

7. *File folders.* Consider providing labeled file folders containing your materials. The folders help listeners keep material together, and make it easy to share with others.

For all important presentations, use leave-behinds. They enable your audience to take your message far beyond the meeting room to influence many people.

Francisco County Sheriff Mike Hennessey says, quote, "Our Garden Project is a tremendously effective crime-prevention program." He cites a study of recidivism—that is, how many inmates return to his jail within two years. Of inmates who do *not* participate in the garden project, 55 percent return to jail. Of the Garden Project inmates, only 24 percent return.

I have a petition that I hope you'll sign at the end of class. It'll be sent to our city and county officials, urging them to set up a garden program here in our community like the ones in Chicago and San Francisco. I'm not claiming that this plan will solve all issues of crime and malnutrition, but it would help improve people's lives.

Let's go over what we've covered. If we set up garden projects in city and county jails, the inmates will have a valuable experience and an opportunity to do something useful. At the same time, we can give fresh fruits and vegetables to needy families.

You can play a part in bringing a garden project to our community. All you have to do is stop by the back table and sign my petition. Thank you.

For other persuasive speeches, see the sample speeches in Chapters 7, 8, and 13 and view videos on connectpublicspeaking.com.

Figure 12.A
This memory aid was given to listeners by a student speaker at the end of a speech on dangerous mercury levels in fish. The card could be kept in a wallet or purse and pulled out at a restaurant or grocery store to help identify the types of fish containing high levels of mercury. (The student derived his information from the Natural Resources Defense Council.)

Resources for Review and Skill Building

connectpublic
speaking.com

Connect Public Speaking provides resources for study and review, including sample speech videos, an Outline Tutor, and practice tests.

Summary

Persuasion means influencing, changing, or reinforcing what people think, believe, or do. When you give a persuasive speech, you should have three key goals: (1) Win over your listeners so that they adopt your view or take a certain action. (2) Know your subject thoroughly. (3) Maintain a high standard of ethical behavior.

There are two major types of persuasive speeches: the speech to influence thinking and the speech to motivate action.

In the speech to influence thinking, your primary goal is to convince people to adopt your position. A subcategory of this kind of speech is the speech of refutation, in which your aim is to knock down arguments or ideas that you believe are false.

In the speech to motivate action, you should tell the listeners exactly what action you want them to take. Whenever possible, encourage them to take some action—even if it's a small, token action—immediately.

Of the many patterns that can be used for the persuasive speech, four are especially effective: the motivated sequence, problem–solution pattern, statement-of-reasons pattern, and comparative-advantages pattern.

Key Terms

comparative-advantages pattern, *331*

motivated sequence, *326*

persuasion, *322*

problem–solution pattern, *330*

speech of refutation, *324*

speech to influence thinking, *323*

speech to motivate action, *324*

statement-of-reasons pattern, *331*

Review Questions

1. What is the goal of the speech of refutation?

2. In a speech to motivate action, why should you try to get listeners to take action immediately?

3. Give three examples of immediate, on-the-spot audience action.

4. What is the goal of the *need* step of the motivated sequence?

5. What is the goal of the *satisfaction* step of the motivated sequence?

6. What is the goal of the *visualization* step of the motivated sequence?

7. What is the goal of the *action* step of the motivated sequence?

8. Which organizational pattern is useful when listeners don't know how serious a problem is?

9. When is the statement-of-reasons pattern especially effective?

10. When is the comparative-advantages pattern most effective?

Building Critical-Thinking Skills

1. Charities often give instructions like these to their fund-raisers: "If people decline to contribute, ask them to give just a token amount, such as a quarter or one dollar." These instructions are sometimes effective in building support for an organization because they follow one of the successful persuasive techniques discussed in this chapter. What is the technique?

2. Which organizational pattern is used in this partial outline (which shows the two main points of a speech)?

    I. Car thefts have risen in frequency throughout the United States.

    II. The number of thefts can be dramatically reduced if owners make their cars less vulnerable.

Building Teamwork Skills

1. Working in a group, create a brief synopsis for a television commercial that uses the motivated sequence. Some possible topics:

    a. Buying a certain brand of toothpaste

    b. Exercising at a spa or gym

    c. Donating blood to the Red Cross

    d. Buying a cellular telephone

2. The text discusses the effectiveness of role play. In a group, brainstorm a list of distracting or disruptive behaviors that audience members sometimes exhibit. Then let each person take turns playing the role of a speaker, while the rest of the group members in sequence act out the bad behaviors. The speaker's job is to respond to each undesired behavior in a firm but friendly manner. After each speaker finishes responding to the disrupters, the group should discuss how the speaker fared both verbally and nonverbally.

Credibility is one of the most important elements in persuasion. Rahul Dravid, a superstar in cricket (India's most popular sport), urges student athletes to balance sports and studies, rather than focus primarily on athletics. When he makes his argument, Dravid has high credibility with India's youth because they know that he practiced what he preaches. He stayed in school and received a college degree in commerce before he became a professional cricket player.

Persuasive Strategies

OUTLINE

Knowing Your Audience
Analyze Listeners
Use a Persuasion Scale
Plan Strategy

Building Credibility
Explain Your Competence
Be Accurate
Show Your Open-Mindedness
Show Common Ground with Your Audience

Providing Evidence

Using Sound Reasoning
Deduction

Induction
Fallacies in Reasoning

Appealing to Motivations
Some Common Motivations
Multiple Motivations

Arousing Emotions

Sample Persuasive Speech
The Outline with Commentary
The Speech as Delivered

OBJECTIVES

After studying this chapter, you should be able to:

1. Describe how to analyze listeners, using a persuasion scale.

2. Explain how to build credibility with an audience in a persuasive speech.

3. Explain how to marshal convincing evidence in a persuasive speech.

4. Distinguish between deduction and induction as tools of reasoning in a persuasive speech.

5. Identify nine fallacies in reasoning.

6. Select motivational appeals for a persuasive speech.

7. Explain how to arouse emotions in a persuasive speech.

It kills one child every 30 seconds. It is malaria, a terrible

disease borne by mosquitoes, and Thomas Bickerton, a United Methodist bishop, is trying to prevent the deaths.[1]

Bickerton raises funds to buy mosquito nets that are treated with insecticide. Ten dollars, he tells his listeners, will buy a net that can save the life of a child. A front-page story in the *New York Times* describes his persuasiveness:

> Addressing a conference of 6,000 Methodist youths in North Carolina last year, Bishop Bickerton held up his own $10 and told the crowd: "This represents your lunch today at McDonald's or your pizza tonight from Domino's. Or you could save a human life."
>
> The lights were so bright that he could see only what was happening at his feet. "They just showered the stage with $10 bills," Bishop Bickerton said. "In 30 seconds, we had $16,000."[2]

Did Bickerton succeed because of his creative use of a $10 bill? While it certainly helped, the main reason for success was his savvy analysis of his audience. He knew they would respond to his plea if he made the act of donating easy, affordable, and immediate. He was using one of the key strategies of persuasion—*know your audience.*

Sulay Momoh Jongo, 7, gets ready to sleep inside a mosquito net in a village in Sierra Leone, a country in West Africa.

Some people think that persuasive strategies are just clever methods to manipulate people. Not at all. While these techniques can be used unethically, you should view them as honorable methods to reach your audience. What could be more honorable than persuading people to pull out a $10 bill to save the life of a child?

In this chapter, we will examine six key strategies that you can use in a persuasive speech.

Knowing Your Audience

The first step in persuasion is understanding your listeners. To truly understand them, you must get inside their minds and see the world as they see it. In the example just mentioned, imagine that instead of Bickerton, there was a different fund-raiser:

> The speaker urges the Methodist youths to take home a brochure about mosquito nets, read it, and then consider sending a donation.

Would this speaker be as successful as Bickerton? Definitely not. He would be revealing an unawareness of how his listeners think and act. Most youths would be far less likely to mail a contribution than to pull out $10 on the spot.

Here are some strategies for understanding your audience:

Analyze Listeners

How can you find out where listeners stand? Gather information about them in advance (see Chapter 4). For example, you can get the names of a few listeners and interview them (on the phone or via e-mail) to find out how much they know on your subject and what their beliefs and attitudes are. If time permits, use a questionnaire to poll all or most of the members of the audience.

Use a Persuasion Scale

For analyzing an audience, consider using the persuasion scale in Table 13.1.[3] On the scale, mark where the listeners are in relation to your specific purpose *before* you speak. Then mark where you hope they will be *after* you speak. Knowing a starting point and an ideal finishing point can help prevent you from giving a speech that fails to connect with your audience.

If your goal is to persuade your audience to switch from diet sodas to healthier beverages, it might be a mistake to assume that the audience is at Stage 5 (convinced of your view and wanting tips on how to find healthy substitutes).

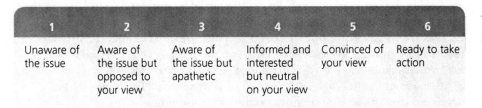

1	2	3	4	5	6
Unaware of the issue	Aware of the issue but opposed to your view	Aware of the issue but apathetic	Informed and interested but neutral on your view	Convinced of your view	Ready to take action

Table 13.1
Persuasion Scale

Tips for Your Career

Perhaps they are really at Stage 1 (unaware of the long-term health hazards of diet sodas). In that case, you should start at Stage 1 and move toward Stage 5 and ultimately end up at Stage 6.

Set a realistic goal. You are not a failure if your listeners fall short of Stage 6. With some listeners, persuading them to move from Stage 2 to Stage 4 is a great triumph.

Plan Strategy

While some audiences may fit neatly into one category or another, many audiences are segmented—that is, you may find 16 listeners opposed to your view, 15 apathetic, 8 already convinced, and so on.

When you have several different segments, to which group should you devote your energies? An obvious answer is: Try to meet the needs of everyone. While this is an admirable goal, it cannot always be achieved. For example, if most listeners know a great deal about your topic but a few are totally uninformed, it would be foolish to spend almost all of your time focusing on the needs of a tiny minority.

The best approach: Try to meet the needs of all listeners, but when this is impossible, choose the group that is most important. If, for example, your pre-speech analysis shows that 21 listeners want guidance on how to deal with angry co-workers and 3 listeners don't think the issue is relevant to their lives, don't focus most of your time and energy on those 3.

Despite the difficulty of meeting the needs of several different segments, there are some strategies you can employ. Using our persuasion scale, let's examine how to reach listeners with *starting* points at each of the six stages. As we proceed, study Table 13.2, which shows an example of how to apply our strategies.

1. **Unaware of the issue.**   For people in the dark on your topic, start by explaining the situation and showing why your ideas are important. Later in the speech, try to convince them to adopt your view.

2. **Aware of the issue but opposed to your view.**   Find out the listeners' reasons for opposing your view and then aim at refuting them. When listeners are strongly skeptical or hostile to an idea, a smart plan often is to delay divulging your central idea until the end of your speech. (This idea will be discussed later in this chapter under inductive reasoning.)

Table 13.2　**Using the Persuasion Scale**

Situation: A speech aimed at persuading listeners to support curtailment of theft from hotel and motel rooms.

Position on Scale	Strategy	Example
1. Unaware of the issue	Explain the problem.	"Thefts from hotels and motels amount to more than $100 million each year. Items stolen are not just towels, but irons and ironing boards, hair dryers, bedspreads, blankets, pillows, wall-mounted telephones, coffee makers, lamps, mirrors, paintings, and TV remote controls."
2. Aware of the issue but opposed to your view	Refute opposing arguments or schemes.	"You may think that the solution is to seek police action, but this is not practical. The police don't have time to investigate and prosecute what they consider minor crimes."
3. Aware of the issue but apathetic	Show that the issue can affect listeners' lives.	"This kind of theft may seem inconsequential, but the American Hotel & Motel Association estimates that to make up for the thefts, hotels and motels have to price their rooms at 10 percent higher than they would otherwise. In other words, you and I must pay extra because of all this stealing."
4. Informed and interested but neutral on your view	Show that your proposal offers the best solution to the problem.	"I propose that hotels and motels require a $100 deposit when a person checks in. Then, when he or she is ready to check out, the room is quickly inspected and if nothing is missing, the $100 deposit is returned."
5. Convinced of your view	Reinforce existing beliefs and give new reasons for supporting your view.	"My proposal should not be an inconvenience for the honest person, and it can ensure that when we check into a room, we won't have to call the front desk and request a coffee maker to replace the one that the previous occupant of the room must have swiped."
6. Ready to take action	Show how, when, and where to take action.	"As you leave today, please sign the petition that details my proposal. I will make photocopies and send them to the headquarters of all the major hotel and motel chains."

Always show respect for opponents and their views. *Never* insult or belittle those who disagree; sarcastic or belligerent remarks make people defensive and all the more committed to their opinion. Try to persuade these people, but if that fails, be content if you can move them a few inches closer to your side. Sometimes the best you can hope for is to plant some seeds of doubt about their position that might someday sprout into full-blown conversion to your side.

3. Aware of the issue but apathetic. "Who cares?" is the attitude of listeners in this category. To break through their apathy, show how the issue affects their own lives.

4. Informed and interested but neutral on your view.   People at this stage need little background information; you can plunge directly into convincing them that your position is correct or superior to other views.

5. Convinced of your view.   For listeners who agree with you, try to reinforce their belief and, if possible, give them new reasons for supporting your position. Although they agree with your view, some listeners may not have considered or endorsed a plan of action; with them, your task is to demonstrate that your plan offers the best approach.

6. Ready to take action.   For speeches aimed at motivating action, this is the stage you want all listeners to reach (although you may not be able to bring every listener this far). Show listeners how, when, and where to take action.

As we have already noted, it is difficult to meet the needs of all listeners when their starting points are at different stages on our scale. But sometimes you can do so. All the examples in Table 13.2 could be integrated into one speech, permitting you to meet the needs of listeners at all six stages.

Building Credibility

For years I had thought that mayonnaise is often the cause of food poisoning. But this is false, says Dr. Mildred Cody, head of the nutrition division of Georgia State University. "Commercially prepared mayonnaise is safe to use," she says. What causes problems at picnics and potlucks is contamination of foods that are often mixed with mayonnaise—such as pasta, potatoes, eggs, chicken, or tuna.[4]

I completely changed my mind about mayonnaise. Why? Because Dr. Cody is a leading authority on food poisoning, and she has investigated the issue thoroughly.

In other words, she has high **credibility**—a major source of persuasiveness in all human communication. Before listeners can accept your ideas, they want to know whether you are reliable, competent, and trustworthy.

In your career, when you want to persuade people who know you well, your credibility boils down to how they assess your ability and your character. If you are a person who is known for honesty, fairness, and competence, you enter the speech with a powerful asset. If you are known for dishonesty, unfairness, or incompetence, you enter with a heavy liability.

In the speech itself, credibility is enhanced if your delivery is enthusiastic and if your speech is clear, well-organized, and well-reasoned.[5] In addition, you can build credibility by adhering to the following guidelines.

Explain Your Competence

If you have special expertise, let your audience know about it—modestly, of course. Don't boast; just give the facts. This enhances your credibility because it shows that you are speaking from personal experience. It says, "I've been there—I know what I'm talking about." Here is how student speaker Lauren Shriver bolstered her credibility during a speech:

> Deep-sea diving is not dangerous—if you follow all the safety rules. I've made over 50 dives myself, and I feel very safe because I'm very careful each time. I never allow myself to get slack and overconfident.

credibility
degree to which a speaker is perceived to be believable, trustworthy, and competent

Ethical Issue

Tips for Your Career

Your boss knows that you strongly oppose a proposed policy, and she asks you to debate the issue with a colleague at the next staff meeting. What is your best approach? Should you demolish your foe with a slashing, take-no-prisoners assault? No, that approach is actually counterproductive.

"Victory is not won by bluster," says Professor Douglas Hunt. "Inexperienced arguers tend to enter the arena like gladiators ready for combat . . . They often allow their commitment to one side of an argument to blind them to the virtues of the other. They argue so aggressively that the audience dismisses them as cranks." Effective arguers, in contrast, "are usually cautious, courteous, and reasonable . . . They understand, anticipate, and even sympathize with the arguments of their opponents . . . They give the impression of being reasonable people whose judgment can be trusted."

Avoid cheap shots—personal abuse or ridicule. For example, a speaker at a public forum on air pollution ridiculed environmentalists as "mushroom pickers who weep at the thought of a butterfly dying." If you throw such poisoned barbs, listeners who agree with you may laugh and applaud your cleverness, but those who are neutral or opposed to your position (the very people you want to win over) may discount everything you say. In fact, your unfairness may elicit sympathy for the other side.

Debate plays an important part in politics. In a contest for a city council seat in San Jose, California, attorney Linda Nguyen, left, gestures during a debate with school board member Madison Nguyen, right. (In the subsequent election, Madison Nguyen won.)

Shriver's information about her diving experience was necessary to give credibility to her remarks. Notice how she inserted her personal background in a modest way.

If you lack personal experience on your topic, you can still enhance your credibility by showing that you have chosen competent sources. For example, if you are speaking on asteroids that might strike the Earth, you can tell your audience that you derived material from two leading experts on asteroids, astronomers Bob Preston and Joán García-Sánchez of the Jet Propulsion Laboratory.

Be Accurate

Sloppiness with facts and figures can undermine your whole presentation. In a speech on child abuse, one student said that 55 percent of American parents abused their children—a statistic that listeners challenged during the question-and-answer period. (A few days later, the student admitted to the instructor that the original source estimated 5.5 percent rather than 55—the overlooked decimal point made a huge difference.) When listeners believe you are wrong on one point, even when it's a small matter, they tend to distrust everything else you say.

Show Your Open-Mindedness

Showing confidence in your ideas is a good thing, of course, but some speakers go to an extreme—they become arrogant and inflexible, refusing to admit any possible problems with their argument.

Audiences distrust fanatical know-it-alls. They prefer a speaker who is open-minded and capable of admitting error or exceptions. In a speech that argued in favor of homeschooling, Patricia Caldwell gave glowing accounts of the success of homeschooled children when they went to college, and then she showed her open-mindedness by conceding that there are abuses:

> In one well-publicized case in Chicago a few months ago, the authorities brought legal action against a husband and wife for not sending their children to school. Their idea of a home school was to make the children— ages 7, 9, and 10—work all day instead of teaching them to read and write.[6]

Was it stupid for the speaker to relate an incident that seemed to negate her central idea (that some parents can do a better job of teaching than the public schools)? No, because she went on to say that bad parent-teachers are rare, and that periodic state inspections can weed them out. Rather than damaging her case, her concession strengthened it, for she showed herself to the audience as fair-minded. If you were a listener, wouldn't you trust her more than someone who asserted that *all* parents are good teachers?

It is especially important to be reasonable and open-minded during the question-and-answer period. I have seen some speakers do a good job in their speech, but when they are asked questions, they become rigid and defensive. They refuse to admit error or to concede that a listener has a good point. These speakers severely damage their own credibility and undo much of the persuasiveness of the speech itself.

Show Common Ground with Your Audience

When you are introduced to someone at a party, you try to find things that you have in common. You ask each other questions ("What is your major?" "Where are you from?") until you hit upon some interest that you share. We try to find common ground because it not only helps us to make conversation but also helps us to feel comfortable with another person.

In a speech, listeners tend to respect and trust a speaker who is similar to themselves, so your job is to show how you are like your listeners. This does not mean compromising your beliefs; it means highlighting those characteristics you share with the audience. This is especially important if some of the listeners are hostile to your ideas. Imagine that you are speaking on gun control, and you know that half the listeners are already against your position. Here's what you can say:

> I'm talking on gun control today. I know that a lot of you are opposed to the position I'm going to take. I ask only that you hear me out and see if my arguments have any merit whatsoever. Though we may disagree on this subject, you and I have at least one thing in common: We want to see a reduction in the number of violent, gun-related crimes in our society.

With this kind of statement, you not only pinpoint common ground (opposition to crime) but also appeal to the audience's sense of fair play.

One of the best ways to build credibility is to show listeners that you share (or have shared) their experiences or feelings. Diana Fisher, manager of the bariatric surgery program at Mission Hospital in Asheville, North Carolina, went from 297 pounds to 125 pounds in just two years—thanks to the same surgical procedure that she now arranges for patients. As part of her job, she explains weight-reduction options to audiences of obese people.[7]

Her first presentation was nearly a failure. As she talked, she was dismayed to see that her listeners were unresponsive, with arms folded. When she asked for questions, there was silence. Then she realized that her listeners had no idea of her personal story. Perhaps they were looking at her and thinking that a thin woman could not know anything at all about the physical and emotional pain of being obese. So Fisher told the audience that she had once weighed almost 300 pounds and had suffered the same agony that they were experiencing. Suddenly, the audience came to life. Some people began crying, and there was a torrent of excited questions.

Now Fisher tells her story at the beginning of every presentation. When listeners see that she has walked the same path that they are treading, they are more inclined to trust her insights on overcoming obesity.[8]

Providing Evidence

When you make an assertion in a speech, it is not enough to say, "Trust me on this" or "I know I'm right." The audience wants **evidence,** or proof. Evidence can be presented in forms such as narratives, statistics, examples, and testimony. For each main point in your speech, choose the evidence that is most likely to prove your point with a particular audience. Ask yourself these questions:

Why did Diana Fisher's audience initially distrust her? See text for the answer.

evidence
the facts, examples, statistics, testimony, and other information that support an assertion

1. Is the evidence *accurate*? Erroneous information would obviously undermine the credibility of your entire speech.
2. Is the evidence *up-to-date*? A research study conducted in the field of medicine in 1986 is almost certain to be outdated.
3. Is the evidence *typical*? An athlete may attribute his success to consuming five banana milkshakes a day, but is his diet common among athletes or is he probably the only one in the world with such a diet?

Here are some tips on using evidence.

Choose evidence from credible sources. While watching TV news one night, I was astounded by this story:

> A New York doctor reports that a patient experienced epileptic seizures whenever she heard the voice of Mary Hart, co-host of the TV show *Entertainment Tonight*. The seizures ceased when she stopped watching the show.

My immediate reaction was total disbelief. What nonsense! Hearing a person's voice cannot cause a seizure. But then the news anchor added:

> The woman was the subject of an article in the *New England Journal of Medicine* by Dr. Venkat Ramani, professor of neurology at Albany Medical College in New York.

Just as quickly as I had dismissed the story, I now believed it. Why? Because the *New England Journal of Medicine* is one of the mostly highly respected medical journals in the world.

Evidence–especially the hard-to-believe variety–becomes much more convincing to the audience if you cite a reliable source. Be sure to give specific details; instead of saying, "a judge," give her name and title: "Sharon Brown, Chief Justice of our state's Supreme Court."

Provide a variety of evidence. In some cases, a single example or statistic may be sufficient to bolster an argument, but in most persuasive situations, multiple support is needed.

Use a vivid personal narrative whenever possible. Imagine that you are planning a speech on drunk driving. If you want to convince your listeners that they could be victimized by a drunk driver, which of the following would be the more persuasive piece of evidence?

1. You tell about an automobile crash in which a drunk driver hit your car and killed one of your passengers.
2. You cite the fact that 25,000 people are killed in America each year in alcohol-related car crashes.

Though you would need to use both of these items in your speech, item 1 would be more persuasive for most listeners. But, you might ask, how can one solitary case be more persuasive than a statistic encompassing 25,000 people? Psychologists have conducted scores of experiments that indicate that one vivid narrative, told from the speaker's personal experience, is much more persuasive than its statistical status would imply.[9] "All other things being equal," writes social psychologist Elliot Aronson, "most people are more deeply influenced by one clear, vivid personal example than by an abundance of statistical data."[10]

Using Sound Reasoning

reasoning
using logic to draw conclusions from evidence

Reasoning, the act of reaching conclusions on the basis of logical thinking, is a part of everyday life. If you take an umbrella with you on a walk because you notice heavy clouds massing in the sky, you are using reasoning to prevent yourself from getting soaked by the rain that may soon fall. While it is true that people are not always logical and rational, it is also true that they frequently can be persuaded by a message that appeals to their powers of reasoning.[11]

Let's look at two popular types of reasoning and then examine some common fallacies of reasoning.

Deduction

Imagine that you are driving a car 15 miles per hour over the speed limit. Suddenly you see a police car parked behind a billboard, with a radar device protruding. You slow down, but you know it is too late. Sure enough, you glance in your rearview mirror and see a second police car with lights flashing.

How did you know that you were going to be stopped? By using **deduction**—a chain of reasoning that carries you from (1) a generalization to (2) a specific instance (of the generalization) to (3) a conclusion. In formal logic, this chain of reasoning is expressed in a form of argument known as a **syllogism:**

deduction

reasoning from a generalization to a specific conclusion

syllogism

a deductive scheme consisting of a major premise, a minor premise, and a conclusion

Major premise (generalization):	Motorists who are speeding when they pass a radar point are stopped by police.
Minor premise (specific instance):	I was speeding when I passed a radar point.
Conclusion:	Therefore, I will be stopped.

Deductive reasoning with a syllogism is one of the most powerful tools of persuasion that a speaker can use. If you can convince your listeners to accept the major and minor premises, the conclusion is inescapable. The listeners are compelled by logic to accept it.

Until her death in 1906, Susan B. Anthony fought for the right of women to vote—a right that was not fully secured until 1920, when the Nineteenth Amendment to the Constitution granted nationwide suffrage to women. In speeches delivered throughout the United States, Anthony used deductive logic as her persuasive strategy. If we put the essence of her speeches in the form of a syllogism, it would look like this:

connectpublic
speaking.com
To see a sample of deductive reasoning, view Video Clip 13.1.

Major premise (generalization):	The Constitution guarantees all U.S. citizens the right to vote.
Minor premise (specific instance):	Women are U.S. citizens.
Conclusion:	Therefore, women have the right to vote.

To us today, this syllogism looks simple and obvious: How could Anthony have failed to persuade every listener? But bear in mind that in the 19th century, many people viewed women as less than full-fledged citizens. In her speeches, Anthony had to convince her audience of both the major premise and the minor premise. Those listeners whom she won over were then obliged by force of logic to accept her conclusion.

In a speech, deductive reasoning is convincing *only if both premises are true and are accepted by the audience as true.*[12] Would an audience be likely to accept the following chain of reasoning?

Major premise:	Cardiovascular exercise improves eyesight.
Minor premise:	Jogging is a form of cardiovascular exercise.
Conclusion:	Therefore, jogging improves eyesight.

The minor premise is true, but the major premise is false, so the entire syllogism is flawed. An audience would reject the conclusion.

Now let's turn to the correct use of deductive reasoning: Student speaker Stephanie Haas wanted to persuade her audience that some types of mushrooms and other fungi are in danger of becoming extinct. She realized that some listeners might think, "Well, no big deal. Why should I be concerned?" So Haas used a syllogism to construct her argument:

What is the error in this syllogism? (1) All pizzas have pepperoni, (2) This is a pizza, (3) Therefore, it has pepperoni.

Major premise (generalization):	All plant species that contribute to public health should be preserved.

Minor premise (specific instance):   Endangered species of mushrooms and other fungi contribute to public health by removing toxins from contaminated soil.

Conclusion: Endangered species of mushrooms and other fungi should be preserved.

If listeners believed both the major premise and the minor premise, they were likely to accept her conclusion.

Induction

induction

reasoning from specific evidence to a general conclusion

While deduction moves from the general to the specific, **induction** proceeds from the specific to the general. Imagine that you are a pediatrician seeing patients one January morning in your office:

• The first patient, age 9, complains of a runny nose, a sore throat, a headache, and muscle aches. She has a fever of 103°.

• The second patient, 7, has similar complaints and a fever of 102°.

• Third patient—same symptoms, plus a fever of 101.5°.

• Fourth patient—similar complaints and a fever of 102.5°.

• Fifth patient—similar symptoms and a fever of 103°.

connectpublic
speaking.com
To see a sample of inductive reasoning, view Video Clip 13.2.

You know from your medical training that these complaints are classic symptoms of influenza (or flu). You know that influenza is communicable disease, striking many people in a community, usually in winter. On the basis of what you have seen, you reason inductively that your community is experiencing an influenza outbreak. You use *specific* evidence (or isolated observations) to reach a *general* conclusion. In reaching this conclusion, however, you must take an *inductive leap.* You cannot prove that there is a flu outbreak simply because of your five patients. You are probably right, but your conclusion has to remain tentative (until further evidence is gathered and the county health department declares an outbreak), because there is always the chance that some other explanation can account for your five patients' illness. Perhaps they have nasty colds or suffer from some new virus; perhaps no other patients with those symptoms will show up at your office during the remainder of the week. The chances are overwhelming that an influenza outbreak *is* the explanation, of course; but the point is that induction, unlike deduction, never leads to a certain conclusion, only a *very likely* one.

The Usefulness of Induction

The inductive method is used frequently by scientists. They make isolated observations and then form a hypothesis. They may note, for instance, that the average temperature is rising each year in Sydney, Tokyo, Cairo, Rome, Copenhagen, Montreal, Lima, Mexico City, and Los Angeles. Therefore—now they take an inductive leap—the entire globe is warming up.

The inductive method has often led to useful discoveries. In World War II, British fighter planes had cockpit covers made of plastic. During combat a cover would sometimes shatter, causing pieces of plastic to become lodged in the pilots' eyes. In pilot after pilot, a British physician observed that the eyes were not damaged or infected by the plastic fragments. This observation led to the use of plastic to make artificial lenses, including contact lenses, for people's eyes.

If the top three cookies taste bitter, we can use inductive reasoning to conclude that all the cookies are bitter.

How to Construct an Inductive Argument

Some public speakers construct their inductive arguments by following three steps: (1) ask a question, (2) answer the question by collecting as much specific evidence as possible, and (3) reach a conclusion based on the evidence. Here is an example:

Question: Do some foods give the brain an energy boost?

Evidence:

Item 1:   U.S. military researchers have found that turkey contains an amino acid that lifts energy levels and helps the brain to manage stress.

Item 2:   U.S. Department of Agriculture scientists say that Brazil nuts can help make you feel more clearheaded and mentally confident.

Item 3:   Researchers at Tufts University have concluded that brightly colored vegetables such as carrots and broccoli are "brain food," loaded with vitamins, minerals, and phytochemicals that maintain brain health and enhance mental performance.

Conclusion: Some foods energize the brain.

If you were using this material for a speech, you would need to flesh it out with additional facts, of course, but it gives you a framework, and it helps you think logically.

When you use inductive reasoning, you will convince an audience only if your evidence is strong. If you have weak evidence, your conclusion will be weak.

A Special Use for Inductive Reasoning

Earlier in this book, you were advised to state your central idea in the introduction of your speech; there is, however, an important exception to this guideline. If listeners are likely to have a negative reaction to your central idea, a wise strategy is to lead them through an inductive chain, saving the central idea for the latter part of the speech.

Student speaker Marilyn Zelinsky wanted to convince her audience that the United States should use punishments other than prison for people who are convicted of minor, nonviolent offenses such as writing bad checks and possessing marijuana. She feared, however, that if she stated her central idea in the introduction, her classmates would consider her a crackpot and fail to take her speech seriously. So she withheld her core concept, choosing to build her case with facts and figures like these:[13]

- "The United States has the largest prison population in the world– 2.3 million. While the U.S. has five percent of the world's population, it has about 25 percent of the world's prisoners."

- "We are the only nation that imprisons people for long periods of time for minor crimes, such as passing bad checks and possessing marijuana. We have 700,000 of these offenders locked up right now."

- "To lock up a prisoner costs the taxpayers an average of $24,500 per year. If we didn't have the 700,000 nonviolent prisoners behind bars, we would have $17 billion to spend on more important things."

- "We can punish nonviolent offenders in other ways, such as house arrest, restitution, and community service."

Toward the end of the speech, she was ready to make her case for alternative sentencing. Her strategy must have worked, because many students, on their evaluation sheets, said they found her argument highly persuasive.

An inductive line of reasoning helps listeners keep an open mind. When they watch you build your case block by block, they are more respectful and appreciative of the central idea when it is finally presented to them. This doesn't mean they will always agree with you, of course, but it does mean that those who are opposed to your ideas will probably see more merit to your case than they would if you announced your central idea in the introduction.

Quick tip: If you have trouble remembering the difference between deduction and induction, keep in mind that they travel in opposite directions. Deduction (think of the word *deduct* in the sense of taking *away*) leads *away* from a generalization; it goes from general to specific, applying a general principle to a specific case. Induction (think of the first two letters *in*) leads *into,* or toward, a generalization; it goes from specific to general, accumulating specific instances that point toward a general idea.

Fallacies in Reasoning

fallacy
an argument based on a false inference

A **fallacy** is an error in reasoning that renders an argument false or unreliable. You should become adept at recognizing fallacies so that (1) you can avoid using them in your own speeches—an ethical speaker would never knowingly mislead an audience—and (2) you can prevent yourself from being influenced by them when you listen to the speeches of others. Here are some common fallacies.

Bandwagon

bandwagon fallacy
equating popularity with truth and proof

"Most voters in our community are supporting Sandra Dawkins for mayor, so jump on our bandwagon as we roll to victory." This is an example of the **bandwagon fallacy,** an argument based on popularity rather than on evidence and reasoning.

Some speakers use public opinion polls to create a bandwagon effect for their argument: "Over 80 percent of Americans believe that beef is an important part of a healthy diet." Although poll results may be interesting, a poll number by itself does not prove the value of anything. A speaker arguing for beef should use nutritional data and other evidence.

Hasty Generalization

hasty generalization
a conclusion that is based on inadequate evidence

A **hasty generalization** is a conclusion that is reached on the basis of insufficient evidence. In a speech on managing credit card debt, a student speaker said that "almost all students on this campus are deeply in debt because of credit cards." When he was challenged in the question-and-answer period by students who disbelieved him, he revealed that he had based his statement on interviews with four friends. If he had polled a larger number of students, he would have seen a different picture.

Red Herring

red herring
diverting listeners from the real issue to an irrelevant matter

In 17th-century England, according to legend, if criminals were being pursued by bloodhounds, they would drag a red herring (smoked fish) across the trail, confusing the dogs and making them veer off into a new direction.

A **red herring** argument distracts listeners from the real issue and leads them toward an irrelevant issue. This trick is frequently used in political debates.

One legislator, for example, may argue for laws protecting the California condor, and then an opponent counters, "How can we even think about birds when our most pressing problems deal with humans? Let's work on taking care of homeless people before we get all hot and bothered about animals."

The fallacy is also used in courtroom battles. If, say, a tobacco company is being sued by the government for endangering the health of citizens, a tobacco-company lawyer might try to divert the jury to a different subject: "Ladies and gentlemen of the jury, the government tells you that tobacco is poisonous, but they say nothing about alcohol. They say nothing about the 20,000 people killed each year by drunk drivers. I don't see the government suing whisky makers." Lawyers who employ this trick sometimes win their cases, but ethical speakers should never use it.

Ethical Issue

Attack on a Person

Some speakers try to win an argument by attacking a person rather than the person's ideas. For example: "Fitzroy has lived in upper-class luxury all his life, so how can we believe anything he says about government assistance for the poor? He obviously knows nothing about poverty." This **attack on a person,** sometimes known as *argumentum ad hominem* (argument against the man), is unfair and unethical. Fitzroy's arguments should be judged on how sound his ideas are, not on any aspect of his personal life.

attack on a person
criticizing an opponent rather than the opponent's argument

Attacks on a person are often used in the courtroom to discredit a witness ("Ladies and gentlemen of the jury, this witness admits that he's an atheist, so how can we trust him to tell us the truth?") and in politics to discredit a foe ("My opponent has gambled in Las Vegas at least five times. Do you want such a person to manage your tax dollars?"). Though this tactic may sometimes be effective, the ethical speaker never uses it, not only because it is dishonest and unfair, but also because it can backfire and cause careful listeners to lose respect for the speaker.

Your Thoughts

The "attack on a person" fallacy is often effective in political battles. Why do you think this is so?

False Cause

Beware of the fallacy of **false cause**—assuming that because events occur close together in time, they are necessarily related as cause and effect. A president takes office and four months later the unemployment rate goes up 1 percent. Can we say that the president's policies caused the rise in unemployment? It is possible that they did, but other factors may have caused the problem—for example, the economic policies of the previous administration.

false cause
assuming that because two events are related in time, the first caused the second

The fallacy of false cause also can occur when a speaker oversimplifies the causes of complex problems. Take, for example, a speaker who says that *the* cause of cancer is negative thinking. That explanation is simple and understandable—and wrong. While negative thinking may be a contributing factor in cancer, medical researchers say that no one thing has been isolated as *the* cause of cancer. The disease is probably caused by an interaction of several factors, including genetic predisposition, susceptibility of the immune system, the presence of a carcinogenic virus, and environmental irritants. Cancer is too complex to be explained by a single cause.

Building on an Unproven Assumption

Some speakers act as if an assertion has been proved when in fact it has not. Suppose that a speaker tells an audience: "Since distance learning with a computer is more effective than traditional classroom education, all of you should take your college courses on your home computers." The speaker is acting as if the superiority of distance learning is an established fact, when in reality many people disagree. An ethical speaker would first try to prove the merits of distance learning and then urge the audience to support it.

The fallacy of **building on an unproven assumption** (which is also called "begging the question") makes careful listeners resentful. They feel as if they are being tricked into giving assent to a proposition that they don't believe.

False Analogy

When speakers use a **false analogy,** they make the mistake of assuming that because two things are alike in minor ways, they are also alike in major ways. Here is an example: "We can communicate effectively via satellite with people on the other side of the planet, so it should be easy for parents and children to communicate effectively within the intimate environment of their own homes." Upon close examination, this analogy falls apart. Satellite communication between nations is a purely technical matter of transmitting radio and television signals, whereas communication among family members is far more complex, involving psychological subtleties that are beyond the reach of technology.

Either-Or Reasoning

The **either-or fallacy** occurs when a speaker offers only two alternatives, when in fact there are many. For example: "Either we halt the world's population growth, or we face widespread starvation." Aren't there other options, such as improving agriculture and slowing down the rate of population growth?

Stating an argument in stark, either-or terms makes a speaker appear unreasonable and dogmatic. Most problems should be seen as a complex mosaic of many colors—not a simple choice between pure red and pure green.

Straw Man

To win arguments, some people create a **straw man,** a ridiculous caricature of what their opponents believe, and then beat it down with great ease. Here is an example: A defender of the death penalty attacks his opponents by saying, "These people think the life of a convicted murderer is worth more than the lives of the police officers and prison guards who protect us."[14] This is a false statement—it is not an accurate reflection of what his opponents believe—but it creates an easy target, made of straw. He can knock it down, smash it, and make himself look like a victor.

Appealing to Motivations

Motivations are the needs, desires, or drives that impel a person toward a goal or away from some negative situation. People have hundreds of motivations, including love, happiness, and health.[15] If you show your listeners how your ideas can help them satisfy such needs and desires, you increase your chances of persuading them to adopt your point of view.[16] Here are some examples of how student speakers appealed to the motivations of their audiences:

- To raise money to buy food for starving people in Africa, LeeAnne Washington appealed to the motivation that most Americans have to help those less fortunate than themselves.

building on an unproven assumption
treating an opinion that is open to question as if it were already proved

false analogy
creating a comparison that is exaggerated or erroneous

either-or fallacy
presenting only two alternatives when in fact more exist

straw man
a weak opponent or dubious argument set up so that it can be easily defeated

motivations
the impulses and needs that stimulate a person to act in a certain way

connectpublic speaking.com
To see a speaker who appeals to motivations, view Video Clip 13.3.

- To try to persuade listeners to use seat belts at all times in a car, Jason Bradley appealed to the strong drive that people have to protect themselves from harm.

Some Common Motivations

Here are some of the more common motivations that audiences have:

- Love and esteem
- Success
- Recreational pleasure
- Social acceptance

- Health
- Financial security
- Altruism
- Adventure

- Safety
- Self-improvement
- Curiosity
- Creativity

A popular model for analyzing motivations is **Maslow's hierarchy of needs,** created by the late Abraham Maslow, an American psychologist. As shown in Figure 13.1, the hierarchy starts at the bottom with the most basic human needs and ranges upward to more and more sophisticated levels.[17]

At the top is **self-actualization,** where one realizes his or her full potential as a human. Maslow believed that when lower-level needs are present, they will usually take precedence. For example, if you are sleep-deprived and sick (lowest level), you probably will have no energy to engage in a creative activity such as violin playing (highest level).

Maslow's hierarchy of needs
a ranking of human needs from simple to complex

self-actualization
the need of humans to make the most of their abilities

Figure 13.1
Maslow's Hierarchy of Needs

Psychologist Abraham Maslow organized human motivations in a hierarchy that ranged from basic biological needs (at the bottom) to self-actualization needs (at the top).

Table 13.3   **Motivations and Appeals**

Motivation	Appeal
Feeling good	Bicycling works out tension and makes you feel energetic and happy.
Looking good	Bicycling burns lots of calories, so it's ideal for weight control. It also tones up leg muscles.
Long-term health	Bicycling is excellent exercise for heart and lungs, thus helping prevent cardiovascular disease.
Friendship	Being on a bicycle is an instant passport to the world of cyclists. It's easy to strike up conversations with other riders, and you can often make new friends. Cycling also provides an enjoyable activity to share with old friends.
Adventure	With a bicycle you can explore out-of-the-way places, travel long distances in a single day, and experience the thrill of flying down a steep mountain road.
Competition	If you enjoy competing, there are bike races in almost every city or town.

Models such as Maslow's hierarchy can't cover all human needs, but they do remind us of the multiple motivations that can be found in our listeners.

Multiple Motivations

Whenever possible, appeal to more than one motivation. Listeners who are not reached by one appeal may be influenced by another. Suppose, for example, that you were trying to persuade your listeners to take up bicycling. Table 13.3 shows some of the motivations that you could identify, coupled with appropriate appeals.

By appealing to more than one motivation, you increase your chances of persuading the audience. For example, the listener who is already in superb health may not be reached by any of the first three items but might be swayed by one of the last three.

Arousing Emotions

Emotions are spontaneous feelings that can be either positive (amusement, love, joy) or negative (fear, anger, sadness). You can use emotional appeals to stimulate listeners and rouse them to action.

How can emotions be evoked? By using support materials (such as provocative narratives) or powerful language (such as vivid metaphors).

As an example of how emotions can be used effectively, here is an excerpt from a speech by student speaker Ralph Barnes on how people with disabilities are sometimes victimized:

> Theresa Delzatto, 35, of Hartford, Connecticut, is paralyzed from the neck down. She survives on a Social Security check and lives in public housing. Just before Christmas last year, she went to Wal-Mart in her wheelchair to do some Christmas shopping. She went to the courtesy desk and explained that she could not use her arms, and she asked for assistance. An 18-year-old clerk was assigned to take items from the shelves and put them in her cart. When she was ready to pay, the clerk helped out by taking Delzatto's debit card from her purse and handing it to the cashier. But then—believe it or not—the clerk never

returned the card! Instead she and a 17-year-old cousin went on a shopping spree with the card and racked up more than $400 worth of purchases. They were later arrested and charged with larceny, but the money was gone. The theft wiped out all of Delzatto's money. She told the *Hartford Courant,* "I'm at the point where I'm just ready to give in. It destroyed most of my independence." Can you believe that anyone could be so mean—especially at Christmas?[18]

This story was effective in eliciting anger—an appropriate emotion for listeners to experience as they learned of the outrages that are sometimes committed against people with disabilities.

Here are some tips on arousing emotions.

Always combine emotional appeals with rational appeals.   If you appeal only to emotions, you play a risky game, because you give the audience only one underpinning for a belief. Here's an example:

Two speakers were debating the morality of the death penalty for convicted murderers. The first speaker, who was opposed to the penalty, concentrated on the ghastly horrors of electrocution, showing grisly photographs and giving lurid descriptions of charred flesh and prolonged suffering. The second speaker quickly conceded that electrocution was barbaric and argued instead for the death penalty by means of lethal injection, which he described as more humane. He gave philosophical and moral justifications for the death penalty, and then he aroused emotions in the listeners by describing the terrible ordeal of victims of crime and their families. From comments made by listeners at the end, it was clear that the second speaker had convinced previously neutral listeners to adopt his position.

Is it ever appropriate to surprise your listeners?

Regardless of how you feel about this controversial issue, I hope you can see that because the first speaker dealt only with emotions, he let himself be outmaneuvered. There are many sound arguments that can be made against the death penalty; if he had used some of them—in addition to his emotional appeal—he might have won over some listeners to his view.

While people can be swayed by emotional appeals, they also need to think of themselves as rational. They need to have justification for the feelings and passions they embrace in their hearts. If you use logic and emotion together, you have a more powerful speech than if you use either one alone.[19]

Know how to use fear.   Over the years, communicators have wondered how much fear one should evoke in trying to persuade people. For example, if you want to convince an audience to avoid tailgating on the highway, would you be more successful with some low-fear visual aids, such as a chart on traffic fatalities, or with some high-fear graphics, such as a gory, full-color videotape of victims of a terrible car wreck? Research favors the latter. "The overwhelming weight of experimental data," writes psychologist Elliot Aronson, "suggests that . . . the more frightened a person is by a communication, the more likely he or she is to take positive preventive action."[20] Research also indicates that high-fear messages are most effective when they are coupled with specific instructions on how to take action. For example, a high-fear message on rabies would be more persuasive if it included instructions on how to avoid the disease than if it left out such instructions.[21]

Use emotional appeals ethically. Any emotion can be exploited in the wrong way. Fear and loathing, desirable when targeted at an infectious disease, are reprehensible, even immoral, when aimed at a minority group. Unfortunately, some politicians have demonstrated that creating or exploiting fears and hatreds can win elections. If you are an ethical speaker, however, you will never let short-term gain entice you into using such tactics. If, for example, you are trying to mobilize public opinion to save an endangered species of bird, you will not demonize homebuilders who want to build on the bird's natural habitat; you will not foment hatred by falsely portraying them as merciless killers. Instead, you will channel emotional appeals in appropriate ways—by generating sadness over the possible disappearance of the bird or by appealing to the happiness listeners might feel over saving endangered creatures.

To determine whether you are acting ethically, identify each emotion you want to arouse and then answer the following questions.

- Do you avoid scapegoating any person or group?
- Does the emotion reinforce, rather than replace, solid evidence and sound logic? (If not, is it because your case is unsupportable and illogical?)
- In arousing this emotion, are you treating the issue and the opposing side with fairness? (Put yourself in the shoes of an opponent and see if your treatment looks fair from that perspective.)

If you cannot answer yes to all three, your ethical footing is shaky. You should omit the emotional appeal or alter the speech.

Develop the emotional appeals inherent in some pieces of evidence. Often you don't need to hunt for emotional appeals to add to your accumulation of evidence. All you need to do is develop the evidence already collected so that it moves the listeners. Let's say that while preparing a speech on the appalling murder rate, you found this statistic: about 25,000 homicides occurred in the United States last year. You can state that figure in your speech and then develop it for emotional impact: "That means that every 22 minutes, another American is shot . . . stabbed . . . beaten . . . or strangled to death." By expressing a fact in this dramatic way, you help your listeners feel the magnitude of the problem. Note that vivid language ("stabbed," "beaten," and so on) enhances the emotional impact.

Sample Persuasive Speech

The following speech by Turron Kofi Alleyne uses the problem–solution pattern. The outline is presented first, with a commentary in the margin. To view a video of the speech, visit www.connectpublicspeaking.com.

The Outline with Commentary

Would You Vote for Aardvark?

Commentary

General Purpose: To persuade

Specific Purpose: To persuade my listeners to support the rotation of names on ballots

Central Idea: Rotating names on a ballot can eliminate the unfair advantage that some candidates enjoy.

INTRODUCTION

I. Attention Material
  A. Imagine running for political office.
  B. Then imagine you lose because your name is not the first on the ballot.

Asking listeners to imagine themselves in a scenario is an effective attention-getter.

II. Orienting Material
  A. This unfairness happens all over the world.
  B. The first name on the ballot gets an advantage over all other names.
  C. Let's explore the problem and then look at the solution, which is rotation of names.

(*Transition:* Let's examine the problem first.)

BODY

I. The first name on the ballot gets 2 to 4 percent more votes than other names, according to researchers.

The speaker devotes the first half of the body to the problem.

  A. Although it doesn't guarantee victory, it gives an unfair reward.
    1. Imagine Anne Adams and Linda Yates are running for mayor. (Show slide.) [See Figure 13.2.]

    A hypothetical example and visual aids help the audience see what is happening.

      a. Adams gets the 2 to 4 percent advantage.
      b. This could provide victory in a close race.
    2. Let's use a 2 percent example.
      a. Adams wins, 51 to 49 percent. (Show slide.) [See Figure 13.3.]
      b. But if names are reversed, Yates wins, 51 to 49 percent.
  B. Some voters prefer whichever name is first.
    1. Dr. Jon Krosnick of Stanford University thinks he knows why.

    Citing a researcher enhances the credibility of the speech.

    2. These voters are totally ignorant about the candidates or they are undecided.
    3. But they feel obligated to vote, so they mark the top name.
  C. It is common in minor elections for the first-listed candidate to win.
    1. Statistics professor Don Piele studied elections results of the past 26 years for the Racine Unified School District.

    Research information provides good evidence to back up the speaker's point.

(continued)

2. Candidates were much more likely to win if their name was listed first.

(*Transition:* Let's turn to the solution.)

II. A simple solution is to rotate all names.

    A. Each candidate gets the top slot an equal number of times.

    B. Let's expand our original example. (Show slide.) [See Figure 13.4.]

       1. Yates, Adams, and Garcia are running.

       2. One third of voters would see Yates first, one third would see Adams first, and one third would see Garcia first.

       3. This is fair because each person would get the 2 to 4 percent bounce on an equal number of ballots.

    C. Rotation has been tried in some states and counties.

       1. In Ohio, rotation is by precinct.

       2. Dr. Krosnick says Ohio has the fairest election system in the nation.

       3. In other areas, there are campaigns to adopt the rotation system.

    D. Throughout the world, some nations are trying to set up fair systems.

       1. Reformers are at work in nations that list names alphabetically, including Ireland, Australia, and New Zealand.

       2. In New Zealand, some candidates change their name to Aaronson, Abbey, and Abernathy to get the top spot. (Show slide.) [See Figure 13.5.]

       3. One New Zealander changed his name to Aaron A. Aardvark.

          a. He has not yet run for office.

          b. Some New Zealanders hope to change to a rotation system before he chooses to run.

(*Transition:* Let's sum up.)

CONCLUSION

I. Summary

    A. The first candidate listed on a ballot gets an unfair 2 to 4 percent edge.

The second half of the body is devoted to the solution.

Showing that the proposed solution actually works is a powerful argument.

Humorous information enlivens the speech.

A complete-sentence outline helps speakers organize material intelligently. For actual delivery, however, a speaker should not read the outline but, instead, use brief notes that are based on the outline.

  B.   The solution is a rotation system with each
       candidate listed first an equal number of times.

II. Clincher

  A.   Please support the rotation system in your
       community and state.

  B.   We can't let Aardvarks win all elections.

*The speech closes with a graceful
finale.*

BIBLIOGRAPHY

Block, Dustin. "Ballot Bias? Exploring the Name-Order
    Effect in Local Elections." *The Journal Times* [Racine,
    WI] 23 Mar. 2003: 1+. Print.

"Does New Zealand Need to Rotate Candidate Names?"
    Scoop Independent News. 12 Mar. 2006. Web. 4 Aug.
    2008.

Koppell, Jonathan, and Jennifer A. Steen. "The Effects
    of Ballot Position on Election Outcomes." *Journal of
    Politics* 66 (2004): 267–281. Print.

Krosnick, Jon A. "In the Voting Booth, Bias Starts at the
    Top." *New York Times* 4 Nov. 2006: 27. Print.

VISUAL AIDS

*Four PowerPoint slides illustrating technical points
in the speech*

The Speech as Delivered

Here is the transcript of Turron Kofi Alleyne's speech, which uses the problem–
solution pattern. Notice that the speaker uses the ideas of the outline without using
the exact wording. In an extemporaneous speech, a speaker does not read or
memorize a speech but speaks from brief notes.

connectpublic
speaking.com
View the video of the
speech.

Would You Vote for Aardvark?

Imagine that you are running for a political office and your name is on the ballot. Now imagine that
    you lose this election simply because your name is not the first one listed on the ballot.

Now this would be unfair, of course, but this unfairness happens throughout this country and
    throughout the world—the name that is listed first on the ballot gets an advantage over all the
    other names. Today I want to show you the full extent of this unfairness and then offer you an ideal
    solution—rotating the names.

Let's start by looking at the problems. Studies by political scientists reveal that the first name on the
    ballot gets two to four percent more votes than it would get if it were listed later. This doesn't
    mean that the first name wins all the time. No, it just means that the first name gets an unfair

Figure 13.2
The first name listed on a ballot gets 2 to 4 percent more votes than it would receive if it were listed lower.

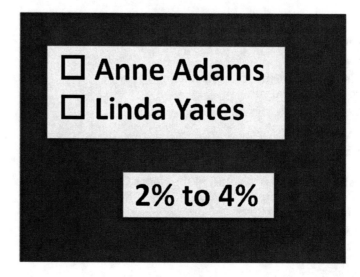

boost. Here's how it works: *[The speaker shows the PowerPoint slide in Figure 13.2.]* Let's say Anne Adams and Linda Yates are competing for mayor of a city. And merely by being first, Adams will get a two to four percent advantage. Now in a close election, that can make the difference between winning and losing. Let's use an example with a two percentage advantage. *[The speaker shows the slide in Figure 13.3.]* Imagine Adams wins 51 percent to 49 percent. But if Yates were listed first, she would get the advantage, and she would win 51 to 49 percent.

The problem is that some voters favor whichever name is listed first, and this raises the question, Why? Dr. Jon Krosnick, a professor of communication, political science, and psychology at Stanford University, has a theory. He says that some voters know nothing about the candidates, or maybe they're undecided and unable to make a decision. Yet, at the same time, these voters feel obligated to vote, so they just grab the name on the top.

Figure 13.3
In a close election, being the top name on the ballot can guarantee victory.

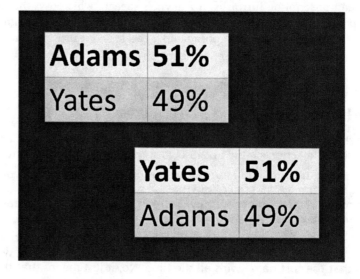

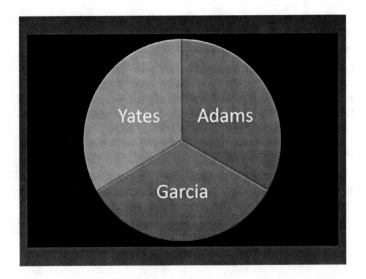

Figure 13.4
If these candidates vied in a rotation system, each name would be listed first for one-third of voters.

Researchers say that in minor elections—for president of a local school board, for example—it is common for candidates to win simply because they got the top spot on the ballot. Don Piele, a statistics professor at the University of Wisconsin–Parkside, reviewed school board election results from the past 26 years at Racine Unified School District. He found that candidates listed first on the ballot were far more likely to win than those that were listed later.

This situation is obviously unfair, so what is the solution? It's simple: Names should be rotated on the ballots. Each candidate's name should appear first an equal number of times. Let's take our earlier example and expand it. *[The speaker shows the slide in Figure 13.4.]* Let's say that Yates, Adams, and Garcia are the candidates. One third of the voters would see a ballot with Yates first. One third of the voters would see Adams first, and one third would see Garcia first. This would provide fairness because each candidate would enjoy the two to four percent advantage an equal amount of times on the ballots.

Has this system been tried anywhere? Yes, some states and counties rotate names so that each candidate is at the top spot an equal number of times. Dr. Krosnick of Stanford says that in the state

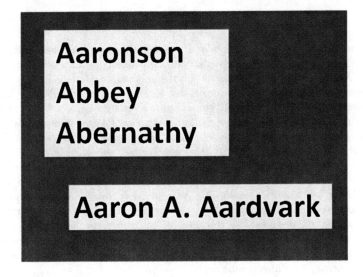

Figure 13.5
In countries with ballots by alphabetical order, some candidates change their names in order to be the first name on the ballot.

of Ohio, candidate names are rotated from precinct to precinct. As a result, Ohio has the fairest election system in the nation, according to Dr. Krosnick. In many other areas, there are people who are campaigning to get their state to change to a rotation system.

The United States is not the only country that is trying to get a fair deal for the candidates. No. In several countries that list their candidates' names alphabetically, such as Ireland, Australia, and New Zealand, reformers are fighting to change to a rotation system. For years, New Zealand has seen some candidates change their names [Figure 13.5] to Aaronson, Abbey, and Abernathy in order to get the top listing on the ballot. One man in New Zealand has changed his name to Aaron A. Aardvark. He has not run for office yet, and some New Zealanders are hoping their nation can change to a rotation system before he can get his name at the top of all the ballots.

Let's review what we've covered. We have seen the name listed first gets a two to four percent advantage over all the other names, and this is simply not fair. The solution is to have names rotated so that each candidate's name appears on top for an equal number of voters.

I urge all of you to support the rotation system in your state, in your community. After all, we can't have the Aardvarks of the world win all the elections.

Resources for Review and Skill Building

connectpublic
speaking.com

Connect Public Speaking provides resources for study and review, including sample speech videos, an Outline Tutor, and practice tests.

Summary

To be effective in persuasion, you must have a thorough *knowledge of the audience.* Find out exactly where your listeners stand concerning your view. Are they opposed, apathetic, neutral, or already convinced? Then plan a strategy to move them toward your position.

During a persuasive speech, enhance *credibility* with the audience by explaining your competence, by being honest and careful with speech material, by remaining open-minded, and by showing common ground with listeners.

Build your case by using strong *evidence* (such as statistics, examples, and testimony) that is accurate, up-to-date, and typical. Try to use a variety of sources, all of them reliable and reputable.

Use sound *reasoning* as a powerful tool of persuasion. Two popular forms are deductive reasoning, in which

you take a generalization or a principle and apply it to a specific case, and inductive reasoning, in which you observe specific instances and then form a generalization. In using logic, avoid these fallacies: bandwagon, hasty generalization, red herring, attack on a person, false cause, building on an unproven assumption, false analogy, either-or reasoning, or straw man attacks.

Whenever possible, appeal to listeners' *motivations*– their needs, desires, and drives that impel them toward a goal or away from some negative situation. Focus on the listeners' needs, not your own. If possible, appeal to more than one motivation, and anticipate conflicting needs.

Finally, try to arouse the listeners' *emotions,* making sure that you always combine emotional appeals with rational appeals, and that you always use emotions ethically.

Key Terms

attack on a person, *357*

bandwagon fallacy, *356*

building on an unproven assumption, *358*

credibility, *348*

deduction, *353*

either-or fallacy, *358*

evidence, *351*

fallacy, *356*

false analogy, *358*

false cause, *357*

hasty generalization, *356*

induction, *354*

Maslow's hierarchy of needs, *359*

motivations, *358*

reasoning, *352*

red herring, *356*

self-actualizations, *359*

straw man, *358*

syllogism, *353*

Review Questions

1. Why are sarcastic remarks inappropriate when directed toward listeners who are hostile to your view?

2. Why is it a good idea in many cases to tell the audience why you are competent to speak on your particular subject?

3. How is an audience likely to react if you are careless with your facts and ideas?

4. Which is more persuasive with the typical audience: one vivid personal narrative or a series of statistical data?

5. What is the difference between deduction and induction?

6. Why should a speaker never use the logical fallacy called "attack on a person"?

7. What is the "straw man" fallacy?

8. What is a "red herring" argument?

9. List at least five motivations that all listeners have.

10. Why should emotional appeals always be accompanied by rational appeals?

Building Critical-Thinking Skills

1. One of the most influential books in American history, *Silent Spring,* was published in 1962 as a warning against the health hazards of pesticides. Its author, Rachel Carson, was attacked by a scientist who questioned her concern for future generations because she was an unmarried woman with no children. What fallacy of reasoning was the scientist using? Why was the criticism invalid?

2. A TV commercial shows a video of an attractive young couple running barefoot on a beach while a voice says, "ABC multivitamin supplements—just one a day for the rest of your life." Identify the motivational appeals contained in the commercial.

Building Teamwork Skills

1. In a survey reported by *Health* magazine, 89 percent of adults said they know they should exercise three times a week for good health, but only 27 percent actually do. In a group, compile a list of excuses that people might use for not exercising. Then, for each excuse, brainstorm strategies that a speaker could use to discourage it.

2. Working in a group, list the motivations that students in a typical high school class are likely to have. Then brainstorm how an Army recruiter could appeal to each motivation in a speech aimed at persuading the students to join the military.

TV personality Matt Gallant gives an inspirational speech at the University of Rhode Island after receiving an honorary doctorate. Inspirational speeches are one of six special types of speeches discussed in this chapter.

chapter 7

Special Types of Speeches

OUTLINE

Entertaining Speech
Techniques for Entertaining
Sample Entertaining Speech

Speech of Introduction

Speech of Presentation

Speech of Acceptance

Speech of Tribute
Wedding Speeches
Toasts
Eulogies

Inspirational Speech

OBJECTIVES

After studying this chapter, you should be able to:

1. Prepare an entertaining speech.
2. Prepare a speech of introduction.
3. Prepare a speech of presentation.
4. Prepare a speech of acceptance.
5. Prepare a speech of tribute.
6. Prepare an inspirational speech.
7. Identify potential pitfalls in using humor in a speech.

In some parts of America in 1955, African Americans were treated as second-class citizens, and they suffered many indignities, such as being forbidden to go to school with whites and being forced to stand in public buses if a white passenger needed a seat. On December 1 of that year, a woman named Rosa Parks was riding a city bus in Montgomery, Alabama, and she refused the bus driver's order to give up her seat to make room for a white passenger. She was arrested and later convicted on a charge of disorderly conduct.

Parks's dramatic resistance to racial injustice—and the international attention it created—played a major role in the struggle for racial equality in the United States.

When Rosa Parks died in 2005 at the age of 92, she was eulogized by another famous African-American woman, Gwen Ifill, senior correspondent for the PBS television network. Here is an excerpt from her speech:

> With a solitary, sacrificial act, she became the kind of black woman I would spend the rest of my life striving to be . . . the kind of woman who bristled at injustice because she worshipped a just God . . . the kind of woman who did not have to raise her voice—ever—because she possessed the gift of that kind of quiet moral authority that can silence a room, or a nation.[1]

Gwen Ifill appears on NBC's *Meet the Press* program.

Ifill's eulogy is an example of a special kind of speech that will be discussed in this chapter. Though most of the speeches that you will give in your lifetime will probably be informative or persuasive, there are occasions when you may be called upon to give other kinds—an entertaining speech at a banquet, a brief speech introducing the main speaker at a convention, a few words announcing the presentation of an award, a eulogy at a funeral to honor a close friend, an acceptance speech to thank an organization for giving you an award, or an inspirational speech to lift the morale of your subordinates or fellow employees.

Entertaining Speech

An **entertaining speech** provides amusement or diversion for the audience. It can be given in any setting, from classroom to convention hall. It is sometimes referred to as an "after-dinner speech" because it is often given after a meal. People who have just eaten want to sit back, relax, and enjoy a talk. They don't want to work hard mentally. They don't want to hear anything heavy and negative.

entertaining speech
an oral address designed to amuse or engage listeners

An entertaining speech can contain a few elements of persuasion and information, but the primary goal is not to persuade or inform, but to create an interesting diversion—an enjoyable experience—for the audience.

Techniques for Entertaining

To entertain, do you have to tell jokes that elicit loud laughter? Not necessarily. Joke telling is just one option among many. (See the Special Techniques feature "How to Use Humor" in this chapter.) Here are some other devices you can use to entertain an audience.

Anecdotes, Examples, and Quotations

Using a single theme, some speakers string together anecdotes, examples, or quotations as if creating a string of pearls—one bright jewel after another. In a speech on the crackpot predictions that so-called experts have made over the centuries, Sarah Caldwell-Evans gave her audience one astonishing quotation after another. Here's an instance:

> When women began to enter all-male professions at the beginning of the 20th century, many prominent men warned that such work would be disastrous for women. Here's what a professor at Berlin University, Hans Friedenthal, said in 1904: "Brain work will cause the 'new woman' to become bald, while increasing masculinity and contempt for beauty will induce the growth of hair on the face. In the future, therefore, women will be bald and will wear long mustaches and patriarchal beards."

Entertaining Speech topic: My quest for the best ice cream flavor

Narratives

An interesting journey, an exciting adventure, or a comical sequence of events can make an enjoyable speech, even if the story is serious. For example:

- A speaker related her encounter with a grizzly bear while backpacking in the Rocky Mountains.

Special Techniques

How to Use Humor

"Cats are smarter than dogs," says comedian Jeff Valdez. "You can't get eight cats to pull a sled through snow."

If used effectively, humor is a good way to keep an audience interested in your speech. It creates a bond of friendship between you and the listeners, and it puts them into a receptive, trusting mood. Here are some guidelines.

1. Use humor only when it is appropriate. A speech about a solemn subject such as euthanasia would not lend itself to an injection of humor.

2. Tell jokes at your own risk. A popular kind of humor is the joke—a funny story that depends on a punch line for its success. If you are an accomplished humorist, you may be able to use jokes effectively, but I don't recommend that any novice speaker use them, for these reasons:

- Jokes usually don't tie in smoothly with the rest of the speech.

- Few speakers (whether experienced or inexperienced) can tell jokes well.

- A joke that is successful with your friends might bomb with a large audience.

- The audience may have heard the joke already.

- Listeners may not be in a receptive mood.

I have seen speakers tell a joke that no one laughed at—not one single person. Maybe the audience had heard the joke before, or maybe it was too early in the morning or too late in the evening. Whatever the reason, a joke that fizzles can be devastating to the speaker's morale, and it can lessen the impact of the speech.

"But it looks so easy on TV," some students say. It looks easy and *is* easy because TV joke tellers have advantages that most speakers lack: They have studio audiences that are predisposed to laugh at virtually any joke the comedians tell. (Your audiences will probably not be poised for laughter in this way.) They have gag writers who test the jokes out before they are used. Most important of all, they are talented performers who have years of joke-telling experience.

3. Use low-key humor. A mildly amusing story, quotation, or observation—although not as spectacular as a side-splitting joke—can be effective. The best thing about low-key humor is that it's safe. While the success of a joke depends on the audience laughing immediately after the punch line, the success of a light story or a witty observation does not depend on laughter—or even smiles. Sometimes the only audience response is an inner delight. In a speech on the elaborate cheating systems that some students use on tests, student speaker Henry Mandell said:

> There is one method of cheating that guarantees that you won't be caught. The night before a test, make a cheat sheet. Memorize it. Then tear it up to destroy the evidence. The next morning, you'll do well on the test.

Mandell was using the kind of wry humor that does not depend on belly laughs. It was not a joke. If the listeners laughed or smiled, fine; if they didn't, no harm was done. It was still enjoyable.

- A police officer gave an hour-by-hour account of the extraordinary security measures taken by the Secret Service when a presidential candidate made a campaign stop in one city.

- One speaker told of the mishaps and misunderstandings that caused her to arrive late and frazzled at her wedding.

Descriptions

You can entertain with vivid descriptions of fascinating places, interesting people, or intriguing objects. For example:

- To give her audience an impression of the bright colors and exotic varieties of birds in the Amazonian rain forest, one speaker showed color slides she had taken of birds in a Brazilian zoo.

- At the meeting of a culinary club, the chef of a gourmet restaurant gave an after-dinner talk in which he described various French pastries. As the chef discussed each type of pastry, a sample was served to each listener.

4. Always relate humor to the subject matter. Never tell an amusing story about a farmer unless your speech is about farming and the story ties in with the rest of the speech.

5. Never use humor that could possibly offend any person in the audience. Avoid humor that is sexual. Avoid humor that targets members of any group in society (racial, ethnic, religious, political, gender, and so on). Even if the audience contains no members of a particular group, you are unwise to ridicule that group because you risk alienating listeners who dislike such humor.

6. Never let your face show that you expect laughter or smiles. If you say something that you think is hilarious, don't stand with an expectant grin on your face, waiting for a reaction. If no one smiles or laughs, you will feel very foolish. And remember, failure to get any smiles or laughs doesn't necessarily mean that the listeners did not appreciate your humor. As mentioned in guideline 3, many kinds of humor elicit only an inner delight.

7. Consider using self-deprecating humor in some situations. Benjamin Franklin was a speaker who was willing to poke fun at himself in a speech. For example, he liked to tell audiences about an incident that occurred in Paris while he was attending a public gathering that featured many speeches. He spoke French, but he had trouble understanding the formal, rhetorical language of French orators. Wishing to appear polite, he decided that he would applaud whenever he noticed a distinguished woman, Mme. de Boufflers, express satisfaction. After the meeting, his grandson said to him, "But Grandpapa, you always applauded, and louder than anybody else, when they were praising you."

Many good speakers tell humorous anecdotes at their own expense because it's an effective way to build rapport with the audience—to create a bond of warmth, trust, and acceptance. Franklin's listeners must have been delighted to learn that the Great Man was capable of committing a faux pas, just like everyone else, and they loved him all the more.

Self-deprecating humor has two bonuses: (1) When you tell about something you did or said, there is no danger that the audience has heard it before. (2) You don't risk offending anyone—your target is yourself, not some group.

Two notes of caution:

- Poke fun at any aspect of yourself except your nervousness. (In Chapter 2 we discussed why you should never call attention to your jitters.)

- Don't use self-deprecating humor if you have not yet established your expertise or authority. For example, if you are a new employee who is making a presentation to the board of directors of a corporation, self-effacing humor could weaken your credibility. By contrast, if you are a manager whose confidence and power are well-known to your audience of subordinates, laughing at yourself can build rapport.

An entertaining speech does not need to be as elaborately structured as an informative or persuasive speech, but it should have a unifying theme—in other words, all your material should tie together—and it should have the standard three parts of a speech: (1) an introduction to gain the attention and interest of the audience, (2) a body that develops the theme in satisfying detail, and (3) a conclusion that provides a graceful finale.

Choose a topic that you find enjoyable, and as you deliver your speech, try to share your enjoyment with the audience. Be light and good-natured. Have fun along with your listeners.

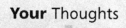

Your Thoughts

Psychologists have discovered that humor can improve a person's problem-solving abilities. Why do you think this happens?

Sample Entertaining Speech

Below is a sample entertaining speech, delivered by student speaker Terry Triplett.[2]

The Names Are Real

This is no joke. At Texas Tech University, the director of the Water Resource Center is Dr. Ken Rainwater.

Tips for Your Career

Tip 14.1 Move Listeners Together

If your listeners are spread apart in a large room or an auditorium, try to move them together if possible. Let's say you have 15 people scattered about in a large hall. It will be easier to make contact with them if you ask them to move to seats at the front and center.

Moving them together is especially important for entertaining talks. Nightclub comedians make sure tables are pushed close together because they know that patrons are more likely to laugh if they are jammed together in warm coziness. Some comedians are reluctant to tell jokes to an audience widely scattered in a large room. People feel isolated, and they are afraid that if they laugh, they will be conspicuous. (Have you ever noticed that funny movies are funnier if you see them in a packed theater than if you see them in a sparsely attended theater?)

Dr. Rainwater is an example of a person whose last name suits his or her profession. I want to share some other examples with you.

According to a recent article in *The Chronicle of Higher Education,* there are a number of professors who have apt names: Michael Greenwood is professor of forest-ecosystem science at the University of Maine, David Music is professor of church music at Baylor University, Stephen Pope is associate professor of theology at Boston College, Randall Toothaker (pronounced "toothacher") teaches dentistry at the University of Nebraska's College of Dentistry, and Ernest Fish is director of the Texas Tech Wildlife and Fisheries Management Institute.

In the world beyond college campuses, the *New York Times* lists some well-suited names—a lawyer in Bellevue, Washington, named David J. Lawyer; a famous Detroit Tigers first baseman named Cecil Fielder; a poet named William Wordsworth; a novelist named Francine Prose; and a TV weather reporter named Storm Field.

All of the names I am giving you today are real names—not stage names or made-up names. When I heard that a national poker champion is named Chris Moneymaker, I was suspicious, but he swears that Moneymaker is his real name. He explains that his ancestors came from Germany, where some people were named for their professions. His family made silver and gold coins. When they came to America, their name was translated into the English word "Moneymaker."

Are all these names and professions just a coincidence? Some people think so, but others think that a person's name influences his or her decisions about a career. Did their names nudge Paul Horn to become a career musician and Robert Bugg to conduct insect research at the University of California?

The *Journal of the American Medical Association* reports that in the United States there is a doctor named Rash, who is a dermatologist, and one named Bone, who is an orthopedic surgeon. There are 10 physicians named Blood and 22 named Needle. Did their names inspire them to enter medicine?

Whether it's a matter of coincidence or destiny, these connections are intriguing. Here are some examples from a list compiled by the advice columnist "Dear Abby": The manager of a sleep disorder clinic in Jonesboro,

Arkansas—Joe Yawn. A psychiatrist in Texas—Paul Looney. An undertaker in Missouri—Richard Dye.

And my favorite of all the names I came across—a liquor store owner in Hereford, Texas, who is named Joe Boozer.

Speech of Introduction

The **speech of introduction** is designed for one speaker to introduce another to an audience. For example:

- At a meeting of her civic club, Paula Moreno spoke briefly on why she was supporting a particular candidate for Congress and then turned the lectern over to the candidate.
- Theodore Lansing, a university librarian, stood up in front of 1,500 delegates at a national librarians' convention and introduced the keynote speaker, a renowned writer of science fiction.

When you introduce one friend to another, you want them to get interested in each other and to like each other: When you introduce a speaker to an audience, you want to achieve the same goal. You want speaker and audience to be interested in each other and to feel warmth and friendliness.

An introduction should mention the speaker's name several times (so that everyone can catch it), and it should give background information to enhance the speaker's credibility with the audience. Your tone of voice and facial expression should convey enthusiasm for the speech to come.

Here are some guidelines for speeches of introduction.

Interview the speaker in advance.   Ask him or her exactly what should be covered in the introduction. For example, should you discuss the significance of the topic (to help prepare the audience for the speech)? Should you tell the audience to hold questions until the end of the presentation?

Verify name and pronunciation.   Ask the speaker these questions:

- "What name do you want me to use?" If you are introducing Dr. Elizabeth Wilson, don't assume that she prefers to be called "Dr. Wilson." Perhaps she prefers the informality of "Elizabeth" or even her nickname, "Liz."
- "How do you pronounce your name?" If the speaker has a name like Neophetos Apostolopoulos, you obviously need help. Practice saying it in advance so that you don't stumble during the introduction. For easier names, don't always assume you know the correct pronunciation. A speaker named Mia may pronounce her name ME-UH, or she may prefer MY-UH. Eva can be EE-VUH or AYE-VUH. Common names like Megan and Ralph have at least two different pronunciations.

Tell the speaker what you plan to say.   By doing so, you can avoid this nightmare: a speaker is about to talk to an audience of 1,000 people, and suddenly she realizes that the person introducing her is telling the very anecdote that she had carefully planned as the opener of her speech. Such nightmares actually happen, say experienced speakers, but they won't happen to you if you reveal your plans to the speaker, and then omit duplications.

Set the proper tone.   When you introduce someone, you help set the tone for the speech to follow. Be careful to set the right tone—a humorous tone for a humorous speech, a serious tone for a serious speech.

Keep it short.   A good rule of thumb is to keep an introduction under three minutes. After all, an audience wants to hear the speaker, not the introducer.

Avoid exaggeration.   If you exaggerate the speaker's abilities or credentials, you build up unrealistic expectations in the audience. Consider this kind of introduction: "Our speaker tonight is a funny person who will have you laughing so hard you'll be rolling in the aisles." Or: "The speaker will give us insights that are wise and brilliant." Such statements can cause speakers to become overly anxious because they feel pressure to live up to the excessive praise.

The following introduction of Joseph Conte was delivered at a meeting of a genealogical society; the introducer had consulted with Conte in advance to make sure that he did not steal any of the speaker's speech.

> Our speaker tonight, Joseph Conte, will talk to us about how to set up a computerized ancestry record. Mr. Conte brings a lot of personal experience to this subject. The great-grandson of immigrants from Italy, he has traced his own family roots back to Florence. He has put all of his genealogical records onto a computer, using a program that was created by a Mormon group in Salt Lake City. Mr. Conte has a background of expertise in scholarly detective work: For the past decade he has been a researcher for the National Archives in Washington, D.C., specializing in 19th and 20th century immigration. Mr. Conte, welcome to our society and thank you for taking the time to share your knowledge with us.

Speech of Presentation

Awards or honors are often bestowed upon individuals for their service to business, institution, community, church, or club. It is customary for a brief speech to be made before the award is presented.

speech of presentation
an address designed to formally present an award or honor

The **speech of presentation** should include the following elements: (1) any background information that would help the audience understand the purpose of the award, (2) the criteria used for selecting the recipient, and (3) the achievements of the recipient.

In many cases, it is customary to withhold the name of the recipient until the very end of the speech, as a way of building suspense.

Humor is usually inappropriate. If you try to make a joke about the recipient, you may seem to be belittling him or her. At one company banquet, a department head gave an award for 10 years of service to a subordinate and used the occasion to tease him with a mock insult: "The only reason we keep him on the payroll is because his father worked here for 40 years." The "humor" was similar to the kind of bantering that the boss and the subordinate engaged in during a typical workday, but at the awards banquet, with his family present, the subordinate felt humiliated.

Here is a model speech of presentation delivered by Meredith Brody at the annual meeting of a community theater:

> The John Cleese Award is given each year to the top actor or actress in our theater. As most of you know, the award is given in honor of the British actor John

Cleese of *Monty Python* and *Fawlty Towers* fame. The winner is selected by ballots circulated to all our members. Our winner this year is a seasoned veteran of our stage, a person who always performs with intelligence, audacity, and élan. I am pleased to announce that the winner of the third annual John Cleese Award is . . . James Colton!

Speech of Acceptance

If you are ever given an award, a promotion, or some other sort of public recognition, you may be called upon to "say a few words." Giving a **speech of acceptance** is difficult because you want to sound appreciative without being syrupy, and you want to sound deserving without being egotistical. Here are some guidelines.

speech of acceptance
oral remarks made by the recipient of an award or honor

Thank those who played a part in your achieving the honor.   If a few individuals made your recognition possible, mention them by name; if a lot of people did, mention the most important contributors to your success and say something like this, "There are many others but they are too numerous to name. Nevertheless, I am grateful to all of them."

Thank the organization giving you the award and recognize the work it is doing.   If, for example, you are cited by the United Way as top fund-raiser of the year, spend a few moments extolling its great work.

Be brief.   I have seen some ceremonies marred because an award recipient viewed the acceptance speech as a chance to expound on his or her pet ideas. If you deliver a lengthy oration, the people who are giving you the honor may regret their choice. Make a few sincere remarks—and then sit down.

Here is a sample acceptance speech, given by Rita Goldberg, who was honored by a chapter of the Lions Club for her work on behalf of people with disabilities.

> I want to thank you for choosing me to receive your Distinguished Service Award. In the past year I couldn't have accomplished half of what I did without the help of Henry and Judith Fletcher. I am grateful to them for their valuable assistance. And I am grateful to you Lions for setting up programs for the visually impaired. Because of your compassion and your work, you have made it easy for volunteers like me to help the disabled. Again, thank you for this honor.

Speech of Tribute

A **speech of tribute** praises or celebrates a person, a group, an institution, or an event. It conveys gratitude, respect, or admiration. For example, the leader of a veterans' organization might pay tribute on Memorial Day to comrades who had died in combat. At a retirement banquet, you might give a brief talk lauding the work of a colleague who is stepping down after 25 years.

A speech of tribute should be completely positive. It is never appropriate to point out faults or dredge up old disputes.

Let's examine three popular types of tribute speeches—wedding speeches, toasts, and eulogies.

speech of tribute
an oration in praise of someone or something

connectpublic
speaking.com
To see a sample speech of tribute, view "Three Celebrity Heroes."

Wedding Speeches

Weddings are celebrated in many ways, depending upon religious, ethnic, and family traditions. Many of these traditions call for brief speeches of tribute at the rehearsal dinner and the wedding reception. The remarks may be delivered by members of the wedding party, parents, grandparents, siblings, and friends. Here are some guidelines.

Focus on the couple.   Instead of dwelling on your own experiences and emotions, talk mostly about the wedding couple and their love and future happiness.

Be brief, but not too brief.   If you speak for only 15 seconds, saying that the honorees are wonderful people whom everyone likes, you are not giving them the respect that they deserve. Say something specific and heartfelt, but keep your remarks under three minutes.

Don't say anything that could embarrass anyone in the room.   You've seen the movies in which a wedding celebration is marred when the best man reveals humiliating details about the groom or says something that is insulting to the bride. Such behavior is not limited to the movies. In real life, people make major blunders. Never mention ex-boyfriends or ex-girlfriends. Never tease about past misdeeds, goofy habits, or unfortunate shortcomings. For this occasion, focus entirely on the positive.

Consider using an appropriate poem or quotation.   Anthologies and the Internet are full of apt quotations, such as this one by an ancient Chinese philosopher

Brief speeches are customary at wedding celebrations.

Lao Tzu: "To love someone deeply gives you strength. Being loved by someone deeply gives you courage."[3] Or you can use a lighter touch, like this poem by Ogden Nash:[4]

> *To keep your marriage brimming,*
> *With love in the wedding cup,*
> *Whenever you're wrong, admit it;*
> *Whenever you're right, shut up.*

If you create videos, make them short and tasteful. A speech of tribute on a DVD, accompanied by photos and favorite pieces of music, can be a delightful part of the occasion if you keep it short, and if you avoid surprise photos: No pictures of "exes." No mortifying snapshots of inappropriate behavior at a party. Concentrate on the couple, using upbeat, happy images.

End with a toast. It's customary, and the perfect way to complete your speech. (In the next section, we will discuss the art of toasting.)

Toasts

> I'd like to propose a toast to Miriam Steele, who has devoted 27 years to this company, giving us creativity, integrity, and a friendly ear to tell our troubles to. Miriam, we will miss you, and we hope your retirement years are filled with much happiness and abundant good health.

When is it a bad idea to use water for a toast?

A toast is a short tribute spoken as glasses are raised to salute people, occasions, or things. Toasts are offered at graduation celebrations, family get-togethers, class reunions, retirement dinners, wedding celebrations, and many other events.

Traditionally, the glasses contain wine, but in the United States and Canada, any beverage can be used—even water. In other countries or with international guests, don't use water, because some cultures interpret it as disapproval of the toast.[5]

Announce a toast by raising your glass and saying, "I'd like to propose a toast." Participants show their agreement by raising their glasses and, at the end of the toast, lightly touching them against the glasses of those nearby. Then everyone takes a sip to "seal" the toast.

Here are some guidelines.

Strive for sincerity, warmth, and brevity. At a party celebrating a college graduation, a classmate gave this toast: "Here's to Paul. May your future be filled with work that you enjoy and friends that bring you as much happiness as you have brought to us."

Don't read a toast. Prepare your toast, practice it at home, but don't bring a manuscript to the table.

Avoid all forms of teasing. A toast honoring a couple on their 35th anniversary should not include references to memory lapses, wrinkles, and weight gain.

Browse the Internet for ideas. You can combine your own words with toasts that are found on the Internet. For example, at a wedding celebration, a friend of the newlyweds gave this toast: "Maggie and Zack, may your days be filled with wonder and grace, and (to quote a wedding toast popular in Mexico), I wish you health, love, happiness–and enough money to enjoy them."

Eulogies

eulogy
a laudatory oration in honor of someone who has died

An especially important kind of tribute speech you may be asked to make is a **eulogy**–a speech of praise for a friend, relative, or colleague who has died. A eulogy should be dignified, without exaggerated sentimentality. (Though humor is usually out of place in a eulogy, it is sometimes appropriate: One student described the funeral of an uncle who had been a "colorful character" well known for his storytelling abilities; in one of the eulogies for this uncle, the speaker recited some of the humorous tales, and everyone smiled in warm remembrance of the yarn-spinning uncle.)

A eulogy should focus on the *significance* of the person's life and deeds, rather than on a mere recital of biographical facts. In other words, how did this man or woman enrich our lives? What inspiration or lessons can we draw from this person's life?

Your Thoughts **?**

A new trend is to deliver a eulogy in the presence of an elderly person *before* he or she dies. Do you think this is a good idea? Explain your answer.

inspirational speech
an address that tries to stimulate listeners to a high level of feeling or activity

Inspirational Speech

The goal of the **inspirational speech** is to stir positive emotions–to help people feel excited, uplifted, encouraged. You may need to give inspirational speeches at various times in your life. Let's say, for example, that you are manager of an office or a department, and you give your staff an upbeat, "you-can-do-it" speech to motivate them to do their best work. Or you coach a children's soccer team and you give the boys and girls a "pep talk" before a game to encourage them to play well.

The inspirational speech is similar to the persuasive speech, with the two purposes often overlapping. The main difference is that in the inspirational speech, you devote yourself almost solely to stirring emotions, while in the persuasive speech, you use emotional appeals as just one of many techniques.

Delivery is an important dimension of inspirational speaking. To inspire other people, *you* must be inspired. Your facial expression, your posture, your tone of voice–everything about you must convey energy and enthusiasm.

An inspirational speech should tap the emotional power of vivid language. An example of effective use of language can be found in a speech delivered by Dan Crenshaw to a support group of parents of children with developmental disabilities. Here is a section from the speech:

> We must learn to live fully and joyfully in the here and now, setting aside all our pain from the past and all our worries about the future. Fulton Oursler said, "We crucify ourselves between two thieves: regret for yesterday and fear of tomorrow."
>
> If we live in the past or in the future, we miss what today has to offer.
> We miss the glistening beauty of a puddle of water.
> We miss the soothing melody of a love song.
> We miss the glint of wonder in a child's eyes.
> We miss the lingering aroma of fresh-baked cinnamon rolls.
> We miss the beautiful arrangement of clouds in the sky.

We miss the satisfaction of rubbing a dog's fur.

The past is over. Think of it as a bullet. Once it's fired, it's finished. The future is not yet here, and may never come for us. Today is all we have. Treasure *today*, celebrate *today*, live *today*.[6]

Crenshaw made effective use of the techniques of *repetition* and *parallel structure*.

Resources for Review and Skill Building

connectpublic
speaking.com

Connect Public Speaking provides resources for study and review, including sample speech videos, an Outline Tutor, and practice tests.

Summary

While informative and persuasive speeches are the most frequent types, there are occasions when a speech must serve other purposes. When you need to entertain an audience, as in an after-dinner talk, your remarks should be light and diverting; any elements of information or persuasion should be gracefully woven into the fabric of entertainment. One device for an entertaining speech is to string together anecdotes, examples, or quotations on a single theme. Extended narratives or descriptions also can be entertaining.

Using humor in a speech is an effective way to create a bond of warmth and friendliness with an audience. Be cautious in telling jokes because they can be risky, and listeners may have heard the joke already. A safer type is low-key humor, such as a mildly amusing story, quotation, or observation. Whatever humor you use should relate to the topic and not be offensive to any person in the audience.

When you are asked to introduce a speaker, convey enthusiasm for the speaker and the topic, and give whatever background information is necessary to enhance the speaker's credibility.

When you make a speech of presentation, focus your remarks on the award and the recipient. When you are called upon to "say a few words" in acceptance of an award or a promotion, thank the people who gave you the honor and acknowledge the help of those who made your success possible.

When you give a speech of tribute, praise the person, group, institution, or event being honored, avoiding any negativity. Three types of tribute speeches are wedding speeches, toasts, and eulogies.

When you speak to inspire an audience, devote yourself to stirring emotions, using a dynamic delivery to convey your energy and enthusiasm.

Key Terms

entertaining speech, *373*

eulogy, *382*

inspirational speech, *382*

speech of acceptance, *379*

speech of introduction, *377*

speech of presentation, *378*

speech of tribute, *379*

Review Questions

1. Why would an informative speech on a difficult, highly technical subject usually be inappropriate for an after-dinner audience?

2. In what situation is self-deprecating humor inadvisable?

3. List three guidelines for the speech of acceptance.

4. What is the function of the speech of tribute?

5. What are the risks that a speaker takes when telling a joke?

6. If you are asked to introduce a speaker, why should you coordinate your remarks beforehand with those of the speaker?

7. When introducing a speaker, some introducers use the speaker's first name, others use the last name. What advice does the text give on this issue?

8. In which kind of special occasions speech does the speaker often withhold an honoree's name until the last sentence?

9. What should be the focus of a eulogy?

10. What is the main difference between an inspirational speech and a persuasive speech?

Building Critical-Thinking Skills

1. One speaker told his audience, "Before I left for this speech, my wife gave me some advice: 'Don't try to be charming, witty, or intellectual. Just be yourself.'" What kind of humor is the speaker using?

2. "Our speaker tonight," says the master of ceremonies, "will outline the five key steps in rescuing a person who is in danger of drowning. Let me give you a quick preview of these steps." What mistake is the master of ceremonies making?

Building Teamwork Skills

1. Working in a group, decide on a topic and then prepare and deliver an entertaining talk, with each member of the group speaking in turn. Some possible topics:

   a. An embarrassing moment

   b. Good vacation spots

   c. The weird behavior of pets

2. In a group, choose a person (living or dead) whom everyone admires. Create a speech of tribute to that person.

In a brainstorming session, executives at a novelty company in Connecticut came up with the idea of putting pumpkin faces on leaf bags, transforming the bags from unsightly trash containers into autumn decorations. The company has sold millions of them. Brainstorming, which is discussed in this chapter, is one of the best ways for small groups to solve problems and create new ideas.

Speaking in Groups

OUTLINE

Meetings
Responsibilities of Leaders
Responsibilities of Participants
The Reflective-Thinking Method

Group Presentations
Team Presentation
Symposium
Panel Discussion

OBJECTIVES

After studying this chapter, you should be able to:

1. Serve as a leader or a participant in a small group meeting.

2. Describe the responsibilities of both leaders and participants in small groups.

3. Identify and explain the seven steps of the reflective-thinking method.

4. Prepare and deliver a presentation as a member of a team.

5. Participate in a symposium.

6. Serve as moderator or panelist in a panel discussion.

You can bolster your career if you know how to work well in a group.[1] Here is what research shows:

- If you show that you have had experience in working on a team, you improve your chances of getting a job. "Experience on a team has become one of the top requests among recruiters looking over job candidates," says Dr. Mary Ellen Guffey of Los Angeles Pierce College.[2]
- Once employed, if you establish a reputation as an effective team member, you enhance your chances for promotion.[3]

Why is working on a team so important? Much of the work of society is done by small groups, such as a team of scientists who develop new medicines, a committee of educators who improve a curriculum, a group of neighbors who try to reduce crime, and a crew of workers who devise a labor-saving method of production.

Teamwork produces impressive results. University students from Madrid, Spain, stand in front of the solar-powered house they designed and built in Washington, D.C. From left: Mana Sagtatio Perez, Yanitra Huertas, Leticia Rojo Bernavdez, Joara Comemburger, and Lucia Lucas.

Small groups have some advantages over the individual. Members of small groups can pool their resources, ideas, and labor. They can catch and correct errors that might slip past an individual. According to Yale psychologist Robert Sternberg, a group often has an IQ (or intelligence level) that is higher than the IQ of any individual in the group.[4]

In this chapter, we will look at working in groups and then discuss making presentations as a group.

Meetings

A meeting is often the best way for small groups to plan and carry out their collective work. Sounds simple, but there is a problem: the majority of business and professional people say (in surveys) that most meetings are unproductive and a waste of time.[5]

Fortunately, this problem can be solved. To have a productive meeting, group leaders and participants should follow well-established principles of effective group communication, as explained below. Let's start with the role of group leaders.

Responsibilities of Leaders

No matter what kind of group you are asked to lead—whether a committee to plan the office holiday party or a team to handle client complaints—your general responsibilities will be the same.

Make Sure You Need a Meeting

It is a mistake to hold a meeting just because "we always have a staff meeting every Friday afternoon." If there is nothing significant to discuss or act upon, a meeting is a waste of valuable time. If you simply need to share information, use e-mail or memos. But call a meeting when

- You need to develop ideas, gain consensus, plan, and follow up.
- You must share information that is sensitive, is emotionally charged, or could be misinterpreted.
- You need to build teamwork and cooperation.

Make Sure Group Members Know Purpose and Scope

In advance of the meeting, all participants should be clearly informed of the purpose of getting together. Otherwise, people will walk in saying, "Why are we meeting?" Letting people know in advance gives them the opportunity to be thinking about the task.

Just as important, make sure group members know how their work will be used. Does the group have the authority to make and carry out a decision, or is it merely being asked to make a recommendation? Can the group's decisions be overruled by a higher authority?

When the meeting begins, you should quickly review the group's purpose and scope of power—to refresh everyone's memory.

Set the Agenda and Length of Meeting

An **agenda** is a list of items that need to be covered in a meeting (see Table 15.1). When there is no agenda, groups are unfocused—they spend time and energy on minor items and never get around to the major issues. A study of meetings by the 3M Corporation found that "a written agenda, distributed in advance, is the single best predictor of a successful meeting."[6]

agenda
document listing what is to be accomplished during a meeting

You don't need to set the agenda by yourself. Ask participants in advance to submit their ideas and concerns. You will not only get good ideas but also assure the participants that their input is valued and will be heard.

Arrange the agenda so the most important items are discussed first. Consider allocating an appropriate amount of time for each item.

Table 15.1
Sample Agenda

	AGENDA **Advertising Committee** September 5, 2009, 2:00–2:55 p.m. Frazier Conference Room
Committee Chair:	Janet Moore
Committee Members:	Melissa Casey, Anne Hansen, Daniel Madden, Michael Pulaski, Luis Rodriguez, and Allison Schwartz.
Objective:	To decide the best outlet for our spring advertising campaign
Agenda Items:	
I.	Call to order
II.	Approval of last meeting's minutes
III.	Approval of agenda
IV.	Discussion of TV advertising options (10 minutes)
V.	Discussion of Web options (10 minutes)
VI.	Discussion of magazine options (10 minutes)
VII.	Vote on our recommendation to the company president
VIII.	Suggestions for next meeting's agenda
IX.	Committee chair's summary
X.	Adjournment

Early in the meeting, get the group's approval of the agenda in case new issues have come up that need to be addressed.

Many people automatically schedule meetings for one hour, perhaps because of the traditional 50-minute class length. Instead, estimate the time you really need. Holding quick meetings (sometimes with everyone standing up) can be an effective way to keep the group focused. When you have a long agenda, or complex issues, having one long session can be more effective than several meetings that break up your momentum.

Your Thoughts **?**

Why do you think that some managers hold short meetings with everyone standing up?

Start on Time

Start your meetings on time and thank those who are there. When latecomers arrive, tell them where you are on the agenda and let them catch up. Waiting to start your meeting until everybody shows up is almost always a mistake.

- It rewards the latecomers, effectively "training" them–and those who arrived on time–to come later and later.
- It wastes the time of those who arrived on time and tells them you don't appreciate their punctuality.

Of course, there are sometimes valid reasons for starting late, such as a traffic tie-up or an office emergency. When this happens, make sure your group knows the reason for the delay and invite them to take a break and return at a specified time.

Set the Tone

Greet people as they arrive. Set an appropriate tone. Usually it will be friendly and upbeat, but more serious if the purpose of the meeting is to share bad news. In any case, always thank your participants for coming.

If some of the participants are newcomers, make sure they are introduced to everyone else.

Make Sure Minutes Are Kept

If the group is not a formal committee with a previously designated recorder, appoint someone to take notes and later prepare **minutes** of the meeting. Minutes are a record of what was discussed and accomplished during a meeting. They should be circulated to group members as soon after the meeting as possible. While minutes are obviously valuable for absentees, they are also important for people who were present—to remind them of their responsibilities for the next meeting. Minutes should consist of five elements: (1) agenda item, (2) decision reached, (3) action required, (4) person(s) responsible for taking action, and (5) target date for completion of action. At each meeting, the minutes of the previous session should be briefly reviewed to make sure that tasks have been completed.

minutes
written record of what occurred at a meeting

Guide—Don't Dominate—the Discussion

Your challenge is to set the direction of the meeting while encouraging free and productive group participation. This is more than politeness; it's good strategy. Group members feel a commitment to the plans and decisions if they have helped to formulate them. Now it is *their* idea, *their* policy.

- Don't let anybody take over the conversation, including yourself. If any one person is doing most of the talking, you may have to gently but firmly intervene: "Those are excellent points . . . I'd like to hear how others are reacting to what you just said."

- Draw out participants who aren't speaking up—but don't put them on the spot. "Carlos, you've had experience with writing proposals. Are you seeing anything we're overlooking?"

- Encourage free discussion, but don't permit attacks on people or ideas.

- Address side conversations directly: "Brent and Ashley, it looks as if you've come up with something interesting. Could you share it with all of us?" They will either grin sheepishly and return to the group or share their thoughts—and they may be shy and welcome the invitation to give their input.

- Summarize periodically. Sum up what has and has not been decided, saying just enough to help the participants keep their bearings. "OK, we've decided to recommend A and B to the board for approval, but it looks like we're stuck on C until Jahquil gets numbers from Finance. Let's go on to item D."

- When you near the agreed-upon time to end the meeting, summarize what the group has accomplished, set the time and place for the next meeting, and make sure all participants know their assignments for the next meeting. Express appreciation for the work that the group has done.

- After the meeting, make sure that minutes are written and distributed to each participant and that all participants carry out their assignments.

Responsibilities of Participants

While leadership of a small group is important, the participants themselves play a vital role. People working together can combine their insights and energies to achieve goals that would be unattainable by a lone individual. The key is cooperation. "The secret of a successful team is not to assemble the largest team possible, but rather to assemble a team that can work well together," says Dean Kamen, founder of FIRST (For Inspiration and Recognition of Science and Technology).[7]

Here are guidelines to keep in mind.

Prepare for Every Meeting

Take time to review the agenda and the key players. Do whatever research, background reading, and interviewing you need to strengthen your position on issues to be discussed. Bring any documentation needed.

Arrive Early

Show up a few minutes before the meeting time. You'll look–and be–more in command, and you'll have a chance to touch base with others.

Participate

Join the discussion and contribute your ideas and opinions. It can be as simple as voicing agreement with a team member or asking a question. If you tend to be shy in group settings, speak up early. The longer you wait, the harder it will be.

Watch your body language. Nonverbal behaviors, such as facial expressions and posture, speak more powerfully than words. If you slump in your chair and don't make eye contact, people will assume you are bored or negative. Instead, sit in an alert but relaxed posture with an open, friendly expression. Make eye contact with those speaking. Smile and nod agreement when appropriate–everyone who speaks up appreciates positive feedback.

Have the Courage to Disagree

You've undoubtedly been part of a group in which everybody seemed to agree with an idea or an approach until one member expressed reservations–and then almost everybody jumped in to say they, too, had concerns. A good way to open the conversation to many points of view is to ask a question. Focus on the *issue,* not on people: "How can we be sure we draw a big enough audience to justify the expense?" As group members respond, they may realize that the idea *is* unworkable–or you may realize it has merit. You can help your group avoid making a decision in false unanimity.

Don't Work from a Hidden Agenda

hidden agenda
an ulterior motive

A group's work can be sabotaged if some members pretend to be committed to the goals of the group but in reality have **hidden agendas**–that is, unannounced private goals that conflict with the group's goals. One frequent hidden agenda is the desire to curry favor with a superior. One or more members of a committee will agree with the chairperson–the boss–even though they feel strongly that the boss's ideas are flawed. They would rather see the committee's efforts fail than go on record as disagreeing with their superior.

Ethical Issue

Don't Carry On Private Conversations

A whispered conversation by two or three participants is rude and insulting to the speaker; it is also damaging to the work of the group, since it cuts off teamwork and undermines cooperation.

What's wrong with whispered conversations?

The Reflective-Thinking Method

For every human problem, the American essayist H. L. Mencken said, "there is always an easy solution—neat, plausible, and wrong." Unfortunately, many business and professional groups leap at easy but wrong solutions. In the 1980s, when Coca-Cola began to lose market share in its battle with Pepsi, the "neat, plausible" solution was to change the Coca-Cola formula and make it as sweet as Pepsi—an easy solution that turned out to be a huge blunder. Sales plummeted because millions of Coca-Cola lovers disliked the new Coke. Soon the embarrassed company resumed making the original formula (which was sold as Coca-Cola Classic).

A more effective technique for solving problems is the **reflective-thinking method,** a step-by-step procedure derived from the writings of the American philosopher John Dewey.[8] These steps should be taken in the order given below.

reflective-thinking method
a structured system for solving problems

Define the Problem

Defining a problem clearly and precisely can save time and (in the business world) money. Here are some tips.

Phrase the problem in the form of a question.   Instead of "We have traffic jams on our campus," say, "How can we eliminate the traffic jams that occur on our campus every afternoon?" The question format helps create a probing, problem-solving atmosphere. Make sure the question is open-ended (that is, not one that can be answered by a simple yes or no).

Avoid wording that suggests a solution.   If you say "How can we finance the hiring of more security officers to eliminate traffic jams on campus?" you are stating that you already know the best solution. You risk cutting off discussion that might lead to a different solution—one that is even better than hiring more security officers.

Avoid vagueness.   Be as specific as possible. Instead of "How can we improve our campus?" say, "How can we discourage people from littering the campus with trash?"

Analyze the Problem

A problem-solving group should scrutinize the problem to learn as much as it can. Key questions that should be asked are

- What are the causes of the problem?
- What are the effects of the problem? (How severe is it? Are many people affected or just a few?)

In the Coca-Cola fiasco, corporate planners should have tried harder to determine the real cause of Coke's loss of market share to Pepsi. Was it the taste of

Coke? Did people prefer a sweeter drink without the traditional Coca-Cola zing? Coca-Cola's management thought so, and their blunder flowed from this faulty analysis.

If you own a restaurant, and some of your customers have complained about slow service, your problem-solving team should focus on causes. Is slow service caused by the servers? If so, is it because they are lazy or inefficient, or is it because each of them is assigned too many tables? Or can the slow service be blamed solely on the cooks? If so, is it because they are lazy or inefficient? Or are they understaffed?

You need to get a clear picture of the cause of a problem before the problem-solving process can continue.

Establish Criteria for Evaluating Solutions

Imagine you are on a task force assigned to solve this problem: many students can't find an available computer on your campus when they need one for their assignments. After hours of study and discussion, your group recommends that the college open a new computer lab in the library and stock it with 50 new computers. Total cost: $200,000. But the idea is quickly shot down by administrators. It's four times what the college can afford. Now it's back to the drawing board for you and your task force. Your group could have saved itself much time and effort if it had known that it could recommend spending no more than $50,000.

This scenario shows why a group should write down the criteria—the standards or conditions—by which to judge a solution. To establish criteria, a group should ask these key questions:

- What must a proposed solution do?
- What must it avoid?
- What restrictions of time, money, and space must be considered?

Criteria should be rank-ordered according to importance. For the computer problem, the task force might end up with these criteria: (1) A computer lab must not cost more than $50,000. (2) It must contain computers that are compatible with those used in engineering and business classes. (3) It must be accessible to students from 8 a.m. until midnight.

Suggest Possible Solutions

When a group takes its next step—suggesting possible solutions—it must show patience and avoid leaping at the first idea that comes along. Putting a wide variety of possible solutions on the table can enhance the chances of making a sound decision.

brainstorming
generating many ideas
quickly and uncritically

One of the best techniques for generating potential solutions is **brainstorming:** participants rapidly, and at random, volunteer ideas while the group leader (or designated person) writes them on a board or pad. Many of the ingenious products that we use daily were invented or improved as a result of brainstorming. For example, consider the digital camera that we use to take photos. The image-capture chip in the camera was invented in a one-hour brainstorming session by two engineers who were under pressure to produce or lose their funding.[9]

For brainstorming to work effectively, there must be an atmosphere of total acceptance—no one analyzes, judges, ridicules, or rejects any of the ideas as they are being generated. Nothing is too wild or crazy to be jotted down.

Total acceptance is vital because (1) it encourages the flow of creative thinking and (2) an idea that seems far-fetched and impractical at first glance might eventually prove to be a good idea. In New York City, the Gaia Institute wanted to develop a prototype of a rooftop garden so that someday gardens can be built throughout Manhattan to help clean the air, cool the city, and provide fresh vegetables. But there was a major problem: How can you have soil rich enough to grow plants yet light enough that the roof doesn't cave in? One idea sounded strange when it was introduced, but it proved to be fruitful when it was tried: mix soil, which is heavy, with shredded polystyrene, which is light. The resulting compost worked; the soil was rich enough to grow vegetables but not so heavy as to cause the roof to collapse. If the prototype is copied elsewhere, there will be a bonus: the gardens can help solve the ecological problem of how to dispose of polystyrene found in thrown-away Styrofoam cups.[10]

Choose the Best Solution

After the brainstorming session, a group should analyze, weigh, and discuss its ideas to come up with the best solution. The solution chosen must meet the following standards:

- The solution must satisfy the criteria previously established.
- The group must have the authority to put the solution into effect (or recommend that it be put into effect).
- The solution must not solve one problem but create another.

Decide How to Implement the Solution

A solution may sound fine, but can it be realistically implemented? The next step is to decide how to put the solution into action.

Suppose a campus task force decides that the solution to a shortage of computers is for the college to buy laptop computers and rent them to students for the school year. How will this be carried out? Who will be in charge of the rentals? What will happen if some computers are lost or stolen? Is there money available for repairs?

Decide How to Test the Solution

Many groups hammer out a solution to a problem but never follow up to determine whether their solution really solved the problem. The last task of the problem-solving group is to decide how to find out if the solution really works.

If a group recommends hiring more security officers to solve traffic jams on campus, it could design a follow-up study to test its solution. If student motorists now require about 15 minutes to exit the campus in the afternoon, the group can set up a test like this: If the hiring of more officers results in an average exit time of 9 or more minutes, the solution has failed to alleviate the problem. But if the average exit time is less than 9 minutes, the solution is effective.

Group Presentations

In your classroom, career, or community life, you are likely to speak publicly as part of a group. Three popular ways of presenting are the team presentation, the symposium, and the panel discussion.

Team Presentation

team presentation
a well-coordinated presentation made by members of a group who focus on a common goal

Teams play an important role in the business and professional world, and sometimes they are called upon to deliver a presentation to an audience. A **team presentation** is like a speech given by an individual except that the content is divided, with each member delivering a different section. For effective team presentations, here are some guidelines.

Designate Roles

To keep the group on track, choose a project leader. He or she should conduct meetings (along the lines discussed earlier in this chapter) to determine key issues: Who will do the various research tasks? Who will deliver which section of the presentation? When will the assignment be due?

Prepare Content

Use all the steps you have learned for an individual speech. Analyze your audience, create a specific purpose and a central idea, develop an outline, and gather materials (especially visuals).

Plan Your Time

Going over your time limit can destroy your credibility and irritate your audience. Time every minute of your presentation. Leave plenty of time for questions and discussion—this is the most challenging part of your presentation, and the one most likely to win approval or lose it.

Practice, Practice, Practice

It is more important to rehearse when you do a group presentation than when you present alone. Practice many times, using all of the equipment and visual aids that you will be using on the big day. If you must travel to another city to give the presentation, take your own equipment—it can be risky to use unfamiliar equipment. In some situations, your team members may live in different parts of the globe, communicating by e-mail, telephone, or videoconference. To avoid being out of sync with one another, you and your teammates should come together several days before a presentation to practice together in the same room.

Get Feedback during a Practice Session

This is a critical—and commonly overlooked—key to success. Find at least one person who is typical of your audience and who has not heard your presentation so he or she can provide a fresh, unbiased viewpoint. Use the feedback to make necessary alterations.

Prepare for the Question-and-Answer Period

Compile a list of likely questions from the audience. For each question, decide the best answer and designate which team member will deliver it.

Plan for Emergencies

Identify potential problems such as equipment failure or a cancelled flight, and how you will manage them. For example, be ready to print hard copies of your PowerPoint slides in case the multimedia projector malfunctions.

Your Thoughts **?**

How should a team handle the possibility of one member being sick and absent on presentation day?

Support One Another

Strive for harmony in the presentation. It looks bad if one team member contradicts or criticizes another in front of the audience. I once saw a team of architects give a presentation, at the end of which the senior architect on the team rose and apologized for the poor speaking skills of a young team member. His remarks were unnecessary—a gratuitous slap in the face—and they reflected poorly on him and the firm.

Listen to the Presentation Attentively

While your teammates are presenting, don't review your notes, check your Black-Berry, or whisper comments to others. These distractions signal to your audience that what's being said isn't important.

Symposium

A **symposium** is a series of brief speeches on a common topic, each usually discussing a different aspect of the topic. Every year, for example, Mt. Sinai School of Medicine in New York City holds a symposium on autism, with five to eight medical researchers speaking on various aspects of autism. One might discuss diagnosis, another might recommend a certain treatment, and another might explore possible cures.

symposium
a meeting featuring short addresses by different people on the same topic

Unlike the team presentation, the speakers in a symposium do not necessarily agree with one another. Sometimes they are not required to coordinate their remarks, although it is a good idea to do so, to avoid excessive duplication of material.

A symposium is conducted by a moderator, who gives a brief introduction of each speaker and manages a question-and-answer period after the speeches.

Symposium speeches are supposed to be brief, and each speaker should be careful to stay within time limits. If a speaker is long-winded, the moderator should intervene and politely ask him or her to yield to another speaker in the interest of fairness.

When you prepare and deliver a speech as part of a symposium, use the same skills and techniques as those of solo speechmaking, with an introduction, a body, and a conclusion.

Panel Discussion

In a **panel discussion,** a team converses on a topic in front of an audience. A panel is usually made up of three to eight team members and is led by a moderator. A common pattern is for panelists to give a brief opening statement and then discuss the subject among themselves, with the moderator guiding the flow. At the end of the discussion, the audience is usually invited to ask questions.

panel discussion
consideration of a topic by a small group in the presence of an audience

Because of the variety of viewpoints and the liveliness of informed conversation, audiences enjoy a good panel discussion.

Guidelines for the Moderator

Much of the success (or failure) of a panel discussion is determined by the moderator. He or she must keep the discussion moving along smoothly, restrain the long-winded or domineering panelist from hogging the show, draw out the reticent panelist, and field questions from the audience. Here are some guidelines to follow when you are a moderator.

Laura von Bertouch, an occupational therapist and captain of a women's basketball team, participates in a panel discussion at Bethlehem College in Sydney, Australia. Joining her are captains of three other teams. The panelists discussed the future of women's professional basketball.

Arrange the setting. You and the panelists can be seated at a table facing the audience. Or, even better, you can be seated in a semicircle so that all members of the panel can see one another while still remaining visible to the audience. A large name card should be placed in front of each panelist so that the audience will know the participants' names.

Brief panel members in advance. Well before the meeting, give panel members clear instructions on exactly what they are expected to cover in their opening remarks. Are they supposed to argue the "pro" or the "con" position? Are they supposed to speak on only one aspect of the topic? (For information-giving discussions, you may want to assign each panel member a subtopic, according to his or her area of expertise, so that there is not much overlap among speakers.) Instruct the panelists not to bring and read written statements, but tell them that they are free to bring notes.

Before the meeting, prepare a list of items that you think should be discussed. This ensures that no important issues are inadvertently omitted. If the discussion begins to lag or go off into irrelevancies, you will have fresh questions ready.

Prepare and deliver an introduction. At the beginning of the program, introduce the topic and the speakers, and explain the ground rules for the discussion; be sure to let listeners know if and when they will be permitted to ask questions.

Moderate the discussion. Give each panelist a chance to make an opening statement (within the time constraints previously announced) and then encourage the panelists to question one another or comment upon one another's remarks. Be neutral in the discussion, but be prepared to ask questions if there is an awkward lull or if a panelist says something confusing or leaves out important information. Listen carefully to what each panelist says so that you don't embarrass yourself by asking questions on subjects that have already been discussed.

Maintain friendly, but firm, control. Don't let a panelist dominate the discussion. During the question-and-answer session, don't let a member of the audience make a long-winded speech; interrupt kindly but firmly and say, "We need to give other people a chance to ask questions." If a panelist exceeds the time limit for opening remarks or monopolizes the discussion time, gently break in and say, "I'm sorry to interrupt, but let's hear from other members of the panel on their ideas concerning . . ." If a reticent panelist says very little, draw him or her out with specific, pertinent questions.

Be respectful of all panelists, including those with whom you disagree. Think of yourself not as a district attorney who must interrogate and skewer criminal defendants but as a gracious host or hostess who stimulates guests to engage in lively conversation.

Ask open-ended questions. For example, ask "How can we make sure our homes are safe from burglars?" rather than "Is burglary on the increase in our community?"

End the program at the agreed-upon time. Wrap up the proceedings on time and in a prearranged way, perhaps by letting each panelist summarize briefly his or her position. You may want to summarize the key points made during the discussion. (To do this, you would need to take notes throughout the program.) Thank the panelists and the audience for their participation. If some members of the audience are still interested in continuing the discussion, you may want to invite them to talk to the panelists individually after the program is over.

Guidelines for Panelists

If you are a member of a panel, here are some guidelines to keep in mind.

Prepare for the discussion in the same way you prepare for a speech. Find out all that you can about the audience and the occasion: On what particular aspect of the topic are you expected to speak? Who are the other panelists and what will they cover? Will there be questions from the audience? What are the time constraints?

Prepare notes for the panel, but not a written statement. If you read your remarks, you will spoil the spontaneity that is desired in a panel discussion. In addition to notes, you may want to bring supporting data (such as bibliographical sources or statistics) from which to draw in case you are asked to document a point.

Respect the time limits set by the moderator. If, for example, you are asked to keep your opening remarks under two minutes, be careful to do so.

In the give-and-take of the discussion, be brief. If the other panelists or listeners want to hear more from you, they will ask.

Stay on the subject. Resist the temptation to ramble.

Tips for Your Career

Be respectful and considerate of your fellow panelists. Don't squelch them with sarcasm, ridicule, or an overbearing attitude. Don't upstage them by trying to be the one to answer all the questions from the audience.

Listen carefully to the comments of other panelists and members of the audience. If some people disagree with you, try to understand and appreciate their position instead of hastily launching a counterattack. Then be prepared to follow the next guideline.

Be willing to alter your position. If you listen with an open mind, you may see merit in others' views, and you may decide that you need to modify your original position. Though such a shift may seem like an embarrassing loss of face, it actually causes the audience to have greater respect for you. It shows you are a person who possesses intellectual courage, flexibility, and integrity.

Resources for Review and Skill Building

connectpublic
speaking.com

Connect Public Speaking provides resources for study and review, including sample speech videos, an Outline Tutor, and practice tests.

Summary

Small groups are important elements in business and professional life, and much of the work of small groups is done in meetings. To lead a meeting, establish an agenda and make sure that it is followed; encourage all members to participate in group discussions; and guide the discussion to make sure that it stays on the subject. When you are a participant in a small group meeting, enter the discussion with a positive attitude and an open mind.

One of the most effective agendas for problem solving is known as the reflective-thinking method. It involves seven steps: defining the problem; analyzing it; establishing criteria for evaluating solutions; suggesting possible solutions; choosing the best solution; deciding how to implement the solution; and deciding how to test the solution.

Sometimes groups appear in public to discuss or debate an issue. Three popular formats are team presentations, the symposium (a series of brief speeches on a common topic), and the panel discussion (an informal presentation involving a moderator and panelists).

Key Terms

agenda, *389*

brainstorming, *394*

hidden agenda, *392*

minutes, *391*

panel discussion, *397*

reflective-thinking method, *393*

symposium, *397*

team presentation, *396*

Review Questions

1. Why is an agenda necessary for a meeting?

2. Why is nonverbal behavior important in a group meeting?

3. If you disagree with what everyone else in the group is saying, what should you do?

4. What does a group do when it brainstorms?

5. In what ways does a team presentation resemble an individual speech?

6. What is a hidden agenda?

7. What are the seven steps of the reflective-thinking method?

8. What should a group leader do after a meeting?

9. What are the duties of the moderator in a panel discussion?

10. What are the duties of panelists in a panel discussion?

Building Critical-Thinking Skills

1. A football huddle is a type of group meeting. Fran Tarkenton, former star quarterback for the Minnesota Vikings, says, "Many of my best plays were the result of input by other team members. For example, outside receivers often told me that they could run a specific pattern against the defense, and we adjusted to run those plays. I would guess that 50 percent of my touchdowns came about by my receivers suggesting pass patterns." How could Tarkenton's insights be applied to business meetings?

2. Some communication experts say that group meetings lose a great deal of their effectiveness when group members number more than 12. Assuming that this statement is true, what would account for a decline in effectiveness?

Building Teamwork Skills

1. In a group, use the steps of the reflective-thinking method (as shown in this chapter) to discuss how to solve a problem on your campus or in your community. Choose a leader to guide the discussion.

2. Using guidelines from your instructor, conduct either a symposium or a panel discussion to present the findings from the problem-solving assignment in item 1.

A

Sample Speeches

Persuasive Speech
Too Much of a Good Thing
Arlene Chico Lugo

Speeches Online

Too Much of a Good Thing
Arlene Chico Lugo

Below is a persuasive speech that uses the problem-solution pattern. To see the video of the speech, go to www.connectpublicspeaking.com.

There's an old saying that I am sure many of you out there have heard. [*The speaker shows poster in Figure A.1.*] "Too much of a good thing is wonderful." Is this true? **1**

The newsletter *Harvard Women's Health Watch* published a story about a young woman who went sailing one Friday afternoon. Now while she was sailing, she sustained a back injury that caused her a lot of pain. Over the course of the next three days she began to take a pain medication called acetaminophen. Now this is a very common pain medication most commonly known as Tylenol. Not only did she take this medication, but she also took twice the recommended dosage of it. And four days later, she died on the way to the hospital due to liver failure. Apparently she did not know that taking too much pain medication can cause liver failure and sometimes death. **2**

This same newsletter, *Harvard Women's Health Watch,* estimates that overdoses of pain medication cause 56,000 visits to the emergency room every year as well as 458 deaths. It is a common trap to think that if a little bit of something is good, then a great deal of it is even better. I'm here today to tell you that too much of a good thing can sometimes be bad for you. **3**

Let's start by looking at the problem a little bit more closely. Many people are unaware of the dangers of taking excessive amounts of medicines and supplements. For example, the popular sleep aid, Ambien: if you take the recommended dose, it will make you drowsy so that you can go to sleep. So taking more will just make you go to sleep faster, right? That may be so, but it can also lead to a reduction in breathing, a coma, and even death. This information is according to Dr. Daniel F. Kripke, professor of psychiatry at the University of California at San Diego, who is the author of *The Dark Side of Sleeping Pills.* **4**

The General Practitioner, a medical journal, says that taking too much ibuprofen (which is another very common pain medication most commonly known as Advil) can cause gastrointestinal bleeding within just three days of overuse. **5**

Too much of a good thing is wonderful.

Figure A.1
Does this old saying apply to medicine?

6   Dr. Bill Edwards, the director of inpatient care at the Children's Hospital in Peoria, Illinois, tells the story of a child who displayed symptoms of a brain tumor. This includes dizziness, pressure in the head, headache, blurry vision—these are all symptoms of a brain tumor. But tests reported no brain tumor. After further testing, they did discover that this child had an overdose of vitamin A. Can vitamins be toxic? The answer is yes—if they are taken in large amounts. According to Dr. Joshua Hamilton, professor of toxicology at Dartmouth College, an excess use of vitamin B_6 can cause nerve damage to the arms and legs. An excess use of vitamin C can cause kidney stones. And an excess use of vitamin D can cause damage to the kidneys.

7   Now that we have examined the problem, what's the solution? It's important to be cautious and well-informed. Collaborate with doctors on what pills and supplements and vitamins you should be taking. Always take the recommended dosage—never more. Be aware of complications because even though you might be taking the recommended dosage, there could still be toxic interactions with the medications that you are taking. Try making a list of all the vitamins and supplements and medications that you're taking and show them to your doctor or your pharmacist to make sure that there aren't any toxic interactions. Educate yourself by consulting health books or health magazines and newsletters. Another good source of education is the Internet but you've got to be very careful with that. Only use reputable sources such as the health sections in ABC.com, MSNBC.com, or CBS.com.

8   Dr. Kathi Kemper, the author of *The Holistic Pediatrician,* warns against using common search engines such as Google. The reason for that is this: Remember the child who had an overdose of vitamin A? Well, his parents were influenced by a Web site claiming that Vitamin A was a cure for children who were hyperactive and had trouble concentrating in school. So you can see where getting the wrong information can be very harmful to you and your children. These Web searches turn out hundreds of sites that talk about vitamin A or any other medication or supplement that you might be investigating, but these sites are also dedicated to selling a product. So you can't trust them to be objective.

9   So, let's sum up what we've talked about today. Painkillers and vitamins are good for you, but they can be harmful when taken in excessive amounts. Collaborate with doctors and pharmacists to know what supplements and what medications you should and shouldn't be taking. Always stay within the recommended dosage—never more. Keep yourself informed by consulting books and magazines and *reliable* Web pages. So, now that you've seen that

Figure A.2
When it comes to pills, this concluding quotation is more accurate than the speaker's opening quotation.

Too much of a good thing can be awful.

you can't always accept the old saying, "Too much of a good thing is wonderful," maybe you'll agree that there's another old saying that offers some better advice. [*Speaker shows poster in Figure A.2.*] "Too much of a good thing can be awful."

Speeches Online

To view 22 videos of full-length speeches, go to www.connectpublicspeaking.com. Included are all the major speeches printed in this book, plus the speeches below:

- **Wedding Crashers**
  Dave Reed

Can a Hollywood movie prompt thousands of people to crash real-life weddings? One speaker investigates.

- **Do You Need Detox?**
  Steven Kaplan

Is your body clogged with impurities? Do you need detoxification? Two speeches ("needs improvement" and "improved")
show the wrong way and the right way to find reliable information on this issue.

- **Humanoid Robots**
  Joe Haupt

Are robots likely to equal human intelligence and capability in this century?

- **Are You Being Overcharged?**
  Laura Valpey

Problem: many consumers are overcharged because of scanning errors. What is the solution?

- **How to Make Avocado Salsa**
  Nick Amick

Two contrasting speeches illustrate the wrong way and the right way to give a demonstration speech.

- **Scars and Bruises**
  Christine Fowler

A self-introduction speech by a student who grew up with many scrapes and falls.

- **Plus much more:**

* Nine additional full-length speech videos
* 33 video clips showing elements of speeches (such as "conveying the central idea" and "providing transitions")

B

appendix

Communication in a Multicultural Society and World

OBJECTIVES

After studying this appendix, you should be able to:

1. Define *intercultural communication*.

2. Compare and contrast culture and co-culture, ethnocentrism and cultural relativism, melting-pot philosophy and cultural pluralism.

3. Compare and contrast the following: individualism and collectivism, high-context communication cultures and low-context

communication cultures, high-power-distance cultures and low-power-distance cultures, masculine and feminine cultures.

4. Identify the various groups that influence our cultural identity.

5. Discuss how technology is bringing diversity into our lives.

6. Identify techniques you can use to reduce the strangeness of strangers.

Have you ever drawn a conclusion about or ascribed

positive or negative characteristics to someone without really knowing him or her? Do you believe another person ever formed an opinion of you or judged you without really knowing you? If you answer yes to either of these questions, it is likely that stereotypes played a role.

Stereotypes express the knowledge, beliefs, and expectancies we have for the members of a particular group.[1] While some of the stereotypes we hold of any cultural group are positive, others are astoundingly negative and overly generalized. While some contain kernels of truth, others keep us from identifying misconceptions. For which groups of people do you have positive and negative stereotypes? And what do the members of these groups think of you? How does each of your evaluations influence whether or not you interact with one another? For example, many Muslims in the United States are asking that others view them more objectively and stop treating them with suspicion. They want stereotypes of them abandoned, saying that individuals should be able to distinguish between mainstream Muslims and those belonging to the radical fringe.[2]

It's not just relationships with Muslims that are suffering. Relations between African Americans, Hispanics, and Asian Americans are also complicated by the stereotypes we hold of one another. Yet all these groups share a common desire and need—to get along better with each other.[3] Stereotyping is just one of the topics we address in this chapter as we explore a host of factors that influence our ability to communicate in a multicultural society and world.

globalization
the increasing economic, political, and cultural integration and interdependence of diverse cultures

diversity
the recognition and valuing of difference

glocalization
how globalization affects and merges with local interests and environments

multiculturalists
persons respectful of and engaged with people from distinctly different cultures

Globalization, Diversity, and Glocalization

In the *age of globalization*, the likelihood of working and living with people from all over the world increases daily. **Globalization** is the increasing economic, political, and cultural integration and interdependence of diverse cultures—the worldwide integration of humanity. Globalization is related to two other concepts—*diversity* and *glocalization*. **Diversity** is the recognition and valuing of difference, encompassing such factors as age, gender, race, ethnicity, ability, religion, education, marital status, sexual orientation, and income. **Glocalization** is a newer concept describing how globalization affects and merges with local interests and environments. All three forces affect communication. Because it is now critical to learn about other cultures and to refrain from stereotyping them, embracing diversity is becoming more important than ever.[4]

Digital technology is helping to erase the notion of territorial boundaries between countries, gradually eroding the idea of the term *nation*. People we once considered strangers are now friends and co-workers, creating the need for us to be **multiculturalists**—persons respectful of and engaged with people from distinctly different cultures. An early observer of how the mass media affect behavior and thinking, Marshall McLuhan predicted many years ago that our world would become a global village.[5] He was right. We are now linked physically and electronically to people around the globe. In addition to using the Internet with increasing frequency, many of us move—for personal or professional reasons—a number of times during our lives.[6] We also travel regularly to other countries, some of us to visit relatives (one in five Americans was born abroad or has at least one parent who was), others to represent an employer, and still others to vacation.

We differ, however, in our willingness to embrace diversity. In the book *Bowling Alone,* written at the turn of this millennium, author Robert Putnam reported that reciprocal and trustworthy social networks were on the decline, a fact he attributed, at least in part, to racial diversity. Putnam reported that we were doing more and more things alone, but why? After studying 30,000 people across the United

BALDO   **BY CANTÚ AND CASTELLANOS**

What does this cartoon suggest about the propensity to stereotype? Can you supply an example from your own experience that demonstrates why identifying people belonging to a group in fixed, limited, and simplistic ways impedes communication?

States, Putnam discovered a correlation between ethnically mixed environments and the withdrawal from public life. He found that people living in diverse communities tended to "hunker down." Sadly, they were more likely to distrust their neighbors–whether they shared the same or a different race, a similar or different background.[7] Do you think this is still true? Are the "gay community" and the "African-American community" communities even though they lack diversity? The world of work reveals a different story. In organizations, people with *identity diversity* (people who come from different races and religions) and *cognitive diversity* (people who have different outlooks and training) come together to do the organization's work. Thus, the challenge we face is to follow the lead of diverse organizations and create a new and broader sense of "we," that is, to harness diversity to build community.[8]

Your Thoughts

How does the world in which you are growing up differ from the one in which your parents or caregivers grew up?

The remainder of this chapter will sensitize you to the ways cultural values and habits influence interaction. Learning about such differences will help you (1) appropriately respond to varied communication styles, (2) recognize the need to expand your choices as a communicator, and (3) increase the effectiveness of your interactions with persons of different cultures.

Defining Intercultural Communication

Whenever cultural variability influences the nature and the effects of communication, **intercultural communication** is at work. Thus, when we speak about intercultural communication, we are concerning ourselves with the process of interpreting and sharing meanings with individuals from different cultures.[9] In actuality, intercultural communication comprises a number of forms. Among its many variations are **interracial communication** (which occurs when interactants are of different races), **interethnic communication** (which occurs when the communicating parties have different ethnic origins), **international communication** (which occurs between persons representing political structures), and **intracultural communication** (which includes all forms of communication among members of the same racial, ethnic, or other co-culture groups).[10]

Cultures and Co-Cultures

To become more adept at communicating with persons who are culturally different from ourselves, we need to learn not only about their cultures but also about our own. A **culture** is the system of knowledge, beliefs, values, customs, behaviors, and artifacts that are acquired, shared, and used by its members during daily living.[11] Within a culture as a whole are **co-cultures;** these are composed of members of the same general culture who differ in some ethnic or sociological way from the parent culture. In our society, African Americans, Hispanic Americans, Japanese Americans, the disabled, gays and lesbians, cyberpunks, and the elderly are just some of the co-cultures belonging to the same general culture.[12] (See Figure 2.1.)

Have you ever felt like an outsider? Persons who believe they belong to a *marginalized group*–that is, a group whose members feel like outsiders–have a number of options to choose from regarding how they want to interact with members of the dominant culture or even if they want to interact with them at all. Have you or has anyone you know used any of the following strategies?

intercultural communication
interaction with individuals from different cultures

interracial communication
the interpreting and sharing of meanings with individuals from different races

interethnic communication
interaction with individuals of different ethnic origins

international communication
communication between persons representing different nations

intracultural communication
interaction with members of the same racial or ethnic group or co-culture as yours

culture
a system of knowledge, beliefs, values, customs, behaviors, and artifacts that are acquired, shared, and used by members during daily living

co-cultures
groups of persons who differ in some ethnic or sociological way from the parent culture

assimilation
the means by which co-culture members attempt to fit in with members of the dominant culture

accommodation
the means by which co-culture members maintain their cultural identity while striving to establish relationships with members of the dominant culture

separation
the means co-culture members use to resist interacting with members of the dominant culture

Co-culture members who use the strategy of **assimilation** attempt to fit in, or join, with members of the dominant culture. They converse about subjects that members of the dominant group talk about, such as cars or sports, or they dress as members of the dominant culture dress. They give up their own ways in an effort to assume the modes of behavior of the dominant culture. In comparison, co-culture members who use the strategy of **accommodation** attempt to maintain their cultural identity even while they strive to establish relationships with members of the dominant culture. A gay or lesbian who takes his or her partner to an occasion in which members of the dominant culture will be present, such as a company or family celebration, is using the strategy of accommodation. On the other hand, when members of a co-culture resist interacting with members of the dominant culture, they employ the strategy of resistance, or **separation.** Because these persons, such as Hassidic Jews, prefer to interact with each other rather than have contact with persons they perceive to be outsiders, they tend to keep to themselves.

Members of co-cultures can practice *passive, assertive, aggressive,* or *confrontational* communication approaches in their efforts to accomplish their objectives relative to the dominant culture. Co-culture members who practice a *passive* communication approach seek to avoid the limelight; they accept their position in the cultural hierarchy. Rather than defend their ways and oppose others, they embrace the cultural beliefs and practices of the dominant culture. Recent immigrants to the United States who desire to attain citizenship may choose this path, hoping to blend in so that they do not disturb the status quo. Co-culture members who employ an *assertive* communication approach may seek to communicate a shared cultural identity with members of the dominant group; they want others to accommodate their diversity. They are receptive to rethinking a number of their ideas, give up or modify some, and hold strong with regard to others. After the September 11, 2001, terrorist attacks, for example, many Arab Americans spoke openly of their patriotism, their support for the war against terror, and their desire for others to allow them to live according to their values and beliefs. Co-culture members who opt to display a more *aggressive* communication approach defend their own beliefs and traditions with intensity and may find themselves perceived by members of the dominant culture as "hurtfully expressive" or "self-promoting." They make it difficult for members of the dominant culture to

Work It Out **?**

What does the following quote featured on a wall at the Holocaust Museum in Washington, D.C., suggest about the importance of understanding and accepting diversity?

In Germany, the Nazis first came for the communists, and I didn't speak up because I wasn't a communist. Then they came for the Jews, and I didn't speak up because I wasn't a Jew. Then they came for the trade unionists, and I didn't speak up because I wasn't a trade unionist. Then they came for the Catholics, but I didn't speak up because I was a Protestant. Then they came for me, and by that time there was no one left to speak for me.

ignore their presence or pretend they do not exist.[13] They adopt this strategy to de-marginalize themselves and actively participate in the world known to members of the dominant culture. In their early years as a group, the members of Act Up, a gay rights organization employed this approach. (See Table 2.1.)

Many theorists believe that understanding both the general culture and its co-cultures is essential for effective communication. Merely knowing another's language, jargon, or argot or sharing some but not all of a group's values does not necessarily ensure understanding. It is also necessary to become aware of the norms and rules of the culture or co-cultures that might influence the nature of interactions you have with its members, whether those interactions occur in public or in private.

Thus, when you and the individuals with whom you are interacting belong to different cultures, for you to understand each other, you each need to consider the role culture plays in shaping your communication. According to cultural anthropologist Edward T. Hall, culture is communication and communication is culture.[14] Culture teaches you how to think and what to think about. Culture teaches you what is beautiful or ugly, helpful

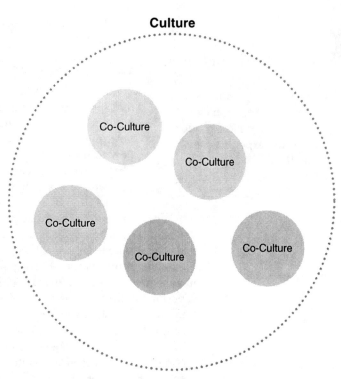

Figure B.1 A Culture and Its Co-Cultures.
The term *co-culture* is preferred over *subculture* because the prefix *sub* denotes inferior status. A co-culture is a culture within a culture.

Using more than one language on a sign fosters communication with the members of a co-culture.

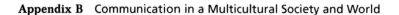

Your Thoughts **?**

Were you ever the only person of your age, race, ethnicity, or sexual preference in a group? How did the experience make you feel?

or harmful, appropriate or out of place. Culture is the lens through which you view the world; it is the mirror you use to reflect and interpret reality.[15]

Culture Guides Communication

Among the lessons taught by culture are how to say "hello" and "goodbye," when to speak or remain silent, how to act when you're angry or upset, where to focus your eyes when functioning as a source or receiver, how much to gesture during speech, how close to stand to another, and how to display happiness or rage at another's actions. By teaching you lessons like these, culture guides behavior and communication. It tells you who you are, how to act, how to think, how to talk, and how to listen.[16]

When cultures meet, when we interact with persons whose values are different from ours or whose behavioral norms differ from our own, we must first recognize and acknowledge our differences. We must come to accept diversity if we are to be able to process other cultures' influences and communicate with each other in a meaningful way. **Ethnocentrism,** the tendency to see your own culture as superior to all others, is a key characteristic of failed intercultural communication efforts. Persons who are ethnocentric experience great anxiety when interacting with persons from different cultures. Quick to utter statements like "They take our jobs," "They're everywhere," and "They're just not like us," those who embrace ethnocentrism lack cultural flexibility and are particularly unprepared to meet the challenges posed by our society and our world today.[17] The more ethnocentric you are, the greater your tendency is to view groups other than your own as inferior. As a result, you tend to blame others for problems and seek to maintain your distance from them.[18]

Cultural relativism is the opposite of ethnocentrism. When you practice cultural relativism, instead of viewing the group to which you belong as superior to all others, you work to try to understand the behavior of other groups on the basis of the context in which the behavior occurs rather than from your own frame of reference.

Two other factors, stereotypes and prejudice, also influence how we react to persons from cultures different from our own. As we noted at the opening of this chapter, **stereotypes** are mental images or pictures we carry around in our heads; they are shortcuts, whether positive or negative, that guide our reactions to others.[19] When attached to the way we view the world, stereotypes generate unrealistic pictures of others and prevent us from distinguishing an individual from a group. Racial profiling is just one example of how stereotyping affects worldview.

Prejudice describes how we feel about a group of people whom, more likely than not, we do not know personally. A negative or positive prejudgment, prejudice arises either because we want to feel more positively about our own group or because we feel others present a threat, real or not.[20] Prejudice leads to the creation of in-groups and out-groups, with out-group members becoming easy targets for discrimination. Because of the negative expectations that stereotypes and prejudice produce, we may try not to interact with people who are the objects of our prejudice. (We discuss stereotypes and prejudice again in Chapter 4.)

ethnocentrism
the tendency to see one's own culture as superior to all others

cultural relativism
the acceptance of other cultural groups as equal in value to one's own

stereotypes
mental images or pictures that guide our reactions to others

prejudice
a positive or negative prejudgment

Separation	Passive	Lunching alone, living in an area with similar people
Accommodation	Assertive	Wearing a yarmulke to work, wearing a sari to a party
Assimilation	Aggressive, confrontational	Staging a protest

Table B.1
Preferred Strategies and Communication Approaches of Marginalized Groups

Taking the Demographic Picture: Diversity in Focus

To what extent has the amount of contact you have with persons of diverse cultural backgrounds changed since you were a child? When you were younger, you were more apt to interact with persons just like yourself. Your experience today most likely is different. Continuing developments in technology and changes in demography are influencing the nature of our interactions.

Intercultural communication is now the norm. In fact, living in the United States gives you an incredible opportunity to interact interculturally without having to pay for international travel. But it hasn't always been that way. Years ago, the United States embraced a **melting-pot philosophy.** According to that theory, when individuals from other countries came here, they lost or gave up their original heritage and became Americans. The national motto, *E pluribus unum*–a Latin

melting-pot philosophy
the view that different cultures should be assimilated into the dominant culture

Culture is the lens through which we see the world. Can you provide an example of how your culture has influenced your view of events?

Your Thoughts **?**

Compare and contrast the lessons taught you by your culture with the lessons taught peers by other cultures.

cultural pluralism
adherence to the principle of cultural relativism

phrase meaning "one out of many"—reflected this way of thinking. It was believed that diverse cultural groups should be assimilated into the parent, or dominant, culture.

Over time, this philosophy was replaced by one that stresses **cultural pluralism.** Cultural pluralists advocate respect for uniqueness, tolerance for difference, and adherence to the principle of cultural relativity. In a multicultural society, every group, it is believed, will do things differently, and that's OK.

Demographers tell us that diversity will shape our country's future. According to U.S. Census Bureau statistics, the five largest ethnic groups are composed of people who identify themselves as White (207.7 million), African American (36.6 million), Hispanic (38.8 million), Asian American (12.7 million), and Native American (3.5 million). Hispanics are now the largest minority group, followed by African Americans, Native Americans, and Hawaiian Pacific Islanders.[21] In one generation, minorities may become the majority. (See Figure 2.2.)

The United States is the most demographically diverse country in the world. Because of this and because of advances in communications and transportation, we will continue to experience an increasing number of contacts with members of other cultures. This alone makes it especially important for us to be able to understand and interact with persons of different backgrounds, nationalities, and lifestyles. We are truly interconnected with all of humanity.

Skill Builder

Ethnocentrism versus Cultural Relativism

Evaluate the extent to which you display culturally ethnocentric or culturally relativistic tendencies by labeling the following statements true or false. For each statement, provide an example of behaviors you used when interacting with or attempting to avoid interacting with a member of another culture. Be specific.

1. I would rather communicate with someone like me than with someone unlike me.
2. I can cooperate with people like me, but I find it difficult to cooperate with people unlike me.
3. I trust those who are like me more freely than I trust those who are different from me.
4. I am less fearful when I am around people like me than when I am around people unlike me.
5. I go out of my way to be with people like me.
6. I go out of my way to maintain my distance from people unlike me.

7. I am much more apt to blame people unlike me for causing trouble than I am to blame people like me.
8. I use my frame of reference to assess the rightness of the behaviors of people like and unlike me.
9. I believe that people unlike me threaten my ability to succeed.
10. I believe that people unlike me should make an effort to become more like me.

What do your answers and examples tell you about the extent to which you and others practice ethnocentrism or cultural relativism? Are there some cultures different from your own that you are more comfortable with than others? Why do you think that is so? Are you content with your responses? Why or why not? What steps are you willing to take, if any, to minimize the potentially negative effects of ethnocentrism?

Figure B.2
Source: New York Times,
August 14, 2008, p. A18.

Majority minorities

The Census Bureau projects that the share of ethnic and racial minorities will reach 54 percent of the total United States population and surpass that of non-Hispanic whites by 2042.

Hispanics can be of any race
Source: Census Bureau

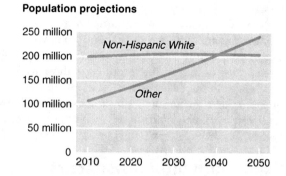

Population projections

Non-Hispanic White

Other

Racial and ethnic breakdown

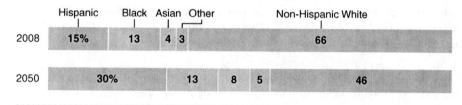

	Hispanic	Black	Asian	Other	Non-Hispanic White
2008	15%	13	4	3	66
2050	30%	13	8	5	46

Percent minority by age group

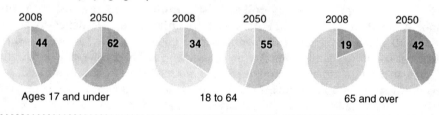

2008	2050	2008	2050	2008	2050
44	62	34	55	19	42

Ages 17 and under   18 to 64   65 and over

The Intercultural Communication Imperative: Reduce the Strangeness of Strangers

While intercultural communication is inevitable, we are neither as effective nor as successful at it as we could be. The reason is clear: Not all of us work hard enough to understand or to be understood by those with whom we differ.

According to intercultural communication theorists Larry A. Samovar and Richard E. Porter, there are too many of "us" who do not work as hard as we should at intercultural communication simply because we do not wish to live or interact with "them."[22] Too many of us have adopted an "us versus them" mentality, which prevents us from effectively meeting the challenges cultural diversity presents. To counter this, we need to conduct ourselves in a manner designed to reduce the strangeness of strangers; that is, we need to open ourselves to differences by adding to our storehouse of knowledge, by learning to cope with uncertainty, and by developing

Your Thoughts

Identify the extent to which ethnocentrism and/or cultural relativism affects you or those you know.

- What steps have you taken to reduce the strangeness of strangers?
- Have you ever considered your culture superior to another culture? How did your feelings influence your relationship with members of that culture?
- Indicate where you fall on each of the cultural dialectics described in this section. Are your preferences different from those displayed by your parents? Are they different from those practiced by your grandparents? If so, how?

an appreciation of how increasing our cultural sensitivity will positively affect our communication competence.

We take a giant step toward improving intercultural communication by accepting the fact that our culture is not superior to others. Nor should we base our behavioral expectations for the members of other cultures on our own culture's norms. To do so would cause us to label the responses of those who belong to other cultures as foreign or strange. To the extent that we are able to use our understanding of another's culture to reduce the number of misunderstandings between us, to the extent that we do not interpret the behavior of others on the basis of our own frames of reference, we take further steps toward reducing the strangeness of strangers.

Exploring Cultural Dialectics

Let's continue by focusing on four variables used to distinguish cultures: (1) individualism versus collectivism, (2) high-context versus low-context communication, (3) high power distance versus low power distance, and (4) masculine or feminine culture. Identified by Hofstede, Kluckhohn and Strodtbeck, and Hall, these dialectics reveal a culture's values and help us make comparisons across cultures.[23]

Individualism versus Collectivism

The cultural dimension of individualism versus collectivism reveals how people define themselves in their relationships with others. **Individualistic cultures,** such as those of Great Britain, the United States, Canada, France, and Germany, stress individual goals, whereas **collectivistic cultures,** represented by many Arab, African, Asian, and Latin American countries, give precedence to group goals. Individualistic cultures cultivate individual initiative and achievement, while collectivistic cultures tend to nurture group influences. This means that, while the "I" may be most important in individualistic cultures, the "we" is the dominant force in collectivistic ones. In collectivistic cultures the individual is expected to fit into the group; in individualistic cultures emphasis is placed on developing a sense of self.

High Context versus Low Context

A second way cultures vary in communication style is in their preference for high-context or low-context communication. Cultures with **high-context communication** systems are tradition-bound; their cultural traditions shape the behavior and lifestyle of group members, causing them to appear to be overly polite and indirect in relating to others. In contrast, cultures with **low-context communication** systems generally encourage members to exhibit a more direct communication style. Members of low-context cultures tend to gather background information when meeting someone for the first time. Thus, they will ask people they have just met where they went to college, where they live, and who they work for. Persons from high-context cultures are much less likely to ask such questions.[24] In addition, persons from low-context cultures are apt to feel that they have to explain everything rather than rely on nonverbal, contextual information as demonstrated by those who display a preference for high-context communication. In contrast, persons who believe that most messages can be understood without direct verbal interaction reveal their preference for high-context communication. Asian cultures typically emphasize high-context communication, whereas Western cultures typically represent low-context communication systems. For example, the Japanese have traditionally valued silence, believing that a person of few words is thoughtful, trustworthy,

individualistic cultures
cultures in which individual goals are stressed

collectivistic cultures
cultures in which group goals are stressed

high-context communication
a tradition-bound communication system which depends on indirectness

low-context communication
a system that encourages directness in communication

and respectable. Thus, the Japanese spend considerably less time talking than do people in the United States. This orientation also helps explain why the Japanese often perceive self-disclosures during interaction as socially inappropriate.

High Power Distance versus Low Power Distance

Power distance measures the extent to which individuals are willing to accept power differences. Individuals from **high-power-distance cultures,** such as Saudi Arabia, India, and Malaysia, view power as a fact of life and are apt to stress its coercive or referent nature. Superiors and subordinates in these countries are likely to view each other differently; subordinates are quick to defer to superiors. In contrast, individuals from **low-power-distance cultures,** such as Israel, Sweden, and the United States, believe power should be used only when it is legitimate; thus, they are apt to employ expert or legitimate power. Superiors and subordinates from low-power-distance countries emphasize their interdependence by displaying a preference for consultation; subordinates will even contradict their bosses when necessary.[25]

Masculine versus Feminine Culture

Cultures differ in their attitudes toward gender roles.[26] In highly masculine cultures, members value male aggressiveness, strength, and material symbols of success. In highly feminine cultures, members value relationships, tenderness in members of both sexes, and a high quality of life. Among highly **masculine cultures** are Japan, Italy, Germany, Mexico, and Great Britain. Among highly feminine cultures are Sweden, Norway, the Netherlands, Thailand, and Chile. Masculine cultures socialize mem-

high-power-distance cultures
cultures based on power differences in which subordinates defer to superiors

low-power-distance cultures
cultures that believe that power should be used only when legitimate

masculine cultures
cultures that value aggressiveness, strength, and material symbols of success

- What roles or rituals are used to celebrate the achievements of persons belonging to an individualistic culture? To a collectivistic culture? Which culture would feature a "salesperson of the year" award? Which would reward the achievements of the team?

Exploring Diversity

Understanding Other Cultures

Make a list of individuals whose cultural backgrounds differ from your own and with whom you have recently communicated. How many of the following questions can you answer with respect to each person on your list?

1. How do the individual's feelings about socialization differ from your own?
2. How does the individual's concept of self compare with yours?
3. To what extent do the individual's values and attitudes differ from yours?
4. Which of your behaviors did the individual have difficulty understanding or accepting? Which of his or her behaviors did you have difficulty with?
5. Which of the individuals you interacted with did you find most like you? Most unlike you? Can you identify your

points of similarity and difference?
6. To what extent was the individual more cooperative or competitive than you?
7. In what ways did the individual's use of verbal language differ from your own?
8. In what ways did the individual's nonverbal behavior differ from your own?
9. How did the individual's treatment of time and space differ from your own?
10. In what ways did the individual's thinking processes differ from yours?

For those questions you cannot answer, take the time to conduct research; then answer them.

• What assumptions do the following proverbs lead you to make about the identified culture's members? How can understanding the proverbs a culture embraces help enhance communication with that culture's members?

bers to be dominant and competitive. They tend to confront conflicts head-on and are likely to use a win-lose conflict strategy. In contrast, the members of **feminine cultures** are more apt to compromise and negotiate to resolve conflicts, seeking win-win solutions.

Interpreting Cultural Differences

Where a culture falls on the individualistic-collectivistic, low-context–high-context communication, and power distance scales affects the interactional preferences of its members. In Japanese and Chinese societies, for example, individuals tend to understate their own accomplishments and successes, while members of North American cultures typically are taught to be assertive and take credit for their personal achievements. It appears that individualistic cultures tend to use low-context communication, while high-context communication tends to predominate in collectivistic cultures. Thus, whereas members of low-context communication cultures interact in a direct way with each other, members of high-context communication cultures interact indirectly. For example, North Americans tend to speak directly on an issue, whereas individuals from Japan, Korea, and China prefer to avoid confrontation, to preserve a sense of harmony, and to make it possible for the individuals with whom they are speaking to save face, or maintain self-esteem. Similarly, rarely will one Saudi Arabian publicly criticize another; to do so would label the individual as disloyal and disrespectful.[27] When persons from diverse power-distance cultures interact, unless these differences in orientation are acknowledged, interactions may well result in misunderstandings.

The Cost of Cultural Ignorance

Communicators who fail to realize that persons from different cultures may not look, think, or act as they themselves do run the risk of having those with whom they interact judge them to be insensitive, ignorant, or **culturally confused.** The culturally confused pay a high price. Cultural misunderstandings often lead to lost opportunities and increased levels of tension between people. The following examples demonstrate the extent to which cultural ignorance affects communication:

culturally confused
lacking an understanding of cultural difference

- Showing the sole of a shoe means nothing to observers in the United States or Europe. As a result, when visiting Saudi Arabia, the American and European delegates to a conference thought nothing about crossing their legs and pointing their shoes toward the speaker while listening to his presentation. The speaker, however, was horrified. In Muslim cultures, the gesture is perceived as insulting.[28] Similarly, while crossing your legs in the United States indicates you are relaxed, in Korea it is a social faux pas.

- John, who represented the interests of an American multinational corporation, and Yu-Chen, his Taiwanese counterpart, had difficulty establishing a working relationship. John's eyeblink rate increased as he became more and more nervous, fearing that his efforts to resolve their misunderstanding had reached an impasse. This only made things worse. Blinking while another person talks is considered normal to North Americans; to Taiwanese it is considered impolite.[29]

God helps those who help themselves.
The squeaky wheel gets the grease.
    —(American)
When spiderwebs unite, they can trap a lion.
It takes a whole village to raise a child.
    —(African)
No need to know the person, only the family.
    —(Chinese)
It's the nail that sticks out that is hammered.
    —(Japanese)

- McDonald's fast-food chain unintentionally offended thousands of Muslims when it printed an excerpt from the Koran on its throwaway hamburger bags.[30] Muslims saw this as sacrilegious. The mistake could have been avoided if McDonald's had displayed greater sensitivity and awareness.
- The Japanese view the business card as an extension of a person, while Americans view it as a business formality and a convenience. Consequently, while the Japanese handle business cards with great care, making certain to put them in safe places, Americans are quick to put them away and thus often end up insulting the Japanese.[31]
- Arabs typically adopt a direct body orientation when communicating. Americans employ a stance that is somewhat less direct and thus often find the communication of Arabs aggressive and unnerving. Arabs and South Americans also tend to gesture vigorously when speaking to others, causing the less physical Americans to construe their behavior as inappropriate and unmannerly. It is common in Middle Eastern cultures for both males and females to physically exaggerate responses, while in the United States emotions are more likely to be suppressed. In Japan, individuals may try to hide or mask certain emotions. It is common among Asian cultures to exhibit reserve and emotional restraint.
- Eye contact preferences also differ across cultures. Americans place a high value on eye-to-eye communication and tend to distrust those who fail to look at them directly. The Japanese, in contrast, believe eye contact over a sustained period of time shows disrespect. Among Asian cultures, too much eye contact is deemed intrusive. Arabs, on the other hand, maintain direct eye contact with those they interact with for prolonged periods.
- Americans tend to value personal achievement and individualism. In contrast, Asian and Native American cultures stress group cohesion and loyalty, placing greater emphasis on group rather than individual achievement.

Failing to develop insights into cultural nuances and differences can be costly. Recognizing and responding to differences among cultures allows for more meaningful relationships. At the same time, we need to be mindful that not everyone

Work It Out ?

Research and supply examples of how a failure to understand the customs or language of persons from a different country and culture contributed to a communication breakdown or embarrassed one of the parties.

- Describe a cultural misunderstanding in which you or someone you know was involved. Was it resolved?
- How do you adapt when in the company of people who are more at home with an alternative cultural convention?

Work It Out ?

In Japan, the word for "different" is the same as the word for "wrong." Compare and contrast a culture in which the goal is to become as much like others as possible with a culture in which the goal is to distinguish oneself from others. Which cultural attitude are you most comfortable with?

Imagine you are given the task to create a metaphor for the United States, one that accurately describes the way immigrants are assimilated into U.S. society. How do you think your parents would depict this situation? Why might a person not identify fully with members of his or her own culture until becoming an immigrant in another country?

Ethics and Communication

Through Others' Eyes

Imagine you arrive in the United States from a foreign country. Though perhaps unlikely, also imagine that you are totally unfamiliar with what life in the U.S. is like and totally unknowledgeable when it comes to American pop culture. In fact, you have never viewed American television, watched American films, or listened to American CDs. You do, however, read English fluently. You find a current issue of *TV Guide* and start reading it. Based on your perusal of prime-time programming,

what characteristics would you attribute to Americans? How many of your listed characteristics would you consider positive? Negative?

If asked to summarize your discoveries, what conclusions would you draw about what Americans value? What subjects would you identify as of great interest to them? How would you assess their attitudes toward persons from other cultures? Finally, what suggestions would you like to offer them?

Do you believe any of the following cultural practices are unethical?

- *cockfighting*
- *the withholding of medical intervention, such as a blood transfusion*
- *female circumcision*
- *the stoning of a rape victim*

If you answer yes to any, explain why. If you answer no to any, explain why not. To what extent do your answers support or negate the belief that every culture has a right to its own customs and beliefs?

cultural imperialism
the expansion of dominion of one culture over another culture

from a particular culture exhibits the same characteristics and communication traits.

Being unaware of how others outside a culture view that culture's members can also be costly: Communication researchers Melvin and Margaret DeFleur surveyed 1,259 teenagers from twelve countries whose main contact with Americans was through popular culture including television programs and movies they watched and the music they listened to. Based on these vicarious experiences, in their judgment, Americans were violent, materialistic, sexually loose, disrespectful of people unlike them, unconcerned about the poor, and prone to criminal activity. The DeFleurs concluded that the exporting of American commercialized popular culture contributes to cultural imperialism and helps foster feelings of anti-Americanism.[32]

If imperialism is the expansion of dominion of one country over another country, then **cultural imperialism** is the expansion of dominion of one culture over another culture. Cultural imperialism's critics assert that the news, entertainment, and products of an industrialized country such as the United States overwhelm the national cultures of other countries. They contend that our ethnocentricity leads us to promote our way of life as superior.

There are signs, however, that the reign of American pop culture is beginning to erode. Foreign film successes such as Stephen Chow's *Kung Fu Hustle*, Zhang Yimou's *House of Flying Daggers*, and Ang Lee's *Crouching Tiger, Hidden Dragon* have been successes in the United States. U.S. music charts also regularly feature vocalists from other countries who speak in Spanish or another language, and foreign news services such as Al Jazeera and the BBC are influencing news coverage. Cross-fertilization of ideas inevitably leads to more diversity. Increasingly, we are finding ourselves exposed to mediated and real-life situations involving persons culturally different from ourselves. This exposure contributes to our learning about ourselves and diverse others. According to researchers, the effectiveness of the United States in the global arena depends on our ability to communicate competently with people from other cultures.[33]

Identifying Influences on Cultural Identity

We all belong to a number of groups, including those defined by gender, age, racial and ethnic, religious, socioeconomic, and national identities. Our cultural identity is based on these group memberships.

How we define *gender roles*, for example, affects the way males and females present themselves, socialize, work, perceive their futures, and communicate. U.S. men tend to adopt a problem-solving orientation, while women tend to be relationship oriented.[34] We also have ideas regarding the meaning and significance of *age*, including how persons our age should look and behave. In the United States, large numbers of people place great value on looking youthful and appearing to be younger than they are. In contrast, in Muslim, Asian, and Latin American cultures, people respect, rather than deny, aging. Our *racial and ethnic identities* are similarly socially constructed. Some racial and ethnic groups, for example, share experiences of oppression. Their attitudes and behaviors may reflect their struggles, influencing their attitudes toward contemporary issues such as affirmative action. *Religious identity* is at the root of countless contemporary conflicts occurring in the Middle East, India, and Pakistan. Similarly, *socioeconomic identity* frames how we respond to issues of our day. The significant gap between the ultrawealthy and the middle and working classes in the United States is contributing to their developing different attitudes on a wide array of issues. *National identity* refers to our legal status or citizenship. People from different countries have been U.S. citizens for

Media Wise

The Cultural Storyteller

What stories about other cultures do film and television tell? Over the years, media producers have delivered a mixed message, both using and removing stereotypes from films and television programs. Disney, for example, changed the voice of the original Big Bad Wolf in the *Three Little Pigs* from having a heavy Jewish accent to a falsetto. Similarly, writers revised the lyrics to the opening song in *Aladdin* after complaints by the American-Arab Anti-Discrimination Committee. In the film, however, both Jasmine and her father, though Arabian, speak unaccented, standard American English, while the speech of the "Arabic bad guys" includes foreign accents. How might associating a foreign accent with being evil affect viewers? Like Arabs, who often are presented as sheiks or terrorists, threatening or cunning, Latinos also have been stereotyped in media. Too often, the parts Latinos play are demeaning and reminiscent of pre-civil-rights-era portrayals of African Americans. Latinos are often cast as the criminal, the maid, the crime victim, the harlot, or the male or female buffoon. Imagine seeing yourself portrayed as a victim, or as subservient to the dominant Anglo society. How might such a portrayal affect your perception of yourself and the options you have? How might they affect your view of your culture?

Both film and television are agents of norms and values. What stories are television and film currently telling? To answer this question, watch a week's worth of prime-time programming on a particular station or view a week's worth of highly ranked DVDs. Count the number of characters in each program or DVD that are from another culture. What did you learn from each character about his or her culture? In your opinion, were cultural stereotypes used to develop each of these characters? If so, describe them. To what extent, if any, did what you view reinforce or alter your existing attitudes toward members of that culture? What emotional reactions, if any, did each character trigger in you? Would you say that the shows or DVDs contributed to your having predominantly positive or negative attitudes toward the members of another culture? Finally, using one or two words, identify the key value of each viewed show or DVD. For example, the message of one show or DVD might focus on materialism, the message of another on force and violence.

generations, yet some still perceive them as foreigners. Do you?

In addition to recognizing how gender, racial and ethnic, religious, socioeconomic, and national differences affect cultural identity, we also need to acknowledge the role generational differences play in our communication with one another. Demographers usually classify people into four generations: matures, boomers, gen X, and gen Y. Called "the greatest generation," matures were born between 1900 and 1945. World War II and the Cold War were two of their key defining experiences. Matures are known for respecting authority, following the rules, being loyal to their employing organizations, and respecting timeliness. Boomers, born between 1946 and 1964, came of age during the space race, the civil rights movement, Vietnam, and Watergate. They are famous for questioning authority, displaying a "can-do" attitude, and focusing on how to get their way. The first TV generation, boomers actually had to get off the couch to change channels. Gen Xers, who were born between 1965 and 1982, saw traditional gender roles bend and flex. The Web emerged during their formative years. They are known for seeking a work-life balance, and being loyal to people, not organizations. Gen Y members, born after 1982, are referred to as the millennial generation or digital natives. They are known for being technologically savvy (they podcast, send text messages, blog, and seek a second life). They also have exceedingly high expectations, are proficient multitaskers, and are interested in "whatever they're interested in." They are apt to spend more time with the Internet and media than they do face-to-face with others. One out of three gen Y members is a minority.

Technology and Intercultural Communication

The Internet permeates national boundaries and erodes the connection between location and experience. It enables us to interact more easily with people who have different worldviews than we do.[35]

In your opinion, to what extent, if any, does participating
in a virtual neighborhood or community increase opportunities for learning about diverse cultures?

Technology and computer networks are also changing the traditional definition of a community. When we speak of a communication community today, no longer are we limited to real neighborhoods. Our concept of community has widened. **Virtual neighborhoods and communities** such as Second Life now also populate the communication landscape. Second Life is a virtual world, a social networking site in which users create avatars–alternative selves or images of characters they use to travel around and interact with other users. Why are people seeking a second life? Perhaps the neighborhoods in which they live are not delivering the person-to-person contact they seek. Seeking surrogate neighborhoods and relationships, millions of people communicate online. However, some critics contend that, rather than bringing us together, computer networks are isolating us. What online communities are missing, they assert, is the essence of a real neighborhood, including a sense of location and a feeling of permanence and belonging. Critics also believe that the culture of computing, especially when it comes to the Internet's newsgroups, attracts extreme political positions and contributes to long-standing international conflicts. Advocates, in contrast, assert that it facilitates international dialogue.[36]

Being able to reach so many different people who live in so many different places so quickly gives a new sense of communication power. Wherever we live, we can use the Internet to help bring diversity and new cultures into our lives. Over time, the Internet may change our social and business lives. Through it, we may meet a wider array of people. Sites such as MySpace and Facebook introduce us to new friends and contacts as well as reacquaint us with old friends. The question is whether we will commit ourselves emotionally to our online relationships and alliances or keep them superficial? What kinds of relationships will we develop by meeting online with diverse individuals in distant lands without actually meeting them? Will all voices really be heard? Will we be more or less tolerant of each other? Will we be aware that words posted to global online groups have consequences, just as they do when delivered in person?

We also need to face the fact that, in some places, technology is considered an evil and governments censor the Web in the effort to control what their people see on the Internet. For example, a court order in Turkey blocked people in the country from accessing YouTube after clips were posted on the site that the government believed insulted the memory of that nation's founder. Turkish visitors to the site saw a message in Turkish and English reading, "Access to www.youtube.com site has been suspended. . . ."[37] Despite this and the fact that some bloggers in countries such as Iran are required to register their sites, the numbers of people going online continues to grow.

virtual neighborhoods and communities online, surrogate communities

FOCUS ON SERVICE LEARNING
- Attend a local continuing education session for persons from other countries who want to learn English. Keep a log in which you identify and analyze your reactions to the persons attending, including any stereotypes you have about them. Develop a proposal for teaching an English as a second language (ESL) course for adults on-site at a local factory.

Thinking Critically

Reflect and Respond

Agree or disagree with the following statement; supply reasons and examples that support your position.

Human beings draw close to one another by their common nature, but habits and customs keep them apart.

digital divide
information gap

Increased access to the Internet provided via libraries and schools is helping to shrink the **digital divide** (information gap) in this country. More minorities, elderly, and poor people now go online, democratizing access and decreasing the chances of what some civil rights leaders worried would be a *technological apartheid*. However, gaining access to computers remains a problem in many places around the world because of the lack of or the unreliability of electricity or because of high poverty levels. Reaching and wiring all the world's people is a mammoth challenge. The Internet, however, is one key to preserving the world's languages and cultures.

Communication Skills in Practice

Guidelines for Improving Your Ability to Communicate Interculturally

Having the desire to relate more effectively with persons of different cultures is critical to improving your ability to communicate interculturally. Also important is limiting your reliance on stereotypes that can diminish your success when you interact with others. In addition, you need to be able to reduce your uncertainty levels regarding the persons of different cultures with whom you communicate. Since you do not necessarily share the same communication rules, the degree of ambiguity you feel when interacting with them increases as your ability to predict their responses decreases. The following guidelines should help you increase your tolerance for ambiguity, enhance your ability to handle new situations, and better prepare yourself to meet the communication challenges of today and tomorrow:

Refrain from Formulating Expectations Based Solely on Your Own Culture

When those you interact with have diverse communication styles, it is critical that you acknowledge the differences and accept their validity. By not isolating yourself within your own group or culture, you allow yourself to be more fully a part of a multicultural society and thus a better communicator.

Recognize How Faulty Education Can Impede Understanding

It is important to identify and work to eliminate any personal biases and prejudices you have developed over the years. Determine, for example, the extent to which your family and friends have influenced your feelings about persons from other cultural groups. Do those you have grown up with appear comfortable or uncomfortable relating to persons of different cultural origins? To what extent have their attitudes affected your intercultural communication competence?

Make a Commitment to Develop Communication Skills and Abilities Appropriate to Life in a Multicultural World

While culture is a tie that binds, the creation of the global village makes it essential that you leave the comfort of your cultural niche, become more knowledgeable of other cultures, and strive to be culturally aware.

It is important to familiarize yourself with the communication rules and preferences of members of different cultures so that you can increase the effectiveness of your communication encounters. Your ability to develop intercultural communication skills depends in large part on how many of the following promises you are willing to make:

I will make a commitment to seek information from persons whose cultures are different from my own.

I will try to understand how the experiences of persons from different cultures leads them to develop perspectives that differ from mine.

I will pay attention to the situation and the context when I communicate with persons from different cultures.

I will make every effort to become a more flexible communicator.

I will not insist that persons from other cultures communicate with me on my terms.

Intercultural communication will become increasingly important in the coming years. We hope you feel better prepared to meet your future.

Revisiting Chapter Objectives

1. **Define *intercultural communication*.**   Intercultural communication is the process of interpreting and sharing meanings with individuals from different cultures.

2. **Compare and contrast culture and co-culture, ethnocentrism and cultural relativism, melting-pot philosophy and cultural pluralism.**   A culture is a system of knowledge, beliefs, values, customs, behaviors, and artifacts that are acquired, shared, and used by members. A co-culture is a group of persons who differ in some ethnic or sociological way from the parent culture. Ethnocentrism is the tendency to see one's own culture as superior to all others. Cultural relativism is the acceptance of other cultural groups as equal in value to one's own. The melting-pot philosophy advocates the assimilation of different cultures into the dominant culture. Cultural pluralism acknowledges that other cultural groups are equal in value to one's own.

3. **Compare and contrast the following: individualism and collectivism, high-context communication cultures and low-context communication cultures, high-power-distance cultures and low-power-distance cultures, and masculine and feminine cultures.**   Individualistic cultures stress individual goals. Collectivistic cultures stress group goals. High-context communication cultures are tradition-bound, valuing indirectness. Low-context communication cultures encourage directness in communication. High-power-distance cultures view power as a fact of life with subordinates deferring to superiors. Low-power-distance cultures believe power should only be used if legitimate. Masculine cultures value aggressiveness, strength, and material success. Feminine cultures value relationships, tenderness, and a high quality of life.

4. **Identify the various groups that influence our cultural identity.**   Among the groups that influence cultural identity, and on which cultural identity is based, are those defined by gender, age, racial and ethnic, religious, socioeconomic, national, and generational identities.

5. **Discuss how technology is bringing diversity into our lives.**   For many of us, the Internet facilitates this task. Enabling us to join a wide range of online communities and interact with people who have different worldviews, the Internet enhances our ability to bring diversity and culture into our lives.

6. **Identify techniques you can use to reduce the strangeness of strangers.**
Although the lessons taught by culture influence our communication style preferences, there are techniques we can use to reduce the strangeness of strangers, adding to the storehouse of knowledge that underscores our communication competence and, as a result, increasing our ability to handle the communication challenges of today and tomorrow.

Resources for Further Inquiry and Reflection

To apply your understanding of how the principles in Chapter 2 are at work in our daily lives, consult the following resources for further inquiry and reflection. Or, if you prefer, choose any other appropriate resource. Then connect the ideas expressed in your chosen selection with the communication concepts and issues you are learning about both in and out of class.

Listen to Me

"Square Dance" (Eminem)
"Born in the U.S.A." (Bruce Springsteen)
"Land Down Under" (Men at Work)
"My Woman from Tokyo" (Deep Purple)
"Colors of the Wind" (Vanessa Williams)
"Al Otro Lado del Rio" (Antonio Banderas)

"Imagine" (John Lennon)
"War" (Bob Marley)
"American Idiot" (Green Day)

What do the views of the song's speaker or speakers suggest about the ability they have to meet diversity's challenges?

View Me

Borat	Dances with Wolves
Bend It Like Beckham	The Joy Luck Club
Boys Don't Cry	Brüno
Mississippi Burning	Milk
Gran Torino	American History X
The Terminal	Remember the Titans

How does culture influence the interaction of the characters in the film? What lessons about the effects of culture can be taught through the film?

Read Me

Thomas L. Friedman. *The World Is Flat: A Brief History of the Twenty-First Century*. New York: Farrar, Straus, & Groux, 2005.

Harper Lee. *To Kill a Mockingbird*. Philadelphia: Lippincott, 1960.

Wen Ho Lee. *My Country versus Me: The First-Hand Account by the Los Alamos Scientist Who Was Falsely Accused*. New York: Hyperion, 2002.

Khaled Hosseini. *The Kite Runner*. New York: Riverhead, 2003.

Khaled Hosseini. *A Thousand Splendid Suns*. New York: Riverhead, 2007.

Sherman Alexie. *Reservation Blues*. New York: Atlantic Monthly, 1995.

Eric Weiner. *Geography of Bliss: One Grump's Search for the Happiest Places in the World*. New York: Twelve, 2008.

Discuss how age, gender, ethnic affiliation, family ties, education, beliefs and religion, and/or nationality influence and shape attitudes.

Tell Me

Share with the class the insights you gained from your chosen Listen to Me, View Me, or Read Me selection.

Choose a side and discuss the arguments for or against using English as a universal language.

Key Chapter Terminology

Use the Online Learning Center at www.mhhe.com/
gamble10e to further your knowledge of the following
terminology.

accommodation
assimilation
co-cultures
collectivistic cultures
cultural imperialism
cultural pluralism
cultural relativism
culturally confused
culture
digital divide
diversity
ethnocentrism
feminine cultures
globalization

glocalization
high-context communication
high-power-distance cultures
individualistic cultures
intercultural communication
interethnic communication
international communication
interracial communication
intracultural communication
low-context communication
low-power-distance cultures
masculine cultures
melting-pot philosophy
multiculturalists
prejudice
separation
stereotypes
virtual neighborhoods and communities

Idioms in Translation

get connected – communicate digitally or via the Internet
save face – maintain self-esteem

storehouse of knowledge – information

Culture Cue

In Arabic cultures and other cultures with collectiv-
ist mindsets, the individual is subordinate to the
collective. In the United States, the individual is still
paramount.

Test Your Understanding

Go to the Self Quizzes on the book's Online Learning
Center at www.mhhe.com/gamble10e.Read Me
Thomas L. Friedman. *The World Is Flat: A Brief History of
the Twenty-First Century.* New York: Farrar, Straus, &
Groux, 2005.
Harper Lee. *To Kill a Mockingbird.* Philadelphia: Lippin-
cott, 1960.
Wen Ho Lee. *My Country versus Me: The First-Hand Account
by the Los Alamos Scientist Who Was Falsely Accused.* New
York: Hyperion, 2002.
Khaled Hosseini. *The Kite Runner.* New York: Riverhead,
2003.

Khaled Hosseini. *A Thousand Splendid Suns.* New York:
Riverhead, 2007.
Sherman Alexie. *Reservation Blues.* New York: Atlantic
Monthly, 1995.
Eric Weiner. *Geography of Bliss: One Grump's Search for the
Happiest Places in the World.* New York: Twelve, 2008.
Discuss how age, gender, ethnic affiliation, family ties,
education, beliefs and religion, and/or nationality
influence and shape attitudes.
Be Prepared

appendix

C

Interviewing and Developing Professional Relationships

What does a job interview have to do with communication? A

lot. In fact, when it comes to the kinds of skills that job recruiters look for, interpersonal skills top the list.[1] An employment interview is like an interaction on Match.com. However, instead of two people seeking to determine if they have what it takes to make a love connection, during a job interview, the candidate and the employer usually meet face-to-face to figure out if the organization's corporate culture and needs are a good match with the applicant's values and abilities.

During the course of our lives we all take part in interviews. From our vantage point, an interview incorporates many of the topics and principles of communication we have already discussed. Culture, self-concept, perception, listening, feedback, language and meaning, nonverbal cues, and assertiveness have parts to play in determining your interviewing success. Let us explore the interview process and what you can do to succeed as an interviewee.

The Employment Interview: More than Casual Conversation

In comparison to ordinary conversations, the conversations we enact during employment interviews are planned and designed to achieve specific objectives. Thus, an **employment interview** is the most common type of purposeful, planned, decision-making, person-to-person communication. The person(s) hiring and the candidate(s) seeking to be hired engage in a process of personal contact and behavior exchange, giving and receiving information, to make educated career-related decisions.

The employment interview offers a unique opportunity for the potential employer and employee to share meaningful information that will permit each to determine whether their association would be beneficial and productive. It gives both participants a chance to test each other by asking and answering relevant questions. Employers hope to gather information about you during the interview that your résumé, references, and any personality tests you may have been asked to take do not provide. They also believe the person-to-person approach is an effective way to sell their organization to you. As an applicant, you seek information about the employer and the job during the interview. You can deduce from your interaction with the interviewer what your long-term relationship might be and what life in that organization might be like if you are hired.

Some interviews are over before they begin. Why? Because the interviewer asks a question that he or she thinks is easy but that the interviewee cannot answer. For example, on being asked what she had to offer the company, all one interviewee could respond was, "Hmmmmm, that's a toughie." Then she added, "I was more wanting to hear what you could do for me." The candidate did not get the job. How would you have replied to that question?

It is as a result of a hiring or selection interview that we find ourselves accepted or rejected by a prospective employer—an individual, a small business, a large cor-

---

Dear_____:

We enjoyed having you visit us here (last week) (last month) (recently). Everyone who talked with you was most impressed, and I personally feel that you are one of the most promising young (men) (women) I've seen in a long time. We all wish we could make you an offer at this time. However, . . .

—From a corporation's form letter

Twenty years from now, the typical American worker will have changed jobs four times and careers twice and will be employed in an occupation that does not exist today.

—Jeffrey Hallet

employment interview
the most common type of purposeful, planned, decision-making, person-to-person communication

Media Wise

Piquing Career Interest

Have you found that you or your friends are taking more of an interest in criminal justice and forensics? If so, you are not alone. Even a large number of universities report having increased the scope of courses they offer in criminal justice. To what is this surge in interest attributed? Many people believe it is due to television.

The public appears fascinated with investigation and the justice system, as evidenced by the popularity of television shows such as *The Mentalist, Law and Order, Without a Trace,* and *CSI.* Their popularity has spilled over into the real world, sparking an increasing interest in criminology careers. Even the Nevada law enforcement agency Field Services Division has responded to popular interest in forensic science,

changing its name to Crime Scene Investigations.[2]

In your opinion, to what extent, if any, is the portrayal of criminology careers on television and film contributing to unrealistic career expectations in those who now seek to become criminologists? For example, most of the crimes featured on *CSI*-type shows are solved in an hour, while they might take months or even years to solve in the real world. In addition, the programs on television rarely show the boring days, they reveal the staff working with state-of-the-art equipment that many cities cannot afford, and they have a crimes-solved rate that actual criminologists could never attain.

poration, and so on. The better prepared you are for an employment interview, the better your chances will be of performing effectively and realizing your job objectives. Remember, an interview is not "just talk."[3]

Common Fears

How do you feel about interviewing for a job? Listed here are some fears that interviewees express frequently. Do you share them? Circle the numbers that most accurately reflect your level of interview apprehension: $0 =$ completely unconcerned; $1 =$ very mild concern; $2 =$ mild concern; $3 =$ more apprehensive than not; $4 =$ very frightened; $5 =$ a nervous wreck.

1. I will be asked questions I cannot answer.

    0   1   2   3   4   5

2. I will not dress properly for the interview.

    0 1   2   3   4   5

3. I will appear very nervous.

    0 1   2   3   4   5

4. I will not appear competent.

    0 1   2   3   4   5

5. The interviewer will cross-examine me.

    0 1   2   3   4   5

6. I will be caught in a lie.

    0 1   2   3   4   5

7. I will talk too much or too little.

0 1   2   3   4   5

8. I will have poor rapport with the interviewer.

0 1   2   3   4   5

9. I will undersell or oversell myself.

0 1   2   3   4   5

10. I won't be hired.

0 1   2   3   4   5

Total the numbers you circled to arrive at your "interviewee's anxiety" score.

Your scores indicate how frightened you are of assuming the role of interviewee. If you accumulated 45 to 50 points, you are a nervous wreck; if you scored 35 to 44 points, you are too frightened; if you scored 20 to 34 points, you are somewhat apprehensive; if you scored 11 to 20 points, you are too casual; if you scored 0 to 10 points, you are not at all concerned—that is, you simply do not care.

Contrary to what you might assume, not being concerned at all about participating in an interview is just as much of a problem as being a nervous wreck, and being too casual can do as much damage as being too frightened. An interviewee should be apprehensive to a degree. If you are not concerned about what will happen during the interview, then you will not care about making a good impression and, as a result, will not perform as effectively as you could.

Preliminary Tasks: Preparing the Cover Letter and Résumé

The job of the applicant is to prepare fully for the interview. By completing two documents—a cover letter and a résumé—that are well written and register a positive impression, you provide the interviewer with a preview of who you are and why you are qualified for the position.

The Cover Letter

The cover letter introduces you to the interviewer. It is a brief (usually one-page), well-written letter that fulfills the following six criteria: (1) It expresses your interest in a position; (2) it tells how you learned of the position; (3) it reviews your primary skills and accomplishments; (4) it explains why these qualify you for the job; (5) it highlights any items of special interest about you that are relevant to your ability to perform the job; and (6) it contains a request for an interview. A résumé is always included with a cover letter. Keep the cover letter to one page. The only chance you have to persuade the person opening it to read your résumé can vanish if the reader sees a lengthy letter.

The Résumé

The résumé summarizes your abilities and accomplishments. It details what you have to contribute that will meet the company's needs and help solve the employer's problems. Although formats differ, the résumé typically includes the following:

1. contact information—your name, address, telephone number, and e-mail address

2. job objective—a phrase or sentence that focuses on your area of expertise

3. employment history—your job experience, both paid and unpaid, beginning

with the most recent

4. education—schools attended, degree(s) completed or expected, dates of completion, and a review of courses that relate directly to your ability to perform the job

5. relevant professional certifications and affiliations

6. community service

7. special skills and interests you possess that are revelent to the job

8. references—people who agree to elaborate on your work history, capabilities, and character; reveal only that references are available on request unless you are asked to provide specific references at the time you submit your résumé

Since the average resume gets about 15 seconds of the reader's time, creating an effective one is essential.[4] Also, although sending a video resume may intrigue you, most companies still do not accept them.

Structure: Stages of the Interview

Most effective interviews have a clear structure. The beginning, or opening, is the segment of the process that provides an orientation to what will come. The middle, or body, is the longest segment and the one during which both parties really get down to business. The end, or close, is the segment during which the participants prepare to take leave of one another.

Just as the right kind of greeting at the start of a conversation can help create a feeling of friendliness, so the opening of an interview can help establish rapport between interviewer and interviewee.[5] The primary purpose of the opening is to make it possible for both parties to participate freely and honestly by creating an atmosphere of trust and goodwill and by explaining the purpose and scope of the meeting. Conversational icebreakers and orientation statements perform important functions at this stage. Typical icebreakers include comments about the weather, the surroundings, and current events—or a compliment. The idea is to use small talk to help make the interview a human encounter rather than a mechanical one. Typical orientation remarks include an identification of the interview's purpose, a preview of the topics to be discussed, and statements that motivate the respondent and act as a conduit, or transition, to the body of the interview.

In the body of the interview, the parties really get down to business. At this point, the interviewer and interviewee might discuss work experiences, including the applicant's strengths, weaknesses, major accomplishments, difficult problems tackled in the past, and career goals. Educational background and activities or interests are relevant areas to probe during this phase of the interview. Breadth of knowledge and the ability to manage time are also common areas of concern.

During the close of the interview, the main points covered are reviewed and summarized. Since an interview can affect any future meetings the parties may have, care must be taken to make the leave-taking comfortable.[7] Expressing appreciation for the time and effort given is important; neither interviewee nor interviewer should feel discarded. In other words, the door should be left open for future contacts.

Your Thoughts

In your résumé, do you have the most important information first?

Ethics and Communication

Résumé Padding and Résumé Poaching

1. Résumé padding has been around for a long time. Would you lie on your résumé to get your foot in the door? Would you "fix up" your résumé to help you look better on paper than you really are?

   Not too long ago, Notre Dame's football coach, George O'Leary, had to step down from his head coach position after admitting that he had falsified the academic and athletic credentials listed on his résumé. In your opinion, should O'Leary have been fired for his résumé misrepresentations? Why or why not?

2. It is not merely some résumé writers who are ethically challenged. So are some recruiters. In fact, résumés posted on Internet job boards are not necessarily private or restricted to recruiters and other employers who pay a fee for access. While some sites may sell their résumés, résumé poaching also threatens the privacy of job seekers. The employees of competitive sites have been known to pose as recruiters in order to download thousands of résumés without permission. Persons who post their résumés on supposedly secure sites find themselves harassed by readers who object to their professions. For example, one job seeker in chemistry found herself harassed by activists against animal research.[6] In your opinion, should Internet job search sites be billboards for all to see, or should they be kept private, with recruiters and employers being screened adequately before being given access?

Questions: The Heart of the Interview

Questions are the primary means of collecting data in an interview. Not only do questions set the tone for an interview, but they also determine whether the interview will yield valuable information. Using the interrogatives *what, where, when, who, how,* and *why* throughout an interview lays a foundation of knowledge on which to base decisions or conclusions.

During the course of an interview, closed, open, primary, and secondary questions may all be used, in any combination.[9] **Closed questions** are highly structured and answerable with a simple yes or no or in a few words. Following are examples of closed questions:

Where do you live?
Did you graduate in the top quarter of your class?
What starting salary do you expect?

Open questions are broader than closed questions and are less restricting or structured; hence, they offer more freedom with regard to the choice and scope of an answer. Following are examples of open questions:

Tell me about yourself.
How do you judge success?
Why did you choose to interview for this job?
Describe a time you failed.
Describe a time when you failed to solve a conflict.

Open questions give you a chance to express your feelings, attitudes, and values. For example, let's consider the first question above. "Tell me about yourself" is not a

closed questions
highly structured questions answerable with a simple yes or no or in a few words

open questions
questions that offer the interviewee freedom with regard to the choice and scope of an answer

Skill Builder

Wake-up Calls

1. According to one résumé expert, "The biggest mistake that people are making is that their résumés have no real impact. . . . A good résumé won't get you a job, but it will get you in the door."[8]

   What steps can you take to ensure that your résumé doesn't end up as origami? Describe how you would market yourself so that the person who receives your résumé actually opens it and spends some time reading it. For example, one applicant for a marketing position included her résumé in a package of gourmet coffees that she sent to the potential interviewer with the slogan "Lindsay will wake up your marketing" affixed to the package. Do you think the interviewer read her résumé?

2. Once your résumé gets you in the door, give yourself an interview wake-up call. By exhibiting the following behaviors during your interview, you can help ensure you make the final cut: (1) Refer to the company you are interviewing with by name; (2) make it clear that you have researched the company; (3) respond enthusiastically to information the interviewer shares; (4) back up your answers to questions you are asked with specific examples; (5) use questions to demonstrate your knowledge of the industry and the company.

WORK IT OUT
- For the next few days, keep track of the verbal and nonverbal messages people use when they say hello or good-bye. Which beginnings and endings were particularly communicative?
- Which were ineffective? Did you observe any false starts or false endings? How could they have been avoided?

request for your life story. The interviewer is really asking, "Why should I hire you?" Thus, your task when answering a question like this is to showcase your communication skills by crafting a statement shorter than two minutes, or about the length of an elevator ride, that lets the interviewer know more about you and what you can do for the company, that is, the benefits you will bring to your employer.[10]

Open and closed questions may be either primary or secondary. **Primary questions** introduce topics or begin the exploration of a new area. "What is your favorite hobby?" and "Tell me about your last job" are examples of primary questions—the first is closed; the second is open.

Interviewers use **secondary questions**—sometimes called probing questions—to follow up primary questions. They ask for an explanation of the ideas and feelings behind answers to other questions, and they are frequently used when answers to primary questions are vague or incomplete. Following are examples of secondary questions:

> Go on. What do you mean?
> Can you give me an example?

Interviewee Roles and Responsibilities

primary questions
questions used to introduce topics or explore a new area

An interviewer uses your interview in three ways: (1) to assess your probable performance if hired, (2) to determine if you and the organization's team can work well together, and assuming the first two goals result in a yes, then (3) to persuade you that the organization is a good one to work for.

secondary questions
probing questions that follow up primary questions

What are your roles and responsibilities during this process? You need to speak and listen, and to provide information to help convince the interviewer that you are the right person for the job. At the same time, you need to collect information that will help you decide whether to accept the job if offered it. To accomplish these goals you need to research the organization to which you are applying and try to anticipate the questions the interviewer will ask. In addition, to help control the interview's direction and content, you also need to plan to ask questions. As your questions are answered, you will learn about work conditions and prospects for advancement.

Effective interviewees work hard at self-assessment. In effect, they take stock of themselves to determine who they are, what their career needs and their goals are, and how they can best sell themselves to an employer.

As a prospective interviewee, you will find it useful to prepare by thinking about and answering the following questions:

1. For what types of positions has my training prepared me?
2. What has been my most rewarding experience?
3. What type of job do I want?
4. Would I be happier working alone or with others?
5. What qualifications do I have that make me feel I would be successful in the job of my choice?
6. What type or types of people do I want to work for?
7. What type or types of people do I not want to work for?
8. How do I feel about receiving criticism?
9. What salary will enable me to meet my financial needs?
10. What salary will enable me to live comfortably?
11. What will interviewers want to know about me, my interests, my background, and my experiences?

In addition to conducting a self-survey, the interviewee needs to work to withstand the pressure of the interview situation. Are you prepared to maintain your composure while being stared at, interrupted, spoken to abruptly, or asked difficult questions? Have you practiced enough to keep cool when on the interview hot seat? How do you think you would react if you were asked tough questions? The following questions are favorites among interviewers. How would you answer them?

1. Tell me about yourself.
2. What do you think you're worth?
3. What are you good at?
4. If we hired you, what about this organization would concern you most?
5. What attributes do you think an effective manager should possess?
6. What are your short-term goals? How are they different from your long-term goals?
7. How has your background prepared you for this position?
8. What are your major strengths and weaknesses?
9. How would a former employer or instructor describe you?
10. Why did you leave your last job?
11. What do you consider your greatest accomplishment?
12. What's wrong with you?
13. What would you do if I told you that I thought you were giving a very poor interview today?

WORK IT OUT
- Craft a two-minute response to the question, Why should I hire you? Try out responses on your peers.

The only way to get the accurate answers is to ask the right questions.
—Kevin J. Murphy, *Effective Listening: Your Key to Career Success*

Each party has questions in the interview—both you and the employer. The essence of the interview is to find out the answers to those questions.
—Richard N. Bolles

Your Thoughts ?

What other qualities do you believe interviewers look for in interviewees? If you were an interviewer, what questions would you ask to determine if a person possessed those qualities?

14.   How long do you plan to remain with us if you get this job?

15.   What would you like to know about us?

Some interviewers prefer to ask even more searching questions, such as the following:

Tell me about how you handled the last mistake you made.

Are there things at which you aren't very good?

At your weekly team meetings, your boss unexpectedly begins aggressively critiquing your performance on a current project. What would
you do?

You're in a situation in which you have two very important responsibilities that both have deadlines that are impossible to meet. You cannot accomplish both. How do you handle that situation?[11]

Practice in answering questions like these–under both favorable and unfavorable conditions–is essential.[12] It is important that you know what you want to say during the interview and that you use the questions you are asked as an opportunity to say it. Along the way, you can flatter the interviewer by offering comments such as "I think you've touched on something really important."

The interviewer can, of course, consult a résumé to ascertain information about the applicant–about educational background and previous positions held, for example. However, gathering enough information to evaluate the personal qualities of an applicant is more difficult. Following is a list of personal qualifications, with the questions interviewers typically ask to evaluate them:

WORK IT OUT

• Role-play asking and answering the questions listed here.

1.   *Quality:* Skill in managing one's own career

   Question: What specific things have you done deliberately to get where you are today?

2.   *Quality:* Skill in managing others

   Question: What are some examples of things you do and do not like to delegate?

WORK IT OUT

• Bring five copies of your résumé to class. Working in groups, take turns using the S.T.A.R. system to respond to group members' questions about your resume.

3.   *Quality:* Sense of responsibility

   Question: What steps do you take to see that things do not fall through the cracks when you are supervising a project?

4.   *Quality:* Skill in working with people

   Question: If we assembled in one room a group of people you have worked with and asked them to describe what it was like to work with you, what would they be likely to say? What would your greatest supporter say? What would your severest critic say?

When it comes to answering questions about items listed on your résumé, one career coach suggests using the acronym S.T.A.R. (*s*ituation, *t*ask, *a*ction, *r*esult) as a guide. For example, let's say your résumé notes that you turned around a sales territory in decline, ultimately increasing sales by 10 percent in your first year. The interviewer asks: "How did you do that?" Your job is to walk the interviewer through the process by revealing the situation you faced, how you assessed your task, the action you took, and the result you achieved.[13]

Most employment interviews can be grouped into one of three categories: the behavioral, the case, and the stress interview. In the **behavioral interview,** an employer is looking for specific examples from the prospective employee of times when he or she has exhibited specific skills. When asked a question such as "Tell me about a time you acted in a leadership role," the interviewee might respond, "I was the director of a fund-raising group," or "I was an officer in Women in Communication." In the **case interview,** a company presents the interviewee with a business case and asks for him or her to work through it. To help prepare yourself for such an interview, check out the company Web site beforehand. Some companies post sample cases on their sites. The third type of interview, the **stress interview,** typically includes more than one interviewer firing questions at the interviewee to see how that person handles himself or herself during a stressful situation.

Because the interview is a conversation and not an interrogation, during the course of the interview, the interviewee should ask questions of the interviewer as a means of demonstrating interest in the job and the company.[14] When the interviewee asks questions, the interview becomes more balanced. What kinds of questions should you ask when in the interviewee role? You should not ask questions that you can answer easily by visiting the company's Web site. You should, however, ask questions that seek clarification; for example: "I read on your site that you will be introducing new products. Could you tell me more about how you plan to roll them out?"

In general, interviewees ask questions about the company and corporate culture (rather than about salary or benefits), the industry, the position, and the people in the company. Following are some examples:

Why is this position open?
What would you say are the main challenges of this job?
What will be the priorities in the first 90 days?
With whom will I be working?
How is the department organized, and what will my role be?
How will performance be measured and evaluated?
How are conflicts resolved?
How are decisions made?
Why do you like working here?[16]

To be effective, both interview participants need to work hard. Questioner and respondent constantly exchange information. While one speaks, the other conveys nonverbal information through posture, facial expression, gestures, and so on. You may stop talking during an interview, but that does not mean that you stop communicating. Know what you want to accomplish with your verbal and nonverbal messages.

Impression Management: Effective Interviewing

How well do we need to know someone before we believe we understand him or her? Experience says not very long. According to psychologists Nalini Ambady and Frank Bernieri, the power of first impressions arms us with a kind of prerational ability or intuition for making judgments about others that color the other impressions we gather over time.[17] It becomes a self-fulfilling prophecy. We assume that the way someone behaves in an interview is indicative of the way that person always behaves.

---

behavioral interview
an employment interview in which an employer looks for the employee to provide specific examples of specific skills

case interview
an employment interview in which the interviewee is presented with a business case by the employer and asked to work through it

stress interview
an employment interview in which more than one person fires questions at an interviewee

WORK IT OUT
1. Enumerate the qualities and skills that would make you a good investment for an employer.
2. Enumerate the qualities and skills you need to develop further and plan how to do this.
3. Compose a "Position Wanted" advertisement for yourself.

Skill Builder

Let's Get Tough

Human relations consultant and interviewer trainer Justin Menkes helps employment recruiters learn how to gather a lot of information in a brief period of time. To accomplish this, he suggests they ask questions like those identified in the text. Try your hand at answering one of those questions: You have two very important responsibilities that both have deadlines that are impossible to meet. You cannot accomplish both. How do you handle that situation?

   Which of the following possible responses does your answer most resemble?

1. I'd focus on the project I'm most comfortable with and give it my all.

2. I'd plan carefully, assign segments of the project to others, and multitask so that I could complete both.

3. I'd ask my supervisor which project is most important to the company.

According to Menkes, the first response suggests that the interviewee's focus is on himself or herself, the second response does not answer the question asked, and the third response reveals an interest in the needs of the company and an interest in developing a collaborative relationship.[15]

The adage that first impressions count apparently holds true for job interviews.[18] In fact, the word *interview* is derived from the French word *entrevoir*, meaning "to see one another" or "to meet." What happens when an interviewer and an interviewee meet for the first time? What variables influence the impressions the interviewer forms of the interviewee? Most interviewers make their decisions about an applicant during the course of the interview. In fact, although most decide in the last quarter of the interview whether or not to invite the applicant back, a bias for or against the candidate is established earlier in the interview, often during the first four to six minutes.

What can you do to help the interviewer judge you positively from the outset? Among the steps you should take are the following: (1) Look like the professional the interviewer wants to hire. Keep in mind that you're going on an interview, not a date. (2) Be smart going in. Know about the company, the competition, and industry trends. (3) Be enthusiastic and show that you are happy to be there. Smile, sit up, lean slightly forward, and maintain eye contact. Communicating a high level of energy works in your favor. (4) Vary your pitch and volume. The interviewer will view you more positively if you do not speak in a monotone, whisper, or shout, or if you speak without exhibiting vocal hesitations or signs of physical tension.[19]

According to researcher Lois Einhorn, the amount of time allotted for an interview also sends an important message.[20] She found that interviewees who were not hired had participated in interviews shorter than those of successful applicants. She also found that successful interviewees spoke a greater percentage of the time than their unsuccessful counterparts. In fact, the successful applicants spoke for some 55 percent of the total interview time, whereas the unsuccessful applicants spoke only 37 percent of the time. Seeming to control the interview also leaves an impression. In Einhorn's research, successful applicants initiated 56 percent of the comments made during their interviews, whereas unsuccessful applicants were viewed as followers—they initiated only 37 percent of the comments. It is important for you to send messages that you are active, not passive.

The interviewer's assessment of you will determine whether or not you get the job. The following are some of the negative factors that turn off the interviewer and lead to applicant rejection:

Your Thoughts **?**

What can you do to convey to interviewers that you possess the qualities they seek?

- arrogance
- lack of motivation or enthusiasm
- immaturity
- poor communication skills
- unclear goals
- unwillingness to relocate or travel
- deficient preparation for the interview
- lack of experience
- too sloppy or too slick an appearance[21]

Among the factors leading to your receiving job offers are the following:

- a pleasant personality (likableness)
- enthusiasm
- interpersonal skills
- ability to function as part of a team
- knowledge of the field
- computer literacy
- creativity
- clear purpose and goals
- flexibility and the ability to handle change
- confidence in what you are doing and who you are
- integrity and moral standards
- global perspective
- sense of humor[22]

Believe in yourself.
—The Wizard of Oz, to
Dorothy

You can cement a positive image in three ways. (1) Never ask about vacation, company benefits, and personal days during your first interview. Work, instead, to display your knowledge of the company, understand its goals, and identify how you fit in by asking questions that touch on strategic and tactical issues. (2) End an interview by reaffirming your interest in the position and restating why you believe you will be an asset to the company.[23] View this as your sales opportunity; that is, ask for the order. Saying something like, "I am very interested in the position.

Exploring Diversity

Voices and Impression Management

People from different cultures use their voices differently, a fact that could lead to misunderstandings between interviewers and interviewees. People from the Middle East, for example, tend to speak louder than Westerners, causing Westerners to perceive them as overly emotional. In contrast, the Japanese tend to be much more soft-spoken, leading Westerners to believe that they are extremely polite and humble.

How could such habitual ways of speaking affect the interview process? What can interviewers and interviewees do to diminish such perceptual barriers?

I would welcome the opportunity to work with you and your team," helps communicate that you really want the job. (3) Remember to send a thank you note to the person or persons who interviewed you. An essential step in the job-seeking process, this is also the one job seekers most often forget.[24] One successful job candidate sent her thank you via overnight carrier. Another who had interviewed for a job with Google delivered a handwritten thank you along with cupcakes for the recruiter and five other officials who interviewed him. One letter of the Google name appeared atop each cupcake.[25] Do you think he was hired?

Diversity and the Interview

Culture influences how we conduct ourselves during interviews. For example, in collectivistic cultures such as those in China, Japan, and Korea, interviewees habitually display modesty. If Americans, who are used to stressing their positive qualities, were interviewing in any of those countries, they could be perceived as arrogant and self-centered. On the other hand, if persons from a collectivistic culture were to interview in the United States, they could be perceived as unassertive, lacking in confidence, and unprepared to assume leadership. While Western culture encourages people to be assertive and showcase strengths, Eastern culture traditionally teaches members to be more modest and humble about their personal achievements, qualifications, and experience. Similarly, Native American culture teaches that cooperation is a benefit and that one leads through deeds, not words. Thus, not wanting to appear boastful, Native Americans could also be hesitant to discuss their personal strengths.[26]

There are gender differences in what employees seek in a job. Survey results reveal that most men value compensation above all else, while most women put employee benefits first. Compensation is ranked third on most women's lists, after opportunities for skill development.[27]

Age also correlates with what employees want most in a job. In contrast with all other groups, the under-thirties do not even rank benefits among their top five concerns. What is important to most persons in this age bracket are opportunities to develop skills, chances for promotion, compensation, vacations, and an appealing culture and colleagues.[28]

Interviewers need to be sensitive to and demonstrate their respect for all cultures. Not hiring someone on the basis of age, sexual preference, national origin, or religion is illegal. Despite this, many Muslim workers report having thought about changing their last names to avoid alienating potential employers.[29] Would you ever change your name if you thought doing so would help you get the job you want? Why or why not?

Technology and the Job Search

The Web has changed the way we search for and find jobs. Regularly search online classified ads for job opportunities. In addition to Monster.com, aggregate sites such as Indeed.com and SimplyHired.com link you to job ads all over the Internet, including companies' career pages. Additionally, networking Web sites such as LinkedIn.com and Ryze.com can help you connect with business professionals in your field without your knowing them well or at all.[30]

Applicants should use a company's home page to get background information on the organization and its culture or to e-mail a résumé and cover letter. Following are some Web sites you can consult for information on companies and jobs:

Company Information
www.wsj.com
www.nytimes.com
www.bizweb.com

Job Information
http://stats.bls.gov The Bureau of Labor Statistics Web site, which offers information on positions by state, listing the average salary being paid per position
www.careerbuilder.com
www.NowHiring.com
www.monster.com

Usenet newsgroups, listserv mailing lists, and blogs are three other Internet resources you can use to learn about employment possibilities and company cultures. Of the three, blogs are becoming increasingly popular in electronic recruiting, functioning as a prime means that applicants use to find out about companies. Often they contain information such as what it is like to work at a company as well as what is going on in an industry.[31]

Job seekers also create their own home pages, featuring both their online résumé and business card.[32] A variety of online resources and computer programs exist to help you prepare your résumé. Many provide you with templates that you can complete as is or customize. You can also post your résumé on the Net by e-mailing it to a server.

In fact, more and more companies now request that potential employees submit an electronic résumé (a résumé that is obtained and analyzed electronically by the employer).[33] An electronic résumé includes keywords that describe the person's competencies and skills. Once the employer scans the résumé into the company's computer tracking system, when a job becomes available, the employer can efficiently search the résumés contained in the database by the keywords that describe the characteristics a person qualified for the position should have. Electronic résumés require standard formats and block letters that are plain and simple. A résumé that is going to be scanned should not use boldface type, underlining, or bullets, because these special effects interfere with the scanning process. To facilitate the initial résumé screening, which will be done by a bias-free computer, an electronic résumé typically contains a block paragraph of keywords, which immediately follows the identification information centered above it. Unlike your traditional résumé, which probably contains action verbs such as *communicates well,* your electronic résumé should contain nouns, such as *organizational skills.* A number of Internet sites can help you prepare an electronic résumé. By posting your résumé on a home page, you increase the likelihood that an employer looking for someone with your background and qualifications will access your résumé and contact you directly.

Employers also use computers to add flexibility to currently available interviewing channels. By conducting a computer-assisted interview, for example, employers are able to conduct preliminary conversations with people geographically dispersed from them. In increasing numbers, in addition to telephones and videoconferences, employers are also conducting interviews via e-mail and chat groups. Although these channels do not enable interviewer and interviewee to shake hands with each other, and despite the fact that such interviews will probably not replace face-to-face interviews, they do expand the information resources used by organizations and can be used to supplement face-to-face interviews.[34]

You will want to avoid the following five blunders commonly made by people who use the Internet to search for a job.[35]

1. *Mismerged cover letters.* The interviewee sends a letter that expresses the desire to put skills to work for one company when applying for a job with another company.

2. *Goofy personal e-mail addresses.* Using a name like Snickerdoodle @pastrylover.com or egotisticalking@sold.com can make you look like a less than serious candidate. Use a business-sounding e-mail address instead.

3. *Fun with fonts.* It is a mistake to use bright colors and exotic fonts in résumés or e-mails. Use a plain-text format instead.

4. *Playing out of your league.* Because the Internet makes applying for a job so easy, many applicants apply for jobs for which they are not qualified.

5. *Thinking Send is the end.* Your work is not done when you click Send. Networking and follow-up remain essential components of any job search. Indeed, 61 percent of people surveyed report that networking and referrals remain the best sources for new jobs.[36]

Finally, here are some other warnings.

1. Do not post anything online, including in blogs and discussion boards, that you would not want an employer to see.

2. Do not request an interview or follow up using the too-casual tone of text-speak. Managers who were interviewed believe that text-speak, including the use of emoticons, has no place in interview communications.[37]

Getting a job today has much in common with reality-show contests. Hundreds of job candidates compete, but there will be only one winner.

Looking at the Law: Illegal Questions in Interviews

We have seen that some interview questions are tough and probing. Others concerning age, race, marital status, and other personal characteristics are protected under antidiscrimination statutes and are illegal to ask. The Equal Employment Opportunity Commission (EEOC) is the arm of the federal government responsible for monitoring discriminatory practices in hiring decisions. The guidelines are updated periodically and the laws of the EEOC apply in all 50 states.

According to the EEOC, criteria that are legally irrelevant to job qualifications are discriminatory. Interviewees in all states are protected from answering questions about race, ethnicity, marital status, age, sex, disability, and arrest records. It is important for both interviewers and interviewees to realize which questions are legally impermissible in employment interviews. Both parties to the interview have to be well versed in their rights to be able to protect them. The determining factor in whether a question is lawful is simple: Is the information sought relevant to your ability to perform the job? The following are among the most commonly asked illegal questions:

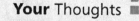

1. Are you physically disabled?
2. How old are you?
3. Are you married?
4. Do you have or are you planning to have a family?
5. What political party do you belong to?
6. Have you ever served time in prison?
7. Is English your native language?
8. What is your religion?
9. Will you need to live near a mosque?
10. Is it hard for you to find child care?
11. Are you a United States citizen?
12. Where were your parents born?
13. Who lives with you?
14. When did you graduate from college?
15. What was the date of your last physical exam?
16. To what clubs or social organizations do you belong?
17. Have you had any recent or past illnesses or operations?
18. How is your family's health?
19. Have you ever been arrested?
20. If you have been in the military, were you honorably discharged?

Your Thoughts

How would you handle being asked an illegal question?

On the other hand, it is legal to ask the following questions:

1. Are you authorized to work in the United States?
2. What languages do you read or speak fluently (if relevant to the job)?
3. Are you over 18?
4. Would you relocate?
5. Would you be willing to travel as needed?
6. Would you be able and willing to work overtime as necessary?
7. Do you belong to any groups that are relevant to your ability to perform this job?
8. What education do you have?
9. Have you ever been convicted of [fill in the blank]? (The crime must be reasonably related to the performance of the job.)
10. In what branch of the armed forces did you serve?[38]

What if an interviewer asks you an illegal question? You can object diplomatically and remind the interviewer that the question is inappropriate. Doing so, however, can make that interviewer defensive and less willing to select you for the job. Another option is to respond to the illegal question with only information that the interviewer could have legally sought from you. That is, you handle the question by answering the part you do not object to without providing any information you do not wish to provide. For example, if the interviewer asks whether English is your native language, you can respond, "I am fluent in English." If he or she asks whether you belong to a political group, you can respond, "The only groups with which I affiliate that are relevant to this job are the Public Relations Society of America and the American Society for Training and Development."

Communication Skills in Practice

Guidelines for Increasing Your Interviewing Effectiveness

As you can see, an interview, like any other interpersonal relationship, requires the cooperation, skill, and commitment of both participants to be effective. Interviewees can benefit from the following guidelines:

Be Prepared

Understand the purpose of the interview; plan or anticipate the questions you will ask and be asked; understand your goals; and be able to communicate those goals clearly.

Practice Sending and Receiving Messages

By its very nature, an interview demands skill at sending and receiving verbal and nonverbal messages. Not only must the parties clearly encode their messages, but they must also be skilled at reading the reactions and checking the perceptions of the other.

Demonstrate Effective Listening Skills

Problems occur in interviews when either the interviewer or the interviewee fails to listen closely to what the other is saying. If participants listen carefully—rather than thinking about what they plan to say next—the interview has a better chance of being productive.

Have Conviction

Ask and answer questions and express your opinions with enthusiasm. If you are not excited by your ideas, skills, and abilities, why should anyone else be?

Be Flexible

Do not overprepare or memorize statements. Think things through thoroughly, and be prepared to handle questions or answers you did not anticipate. Be able to adjust to the other person's style and pace.

Be Observant

Pay attention to the nonverbal signals sent to you and by you. Be sure that the signals you send are positive, not negative. Give the other person your total attention.

Consider the Offer

Both interviewer and interviewee need to consider the ramifications of a job offer. A typical 40-hour-a-week job done for approximately 50 weeks a year adds up to 6,000 hours in only three years. Be sure that your choice is one both you and the organization can live with.

Chart Your Progress

Each time you participate in an interview, fill out a copy of the following evaluation. Circle the number that best describes your response to each question.

a. How prepared were you for the interview?

Not at all prepared   1   2   3   4   5   Fully prepared

b. What kind of climate did you help create?

Hostile climate   1   2   3   4   5   Friendly climate

c. Were the questions you asked clear?

Not clear   1   2   3   4   5   Clear

d. Were the responses you offered complete?

Incomplete   1   2   3   4   5   Complete

e. How carefully did you listen to the other person?

Not at all   1   2   3   4   5   Very carefully

f. How carefully did you pay attention to nonverbal cues?

Not at all   1   2   3   4   5   Very carefully

g. To what extent were you distracted by external stimuli?

Very much   1   2   3   4   5   Not at all

h. How self-confident were you during the interview?

Not at all   1   2   3   4   5   Very confident

i. How flexible were you during the interview?

Not flexible   1   2   3   4   5   Very flexible

j. Would you like to change or improve your behavior for your next interview?

Very much   1   2   3   4   5   Little, or not at all

If your answer to the last question is 1, 2, 3, or 4, consider how you would like to change.

Revisiting Objectives

1. Define *employment interview*. During the course of our lives, we all take part in a number of different types of interviews, as either interviewee or interviewer. The interview is the most common type of purposeful, planned, decision-making, person-to-person communication.

2. Describe the stages of an employment interview. Effective interviews are well-structured interactions. They have a beginning, which provides an orientation to what is to come; a middle, when the participants get down to business; and an end, when the main points are reviewed and the participants take leave of one another.

3. Distinguish between closed, open, primary, and secondary questions. Questions are the heart of the interview and the primary means of collecting data. Four basic types of questions are asked in an interview: closed, open, primary, and secondary. Closed questions are highly structured and can be answered with a simple yes or no or in a few words; open questions are broader and offer the interviewee more freedom in responding. Primary questions introduce topics or begin exploring a new area; secondary questions (probing questions) follow up primary questions by asking for further information. Whatever the type of question, an interviewee must maintain honesty in answering.

4. Perform the roles and responsibilities of an interviewee. Good interviewees work hard during an interview, functioning simultaneously as information seekers, information givers, and decision makers. To be a successful interviewee requires specific preparation. Honest self-assessment, practice in answering typical questions, and mastery of the techniques of impression management are of prime importance. To avoid misunderstanding, you need to be aware of how cultural differences can affect the interview.

Resources for Further Inquiry and Reflection

To apply your understanding of how the principles in this appendix are at work in our daily lives, consult the following resources for further inquiry and reflection. Or, if you prefer, choose any other appropriate resource. Then connect the ideas expressed in your chosen selection with the communication concepts and issues you are learning about, both in and out of class.

Listen to Me

"Working Girls" (10cc)
"From 9 to 5" (Dolly Parton)
"Let the River Flow" (Carly Simon)
"Working Class Hero" (John Lennon)

Each of these songs revolves around the world of work. What do the attitudes expressed in the song suggest about our eagerness and/or preparedness to interview for a job?

View Me

A Few Good Men
Bowling for Columbine
Goodnight and Good Luck
Kinsey
Disclosure

Kramer vs. Kramer
Roger and Me
The Smartest Guys in the Room
Religulous

Interviews play a key role in each of these films. How does the knowledge gleaned through one or more interviews advance the plot?

Read Me

Moises Kaufman. *The Laramie Project*. New York: Dramatists Play Service, 2001.

Studs Turkel. *Working*. New York: Avon Press, 1992.

John Patrick Shanley. *Doubt*. New York: Theatre Communication Group, 2005.

Interviews play a key role in each of these works. Identify the kinds of questions raised by the interviewer(s) that elicited the most useful information from the interviewee(s).

Tell Me

Share with the class the insights you gained from your chosen Listen to Me, View Me, or Read Me selection.

Discuss the most unusual thing that you are aware of happening during an interview to either the interviewer or the interviewee.

Key Terminology

Use the Online Learning Center at www.mhhe.com/ gamble10e to further your knowledge of the following terminology.

behavioral interview
case interview

closed questions
employment interview
open questions
primary questions
secondary questions
stress interview

Idioms in Translation

a toughie – something difficult
cover letter – the letter that precedes a résumé
door should be left open – possibility should be kept open
get you in the door – get you an appointment
provide a platform – give a public forum
telecommute – work from home using a computer or other technology

things do not fall through the cracks – things are not forgotten or overlooked
to roll them out – to introduce [new products]
touched on something – spoke about something
walk the interviewer through – explain to the interviewer

Test Your Understanding

Go to the Self Quizzes on the book's Online Learning Center at www.mhhe.com/gamble10e.

Investigating *Frost/Nixon*

The film *Frost/Nixon* demonstrates how the finesse of the interviewer can lead to unintended revelations on the part of the interviewee. After viewing the film answer these questions with reference to examples taken from it:

1. How does information derived from an interview influence perception and belief?

2. What role does preparation play in an interviewee's performance?

3. In what ways is an interviewee's effectiveness impacted by the assumptions made about the interview?

4. How do nonverbal cues affect judgments made about the interviewee?

5. What lesson from the film can you use when interviewing?Work It Out